HEROIC OPTION

HEROIC OPTION

THE IRISH IN THE BRITISH ARMY

by

JEAN AND DESMOND BOWEN

Pen & Sword
MILITARY

First published in Great Britain in 2005 by
Pen & Sword Military
an imprint of
Pen & Sword Books Ltd
47 Church Street
Barnsley
South Yorkshire
S70 2AS

Copyright © Jean Bowen, 2005

ISBN 1 84415 152 2

A CIP catalogue record for this book is available from the
British Library

Typeset in Plantin by
Phoenix Typesetting, Auldgirth, Dumfriesshire

Printed and bound in England by
CPI UK

Pen & Sword Books Ltd incorporates the imprints of Pen & Sword
Aviation, Pen & Sword Maritime, Pen & Sword Military, Wharncliffe
Local History, Pen & Sword Select, Pen & Sword Military Classics and
Leo Cooper.

For a complete list of Pen & Sword titles please contact
PEN & SWORD BOOKS LIMITED
47 Church Street, Barnsley, South Yorkshire, S70 2AS, England
E-mail: enquiries@pen-and-sword.co.uk
Website: www.pen-and-sword.co.uk

To the Irish soldier past and present
serving in the British Army and to the
Regimental Associations that keep alive
the history of the Irish Regiments
that were disbanded in 1922.

Contents

Irish Regiments in the British Army

INFANTRY

Royal Irish Regiment (18th Foot)

Royal Inniskilling Fusiliers (27th Foot)

Connaught Rangers (88th Foot)

Royal Irish Fusiliers (the 'Faughs')

Royal Irish Rifles

The Prince of Wales's Leinster Regiment (Royal Canadians)

Royal Munster Fusiliers

Royal Dublin Fusiliers

CAVALRY

6th Inniskilling Dragoons

4th Royal Irish Dragoon Guards

5th Royal Irish Lancers

8th King's Royal Irish Hussars

Acknowledgements

Desmond and I worked together on the manuscript for *Heroic Options: The Irish in the British Army* until his death in 1998 when I began the task of finishing it on my own. So many people were helpful along the way. In particular I mention Colonel Robin Charley who kindly allowed me to work in the small library of the Royal Irish Rangers Museum on Waring Street, Belfast. Thanks are extended to the helpful staff of the National Army Museum, London, the National Library of Ireland, Dublin, and special thanks to the late Joan Collett, Librarian at Queens University Library Belfast, who supplied us with valuable references. I am more than grateful to Mr Brereton Greenhous, friend and military historian for National Defence Canada (now retired) who first read our manuscript and liberally used his red pencil, a very necessary task aimed at cutting down our unwieldly and perhaps overly enthusiastic text. This was in line with advice by another friend, Anthony Morris, formerly of Coleraine University, Northern Ireland, an historian who gave me valuable information on what not to do at this time in the publishing business and stressed the use of 'short, snappy sentences'. Thanks also to Jenny Wilson of Carleton University, Ottawa, who provided information on copyright. The Regimental Associations and their museums were prompt and very helpful, my thanks to them all. Thanks also to Michael Lee, Bill McFadzean, Norman Adams and Keith Jeffrey who kindly supplied me with privately owned photographs. Many thanks to the staff of Pen & Sword Books Limited, especially to Brigadier Henry Wilson, Publishing Manager, for his always patient and cheerful e-mails in answer to my *numerous* queries. I cannot adequately express my thanks to my assistant Jo-Anne Cairns, without whose constant enthusiasm and computer skills this work would never have been ready for publication. Finally, although I was always encouraged by our children and I thank them for this, I am told they were somewhat surprised that their mother finished the book!

Preface

It may not in fact be so surprising if, on examination,
an Irish military tradition turns out to be central to the
Irish historical experience, and a key element
in modern Irish identity.

T. Bartlett, K. Jeffery
'An Irish Military Tradition?' in
A Military History of Ireland, p. 2 Cambridge, 1996

This study had its genesis in a pilgrimage in the early 1980s to First World War memorials to the Irish who fought and died at places like Mons, Etreux, Thiepval and Ypres. Shortly afterwards we made our first visit to the Irish National War Memorial at Islandbridge in Dublin where we witnessed neglect verging upon desecration, the result apparently of a government policy of: 'deliberate and mean-spirited ruination'.[1] The contrast with the beautifully maintained monuments to Irish war-dead in Belgium and France could not have been greater. Vandals had destroyed memorial records, fountains were dried up, gardens had been opened to horse grazing, columns were decapitated and the central monument was covered with graffiti. Nor were we the only visitors dismayed by what government policy had allowed to happen to one of the memorable works of Sir Edwin Lutyens who had also designed the Cenotaph in London:

> From all over the world Lutyens scholars came to see his master-piece; came to see and could only wonder at the barbarism of a society and a political culture which could permit this . . . sacrilege; not merely permit it, but exult in it, and make indifference and contempt for those who had died in the Great War a badge of their political identity.[2]

Located in what the *Sunday Times* called a distant backwater, the monument is a magnificent construction that preserves the original wooden Celtic cross from Ginchy on the Somme to honour the 16th (Irish) Division's fallen. Surrounding ponds and flower beds near the River Liffey would provide a beautiful setting for four pavilions housing the many-volumed memorial records of thousands of Irishmen who died serving in the British Army in the Great War.

During the turbulent years of the 1920s many delays occurred in planning for the War Memorial because of nationalist intransigence; consequently work was not begun until 1931. Half the work force were ex-servicemen selected by the British Legion Employment Bureau, while the other half were provided by ex-servicemen from the Irish National Army, which ensured employment. The Irish Free State Government contributed towards the erection of the monument and its future maintenance, with other funds provided by contributions to a trust fund. The memorial park was completed in 1938.

From 1932 the ultra-nationalist Eamonn de Valera and his Fianna Fail (Soldiers of Destiny) republican party dominated Irish political life. During the de Valera era it was not 'politically correct' to recognize the contribution made by so many Irish soldiers to the British Army in times past. In 1939 he agreed to attend the opening ceremony at Islandbridge, but postponed it indefinitely when conscription in the north of Ireland seemed probable. Islandbridge remained 'officially unopened'. Between 1940 and 1970 the British Legion (the Association of Great War Veterans) was allowed to hold its Armistice Day ceremonies at the site, but without government support. By 1970 the monuments and gardens were falling into decay. Fortunately, by 1988 they were being restored and maintained. Memorial plaques are also to be found in most Protestant churches and in Dublin's Adelaide Road Synagogue. It is rare to find remembrance plaques in Catholic churches, such as the moving one in St Mary's Roman Catholic Church in Haddington Road, Dublin. Most Dublin hospitals contain memorials, as do those 'schools across the country with prewar OTCs'. Clongowes Wood College in Kildare is perhaps the only exception among Irish Catholic schools to erect war memorials. Cenotaphs such as the Celtic Cross near Bray Railway Station can be found in most large towns in the south.[3] Some communities opted for practical memorials such as the new electric light installations in St Catherine's Church in Dublin.

During the years of Fianna Fail hegemony the resentment of everything British tended to be bitter and unforgiving. On a visit to Charlesfort, the one-time British bastion near Kinsale, we made the suggestion to a surveyor working on the site that a restoration along the lines of the old

French fort at Louisbourg in Cape Breton Island, Canada, might be a popular tourist attraction. We described to him how during the tourist season the Canadian National Parks Service had Louisbourg Fort garrisoned by university students dressed as eighteenth century French soldiers and we wondered if similar summer employment at Charlesfort might not be provided for Irish university students who could act as British redcoats. The surveyor looked at us quizzically, shook his head and suggested that we knew as well as he the impossibility of an historical reenactment of that sort ever taking place in the Irish Republic. The outlook of the Irish Government may have been an exercise in militant republican virtue, but the introverted clinging remembrance of its struggle for political independence was at the cost of ignoring so much of its history of which it could be proud: clearly the Irish in every generation had influenced significantly the British Army.

Shortly after the First World War books appeared telling the stories of Irish 'regular' career soldiers in the British Army and those who answered the call and joined the Citizen New Army Irish Divisions for the duration of the War. In his *The Tenth (Irish) Division in Gallipoli* (1918) Bryan Cooper writes of its New Army Irish soldiers in that tragic campaign. Cyril Falls's *The 36th (Ulster) Division* (1922) tells of the fate of the Ulstermen and their New Army Division in the war. Very important is Henry Harris's *Irish Regiments in the First World War* (1968), one of the early books to bring together information on the contribution of Irish soldiers fighting as Irish in their Irish regiments and divisions in the British Army.

Signs that the mentality of 'ourselves alone' era of Irish history was passing can be seen in the pioneer work of Irish historians who produced the *Irish Sword,* the Journal of the Irish Military History Society, inaugurated in 1949, wherein scholars were encouraged to produce studies of Irish military history dealing even with a sensitive subject like that of the service of the Irish soldier in the British Army. Happily, this journal continues to publish valuable studies of Irish military history.

The paucity of works recognizing the specific contribution made by so many Irishmen to the Imperial forces is now apparently at an end. The 1990s have seen a number of books dealing with the Irish contribution to the First World War. In 1992 appeared the story of Nationalist Ireland's contribution to the war in the 16th (Irish) Division, and Terence Denman's title is very revealing: *Ireland's Unknown Soldiers*. In his Introduction (page 16) he sums up past attitudes to these Irish soldiers: 'I realized,' he writes, 'that I had stumbled into an historical no-man's land. Despite widespread interest in Britain in the Great War, Irish participation in the conflict is seen as marginal and attracts little serious study.'

Also in 1992 was published Tom Johnstone's valuable study *Orange Green & Khaki*, the story of the Irish Regiments in the Great War 1914–1918. We are conscious that we stand on the shoulders of the many scholars who have provided such valuable insights of a kind often lacking in those important regimental histories that we have also consulted. 'History is about chaps'[4] and in this work we have tried to consider the values, beliefs, as well as the deeds of Irish warriors who, particularly in the First World War when Ireland was struggling for independence, attempted to justify service to both 'harp and crown'. This issue on a personal level was often a conflicting one to soldier heroes like John Lucy and Tom Kettle who explored their own minds and found often contradictory answers. This study is, of necessity, only a glimpse into that vast contribution that Irish soldiers throughout the centuries have made to the British Army. As for women, wives and children have accompanied their husbands to foreign fields from the time of the 'Wild Geese' in 1691.[5] In the First World War Irish women made a courageous contribution serving as nurses and among them were fatalities, but that is another story.

Legions of Irish served in the British armed forces of their day. From the time of the Duke of Marlborough's wars on the continent in the early eighteenth century and during the century's later years when the penal laws against Irish Catholics were in practical abeyance, there was a flood of Irish enlistment. Along with Irish regiments being raised in Ireland between 1793 and 1815, some 159,000 Irishmen were integrated into English regiments. Daniel O'Connell complained in 1812 that Britain was taking 'away our native army from us' and so it was, but this 'army' went quite willingly.[6]

In the British Army there was a long tradition of Irish Protestant officers, members of the Anglo-Irish landed aristocracy and minor gentry families serving in the forces of the crown. Never clearly designated a Junker military class as was their Prussian counterpart, they presented a particular genius in leadership and made a contribution out of proportion to their numbers.[7] Restrictions on Roman Catholics holding commissions or achieving high rank were easing in the late eighteenth century, as Sir Henry Keating's career shows. Another example in the nineteenth century was General Sir William Butler from a minor Catholic branch of the illustrious Butler family. Catholic Irish rankers could be found in large numbers in the East India Company's armies from the seventeenth century and in the Peninsular War they were about half the Duke of Wellington's army and became his much lauded Irish Infantry. Considered the healthiest peasants in Europe, the large and strong Irish often chose their service as an escape from stultifying insular conformity as well as for economic reasons. Doubtful it is that many recruits enlisted merely for 'their pound of bread', and the harshness of army life would have been well known among Irish peasants.

The brawny physique of these Irish peasant lads is well represented by Elizabeth (later Lady) Butler, the celebrated military artist, in her 1879 painting *Listed for the Connaught Rangers* (Bury Art Gallery). Her scene of a small recruiting party in the 1870s which has found two young men willing to take the Queen's shilling could have been enacted any time throughout Ireland in the nineteenth century. They are being marched out of their Kerry glen; one young man, jauntily smoking, is ready for adventure, the other casts a nostalgic glance towards the cabin he has left. Elizabeth Butler has captured the complexities associated with their choice of voluntary exile from their native culture. It is too simplistic to dismiss the Irish recruits in the British Army as mere 'scapegoats, those in debt or in trouble over a girl', to use a phrase of Ernie O'Malley. Her painting was inspired by her husband, Major William Butler, whose essay *A Plea for the Peasant* (1878) argues that the way to improve recruitment for the army was to improve the conditions of the Irish peasants 'since they provide the best fighting stock in the British Army'.[8] The 'redcoat' was a very visible sight in the Irish countryside and very much a part of Irish life. To house the many soldiers more barracks had been built in Ireland than in either England or Scotland; in fact the oldest barracks in Europe was the Royal (now Collins) Barracks in Dublin.[9] These 'green redcoats' were constant reminders of a life of romance and adventure.

This study of the Irish in the British Army is concerned chiefly with their martial prowess, but important also is their contribution to the building of the great empire of which they were a significant part. Wherever the empire expanded the pugnacious Irish were generally to be found at the 'sharp end' in any military force. This was not surprising when Irish recruits came from a society that spawned the phenomenon known as faction-fighting and where, in the words of William Carleton, skill with the shillelagh was 'an integral part of the Irish peasant's education'. Many of them would have been nurtured on the heroic myths found in the oldest Irish epics, such as those of the young warrior Cuchulainn. If we think this is fanciful, in Belfast today can be seen Ulster Protestant paramilitary murals proclaiming their protective role in the community, like that of Cuchulainn, 'ancient defender of Ulster'. Heroism, bravery, endurance, all have been instinctively respected by the Irish of any age, a military spirit with a history dating back to those warrior Celts. It is a heroic spirit that manifests itself in the long service of the Irish to the British crown since the fifteenth century and specifically to the British Army that was formally founded in the seventeenth century. In pursuit of this 'heroic option' we will carry our study to the end of the First World War.

On the eve of departure of Irish emigrants who fled Ireland because of political, social or economic factors or the famine, there was frequently held an 'American Wake' with the singing of sad songs and other expressions of a 'death watch'. Deliberately implanted within the psyche of the emigrant was a haunting sense of guilt for having left the parochial world of Ireland. Often associated with the communal grief was an expression of bitter hostility towards the traditional English authority which was blamed for the continuing emigration of Ireland's young. Those Irish who joined the British Army tended not to share that same sense of guilt largely because of the unique regimental system that had slowly evolved during the eighteenth and nineteenth centuries and which has characterized the British Army. The Irish recruit, especially if he joined an Irish regiment or one deemed to be Irish because of many Irish in it, quickly found a new 'home' and a kind of tribal unity that could transcend determinants of history, geography, folk mythology and the poisonous inculcation of traditional animosities. The cultural traditions of Protestants and Catholics that were so divisive in Ireland could be submerged in their regimental allegiance, while the deep religious faith of the serving Irish Catholic soldier added its own dimension to the army. Their cultural diversity, their intense loyalty and their courage and élan in attack also added 'Irishness' and made the army less 'English'. There were even Irish-speaking soldiers in the eighteenth and nineteenth centuries and perhaps the most popular march in the British Army has been 'St. Patrick's Day in the Morning'. Stories of their humour also abound, as Rudyard Kipling explored in his famous collection *Soldiers Three,* wherein his Irishman Mulvaney tells most of the stories. Through accidents of history as well as trial and error, the British Army has found the secret of pluralist endeavour in incorporating different traditions. Terence Denman has pointed out: 'the British institution that the Irish made the greatest impact on, certainly in terms of numbers, was the army', and he states that little attention has been paid to the Irish as 'a distinct group'.[10]

The allegiance of the Irish to the British Army has always been anathema to Irish Republican Nationalists and a cause for wonder to many others. Henry Harris expressed this well:

> It may strike readers unfamiliar with Irish history as odd that a country constantly rising in arms against its rulers should continue to supply these rulers with a steady supply of loyal first class fighting men. Irish romantic and Nationalist writers tend to play this down or attribute it to the admittedly bad social and economic conditions of the times. . . . A national proclivity to quarrel may have prevented this martial people from uniting

amongst themselves but when properly trained and equipped they have been accepted as among the best soldiers in the world.[11]

The historic Irish regiments in the British Army embodied the heroic tradition. When Major John Doyle (later General Sir John, Bart.) of an old Irish family raised an Irish regiment for the war between France and Britain that began in the late eighteenth century, he appealed to Irishmen in heroic terms. A Dublin newspaper of 7 September 1793 stated that Doyle, 'the Soldiers' friend', had permission from his Majesty to:

> raise forthwith a legion of heroes, the 87th . . . such spirited lads as are desirous of serving in this honourable corps to be called the Prince of Wales' Irish Heroes.[12]

The Irish soldier and his historic Irish regiments have made the British Army the unique organization that it has become and both, we hope, will be seen as part of Ireland's rich heritage.

CHAPTER ONE

Ireland's Warrior People

The warrior cult informed all Celtic mythology . . . it was better to
have a short and heroic life than a long and uneventful one.
                              F. Delaney, *The Celts*, London, 1993, p. 76

From the time that the ancestors of the Irish people, the Celts, appeared
in history their military prowess was recorded by their neighbours who
generally found difficulty in living with them. The Romans feared Celtic
military power, but Celtic auxiliary troops were instrumental in Roman
victories over fierce tribes like the Helvetii of Switzerland and were particularly appreciated by Caesar in the fighting against their Celtic kinsmen,
the Belgic tribes of northern France. By 52 BC independent Celtic tribes
were to be found only in Britain and Ireland.

The Roman historian Tacitus, writing of the first century, viewed the
manner of life of the Irish as the very essence of savagery. A brutal pagan
culture existed in Ireland long after it had disappeared in Europe. In the
ancient Irish Celtic literature the exemplar of martial prowess was Cuchulainn, a heroic being with supernatural powers and a fearsome avatar
for savage people always at war. Irish sagas portray a culture devoted to
the glorification of warfare, in which was a demand for heroism: 'to be
wounded in the back while fleeing from an enemy lost the king his status
in ancient Irish law'.[1]

Long before the actual forming of the British Army Irish soldiers were
in great demand to fight for the British crown. Edward I and Edward II
used Irish mercenaries during their Scottish wars, the hobelars or
mounted lancers being of value in the Scottish terrain. Also in demand by
Ulster chieftains and other Irish warlords were the galloglass or foreign
warriors, heavily armed mercenary foot soldiers, a fiery mixture of Irish,
Scots and Norse blood, 'essentially . . . Gaelic in tongue and custom' from
the Scottish Isles, elite families who, with the lighter armed Irish Kern,
also infantry, became the backbone of most native Irish armies from the
late thirteenth century.[2] Henry VIII employed the savage Irish Kern whose

reputation was such that they were hated in both France and Scotland. He saw that the absence from Ireland of these fierce warriors 'should rather do good than hurt',[3] a viewpoint of Irish soldiers echoed centuries later in penal law times.

During the reign of Elizabeth I Irish soldiers were allowed to serve in the English Army from 1563 and under the Lord Deputy, Sir John Perrott, certain Irishmen were allowed to raise 'companies . . . of their own countrymen'. The Irish Council said, in June 1598, that three-quarters of the Queen's troops then in Ireland were Irish. To the English Ireland was 'full of barbarians' and Elizabeth's courtiers saw with wonder the wholly Gaelic appearance of the second Earl of Tyrone, the great Hugh O'Neill's Celtic party in London, in defiance of previous Tudor legislation:

> Their hair was long: fringes hanging down to cover their eyes. They wore shirts with long sleeves dyed with saffron, short tunics and shaggy cloaks. Some walked with bare feet, others wore leather sandals. The galloglas carried battle-axes and wore long coats of mail. . . .

As one contemporary chronicler recorded, 'they presented a fantastic sight'.[4]

The important Irish rebellion in 1641 led to the civil war in England and ultimately to Charles I losing his crown. By 1642 many Irish soldiers had provided the king with desperately needed manpower. Charles's nephew and Second in Command, Prince Rupert of the Rhine (who would later be Lieutenant General of all the King's Armies), wrote 'gratefully' to the Marquis of Ormond about his 'Irishes' whom he felt 'instinctively to be the best fighters he had ever yet commanded. . . . I am mightily in love with my Irish soldiers.' In 1644 and 1645 the Scots warrior Alisdair Macdonald brought from Antrim (in Ulster) to Scotland wild Irish Kern who together with many of Macdonald's clan fought for Charles under the Marquis of Montrose against the Covenanters.[5]

When King Charles was executed in 1649 Oliver Cromwell and other parliamentarians were resolved to deal with Irish interference in English affairs. In August of that same year Cromwell arrived in Ireland as Lord Lieutenant and Commander in Chief of the Commonwealth Army, with his avenging regiments. Although his terror tactics were widely practiced in war at this time, the Irish would never forget the savagery of the Cromwellian Army at places like Drogheda and Wexford. By the time of Cromwell's death in 1658 deep resentment existed between the Irish and the English. The English were now to be perennially anxious about a resurgence of Irish militarism ideologically supported by the power of the Papacy and continental armies. When the ill-starred House of Stuart returned to the throne and its pro-Catholic sympathies were revealed, most Englishmen thought like a polemicist of 1641:

> Ireland is not unfitly termed a back doore into England: and of what dismall portendence . . . to have the pope the keeper of the keyes of your back dore, . . . if you let Ireland goe, the peace and safety of your own land and nation . . . will soon follow after it.[6]

Origin of the British Army Under Charles II

Charles II, on returning to the throne in May 1660, desired to form a standing army, but the mood in the country was very much against this after the experience of Cromwell's New Model Army, which had been seen as an 'oppressive instrument of political power'. Charles was an astute politician, mindful of his 'royal prerogatives', but, perhaps remembering his father's abuse of them, he did not object when the first action of the Convention Parliament was to disband the Army of the Commonwealth. This disbanding was halted by a timely intervention of history when, in January 1661, a minor insurrection occurred in the City of London and was speedily put down by General George Monck's Coldstream Regiment of former Parliamentarian allegiance and now the 'military instrument of the Restoration' and by Charles's personal guards who had returned with him from exile. This led the way on 14 February 1661 to that 'symbolic gesture' when 'Monck's Coldstream Regiment laid down its arms on Tower Hill and took them up again as the Lord General's Regiment of Foot in the service of the Crown. It is from this date that the Regular Army may be said to have its origin'.[7]

Against Parliament's continuing distrust Charles succeeded in laying the foundation of the Royal or British Army, but Parliament ensured that it would not be easy for him to build up his army beyond the near 7,000 it had in 1681. In Ireland the army of the Irish Establishment was a little larger and, although the Cromwellian garrison of Ireland had been greatly reduced in 1661, it was 'the largest military concentration in the British Isles', and this added considerably to Charles's military resources. Charles's modest Standing Army survived, David Ascoli points out, because of the regimental system, a system whereby, although Charles was the supreme commander of his forces, he left their maintenance to individual regimental colonels. In those early days they literally owned their regiments and, in spite of this invitation to abuse, it was because of this independence that the 'Standing Army was able to withstand for two centuries the hatred, malignity and stinginess of Parliament and the contempt and scorn of every citizen'.[8]

The history of the Royal Irish Regiment gives a picture of that period in the seventeenth century before the first Irish regiments formally became part of the British Army. Charles II raised the Royal Irish Regiment on 1 April 1684 when reorganizing the military forces of Ireland into regiments. These forces until now consisted of a regiment of Irish foot guards raised in England in 1662 and brought to Dublin, and independent troops of cavalry and companies of infantry that had garrisoned important places throughout the island. Many officers by this time had served on the Continent and many in the ranks were descendants of Cromwell's veterans so that when Arthur Forbes, Viscount Granard, was granted the colonelcy of one of these newly raised regiments to be known as Granard's Regiment, all ranks were experienced soldiers. Arthur was the eldest son of Sir Arthur Forbes, Bart, of Castle Forbes, County Longford, and had been a cavalry officer in the Royal Army during the rebellion in the reign of Charles I. A zealous royalist, he was made Marshal of the Army in Ireland after the Restoration. He had been raised to the peerage of Ireland in 1675 as Baron Clanehugh and Viscount Granard, and in December 1684 was created Earl of Granard.[9] The Granards are among the first of those Anglo-Irish families who gave long service to the British Army.

James II followed his brother Charles II to the throne of England in February 1685, a zealous Catholic in a Protestant nation. James tried to put through a policy of genuine civic and religious equality for all his Christian subjects, openly, however, favouring Roman Catholics, who were in fact restrained from holding office under a wide range of penal laws. He defied Parliament, using his royal prerogatives and, alarmingly, introduced Catholic officers into his Standing Army. In March 1685 James ordered that two Catholic officers, Colonels Richard Talbot and Justin MacCarthy, be given regiments, which meant that the statutory requirements for taking the oath of supremacy were being dispensed with. Within months James's policy amounted to turning a Protestant army into a predominantly Catholic army.[10]

That summer Colonel Talbot was ordered to Ireland and began re-modelling James's army, admitting many Catholics. An Irish Catholic champion and brother of the Roman Catholic Archbishop of Dublin, Talbot was an able soldier who in his youth had served in the Irish Catholic Confederacy. James soon raised him to the peerage as the Earl of Tyrconnell and, in 1686, when he was appointed Lord General of the army he ruthlessly carried out a religious purge, dismissing from many regiments all the Protestants in the ranks, replacing them with Catholics. Men were 'stripped of their uniforms and turned penniless and starving upon the world'. Officers were not much better treated, though it took longer to find Catholic officers as replacements. Two of Lord Granard's captains, John St Leger and Frederick Hamilton, were 'disbanded' solely because of their religious beliefs. In protest at these proceedings, Colonel Granard resigned his commission in favour of his son Arthur, Lord Forbes. A bold and daring man, Forbes had learned his trade of war first with the army in France and later in a campaign against the Turks in Hungary. Through political influence and in defiance of Tyrconnell, he retained in his regiment 'more good officers, sergeants, and old soldiers than any other colonel'.[11]

In 1687, when the domineering Tyrconnell was appointed Viceroy of Ireland, alarm among the Irish Protestants spread rapidly. At the same time throughout England was a growing dissatisfaction with James's method of rule and his continual pressuring for the inclusion of Roman Catholics everywhere. English fear of the Papacy was further inflamed by the presence of French Protestant Huguenots, who brought from France stories of atrocities. After Louis XIV's revocation of the Edict of Nantes in 1685, which abolished the civil rights and religious freedoms granted to Huguenots in 1598, they had fled to Ireland, England, Germany and Holland, bringing with them anti-French attitudes. Troubling reports, not always true, of unruly Irish soldiers in England abounded. One of James's newly created Irish regiments under Colonel MacElligot, a tough Kerryman from an ancient Munster family, was made up of Irish Catholics, officers and ill-disciplined troops, rough veterans recently returned from the Low Countries. There is a story of how they shot into a Protestant Church and otherwise terrorized Portsmouth. James's orders to draft some of them into the regiment of the Duke of Berwick (his illegitmate son) stationed at Portsmouth precipitated the revolt of the 'Portsmouth Captains' in 1688. Five of them and their Lieutenant Colonel refused to receive Irish Catholics and were cashiered. This led to rumours that James planned to bring over 'hordes of bloodthirsty Irish Catholics to cut English throats', and to introduce large numbers of them into the army as Tyrconnell had done in Ireland.[12]

Even if the coming of these Irish troops proved to be of incidental importance, further alarm spread when a legitimate son was born to James, a Catholic heir who could break the succession to the British throne, that of the Protestant Princess Mary, daughter of James and wife of the Dutch Prince William of Orange who had expected her to inherit the British crown. A small group of influential statesmen and peers invited Prince William to come to England to save the nation from Catholic tyranny. As a Protestant heading the Augsburg League of Protestant nations against Catholic France William was already committed to bringing England into his ongoing struggle against Louis XIV and to preventing his Uncle James from forming an alliance with Louis. William accepted. It was this political European background that drew Ireland into the subsequent war.

Lord Forbes's Foot was one of the regiments ordered to England from Ireland by James to meet an invasion threat by William of Orange in 1688. It was a difficult time for the regiment in a country where Irish troops, presumed to be Catholics, were looked upon with much suspicion and hostility. The regiment marched to Salisbury where James was mustering his army to meet William's force that had landed at Torbay in Devon in November. But James's world was collapsing; he had managed to so undermine the loyalty of the majority of his people that his statesmen, courtiers and generals, even his own daughter Anne, deserted him. James abandoned his army and fled to France to the protection of Louis XIV. The 'Glorious Revolution' was accomplished without a shot being fired. Most of James's army submitted to William but not all were welcome. William ordered Lord Forbes to disband the Roman Catholics of his regiment and some five hundred officers and men were disarmed and sent to the Isle of Wight. There was much confusion at this time, but Forbes ably kept together some officers, many non-commissioned officers, and about one hundred and thirty privates to remain with the Colours. For the age William was not intolerant of Catholics in ecclesiastical affairs, but he did not welcome them into his army. As for Lord Forbes, he resigned his commission during that winter of 1688–89 on the grounds that, having sworn allegiance to James II, he could bear arms for no other king. The Honourable Edward Brabazon, Earl of Meath, followed as Colonel in May 1689 when William re-officered the now enlarged regiment and Meath's was numbered eighteenth of the infantry of the line to become the oldest Irish regiment in the British Army.

The Irish in the Revolutionary War in Ireland, 1689 – 1691

The 'Glorious Revolution' and the war that followed was an event of enormous significance in Ireland and one with consequences for the Irish in the British Army. Before William's army under Friedrich Herman, the Protestant first Duke of Schomberg, landed near Belfast in August 1689 a civil war had begun in Ulster. On 7 December 1688 occurred the city of Derry's first act of defiance, the closing of the gates against Tyrconnell who had ordered the garrison to be replaced by a regiment he could trust. This famous gesture of the thirteen apprentice boys, although the work of 'hot-headed youth', is still celebrated as part of Ulster's tradition.[13]

In February 1689, when James was considered to have abdicated, the

Crown was offered jointly to William and Mary. Very shortly afterwards William sought Parliament's support for England's new continental allies and he especially stressed the need to secure Ireland as Protestant and not to be used by France. Tyrconnell's control over Ireland together with James's pro-French and pro-Catholic policies ensured that Parliament agreed. It was not until James landed with French troops at Kinsale on the south coast of Ireland in March 1689 in an attempt to recover his crown and was joined by the Irish army raised by Tyrconnell that the Commons voted £700,000 for William's reduction of Ireland. Ireland thus became not just part of but a major site in, a European war, drawn in because of its strategic position and relationship with England. The Irish called it *Cogadh an Dá Ri* – 'the war of the two kings', but because of the involvement of King Louis XIV it might more properly be called, as one Irish historian stated, 'the war of the three kings'.[14] For the Irish it was part of the ongoing struggle between Irish Protestants and Irish Catholics.

Ulster Protestants, not yet well organized, were routed in March at 'the break of Dromore' in east Ulster by James's Irish Army. They then fell back on Enniskillen and Derry, the only towns in Ireland that showed resistance to James, defiantly proclaiming allegiance to William and Mary, while James held Dublin and the southern and western parts of Ireland. Thousands of refugees from the surrounding countryside streamed into these towns and severe food shortages followed. From among these refugees irregular regiments of horse and foot were raised and maintained locally.

When James himself arrived in the north he expected to be well received in Derry as their king, but, approaching the walls of the city in April 1689 with a small army, he was personally fired on and had to retire. Thereafter he left the siege that followed to the command of General Richard Hamilton, while command of the Jacobite Army was given to General Conrad Von Rosen, the senior French general. On 28 July a dilatory relief expedition under the veteran Major General Percy Kirke arrived in transports on Lough Foyle finally ending the siege of one hundred and five days. The ordeal gave the Ulster Protestants their war cry of 'No Surrender', a potent shibboleth for intransigence in use down to the present day to express the mythology of a heroic people under perpetual siege who would rather die than surrender their birthright to 'popish tyranny'.

If the heroism of Derry was a passive but stubborn one, that of the Protestants in the Enniskillen district was very aggressive. Supplied with arms and ammunition brought in through Ballyshannon, the Protestants in the area, who knew they could fight a lengthy defensive war in the marsh and lake land of Fermanagh, found a cavalry leader of genius in Colonel

Thomas Lloyd, a young Roscommon squire often referred to as 'Little Cromwell'. He was prominent in the Enniskillener's victory at Newtownbutler in July 1689, when three thousand troops under command of the veteran Jacobite Justin MacCarthy were routed and their leader was taken captive, later escaping. Appointed to lead the Enniskillen horse was Colonel (later Brigadier General) William Wolseley from England who subsequently settled in County Carlow. His Irish military family in the nineteenth century would give the British Army its famous Field Marshal Sir Garnet Wolseley. Also there was Zachariah Tiffin who became the first Colonel of the formation that was to evolve into the 27th foot, later the Royal Inniskilling Fusiliers, in the British Army.

From these 'irregular' Enniskillen forces, commissions granted by Major General Kirke brought into being a regiment of horse, two of dragoons and three of foot. These Irish levies from Derry and Enniskillen were compared at first by some of Marshal Schomberg's officers to 'a horde of Tartars', and Schomberg himself spoke of them as 'so many Croats'. Their small, hardy horses were not impressive looking, but these 'garrons' proved their worth in the rough Ulster terrain and 'the very ill-mounted and ill-made' Enniskillen and Derry troops soon won the respect of all. On 1 January 1690, by order of William, these forces were brought onto the Royal Establishment and put under Schomberg's Command. He was German, an experienced soldier of fortune who had fought in the Thirty Years' War and had been a Marshal in France, but after the Revocation of the Edict of Nantes as a Protestant he had resigned from Louis' service. He was over seventy years of age. This experienced campaigner thought very little of the twenty thousand troops he brought to Ireland, even the Anglo-Irish officers whom William favoured over their English counterparts. He admired Meath's 18th Foot, which joined the Williamite force in August 1689 and was with the army when, after taking the town of Carrickfergus, Schomberg refused to give battle to James because of his woeful inadequacies in transport, guns, ammunition, food and clothing, and fell back on an entrenched camp at Dundalk. There thousands died of fever and disease in the autumn rains, including the energetic Colonel Lloyd, and especially the English, who would not take the trouble to run up shelters or dig trenches to drain their camping grounds. The 18th Foot seems to have suffered less as Schomberg wrote in October 1689: 'Meath's best regiment of all the army, both as regards clothing and good order and the officers generally good', and he adds, 'The soldiers being all of this province the campaign is not so hard on them as on others'.[15]

The memory of the Battle of the Boyne is kept alive by Protestant Ulstermen on their marching banners in their annual Orange Day Parade with many a depiction of 'King Billy' on his white horse, for William commanded his forces himself. He had found Schomberg to be a 'dilatory commander' and decided he must take over. Arriving in Ulster in mid-June 1690, almost immediately, on 1 July, he was engaged in battle at the Boyne River where James decided to stand to keep William from heading south to Dublin, the key to Ireland. Fighting with the Irish Protestants in King William's army were the English and mercenaries of Danes, Dutch, Germans, and French and Swiss Huguenots; James's Irish Catholic troops were supported by French Infantry, including Germans and Walloons, and some officers from England and Scotland.

William's army was considered the more professional, even with numbers of newly raised and inexperienced men. James's newly organized Irish Army lacked military expertise, especially at battalion and company levels where there were severe shortages of skilled officers to provide leadership and training after Tyrconnell's purge of the old army and 'the long exclusion of Catholics from military life'. Patrick Sarsfield, an important name in Irish history, was one of the few Jacobite professional Irish soldiers. From an old Irish family with estates at Lucan, Sarsfield was a cavalry officer who had served on the continent in Louis XIV's Dutch war and was wounded fighting for James in the Duke of Monmouth's rebellion at Sedgemoor in England. In Ireland, after assisting Tyrconnell to remodel the Irish Army, he had preserved Connaught for James in 1689 and his brilliant cavalry raid outside Limerick destroyed part of William's siege train. In 1690 James promoted Sarsfield to Major General and early in the following year made him Earl of Lucan. There are mixed views of Sarsfield. In James's force he was called 'the darling of the army', and by Williamite generals he was respected far more than were other Irish officers. James, on the other hand, thought him 'a brave fellow, but very scantily supplied with brains, a sentiment Tyrconnell . . . echoed'. G. A. Hayes-McCoy, the Irish historian, sees him as 'a competent . . . a dashing . . . rather than an outstanding soldier '.[16]

To engage James, William had to cross the River Boyne, which his infantry successfully accomplished wading waist-deep at a ford at Oldbridge. Once over, the elderly General Schomberg was killed rallying Huguenots in a sharp fight. William himself led his cavalry across a ford further downstream; his personal escort included four troops of Sir Albert Conyngham's Inniskilling Dragoons, a regiment of English Horse and Lord Cutts's Regiment of Foot. An eyewitness reported that the King 'drew his sword and spoke thus to the Inniskillings: . . . I have heard a great deal of your bravery and now I make no doubt but I shall be an eyewitness of it.' Almost foundering in the mud and hotly fired on, the King leading the cavalry reached the shore where the Inniskillings charged so impetuously they became scattered and fallen on by James's Irish reserves. In the chaos, Lord Cutts's infantry stood firm and William was able to rally the cavalry for a successful charge. Meanwhile, when the other eight troops of Inniskillings were routed and many killed, William again took control, relaunched them into battle, and with the Dutch and Huguenot Horse they 'ten times charged and counter-charged in what was . . . said to be the most savage fighting of the day' until the Jacobites retreated. Conyingham's Inniskilling Dragoons lost about sixty men. Sir Albert was a prominent cavalry leader who, during Tyrconnell's religious purge, had lost his appointment as Lieutenant General of the Ordnance in Ireland. He himself had raised several troops of Dragoons, among them two commanded respectively by his nephew, the valiant Reverend Dr John Leslie, and the reverend Doctor's son.[17]

William's victory at the Battle of the Boyne gained him Dublin. Within three weeks James had fled to France to remain a pensioner of Louis XIV. His army was forced to retire into the interior of Ireland towards Limerick and, remaining mostly intact, fought for another year without much success, but it defeated William at Athlone and Limerick, August 1690, where the 18th Foot had severe casualties including their Colonel the Earl of Meath. William's hopes to finish the war quickly were dashed and he returned to England leaving in command his Dutch General Godard van Reede de Ginkel, a competent professional soldier. Ginkel prepared for a fresh campaign in 1691 against his Jacobite opponent the experienced French General Marquis de St Ruth.[18]

Tiffin's Foot (the future Inniskilling Fusiliers) were in the second attack on Athlone in June 1691, part of a Williamite force that took the town through a clever ruse. The narrow but vital bridge over the Shannon remained broken and Ginkel, his supplies running low, was determined to attempt the ford. He offered pardon to three Danish soldiers, who were under the sentence of death, if they would test the ford's depth and width. When they entered the river the Jacobites took them for deserters because 'we', writes the Inniskilling historian, 'fired seemingly at them in the river'. On their safe return Ginkel retired his troops as if the siege was lifted. While St Ruth, ignorant of an impending assault, was entertaining 'the Ladies and Gentlemen and Officers of the Town and the Camp', picked detachments from the whole army, including Tiffin's Foot hidden in trenches, plunged into the water up to their cravats and reached the opposite bank. The defenders of the breech, taken unaware, fired a confused volley, 'panicked and fled'. Within half an hour Athlone was in Williamite hands.[19] St Ruth withdrew to the west, realizing that the town could not be retaken, and marched to Aughrim in County Galway. At this most decisive battle of the war on 12 July 1691 Ginkel effected a resounding victory amidst fierce fighting and heavy losses in both armies in which the Marquis de St Ruth was killed. The name Aughrim, like that of 'the Boyne', resounds in Irish history.

Sporadic fighting continued in which Sir Albert Conyngham and twenty men 'were murdered in cold blood' when his Inniskilling Dragoons were surprised in their camp at Collooney on 5 September by a larger Jacobite force.[20] On 3 October the Treaty of Limerick formally brought William's Irish campaign to an end. It had been a campaign in which for the first time the recently constituted British or Royal Army went into battle. Irishmen fighting Irishmen on the soil of Ireland and on foreign battle-fields would be a part of Ireland's unfolding history.

After the sudden death of Tyrconnell at Limerick, the chief negotiator for the Jacobite forces was the shrewd Patrick Sarsfield who used all his influence to urge his countrymen to support King James's cause, thereby 'sacrificing to his loyalty his fine estate'. William, anxious to be free of Ireland, promised Lord Lucan that some fifteen thousand Jacobite soldiers would be allowed to go to France in British ships, which they did. These Irish Jacobites in the service of France became the celebrated 'Wild Geese' who in their red coats ironically resembled their Irish counterparts in the British Army.[21]

Surviving the standing down of William's Irish force were the 27th Foot and two regiments of Enniskillen Horse; two dragoon regiments under various titles would evolve into the 5th Royal Irish Lancers and the 6th Inniskilling Dragoons. These regiments raised by Protestants in Ulster began over two centuries of service in the British Army. The 18th Foot was unique because it was the only regiment originally from James's Irish Army to be taken into the British Army by William, possibly, it was said, because of the many Protestants in its ranks.

The 18th Foot began to establish a tradition for valour when the regiment greatly distinguished itself in the Siege of Namur, a fortress King William recaptured from the French in his first successful campaign on the continent in 1695. In the storming of the Terra Nova breach under their able General, the much loved Lord Cutts, nicknamed 'Salamander' for his fiery bravery, the 18th Foot gallantly charged suffering terrible losses and the attack was a costly failure. After they were forced to retire the 18th Foot formed the 'forlorn hope' to lead the breakthrough attack and assist the Bavarians at another breach. William was so impressed by the regiment's heroics at the Terra Nova, that he 'formally conferred upon it the title of the Royal Regiment of Foot of Ireland with the badge of the Lion of Nassau and the motto "Virtutis Namurcensis Praemium".' Desperately wounded at Namur was Robert Parker of the 18th Foot. The son of a Kilkenny farmer, Parker as a boy found he had an aptitude for soldiering and in 1689 ended up in Meath's 18th Foot in which he served throughout William's Irish War. After a long period spent in hospital recovering from his wound he was gazetted to a commission and eleven years later he was Captain Lieutenant and Adjutant of the regiment. Parker suffered another serious wound at Menin, which was a great victory for the famous Marlborough under whom the regiment fought and won much glory. Promoted to Captain of a grenadier company Parker had had a remarkable career for an Irish farm boy and moreover became one of the regiment's four historians.[22]

From the period of the Williamite Wars in Ireland an Anglo-Irish military identity began to emerge. Irish Protestants had rushed to arms to defend their country from the rule of a Catholic monarch and William's victory assured them that Ireland would be Protestant, 'a sister kingdom to England'.[23] It was the prevalence of this political/Protestant mythology that was for some time to bedevil the recruitment of Irish Catholics into the ranks of the nascent Irish regiments and, indeed, the British Army as a whole. Huguenots arriving in Ireland and England had reinforced anti-Catholic attitudes. In the Williamite War there was scarcely any action in which they did not have a presence. The Huguenot General Henri de Massue, Marquis de Ruvigny, Commander of the Huguenot cavalry, was publicly praised by Ginkel for his bravery at Aughrim. When the war ended some Huguenots obtained pensions and settled on an estate at Portarlington, Ireland, given to de Ruvigny who was granted the title Earl of Galway. He served as Commander in Chief in Ireland and twice as Lord Justice in 1697, 1715–16. It was said of de Ruvigny, a strong Protestant and of the inner circle of William of Orange, that he was responsible for the early penal laws but recent scholarship has exonerated him as the victim of a plot to discredit him directed by Louis XIV.[24]

CHAPTER TWO

THE EIGHTEENTH CENTURY 1702–1803
THE IRISH SOLDIER IN FOREIGN FIELDS

The door of the world was opened to him by the English Crown.

General Sir John Hackett, GCB, CBE, DCO, MC, DL
Foreword, p. XI, to *A History of the Irish Soldier*
Brig. H.E.C. Bredin, Belfast, 1987

The Irish and the Jacobite Legacy

The problem for Catholic-Protestant relations in the British Army after the 1697 Treaty of Ryswick was that the political settlement of 1701 provided that British sovereigns were to be Protestant. William III died in 1702 and was succeeded by Anne, second daughter of James II and a strong Protestant, the last Stuart sovereign in England. From the 1690s a series of anti-Catholic penal laws emerged over a period of years to protect the social order from any arrogant changes as had occurred under the Catholic King James. Thus the legacy of the Williamite or Jacobite War had repercussions for the British Army: official British policy forbade the recruitment of Irish natives, Protestants or Catholics. After the war Catholics were not considered trustworthy and it was thought that if the recruitment of Irish Protestants was permitted there could be no certainty that Irish Catholics would not also slip in. Regiments were to recruit in England, as happened in the 27th Foot under their rigorous Colonel Richard Viscount Molesworth, who strictly adhered to the official policy of not enlisting any Irish, even though the regiment was quartered in their own town of Enniskillen. When Sergeant Deering enlisted fifteen Irishmen for the regiment, he was reduced to the ranks. Officers were often cashiered for a similar offence. When Molesworth moved on from the Inniskillings in 1739, it appeared to be Irish in name only. Irish Protestants were officially barred from enlisting until 1756 and Irish Catholics until 1799, but exceptions abounded throughout the eighteenth century.

A formal Irish Establishment was created in Ireland in 1701, an organization that was entirely separate and distinct from the British Army in England, having its own administration and commander in chief with headquarters in Dublin Castle, the cost borne by Ireland. It was much appreciated by Irish Protestants. Its twelve thousand troops allotted by the English Parliament were to safeguard Ireland from attack and also acted as a strategic reserve for the British Army. Whenever a crisis threatened abroad regiments on the Irish Establishment were moved and this would pertain throughout the eighteenth century.[1]

Scholars are not at all certain how many Irishmen served in the British Army in the early eighteenth century. War always provided an excuse to recruit the Irish. In Queen Anne's War of the Spanish Succession (1702–1712) it is estimated that a third of the Duke of Marlborough's men were Irish; presumably all claimed to be Protestant but regimental records for the period are scanty. His army was substantially one of European mercenaries; it would have been easy for any recruit to enlist without too many questions being asked. Nearly half of the many regiments raised for Marlborough for his Flanders campaign were recruited in Ireland and four that escaped the reductions after the war were Irish in origin and composition. The 35th Foot raised in 1701 by Arthur Chichester, 3rd Earl of Donegal, was known for years as the 'Orange Lillies' or the Belfast regiment. The 36th Foot, raised by Viscount Charlemont in the same year, was nicknamed 'The Saucy Greens' both for their Irish origin and their alleged fondness for the fair sex. The 37th Foot was raised by the Irish Protestant cavalryman Thomas Meredith, the Adjutant General of the army who talked of weeding out the 'wretched papists'. The 39th Foot, raised in Ireland by Colonel Richard Coote in 1702, was nicknamed 'The Green Linnets'.

It was a constant temptation for recruiting officers to enlist any likely-looking Irishman into the ranks. If a matter like religious affiliation would not be looked into too closely, neither it would seem was the matter of gender. The female soldier known as 'Mother Ross' was said to have been born Christian Cavenaugh of Dublin. In search of her lost soldier husband, Richard, she enlisted in 1693 as a private in a foot regiment as Christopher Walsh. For thirteen years she served in different regiments, was wounded at Landen, then transferred to the Scots Greys as a trooper of dragoons. Her sex was discovered only when she was again wounded at Ramillies. Two husbands were killed under Marlborough. A third husband was a Welsh Fusilier named Davies, a pensioner in the Chelsea Hospital who survived her. She was granted a pension of a shilling a day by Queen Anne and on her death in 1739 was buried with military honours in the Chelsea Hospital cemetery.[2]

Despite a 1724 general order against any Irish enlistment in the British Army issued by Ireland's Lieutenant Governor, Viscount Shannon, two years later an 'Abstract of the Army on Duty in Ireland' revealed that 5,276 other ranks included 1,356 Irish. In the first half of the century clearly a blind eye was turned against recruiting Irish, at least Protestant Irish, and commanding officers were finding ingenious ways of doing so. An extensive deception by one infantry regiment involved the shipping of Irish recruits to Scotland, there to be dressed in bonnets and plaids, then shipped back and enlisted as Highlanders.[3] In 1726 Hugh Boulter, the Protestant Archbishop of Armagh, urged that those Irish being recruited into the army bring with them 'certificates of their being Protestants and the children of Protestants'.[4] Fear of Catholics was undoubtedly the reason for this, but it shows that Irish *were* being recruited.

By the time of the great conflicts of the Seven Years' War of 1756–1763 in North America, the European continent and in India, it is clear that the British Army was already enlisting a great many Irish, both Protestants and Catholics. In 1755 British infantry regiments arriving in Canada from Ireland were said to be composed almost entirely of 'convicts and Irish Papists'.[5] In February 1757 regiments like the 27th Foot bound for North America 'were instructed to recruit on their way to Cork as many able-bodied men as were necessary to complete their respective corps, and in 1789 most of the officers and over sixty percent of the men were Irish'.[6]

Irish Protestants were early represented in the cavalry. A surviving incomplete inspection return of June 1725 of General Ligonier's Horse reports that, when three troops were reviewed in Dublin, 'The Private men are of good stature . . . and most of them Natives of this Country', and again in 1744 it was recorded that: 'General Ligonier's Regiment of Horse consists wholly of Irish Protestants . . . mostly raised in the north of Ireland'. As time went by colonels like John Ligonier paid only 'lip service' to the order banning recruiting any Irish. For the sons of the Anglo-Irish gentry there was always a place in the British Army beginning in the Williamite War, their preeminence in the army dating from the time of Marlborough. Some Catholics were enlisted in the cavalry, usually the preserve of Protestants. In those early eighteenth century years when the Seventh Dragoon Guards then known as the Fourth Horse, spent a long period in Ireland, so many Roman Catholics were recruited it became irreverently known as the 'Virgin Mary's Bodyguard'.[7]

As the century progressed and to offset the tedium of long years garrisoned in Ireland, cavalry officers became very much part of the social life of the landed gentry. A dashing young officer of Horse was a target for wealthy acquaintances with eligible daughters. 'The Cavalry Corps in

Ireland were extremely select,' wrote Surgeon John Smet of 8th Light Dragoons in 1784; 'it was in the power of colonels of choosing . . . young gentlemen of distinction who might wish to get a commission and who all could easily afford to add a hundred pounds a year to their pay'.[8] By the end of the eighteenth century so popular was the army and so keen was the competition for commissions that Anglo-Irish families were sending their sons to schools that would fit them for a military career.

Appearing in these years was one of the future Irish heroes of the eighteenth century British Army, the Anglo-Irishman Eyre Coote. The Coote family had moved from France to England in the reign of Richard II and a branch had settled in Ireland during the Elizabethan wars, several of whom had noteworthy military careers from that time. Eyre's great-grandfather, the strongly Protestant Chidley Coote, had commanded a regiment of horse in Cromwell's New Model Army. By the eighteenth century the family seat was at Kilmallock in County Limerick where Coote was born in 1726. Like many Anglo-Irish in the British Army, Eyre Coote's father was a clergyman of the Irish Protestant Church. As a young Ensign in the 27th Foot (later Inniskilling Fusiliers) Coote fought in the Jacobite Rebellion, 'the Forty-Five', when the Young Pretender Charles Edward Stuart, 'Bonnie Prince Charlie', raised some of the Highland clans in Scotland with French help. Among the few French fighting in Scotland were 'Irish Piquets', volunteers from regiments of the Irish Brigade in the French Army. Scots as well as the Irish 'Wild Geese' had a tradition of service in France and a Scots/Irish connection developed:

> The Highland Scots recruited by French agents . . . before the '45 rebellion would chiefly have gone into one of the French Irish regiments which also recruited fairly steadily from Ireland. A . . . relatively common language [and religion] between the Irish soldiers and the Highland Scots would have made inter-regimental communication easy and all the officers, Irish or Highland Scots, would have spoken Gaelic.[9]

The wretched Battle of Falkirk, fought in the sleet and snow of January 1746, was a defeat for the British Army, and the Inniskillings, who suffered greatly, were part of the general retreat. Eyre Coote carried the King's Colour, which was only saved from capture by his presence of mind when he tore the Colour from its pole, hid it under his coat and escaped to Edinburgh. For leaving the field of battle Coote, Lieutenants Baldwin Leighton and William Shipton were subsequently court martialled and suspended. Later, when Coote explained that his sole motive for his actions was to save the Colour of the regiment, he was reinstated in 1749 as Lieutenant in the 37th Foot transferring as Captain to the 39th Foot in 1755.[10] Eyre Coote was destined for a distinguished career in India.

The Irish and the Conquest of Canada –
The Battle of Quebec in the Seven Years' War

The British Army, supported by the British Navy, captured Quebec, then the capital of Canada, on 13 September 1759, a victory that brought Canada into the British Empire and posthumous fame to Major General James Wolfe, one of the renowned heroes of the eighteenth century. Beckles Willson in his 1909 biography of Wolfe has claimed an Irish ancestry for him, but a recent historian has claimed an English heritage questioning Willson's documentation. It is to Ireland, however, that we turn to learn of Wolfe's antecedents and very military family. James's grandfather, Edward Wolfe of the Royal Regiment of Irish Footguards, was dismissed from King James II's Irish Army during Tyrconnell's purge of Protestants, served under William III and as a captain in Queen Anne's army. James's father, Edward, first commissioned Ensign in the marines, was in 1717 appointed Captain and Lieutenant Colonel in the 3rd Foot Guards. Eventually, in 1740, he was appointed Adjutant General to a force for Colombia and was then able to pursue patronage and 'interest' for his two sons James and Edward, typical of the eighteenth century British Army and of society in general. James, not yet fifteen, was commissioned in his father's regiment of marines.[11] He advanced rapidly in his career, making his name in the Louisbourg Expedition in 1758, which led to his command of the Quebec Expedition the following year when only aged thirty-two.

Irishmen were prominent in the crucial battle at Quebec. One of two brigadiers Wolfe had chosen was an Irishman, the Honourable Robert Monckton, Colonel of the 2/60th Royal Americans. He was the 'easy-going unlettered' son of Lord Galway with whom Wolfe had served as boy officers in Flanders. Monckton had been in Nova Scotia since 1752; he had taken the French Fort Beausejour and had also served as Lieutenant Governor of Nova Scotia in 1755 when he was involved in the unhappy expulsion of the Acadians. A capable officer and considered valuable because of his North American experience, he returned to England as Lieutenant General and Governor of Portsmouth. Always cheerful, he was the opposite of James Murray, a Scot, Lieutenant Colonel of 15th Foot and the other Brigadier chosen by Wolfe. The impoverished son of Lord Elibank, Murray was fiercely ambitious and envious of Wolfe; they had quarrelled at Culloden, but he had fought well at Louisbourg and this seems to be why Wolfe chose him. The Honorable George Townshend's appointment as the third Brigadier was only because of family connections, one of the most influential Whig families in the eighteenth century. Wolfe accepted him even though he was not to his liking.

Two competent Irishmen were appointed Staff Officers. Major Isaac Barré of the 32nd Foot, born in Dublin of Huguenot parents, was Adjutant General. He would later become an important member of Parliament, opposing taxation of the American colonies. Lieutenant Colonel Guy Carleton of the 72nd Foot, born in Strabane, County Tyrone, was appointed Quartermaster General. Later, in 1786, Carleton, as Lord Dorchester, was Captain General and Governor in Chief of British North America.

The British Army's triumph at Quebec is one of the best known and most romantic actions in the eighteenth century, memorable for its secret nighttime landing and ascent from the *Anse au Foulon* to the heights of the Plains of Abraham. Wolfe's plan was that a forlorn hope of twenty-four volunteers led by Captain William Delaune, Wolfe's Huguenot friend from his own 67th Foot, would find a narrow road leading to the heights. On landing in darkness also, Lieutenant Colonel William Howe and his light infantry discovered that the boats had been carried by the tide downstream beyond the Foulon. He immediately decided to lead his three companies on a hazardous climb up the scrub-covered face of the cliff directly on his front, which had not been part of Wolfe's plan. As Captain John Knox from Sligo, of the 43rd Foot, recalls in his valuable *Journal*, the Highlander Captain MacDonald, one of the first up, speaking French, was able to deceive the French sentries on the heights and send them off. Meanwhile Delaune, ordered by Howe, had found the crucial path up which Wolfe then hurried the remainder of his army to the heights. In the early morning the French General Montcalm found long lines of British redcoats facing the city, some drawn up two deep instead of the usual three. Captain Knox in describing the battle recounts how his own 43rd and the 47th Foot in the centre of the line and holding their fire gave the oncoming French columns 'with great calmness, as remarkable a close and heavy discharge as ever I saw'. The battle was over in a few minutes and both Wolfe and Montcalm were mortally wounded. The French Army fled in confusion. Knox records how in Wolfe's dying last moments he ordered 'Webb's regiment with all speed down to Charles's river to cut off the retreat of the fugitives from the bridge'.[12] Most of the French regulars, driven down the hill and over the river, got away; it would be another year before the conquest of Canada would be fully accomplished. British casualties were heavy in the senior ranks; Carleton and Monckton were seriously wounded and Barré lost an eye.

Captain Knox has also recorded how Irish officers in many regiments kept alive Irish traditions when abroad. His 43rd Foot was filled with Irish, both officers and other ranks, and with his comrades he was 'exiled' for nearly two years in the wilds of Nova Scotia at Fort Cumberland on the hill of Beauséjour where outside the fort lurked Acadians and their Micmac allies who killed and scalped any of the garrison who wandered from the fort. A great relief for the garrison was to celebrate St Patrick's Day. In 1758 and 1759 the Irish officers laid in provisions each autumn for the feast day and there was a considerable expenditure on punch, wine and beer. In the latter year twenty 'Hibernian' officers stood drinks for the other thirty-four who did not share the ethnic good fortune to be Irish. To celebrate, the Irish in the ranks were given an advance in pay and their guard duty was taken over by those who were not Irish. The Colours were hoisted, crosses were worn in hats and a great time was had by all.

The Passing of the Recruitment Problem

After the Seven Years' war, which ended with the Treaty of Paris in 1763, the expanding British Army formed new commitments that resulted in further changes in the recruitment policy for the Irish. With so many soldiers having to serve overseas, the capability of the Irish Establishment to supply reinforcements, or even to protect Ireland against a possible French invasion, was found wanting when Irish Catholics were officially excluded. To quell some of the anxiety of the Irish Protestant Parliament Lord Townshend, now the Lord Lieutenant, assured them of the Crown's promise to keep twelve thousand troops in Ireland, except if invasion or rebellion occurred in Great Britain. He also caused considerable unease in his proposal of 1770 that to build up Protestant numbers on the Irish Establishment only 'papists' should be enlisted for foreign service. As a soldier himself, he had a high regard for Irish Catholic soldiers after the Quebec campaign. When the American War of Independence was making demands for troops, Townshend made the most of the War Office proposal to allow regiments on the British Establishment to recruit Irish Protestants by pressing that Irish Catholics also be recruited. In January 1771 London gave cautious approval which brought about widespread recruitment of Catholics, who, by a statute of 1774, were able to give an oath of allegiance instead of the earlier religious test. By 1775 thousands of Irish were enlisting and of the forty-four battalions serving in America in 1776 sixteen had come from the Irish Establishment and were augmented with Roman Catholics.[13] In the 1770s therefore began the easing of the formal penal laws throughout Ireland.

A result of this can be seen in the career of Sir Henry Sheehy Keating, KCB, the first Catholic to become a general after the higher military grades were opened up to officers of that faith. Born in 1777 into a well-known Irish Catholic family with military connections, he and his brothers were educated at the English Jesuit College in Liege. Gazetted Ensign in the 33rd Foot seeing service in Martinique, by 1800 he had transferred as Major to the 56th Foot, the Pompadours, and was Lieutenant Colonel when the regiment went to India in 1807. Keating was in overall command of the expedition to capture from the French the Island of Bourbon, an important position commanding the trade route from England. In 1810 he accepted the island's surrender and was appointed its Governor. Honours came his way and very pleasing to him was his last appointment as Colonel of his old regiment, the 33rd Foot. As a young Subaltern in 1795 he also became known as the first writer to appreciate that King James did not sufficiently exploit the topographical features at the Battle of the Boyne which, Keating claimed, led to his defeat.[14]

The Irish and the American War of Independence 1775–1783

By one of the paradoxes which haunt Irish history the 'loyalists' of the American war were apt to be Irish Catholics rather than Irish Protestants whose ancestors had established themselves in the eastern seaboard colonies. From the last years of the seventeenth century a steady movement of Ulstermen had taken place to establish in the American settlements a vigorous border population, as prone to quarrel with their German and other neighbours as they had been with the Catholics in Ireland.[15] By the time of the American War of Independence the Scotch-Irish, as the Ulstermen were called, formed the very core of resistance to British authorities. The cause of the war was, in part, the colonists' reluctance to pay British taxes for their continued security, especially the Stamp Act, for in their view the Treaty of Paris of 1763 removed the French threat. Tensions over sovereignty soon developed.

The temper of the colonists had been growing daily because of their grievances and in the face of this threat the Board of Customs Commissioners based in Boston requested more military aid; eventually the 14th and 29th Foot arrived from Halifax, the 64th and 65th Foot from Ireland. They were not welcomed by the population. One encounter was the so-called 'Boston Massacre' of March 1770 when a mob gathered outside the Customs house and an Irish Captain in the 29th Foot, Thomas Preston, and seven of his men were called in. The troops were assaulted by the mob who would not disperse and, when some unknown person shouted 'Fire', the troops did so. Preston frantically ordered them to stop, but five of the mob were killed and six wounded. Preston and his men were imprisoned and, later acquitted, but this unnecessary event has passed into American folk history as an example of British military brutality.[16] It is obvious from the names of the civilians who took part in the clash that some of them were Irish, as were many of the 29th Foot, who were given the nickname 'the Vein Openers'. Tensions in the city escalated, evolving five years later into a revolution, the War for American Independence.

Irishmen in their allegiance to both sides in the war played a leading role. When the American Continental Army captured Montreal it was led by Brigadier General Richard Montgomery of Swords, County Dublin, a graduate of Trinity College, Dublin, who had almost twenty years of service in the British Army. He died leading an unsuccessful assault on Quebec in 1775; opposing him was the Anglo-Irish Major General Guy Carleton, who as Wolfe's Quartermaster General, had been wounded at Quebec and now was Governor of Quebec and responsible for the defence of Canada. When the British landed at Savannah, Georgia, in 1778, fighting with them were the Volunteers of Ireland composed of Irishmen of loyalist sympathies who had deserted from Washington's army and had been enlisted in Philadelphia by Lieutenant Colonel Lord Rawdon. An Anglo-Irishman born in County Down, he succeeded his father as Earl of Moira in 1793. In Washington's Continental Army prominent commanders like Henry Knox, 'Mad' Anthony Wayne and John Sullivan were all of Irish descent. Most outstanding was the Irish-born Edward Hand of King's County, also a graduate of Trinity College, a former surgeon's mate in the 18th Royal Irish Regiment, who would be breveted as Major General in the Continental Army.[17] He took part in the storming of the British works at Yorktown and at this British defeat Brigadier General Charles O'Hara, from County Sligo and future notorious governor of Gibraltar, surrendered on behalf of Major General Lord Cornwallis.

Roger Lamb of Dublin has provided a remarkable account of his experiences in the conflict. A Protestant, in 1773 on his seventeenth birthday he enlisted in the 9th Foot on impulse he writes, to seek adventure and to escape a 'confining' life at home with his store-keeper father. Three fellow recruits who became friends and later fought with him were Irish: Terence Reeves from Belfast, Alexander 'Smutchy' Steel from Limerick, and Richard Pearce, 'the felonious son of an Ulster nobleman' who had to enlist under the assumed name of Harlowe. All of them had found escape by enlisting in the 9th. Lamb enjoyed three years of army life in Ireland, then, in 1776, sailed from Cork for Quebec. He had early been promoted to corporal as he had some schooling. His regiment, the 9th, were part of

Lieutenant General Sir John Burgoyne's much-mauled force and had to surrender at Saratoga in 1777. Eventually Lamb and his fellow prisoners found themselves in a primitive forest camp west of Boston where their guards continually urged them to desert. While there Lamb, now a Sergeant, was sent by his officers to the nearby town of Brookfield to visit two soldiers sentenced to hang for murder, but who, contrite, requested support and forgiveness for dishonouring their regiment. Refreshing himself at a wayside inn, Lamb had a long conversation with the American owner which revealed a not uncommon way of thinking among Irish soldiers throughout the centuries. This gentleman was puzzled that an Irishman, when his people had a reputation for rebelliousness and for being uniformly intolerant of the English king, should yet choose to remain and serve under him in the British Army. Lamb had a forthright answer:

> That sir, I replied, is a calumny which has become hereditary to historians. The reverse is the case: during a matter of twenty reigns . . . the fidelity of Ireland to the Kings of England has been very seldom interrupted. Irish soldiers have often been brought over to England to protect their sovereigns against the insurrections of British rebels.

Lamb maintained stoutly he would 'remain a loyal subject of the king'. He soon arrived at Brookfield and witnessed the execution of the two soldiers, which affected him deeply.

In November 1778 the 9th and the Army began a long march towards the Southern states who, it was said, would shoulder the maintenance of British prisoners. As Lamb approached the Hudson River in New York state, he and two Irish friends decided to escape to New York. Helped by some loyalists and poor people who willingly took bribes, they arrived in New York a week later and joined General Clinton's Army. In New York this 'seeker of glory', offered the chance to return to England, chose to join the famous 23rd Foot, the Royal Welch Fusiliers, renowned for victories at the Boyne and under Marlborough.

With the 23rd Foot Lamb sailed to South Carolina and was several times in action, until he was made a prisoner after Cornwallis's surrender at Yorktown and his fighting days in America came to an end. Already experienced, as 'a temporary surgeon' he was allowed to help with British wounded in a hospital nearby at Gloucester from where he escaped again and set out on an arduous journey on foot, encountering along the way many Irish, both civilians and soldiers. At Frederick Town he was caught and confined in the jail where he nearly starved. His reputation as someone who escaped frequently was well known. On his request to be with other British prisoners who were encamped here he was released to the friendly Captain Eyre Coote of the 33rd Foot, whom he knew. The nephew of Major General Sir Eyre Coote who was still fighting in India, Coote deplored being under parole so he could not escape, but he greatly encouraged Lamb to continue to do so. Finally Sergeant Lamb, after further escapades, rejoined his regiment in New York in time to learn of a peace and surrender by the British of the American colonies. He ended his days very happily in Dublin as a school teacher.[18]

In Ireland the American war brought about an increased militarization of society and a phenomenon was the reappearance of the Volunteer movement, a non-professional soldiery who could assist the regulars in the British army on routine security duties on an unofficial basis. But many were uneasy over the inevitable opening of the ranks to Roman Catholics, whose gentry subscribed liberally to the Volunteer movement. Since 1778, when France entered the war and a series of Catholic relief acts had signalled the ending of the penal laws, more and more Catholics were to be seen among the gloriously uniformed Volunteers who never seemed to stop having parades and reviews. Such volunteering greatly appealed to the Irish, but few of the Volunteer officers showed interest in accepting crown commissions. This was not true of the militia which frequently became the back door into the army.

The Irish Militia and the Rising of 1798

An Irish Militia Act passed in 1793 reactivated the old militia. This was undoubtedly a result of the French Revolutionary War, but there was also a need for a force controlled by the government rather than by individuals, like the leaders of the Volunteers who could be politically suspect with their own agendas. At the same time another Catholic Relief Act of 1793 officially gave Catholics the right to bear arms in Ireland and a Militia Bill further enabled the militia to enrol Catholics to defend their country against a possible French invasion and fight side by side with Protestants, a startling new policy. Previously Catholic soldiers had been chiefly recruited to serve abroad. The militia force was to be drawn by lot from the entire able-bodied male population aged eighteen to forty-five, without regard to religion. Enlistment was for four years and the militiaman was to serve outside the county in which he had joined; officers were mostly Protestant and the men in the ranks overwhelmingly Catholic. 'Substitutes were allowed, and so too were volunteers. Anyone who refused to serve was liable to a £10 fine, and if they would not pay this could be treated as mutinous.'[19] Although most people welcomed the militia as a change from the prevailing set piece encounters of local factions, there were serious riots against it. The *Freeman's Journal* of 24 October 1793 reported an anti-militia recruitment riot in Erris, County Mayo, in which one thousand took part and fifty-two were killed. The *Journal* also noted the absence of religious distinction in the recruitment and there was intense interest in bounties, such as that offered by Lord Doneraile's very liberal assistance to the recruits of the South Cork militia.

In some areas, clearly, recruitment was not a problem. In Limerick City Major Ross-Lewin, from a military County Clare family, reported a quick enlistment without balloting or bounty: 'The Irish are a people naturally fond of the careless, chequered, errant life of a soldier; and as one proof of it, my corps was raised voluntarily in a single day'.[20] For the British Army the Irish militia would be of enormous importance during the Napoleonic wars, for by then these formations had evolved into holding units that provided many of the recruits for regiments, a 'nursery for the regulars'.

The Duke of Wellington at first thought little of the Irish militia units; to him they were an 'embarrassment', but the Irish flooded into his army and in the end he appreciated them. It is estimated that between 1806 and 1813 nearly 29,000 Irish militia were sent to line regiments and not only to designated Irish formations. In 1800, when volunteering from the Irish Militia took place, the 68th Foot, a favourite with Irish Militia men, received about 2,600 men. As the Durham Light Infantry it would join Wellington's army in Portugal eleven years later. The 54th Foot was almost as popular with the Irish: 'in the spring of 1800 the regiment . . . before leaving Ireland . . . had obtained so many volunteers from the Irish militia . . . that a second battalion was ordered to be formed'. Militiamen also enlisted whenever parliament asked for them. In 1801, in the words of one south Cork militiaman when asked to volunteer for England, 'To be sure I will volunteer to England; it will be like going from the kitchen to the parlour'.[21]

At this time the Irish soldier, either Protestant or Catholic, if he did not directly enlist in a regular line regiment, could be found in a militia unit or a local yeomanry corps, raised in 1796 by local worthies as a police force, but, unlike Volunteers, under strict government control. By 1796 there were over 50,000 Irish in the British Army who were deployed around the world. Irish recruitment in all branches of the army was intense in the era following the outbreak of the French War, aided by the ending of the separate Irish Establishment in the Act of Union, 1800. With militarism flourishing in the countryside regular recruits were not hard to find; in the fifteen years preceding Waterloo Irish recruiting was over 90,000, boosted by nearly 30,000 militiamen.[22]

Long before the 'glory' days under Wellington, however, the Irish had a form of fighting put upon them which they almost universally hated: in aid of the civil power, that of engaging in actions against the unruly peasant social class that many came from. Militia were often used side by side with regular troops and, even though the militia units had been levied in some other part of the country, empathy of some magnitude was inevitable. Because of their class identification it was usually easier for officers to carry out their disagreeable tasks, but not always, especially when, in the American War of Independence and during the early years of the French Revolution, privileged people played with ideas of liberty, fraternity and equality.

Such ideas underlay what is known as the '98 Rising when the Irish Militia was among those called upon to put down the rebellion of the United Irishmen and had to fire on their fellow countrymen. Out of the Volunteer movement had come the Society of United Irishmen founded in Belfast in October 1791 when many Protestants, churchmen and dissenters alike were fascinated by the ideology of the French Revolution. Leaders emerged like Theobald Wolfe Tone, a Protestant Dublin lawyer and a French Revolution enthusiast, who talked of the use of arms to obtain independence for Ireland. By 1796 the United Irishmen were building up a military organization in Ulster, and the following year in Leinster an oath to take up arms if necessary was taken despite a harsh Insurrection Act. Military efforts, such as they were, were under the Irish aristocrat Lord Edward Fitzgerald, who, because commissioned in the British Army, had experience in America. He was caught in Dublin in 1798 and shot, dying of his wounds in prison.

However violent it often was, militarily the '98 Rising of the United Irishmen failed due to the lack of preparation of the insurgents and the prompt repressive tactics of the government. In late 1796 when the French Fleet, with Wolfe Tone on board, appeared at Bantry Bay on the west coast of Ireland threatening a landing in support of the United Irishmen, there was no question of the loyalty of the Militia. Some 19,000 strong, the Militia immediately moved with 'great alacrity' from all parts of the country to withstand the invasion. When the crisis had passed it was stated in the House of Lords that 'from Dublin to Bantry not a single man had deserted'. It was a different story only two years later at Killala when the French again appeared and this time did land. In the 'Castlebar Races', as the Castlebar defeat was called, the Irish militia units broke and fled (some defecting to the French, others only in confusion) after they encountered the veteran troops of the French Regulars, but not before they had put up a gallant fight at the Castlebar bridge under Lord Granard's leadership.[23] They redeemed themselves at Ballinamuck, however, and in the Church of Ireland Cathedral in Armagh is the flag of the French 70th Demi-Brigade taken by the Armagh militia after the final French defeat in that battle. Treated with condescension by the military and often mistrust by civilians, the Militia were defended by Lord Castlereagh, the Irish Chief Secretary, who was overly generous in his praise of the Militia who were, in fact, never completely trusted again.[24]

During these years of social unrest in Ireland it was scarcely surprising that some agitators would have infiltrated into the Army ranks and Militia, one example being the 5th Royal Irish Dragoons. Fenian and United Irishmen enlisted in the 5th deliberately to stir up mutiny and when this was discovered in 1799 the regiment was shipped to England, disbanded and struck off the Army List. Queen Victoria ordered the regiment to be re-raised in 1858 but with a new name, the 5th Royal Irish Lancers.

THE IRISH AND EIGHTEENTH CENTURY INDIA

Coote Bahadur

From the seventeenth century Irish were serving in India in the forces of the British Honourable East India Company which had slowly built up its strength, first as a trading company and then an accompanying military body. There was no religious bias nor prohibition against recruitment of Irish soldiers in the Company's army, unlike the British Army during the eighteenth century, so that John Company, as it was known, had long provided careers for the Irish, Catholic or Protestant. Very important for officers was that promotion was by merit not purchase, and this was a boon for the impecunious officer who, under the British Army's purchase system, could be saddled with debt as soon as he embarked upon a military career. A young man had to purchase a commission at regulated prices that varied according to the regiment chosen. Any promotion to a higher rank had also to be purchased, but only when a vacancy occurred. Vacancies caused by deaths on active service or by augmentation of a regiment were usually filled without purchase. Although John Company's Army was separate from the British Army, Irish soldiers in both frequently fought side by side, an association we cannot ignore.

Major Stringer Lawrence, who arrived in India in 1748 as Commander in Chief of the East India Company's military in Madras and then of all India in 1761, was from the professional British Army and was crucial in training and directing the Company's forces in the eighteenth century. In 1754 they were immensely strengthened by the arrival of the 39th Foot, the first regiment of British regulars to serve in India, for which signal

honour it was given the motto 'Primus in Indis'. Joining it shortly after its
arrival was the Anglo-Irish Captain Eyre Coote, he who had survived the
Falkirk scandal of 1746. Already in India was the Englishman Robert
Clive as Lieutenant Colonel in command of troops of the East India
Company, under whose military leadership Coote would serve. Clive had
arrived as a clerk in the Company and subsequently distinguished himself
as a soldier and politician, ultimately to be known as the father of British
India.

With the 39th Foot, commanded by the Huguenot Colonel John
Aldercron, was Lieutenant John Carnac, a Huguenot from the Irish
middle-class. A middle-aged bachelor who supported an elderly mother
and two deaf mute brothers in Dublin, he was known in Calcutta for his
rosy complexion and somewhat fussy ways, but 'he could be . . . a military fire-eater'. He became a great friend of Robert Clive and later
transferred to the East India Company where he became Clive's secretary
and Aide de Camp. Francis Forde, from an Anglo-Irish ascendancy
family, was the senior major in the 39th Foot. This son of the member of
Parliament for Downpatrick, Northern Ireland, had been in India with the
regiment since 1754 to become Colonel Aldercron's Second in
Command. When Clive met Francis Forde in 1756 he immediately held
such a high opinion of him that later, when the 39th returned to England,
he arranged for Forde to join him in Bengal in the East India Company's
service and even helped Forde financially to leave the 39th, in spite of difficulties that arose over Forde's appointment. The historian Mark Bence
Jones calls Forde an 'Anglo-Irishman of sunny disposition and great
ability'.[25]

Captain Eyre Coote, promoted temporary Major by Clive, first came
into prominence at the Battle of Plassey, 23 June 1757 against Surajah
Dowla the Nawab of Bengal, which gained the first battle honour for the
Bengal European Regiment. This brought to an end Clive's Bengal
campaign, a series of small battles with France in the Seven Years' War
that now reached India when both England and France took advantage of
native rivalries. Coote and two hundred men of the 39th Foot were the
only Crown troops in a force which, together with the Company's other
European and mostly sepoy troops, totalled roughly 3,000 men. He was
sent ahead with a detachment to capture the fort of Kutwa that
commanded the road and the river on the way to Plassey, and he organized such a successful 'piece of bluff' that the garrison of some 2,000
Bengali troops fled, abandoning the fort, guns and supplies to Clive. At
Kutwa Mir Jafar, paymaster general of the Bengali Army, was to join Clive
and his army in a palace conspiracy whereby Prince Surajah Dowla would
be deposed and Jafar put on the throne as an ally and protégé of the

Company. Jafar did not appear, but wrote to tell Clive that he would support him. Jafar, however, was playing one side off against the other, a very risky enterprise for Clive that could result in his having to face Surajah Dowla's army of 50,000 alone. When a council of war with his officers was assembled on 21 June 1757 to discuss Clive's next moves Coote, as senior King's officer, was first to vote for immediate attack on the grounds that 'delay might cast damp', and also before French help under M. Law, the French Governor of Cosimbazar, should arrive. Others, including Clive, voted against taking action. Clive changed his mind and the next morning advised Coote that he would attack. In the battle it was clear that a large part of the Nawab's army, commanded by Mir Jafar and other conspira- tors, was ready to defect. Mir Jafar gave the Nawab the treacherous advice not to attack that day, because it was too late and advised the Nawab to withdraw. Clive, seeing this, ordered a general advance. After a fierce rear- guard action, in which only the French gunners continued fighting to the last, the Bengali force fled and Coote participated in the pursuit, but in darkness and without cavalry this was possible for only a few miles. Plassey was a victory for Clive largely due to the unreliability of the Nawab's Army and the treachery of Mir Jafar, who was recognized as the new Nawab of Bengal. Plassey has been called 'a petty action', but it was 'to rank as the first decisive battle in the history of British India'.[26]

Because of Clive's initial indecision 'there were many people [in England], even if Coote himself was not among their number, to give all the credit to him and not to Clive for the victory of Plassey' and this did not help their relationship. Coote was a brave soldier with a quarrelsome temperament, quick to take offence, and difficulties between Coote and Clive had already surfaced after an earlier fracas at Fort William on 2 January where Clive had been incensed by Coote, who, in a seemingly high-handed attitude to Company troops, had taken his orders from Admiral Watson RN, rather than Clive. The Clive/Coote dissension reveals the inter-service dispute between Crown and Company troops when officers of the Crown at times demanded precedence over those commissioned by the Company, many of whom had long experience of Indian conditions and in commanding native troops. After the battle Coote returned to England to settle his affairs and to lay before Prime Minister William Pitt a version of the operations in Bengal quite different from Clive's despatches.

Coote's difficulties with Clive were soon seized upon by the very able Laurence Sulivan, a Protestant Irishman from County Cork who, with experience in India, had risen from being a director of the East India Company in London to become its chairman in 1758. Sulivan, as a competent businessman, was interested in the Company's profit-making and not in Clive's Imperialist view.[27] The tensions between Sulivan and Clive came to a head over military command in India when Major James Kilpatrick, his Second in Command, died of fever in 1757. Clive's recommendation of his other protégé, Major Francis Forde, for command of the troops in Bengal was refused by the Company's directors, who saw the nomination as Stringer Lawrence's preserve. Sulivan then promoted the cause of Eyre Coote, Clive's *bête noire,* as commander in Bengal. Meanwhile Forde, commanding troops of the Bengal European Regiment, acquitted himself well in defeating the French near Condore in December 1758, and in capturing the French coastal settlement of Masulipatam in April 1759, bringing an end to French supremacy in the Deccan. When Coote's appointment became known in a despatch from the directors the unfortunate Forde resigned from the Company; his military career effectively finished, he returned to Ireland. Capable and brave soldier that he was, before leaving India he defeated for Clive a Dutch force in Bengal. In the intricate rivalries in Bengal, Forde could be seen as 'an ill-used man'. Four years later in 1764, under Clive's patronage, he received a Company appointment but was drowned at sea on his way back to India. Sadly Francis Forde died never honoured for his services to his country.[28]

Prominent in helping Forde at Condore and Masulipatam was another Anglo-Irishman Captain (later Major) Ransfur Lee Knox. Born in Sligo into a family of military careerists and churchmen and connected to the Knoxes of Prehen, Co Derry, at the age of sixteen Knox entered the recently founded Royal Military College at Woolwich as a gentleman cadet intended for the artillery. In 1753 he was instead accepted in the East India Company as Ensign, landing at Madras in 1754. Knox had been quickly picked out by Clive and Forde and as Captain was an able commander of Bengal, European and Sepoy battalions. After the Siege of Patna in 1763 Knox was appointed Lieutentant Colonel of a 2nd European Regiment, but died at thirty-four before it was organized, another example of how India claimed the lives of able soldiers through disease.[29] Many years later, in 1824, a Bishop Hebert found his tomb on the banks of the Ganges at Patna bearing the inscription: 'the earthly remains of the truly gallant Major Randfurlie Knox'.

In March 1759 Coote was appointed Commander-in-Chief of the military forces in Bengal and returned to India. While he was still in England the government was persuaded by the East India Company to raise another infantry regiment for Bengal, the 84th foot; 'our trusty and well-beloved Eyre Coote' was commissioned by the King as its Colonel. Now began the long British-French imperial struggle in India and hostilities resumed between the French and the British East India Companies. Both armies were commanded by Irish soldiers of genius: Colonel Eyre Coote and Count Thomas Arthur Lally de Tollendal.

Lally was a descendent of an ancient Galway family; his father, an Irish Jacobite, Sir Gerard Lally was a Brigadier General in the French forces and the younger Lally, commissioned in Dillon's Regiment, served with distinction in the Irish Brigade especially in the victory over the British at Fontenoy. When Lally arrived in India in 1758 in command of a French Expedition, his experienced regiments were filled with officers bearing names like Murphy, O'Kenealey and O'Kennedy. On his arrival in India he immediately took Fort St David and held Pondicherry, but economies by French authorities soon began to limit his effectiveness and furthur operations were unsuccessful.

Coote's victory over Lally was at Wandewash on 22 January 1760, where, in this battle, Coote adopted a two-deep line of infantry as a battle formation nearly half a century before Wellington did so. It was a 'classic confrontation of French column against British line and for the French it was the beginning of the end'. Lally withdrew his battered forces to Pondicherry where, after a siege and without adequate supplies, he surrenderd to Coote in January 1761. He was taken to London, then requested to be returned to France where he was accused of treason and cowardice and, after imprisonment, was beheaded in 1766. Coote paid generous tribute to Lally who had been ill-served by poor support from France: 'There is not another man in all India who could have kept on foot for the same length of time an army without pay and receiving no assistance from any quarter'.[30]

Coote returned to England a hero and a rich man. A period of being a country gentleman followed, with his bride, the daughter of the Governor of St Helena, whom he had met and married while on his way home. Elected a member of Parliament, he sat for Leicester until 1769 when he was appointed Commander-in-Chief in India by the directors of the East India Company. This appointment was short-lived because Coote, with his impatient and 'peppery' nature, could not get along with the Madras Council: 'Only an angel could,' writes Philip Mason, 'it was factious, interfering . . . often corrupt throughout this period.' Never one to tolerate advice from civilians, Coote resigned and returned to England. Knighted in 1771, he accepted yet again, in 1778, the post of Commander-in-Chief of the Company's forces in India with a seat on the Governor General's Council. En route to India Coote heard that France was aiding the American colonies and hostilities with the British broke out again in India. In 1780 Hyder Ali, Prince of Mysore, a brilliant soldier, fed up with the British, declared war and with his son Tippu and a large army began a campaign of ravaging the Carnatic, establishing himself fifty miles from Madras. Coote in Calcutta was sent with troops by Warren Hastings, the first Governor General in India, to take command, preserve British possessions in the Carnatic and restore morale in the Madras Army. As always, Hyder Ali outnumbered him and Coote, tied up by him, had to stay five months at Cuddalore until a French squadron moved from offshore allowing shipping from Madras to bring supplies for Coote's half-starved army and reinforcements by Admiral Hughes's Fleet. On 1 June 1781 Coote led his forces against Hyder Ali in the battle of Porto Novo. A British schooner, opportunely arriving offshore, fired on Hyder Ali's cavalry, killing their leader, and predictably they fled. The victory was not decisive but it saved Southern India for the British. Coote's leadership was highly praised: 'He was everywhere and exposed himself to every danger'. Later that year Coote's victories at Pollilur and Sholinghar proved frustrating; forced to retire to Madras for fresh supplies he could not achieve a successful follow-up. In May of 1782 Coote set out from Madras when he heard that the Mysoreans were again gathering and on 22 June at Arnee the last of Coote's battlefield duels took place against Hyder Ali. Again Coote prevailed, 'the saviour of the Carnatic'. Peace was signed between England and France and the second Mysore War ended.[31]

In the following March a very ill Coote, with his wife and staff, left Calcutta for Madras, urged by his friend Warren Hastings as the man most able to save the Presidency of Fort St George where there was mutinous conduct among the troops and quarrels in the council. Coote died at sea on the voyage shortly before news reached India of the Treaty of Versailles, which restored in full to the British the Indian territories for which Coote had fought so long. He was buried with full honours in St Mary's Church, the oldest Protestant church in Madras.

Eyre Coote is not as well known in British Army history as Gough, who defeated the Sikhs, or Nicholson of the Punjab and Indian Mutiny, or Wellington of the Peninsular War, all Irishmen. His reputation is secure as the Irish soldier who defeated France and the formidable Hyder Ali and won for Britain supreme power in India. 'In the matter of tactics on the field,' the noted military historian Sir John Fortescue writes, 'he seems to have been one of the greatest masters of his own or of any other time . . . He could handle ten thousand men with the ease and precision of a sergeant drilling a squad in the barrack yard.' In organizing his army in Madras Coote was careful to reduce the chronic friction between the King's and Company's officers striving to be fair in assigning commands. Coote's impatience with civilian colleagues and his often imperious and difficult temperament were not helped by failing health in his later years. As a general he was to the sepoys Coote 'Bahadur', a Persian word meaning bold, and in Hindustani a superlative implying courage. Captain Innes Munro of the 73rd Foot (later the Black Watch) spoke of the respect granted to Coote by both sepoy and European troops: 'The soldier's friend, most dear to the soldiers he commanded for his personal bravery, his great likeability, and his affectionate regard for their honour and interests'. He had particularly commended a Highland piper of the 73rd at the Battle of Porto Novo who, with 'astonishing composure', continued to play as he marched up and down during the battle. Coote was the first British commander to mention by name in his despatches NCOs and private soldiers, both British and Indian. Not until over sixty years later would General Sir Charles Napier do the same.[32]

Emulating Coote, perhaps it is fitting to mention Sergeant Speedy, an Irish enlisted man whose career in India is especially valuable, for, after serving in a detachment under Major Kilpatrick, his is the only name recorded as having joined the ranks of the Bengal European Regiment at its formation in December 1756. His story comes from Captain Williams who wrote the *Historical Account of the Bengal Native Infantry* and knew Speedy personally. Speedy had fought in the wars of the Austrian Succession, 1740s, with the 32nd Foot at Dettingen, Fontenoy and Lauffeld where he lost part of a hand. Discharged but fond of adventure, he enlisted again as a soldier in the East India Company and was one of the few to survive the terrible malaria which carried off three-quarters of the detachment sent to Bengal under Major Kilpatrick. He was with the Regiment at Plassey under Clive and at Condore and Masulipatam under Francis Forde. In 1760 he was promoted to Sergeant Major of a sepoy battalion. Captured in the battle at Manji he managed an exciting escape from a native boat that was taking him to his execution. Speedy served in the Bengal European Regiment until his death in 1767 'having led as eventful a life as perhaps any Irish soldier at that time'.[33]

India was the place where many Irish also served as mercenaries, their adventurous spirit and martial ability finding action. Typical of these men was William Gardner, the well-educated son of an Irish Infantry Major. In 1783 an ensigncy in the infantry was purchased for him in England, but, seeking more adventure or faster promotion, he resigned his commission in the British Army to serve the infamous Mahratta Prince Holkar. Gardner soon fell out with Holkar and at one point almost cut him down during an altercation. He then served another prince, Amrit Rao, but, refusing to fight the British, he was imprisoned. In a *Boy's Own Paper* type of adventure he escaped an escort, jumped off a forty-foot precipice, swam a river and eventually joined General Gerard Lake's army. His bravery led Lake to order him to raise and lead a body of cavalry to be recognized as Lieutenant Colonel Gardner's Corps of Irregular Horse. After successive changes of name Gardner's Horse evolved in 1890 into the 2nd Bengal Lancers.

Another example of the Irish mercenary spirit in late eighteenth century India was George Thomas, an Irish Protestant from Roscrea, County Tipperary, a colourful soldier of fortune. The 'accepted story' of Thomas's early life was that he was born in 1756, began his career by running away to sea, deserting his ship in Madras, then setting out to live by his sword in the native armies of Hyderabad and other princedoms. It is thought Thomas had also enlisted in the British Army where he would have been at home for it was full of Irishmen and where, more importantly, he would have learned his undoubted military skills and horsemanship. It is known that he put his knowledge of artillery to good use while fighting against the Sikhs. Recognized as the virtual 'king' of a large tract of Moghul land, by 1801 Thomas's reputation and resources were at their peak when his brigade-size army in the Deccan dominated territory on the Sikh border and pillaged the countryside as far as Delhi. His nemesis in the war between the Indian princes was another mercenary, Pierre Perron, who became a powerful military leader. Thomas's final struggle with Perron and his superior forces was at Hansi, an ancient fortress city deserted and partly in ruins that Thomas had made his capital and head-quarters. Thomas appeared in the fray: 'a huge man in native dress, armed with sword and buckler, his face contorted with fury, and roaring like a bull . . . his arms bare to the shoulder and entwined with tatoo marks . . . It was all in vain'. On 20 December Thomas with great dignity finally surrendered to Colonel Louis Bourquin, commander of Perron's Third Brigade.

Thomas was admired among mercenaries as an honourable man and true soldier in that eighteenth century world of warfare where conventions of chivalry were often observed. British officers under Bourquin persuaded him to allow Thomas to keep his weapons, goods and large family and leave for British territory. Thomas accepted. Before leaving he was received 'with all ceremony' in Bourquin's mess where, inflamed by drink and the thought of his defeat, he took exception to Bourquin's toast to the 'success of Perron's arms' and, 'glaring with fury . . . leaped to his feet and drew his sword yelling, "One Irish sword . . . is still sufficient for a hundred Frenchmen".' Bourquin fled but later was persuaded to return and 'peace was restored'. At age forty-six Thomas, already a very sick man, died in Bengal on 22 August 1802 on his way home to Ireland.

In those days of conflicting alliances George Thomas was known to have intrigued with the British. After his defeat, when talking to Colonel William Francklin, chronicler of the Moghul scene, this proud, boastful man of the sword mourned his 'grand design to conquer the Punjab; "to plant the British standard on the banks of the Attock River" '. Thomas was later admired by the Victorians for his British pluck and daring, and though censured for going native, drinking and keeping a harem, was excused as 'a lovable Irish scapegrace'. Shelford Bidwell writes that this was:

> an inadequate verdict on a man who seized a principality and ruled it so justly that his name was still remembered with affection and respect in the twentieth century and who as a soldier on the Indian scene, if not the equal of a Lake or a young Arthur Wellesley was certainly in the class of Clive or Forde . . . these now forgotten men whose . . . daring put the East India Company in possession of half a sub-continent.[34]

In India also the young Colonel the Honourable Arthur Wesley of the 33rd Foot came into prominence in pursuit of that illustrious career that would later make him a national hero as the great Duke of Wellington. There was not a military tradition in Arthur Wesley's Anglo-Irish gentry family. His father Lord Mornington was a country gentleman at the family estate, Dangan Castle, County Meath and, in 1764, a Professor of Music at Trinity College, Dublin. He also had been a member of the Irish House of Commons and of the Irish House of Lords. Wesley's family, originally from Somerset, England, had accompanied Henry II to Ireland and had slowly amassed land through intermarriage with Anglo-Irish gentry of the Pale. Arthur was born in Dublin in 1769, the same year as Napoleon Bonaparte. He seems to have been close to his family and his older brother Richard, who succeeded his father as the second Lord Mornington and inherited the family's debts, would be generous in purchasing commissions for him in several regiments as Arthur advanced in the British Army. In India, where Richard was Governor General, Arthur acted as Richard's unofficial military secretary and Henry, his younger brother, Richard's private secretary. After Eton Arthur's family did not consider him fit for anything but a military career and at seventeen he was packed off to the historic Royal Academy of Equitation at Angers, France, with the sons of the Irish Lords Walsh and Powerscourt, along with some French nobility. There Arthur learned to write and speak French fluently. On his eighteenth birthday in 1787 with family help he was gazetted Ensign in the 73rd Highlanders, and at the end of the year Lieutenant in the 76th regiment. By 1788 he was back in Ireland as Aide de Camp to the Viceroy and from 1790 he served as MP for the family seat of Trim.

Wesley was very much involved in Anglo-Irish affairs. He was always 'enlivened by the pleasures and scandals of Dublin life' in his duties at

Dublin Castle as MP and as a young Lieutenant in the 41st Foot. In this Anglo-Irish society Arthur found his wife, the Honourable Catherine (Kitty) Pakenham, daughter of Lord Longford whose town house was in Rutland Square, Dublin, where the Morningtons also had a house in nearby Merrion Street. Robert Stewart, of the famous Anglo-Irish Londonderry family and a fellow member of Parliament, was another of Arthur's childhood friends who later, as Secretary for War, was always someone he could turn to for advice and help, especially when he was in the Peninsula.

Arthur Wesley's passionate concentration on his career as a professional soldier was, at least in part, influenced by his determination to wed Kitty Pakenham after his first proposal of marriage had failed. Among several obstacles to their marriage was the disorderly impoverished state of the Wesley family's affairs and the sale by Richard of both Mornington House in Dublin and the Dangan Castle estate which represented for the Pakenhams 'a desertion of Ireland'. The scandal attaching to Richard's irregular union and profligate lifestyle did not help Arthur's cause. He was made to understand by Lord Longford that family approval of such a match with 'a younger son with little chance of inheritance' whose interests were only gaiety and music was very unlikely. When Lord Longford, Kitty's father, died shortly after, it was the then Lord Longford, Kitty's brother Tom, who informed Major Wesley his proposal of marriage was rejected.[35]

Wellesley Bahadur

As Lieutenant Colonel of the 33rd Arthur Wesley was beginning to develop a professional interest in matters military and a skill in attention to detail. In his first experience of action in the field, in Holland in September 1794, he commanded a brigade in Lord Moira's force sent to reinforce the army of the Duke of York in Flanders and was commended for his handling of it. The expedition, however, was poorly led and the 33rd joined other regiments in a prolonged and undisciplined retreat in bitter winter weather. It was a shocking experience and the neglect of the men and the lack of supply-services was a salutary lesson for the young Wesley. He would later complain, 'I was on the Waal [river] . . . from October to January . . . and during all that time I only saw once one General from the headquarters'[36] – a complaint echoed over a century later in the First World War by the young Lieutenant Bernard Montgomery, also of Irish stock. Returning reluctantly to Ireland and his aide de camp duties, Wesley deplored the scandalous traffic in commissions; however, purchase itself was not an issue. It was with relief that he left Ireland for

India, joining his regiment at Cape Town, promoted a full Colonel in the Army by seniority at twenty-seven.

Arriving at Calcutta in February 1797 Wesley found that the Irish were a major element in its social life and he was prevailed upon, as a newly arrived Irishman, to preside at the annual St Patrick's day dinner. Much socializing and drinking went on, especially in the mess of the 33rd and with two new companions, the Irish Major General John St Leger, a friend of the Prince of Wales and recently arrived with the Royal Establishment in Bengal, and William Hickey, a memoirist of the East India Company who for many years was an attorney in Calcutta. Wesley's interest in Calcutta society, however, was fleeting; he had come to India in the interest of his military career and, having spent his time studying books on Indian campaigns, he became increasingly impatient with the numerous dinner parties. About this time Arthur signed himself for the first time as Wellesley, not Wesley, a reversion to an old spelling of the family name, a practice begun by Richard who saw it as being more distinguished.[37]

When Richard Lord Mornington arrived as Governor General in May 1798 he decided to put an end to the suspected ambitions of the ruler, Tippu Sultan, the Tiger of Mysore and son of Hyder Ali, who was reported to be associating with the French. He astutely 'seduced' mercenary officers, like Gardner and Thomas, by letting it be known that if they left the service of Perron or of the Mahrattas and 'reported to the British', the Company would guarantee their pensions. The ensuing Battle of Seringapatam in 1799 brought an end to Tippu and military honour to Arthur Wellesley who, in General Harris's army, commanded a large force that included his own 33rd Foot, Madras troops of the East India Company and battalions of Britain's ally the Nizam of Hyderabad. His command of the latter greatly angered Major General David Baird, a tough Scottish giant who thought he should have been appointed: he was older than Wellesley and, having once been a prisoner in Tippu's dungeons, had wished for a chance for revenge. Ordered to attack at night the Sultanpettah Tope, a dense grove of bamboo, Wellesley had not been able to reconnoitre the ground. He nevertheless deeply regretted his failure and the deaths of his men. Some said he escaped a reprimand only because of his brother's position. Wellesley, given a chance to make amends, took the Tope without loss the next morning, 6 April. In early May a successful attack on Seringapatam's defence works went in. Baird volunteered to lead the assault of two columns and did so with great enthusiasm and skill, while Wellesley commanded a third, in reserve. Tippu Sultan was found dead. Wellesley emerged from this victory having made an enemy of Baird who expected to be Governor of Seringapatam, the honour going to the well-connected Wellesley.[38] By the time of Wellesley's great victory at Assaye in September 1803 against the Mahratta forces of Doulot Ráo Scindia, where he won much respect as the Major General in the Company's services who finally restored order in the Deccan, he had begun to display the innate coolness under fire and moral authority among his troops that was to characterize him in the Peninsular War. But Wellesley would later observe that this battle was 'the bloodiest I ever saw'.

Raising of Irish Regiments for the British Army and the Revolutionary War in France

During these years Irish regiments were among the many raised in the British Army that would serve under Wellesley when France declared war on Britain in 1793. Already mentioned is the 87th Foot, Major John Doyle's legion of 'Irish Heroes' raised in September 1793. Three months later the 89th Foot was raised in Dublin by Colonel William Crosbie. In 1798 Major Lord Andrew Blayney of Castle Blayney, Monaghan, purchased the lieutenant-colonelcy of this regiment which then acquired the nickname 'Blayney's Bloodhounds' said to be from chasing rebels in the '98 United Irishmen Rising. Hard on the heels of the 87th and 89th, in 1793 the 83rd Foot was raised in Dublin by Colonel William Fitch, a brave benevolent commander who was killed in action in Jamaica in 1795. Their nickname of Fitch's Grenadiers was a rather ironic sobriquet because grenadiers were by tradition always chosen from the tallest troops and Fitch's men were mostly of diminutive stature. The 86th, not at first an Irish regiment, was also raised in 1793, in Shropshire, England, by Major General Sir Cornelius Cuyler and almost immediately moved to Ireland where the number 86 was allotted to it. In 1812, in recognition of their capture of the French island of Bourbon in 1810, the 86th was granted the title The Royal County Down Regiment of Foot and permitted to wear on their buttons insignia of the Irish harp and crown. Later in the nineteenth century the 83rd and 86th would become 1st and 2nd battalions of the Royal Irish Rifles and the 87th and 89th would be the Royal Irish Fusiliers

Of the regiments raised in 1793 the one with the reputation for being most Irish was the 88th Foot, the Connaught Rangers, 'some of whom knew only enough English to get by on parade'. [39] Its first colonel was the Honorable Thomas de Burgh, later the Earl of Clanricarde. With one or two exceptions all its officers were Irish, the sons of gentlemen belonging to septs or families that had some relationship with the colonel. Many of these officers raised recruits from their estates or communities in

Connaught and from the beginning a strong 'familial' spirit soon merged with a regimental allegiance that was uniquely treasured. It was the only regiment raised at this time with a territorial designation. The regimental spirit of the Connaught Rangers was early evident in a fracas with the Derbyshire militia at Eastbourne, England, where the militia were so impressed with the fighting prowess of the 88th that some two hundred of them were persuaded to transfer into the Rangers. In late 1808 when ordered to the Peninsula, the commander of the 88th was Major Vandeleur of the Vandeleur family whose younger sons were classic Irish Junkers.

In the late eighteenth century the process was well underway that gave Wellington's army in Spain its very Irish character with 'no fewer than fourteen Irish regiments' and as he estimated an Irish presence of '30 per cent' in other regiments.[40]

CHAPTER THREE

The Irish in the Peninsular War,
in North America and at Waterloo

Over the hills and over the main
To Flanders, Portugal and Spain

Traditional Eighteenth Century
British marching song.

Major General Sir Arthur Wellesley, whom Napoleon would disparagingly call the 'Sepoy General', returned to Britain in 1805 after an absence of eight years in India a hardened campaigner with a capacity for handling large bodies of men under fire and attention to detail that would become legendary. Showered with honours including his KCB and thanked by Parliament with a fortune, his financial troubles disappeared. Despite these plaudits the senior military command he really wanted did not come his way. He was given command of a brigade to Hanover, a brief 'abortive expedition', followed by command of a brigade guarding the coastline at Hastings. There seemed little regard for anyone who had served in India, nor had he sufficient European experience for a higher appointment. Wellesley accepted stoically the limitations at this time in his career, for in military matters his duty was to serve the King wherever he was sent.[1] The concept of duty would be his abiding principle throughout his life.

Wellesley could now open negotiations to resume his courtship of Kitty Pakenham despite the many intervening years. In April 1806 they married in Dublin in what proved to be a union far from ideal. The marriage certainly extended Arthur Wellesley's connection with the Anglo-Irish class; Kitty's brothers Sir Edward and Sir Hercules Pakenham, both young army officers, would serve under him and become devoted to their brother-in-law. A close bond developed between Wellesley and a former rival for Kitty's hand, Galbraith Lowry Cole, who also served under him. The son of Lord Enniskillen, Lowry was a young Anglo-Irishman of impeccable background, an old friend of Kitty's family and a career soldier like Arthur. At twenty-one he was gazetted Major in the 86th Foot, followed by a colonelcy in the Coldstream Guards. He had also commanded a regiment in the Irish Rebellion of 1798 and was wounded at Vinegar Hill. Lionized by family and friends, including the Pakenhams, Lowry was elected MP for County Fermanagh.[2]

Wellesley became a member of Parliament for Rye while he was at Hastings, advised to do so by his old friend Robert Stewart, now Lord Castlereagh and Secretary for War, to defend the honour of his brother Richard accused of sharp practices in India by a fellow member of the Commons. Wellesley was a soldier not a politician and became impatient while Napoleon was striding across Europe with his armies. He petitioned Castlereagh many times for a command, reminding him that by remaining in a 'large civil office', by which he meant his position as Chief Secretary of Ireland appointed in April 1807, he 'might lose the confidence and esteem of the officers and men of the army'. At last Wellesley achieved his necessary service in Europe when in August 1807 he joined an expedition to Denmark to force the Danes to give up their fleet before the French seized it. A more experienced officer was his Second in Command, a 'minder' but a tactful man, and Wellesley soon took over and led his brigade in a successful attack at Köge which brought about Copenhagen's surrender on 6 September.

Wellesley – Early Days in the Iberian Peninsula

Lieutenant General Sir Arthur Wellesley (the Duke of Wellington from 1814) is chiefly remembered for nearly 'seven years of patient and brilliantly successful warfare in the Peninsula by which the British expeditionary force was brought from a beach in Portugal to the recovery of Spain and a victorious invasion of Napoleonic France'[3] and the defeat of Napoleon at Waterloo. In October 1807 Napoleon declared war on Portugal and General Junot invaded and occupied Lisbon. The following May Napoleon replaced the popular Spanish King Ferdinand VII with his own brother Joseph Bonaparte. Spain erupted and revolts against the French took place throughout the country. In 1808, when Wellesley and Napoleon were entering their fortieth year, deputations from Spain in June, and Portugal in July, went to England to appeal for help to withstand the French power and Britain responded. Wellesley, who was already assembling a force in Cork to support revolutionaries in Venezuela against Spain, was ready and willing. When he instead set sail for Corunna in northern Spain in July his orders were 'to drive [General] Junot out of Portugal'.[4]

Wellesley, now the youngest Lieutenant General in the army, with his small force landed at Oporto, Portugal in August 1808 and immediately used Colonel (later Major General Sir) Nicholas Trant, a Portuguese-speaking Irishman, as the liaison officer with the Portuguese General Bernardin Freire. The Battle of Vimeiro on 21 August was a clear victory for the allies, with the Portuguese fighting under Trant. Wellesley outmanoeuvred the French by using his reverse slope tactic that would become famous in the Peninsular War: he kept most of his redcoat infantry behind the ridge out of sight with orders to hold their fire until the last moment when, at a command, they rose in two thin lines to pour murderous rapid musket fire into the densely-packed advancing French columns. The French fled; Junot's casualties were twice those of the British, including three generals. Unfortunately, arriving on the scene were two British generals senior to Wellesley, Dalrymple and Burrard, who forbade pursuit of the demoralized French. The result of this folly was the Convention of Cintra whereby the defeated French were allowed to leave Portugal and even to be carried back to France in British ships. Arthur Wellesley was recalled to Britain to defend himself in the military inquiry into the Convention. The Court of Inquiry, loathe to blame the generals, accepted the Convention, but neither Dalrymple nor Burrard ever held command again. Wellesley was always to regret signing the armistice document for which he said he was not responsible, not being commander of the force.[5] He then reluctantly returned to his Parliamentary duties as Chief Secretary for Ireland.

Meanwhile the able and canny Scot Sir John Moore was ordered into Spain against the French to support a very divided Spanish army; an Irish soldier of fortune, General Joachim Blake, commanded the troops from Galicia. When Moore reached Salamanca he was told that Blake's forces had disintegrated and the French were scattering the rest, bringing massive reinforcements into Spain. Then came news of the fall of Madrid. Finally, on 23 December Moore learned that Napoleon himself was leading his army north from Madrid to attack him. He led his unwieldy army courageously through towns in northern Spain, over icy roads, pressed hard by Napoleon's forces and then up into the harsh mountains of Galicia. ' "The English are running away . . ." boasted Napoleon' and by 2 January 1809 he left for Paris leaving command to Soult. Finally on 10 January Moore's army descended to the Spanish Port of Corunna, but before the army could be safely evacuated by the Fleet the Battle of Corunna took place. Moore's exhausted army fought bravely but he did not survive the fierce fighting.[6] As Moore lay dying on 16 January he was held by his inseparable friend and Adjutant General, Colonel (later Lieutenant General) Paul Anderson, a native of Waterford. Anderson had joined the 51st Foot in 1791 when Moore commanded the regiment, had been Brigade Major under him in the West Indies and was with him during '98 in Ireland and in many campaigns. The French, also weakened, did not prevent the army's departure and the successful Retreat from Corunna became one of the famous episodes in the British Army.

When the Irish Major Charles Napier of the 50th Foot was wounded several times at Corunna there is an amusing story of how he tried to limp back to his own lines with a shattered ankle and was taken prisoner. Stabbed in the back, he was saved by a French soldier who intervened when other French soldiers robbed and nearly clubbed him to death. Napier was nearly killed again by a 'wild and rude Irishman' in his regiment named Hennessy. This obstinate soldier rushed at Napier's captors brandishing his musket, but when Napier shouted that they surrender as he was wounded and a prisoner Private Hennessy shouted back in his less than intelligible brogue:

> 'Surrender! Why should I surrender?' . . . 'Because there are at least twenty men upon you.' 'Well, if I must surrender, there! There's my firelock for you. . . . Stand away ye bloody spalpeens,' he roared at them. . . 'I'll carry him myself. Bad luck to the whole bloody lot of ye'.[7]

And so, still cursing, he helped the suffering Napier to a farm house where he was imprisoned. Napier survived with the help of a French officer who was a fellow Mason and, paroled in 1809, he was soon back in the Peninsula.

Wellesley's friend the gruff Major General William Carr Beresford was another important Anglo-Irish commander in the Peninsula. He was invited by the Portuguese to reorganize their army and given the rank of Marshal of the Portuguese forces. The illegitimate son of one of the greatest Irish landowners, the Marquess of Waterford, Beresford had learned to speak Portuguese when he was Governor of Madeira. He had been sent to the military school at Strasbourg, had served in North America, India, Egypt and the Cape of Good Hope, had been captured during the taking of Buenos Aires and had fought with distinction at Corunna. Wellesley always trusted him and often said that Beresford was 'the best officer we have for the command of an army'. Indeed the successful and efficient Portuguese Army in the Peninsula was largely his creation. Beresford was also valuable to Wellesley on the home front; as brother of the Marquess of Waterford his political clout was considerable.[8]

The British Army faced a formidable foe in the Peninsula. The revolutionary fervour of the French Revolution gave an *élan* to Napoleon's conscripted fourteen French armies, while their discipline made the French military machine a frightening power. The British Army clearly had to learn a new technique of war. Encouraged by the Duke of York, Commander-in-Chief of the British Army who was interested in light infantry tactics, a reforming movement took place. Light infantrymen operating separately from the rigid regular lines had already been accepted by Sir John Moore. Then in 1800 an Experimental Corps of Riflemen was created from men drawn from the pick of fifteen regiments, armed with the new Baker rifle, harder to load but more accurate up to 300 yards, and clothed in bottle-green uniforms for protective covering. Brought into line in 1802 the Rifle Corps moved to Shorncliffe, General Sir John Moore's area of command, and there he directed and trained the Light Infantry Rifle Corps. Moore, in his selection of personnel for the new Light Infantry Rifle Corps, wrote that men should be young 'not so much . . . men of stature as . . . intelligent, handy, and active'. All the men were encouraged to think and act for themselves.[9]

Wellesley himself had studied 'France's Revolutionary armies [that] had swept across . . . Europe in dense columns behind a screen of *voltigeurs* and *tirailleurs*', effective new formations. He also studied the tactics used in the forests of America by the innovative Colonel Bouquet, the Swiss officer who commanded the 60th (Royal) American regiment (later the King's Royal Rifle Corps), raised to counter the marksmanship of French Canadian backwoodsmen in fighting that had no rigid rules. In Portugal Wellesley ordered a permanent company of riflemen be attached to his brigades.[10] These Rifle units particularly appealed to the Irish. The adventurous, independent thinking encouraged in riflemen is well exemplified in Bernard Cornwell's novels of the Peninsular War where he follows the careers of his swashbuckling characters Rifleman Richard Sharpe and his Irish sidekick Sergeant Patrick Harper as Sharpe climbs the promotion ladder without purchase. They proudly wear their 'jackets of green' and black equipment rather than the 'white pipe-clay of the scarlet-coated' Line regiments.

In April 1809 Wellesley resigned as Chief Secretary for Ireland and returned to Lisbon to take command of the British Army after Moore's death. Working with Beresford's flanking advance, Wellesley skilfully took Oporto on 12 May. In July he crossed into Spain, joining forces with the aged and frail Spanish General Cuesta, who proved to be an unreliable ally and failed to provide promised food for the allied forces. The Battle of Talavera, which followed on 27 and 28 July against the French Army commanded by Marshal Victor, was a Pyrrhic victory for Wellesley's army. Wellesley again used his successful tactic of keeping his troops on the reverse side of the Medellin Ridge, a key position he occupied. When the French columns climbed to the crest they were suddenly met by an extended line of infantry who fired concentrated and deadly volleys.

According to regimental records, the first British shot fired at Talavera was by a Connaught Ranger named Thomas Kelly. The 88th lost 136 men in the two days of fighting. Of Talavera Wellesley said, 'Never was there such a Murderous Battle!!'; he was hit but not hurt. This battle marked the last time that Wellesley trusted the Spanish Army; always there was trouble over supplies and General Cuesta had abandoned to the French some 1,500 British wounded in Talavera. For this victory Sir Arthur Wellesley was honoured with the title Viscount Wellington of Talavera and of Wellington and Baron Douro of Welleslie in the county of Somerset. From September 1809 he signed himself Wellington.[11]

The Connaught Rangers' exploits in the Peninsula come to us first hand through the very gifted military diarist William Grattan, who joined the Connaught Rangers as an ensign in 1809. A member of a well-known Dublin family, among his relatives was a cousin Thomas Colley Grattan the novelist, and a more distant relative was the Irish statesman Henry Grattan. William's vivid recollections of his Irish comrades, both in and out of battle, include comments on tensions between the Connaught Rangers and the newly appointed 3rd Division Commander under whom they served, Major General Thomas Picton, a Welshman. Picton brought with him a tarnished reputation as Military Governor of Trinidad following accusations of mismanagement. George III stood by him and he survived to be asked by Wellington to join him in the Peninsula, there to gain a reputation second only to Wellington himself as one of the most colourful characters in that campaign, his division becoming known as the 'Fighting Third'.

On Picton's first parading of his division two 'marauders' of the 88th were brought forward on a charge of stealing a goat. Very much against looting, Picton immediately ordered a flogging in front of all. Then, turning to the 88th, he said, 'You are not known in the army by the name of "Connaught Rangers", but by the name of Connaught *footpads*!' He also made reference to their country and their religion. The Connaughts' Colonel Alexander Wallace took issue with this, but later recorded for Grattan how Picton apologized to Wallace and senior officers of his division for his remarks, explaining he had not been correctly informed about the Rangers' conduct. The 88th was 'a fine fighting regiment' and steady on parade thanks to the iron hand of its Scottish Commander Colonel Wallace, but it was known that its 'conduct off parade was appalling for then it drank, looted, robbed and burned with the same un- restrained enthusiasm that it showed in battle', an enthusiasm that gained eleven battle honours in the Peninsula while earning their nickname 'the Devil's Own'. Grattan claimed Picton never uttered a 'harsh expression towards the regiment again', but he adds that, during the four years the

Connaught Rangers were under his command, although many deserved it, no officer of the 88th was recommended for a promotion. Wellington's comment on Picton was that he was a fine soldier, brave, impulsive but 'as rough, foulmouthed a devil as ever existed'. In spite of Picton's strong language and reputation the experience of soldiers in the very Irish 2/83rd Foot was that they always thought him a 'kind' general who 'often did his best to get obscure merit rewarded'.[12]

Although Wellington lost faith in his Spanish allies as regular field formations, the historian David Gates writes: 'Without the Spanish Army it is doubtful that the Allies would have won the war'. Frequently, he adds, 'Wellington owed his salvation to the intelligence role of [the Spanish] guerrillas'.[13] Very important to him also were two Irish Catholics from seminaries in Spain and Portugal who would provide him with invaluable military information. One was James Doyle, an Augustinian who left his studies for the priesthood at Coimbra University when he was called up into the Portuguese Army; he refused the rank of major and instead volunteered to collect and supply information. He was to become the famous 'J K L', political bishop of Kildare and Leighlin during Ireland's Catholic Emancipation crisis. Another was Dr Patrick Curtis, Professor of Astronomy and Rector of the Irish College in Salamanca, which became a major British hospital. He became the Roman Catholic Primate in Ireland from 1819–1832. Both men served Wellington as 'irregulars' or spies and he kept in touch with both when the Peninsular War ended.

There was much criticism of Wellington in the British press when he retreated from Spain to Portugal after his victory at Talavera. To him, Portugal must be protected and Lisbon retained as a European base. With this in mind in September, leaving his army at Badajoz, Wellington rode out secretly from Lisbon with his chief engineer and scouted the rugged territory to the north and the coast. The result of his forays was the Lines of Torres Vedras or, more precisely, groups of hill forts and redoubts that his engineers, with Portuguese labourers, would fortify over the following months, constructing extensive gun emplacements, earthworks and trenches that incorporated the little town of Torres Vedras near the sea. These Lines would provide an impregnable position, a safe haven for his army that would astonish the French when discovered a year later. Very important also, Wellington, now in command of the sea, could use the coast for supplies and embarkation of his army if necessary.

In the spring of 1810 Marshal André Masséna, Napoleon's 'ablest general', began his advance into Portugal; his orders were, according to reports Wellington received, 'to drive the British into the sea'.[14] Marshal Ney, Masséna's 'dashing' Second in Command, captured Ciudad

Rodrigo in July 1810, followed in August by the accidental explosion and surrender to him of Almeida town and garrison on the Portuguese frontier. The road to Portugal was now open to Masséna. He, however, in continuing his advance into Portugal to Coimbra chose a most difficult northern route and this information gave Wellington the opportunity to bring Masséna to battle at a site of Wellington's own choosing, the formidable ridge of Busaco, an immensely strong position lying across Masséna's advance. The Battle of Busaco on 27 September went to Wellington, although his Anglo-Portuguese Army was outnumbered. When the fog lifted the 8th Portuguese and the 45th Foot, a regiment filled with Irish who had won the nickname 'The Old Stubborns' at Talavera, joined with the equally tough Irish Connaught Rangers in a magnificent early morning attack on the flank of an exhausted advancing French column which had not yet arrived at the crest of Busaco Ridge. Under the flashing Irish bayonets, the mass of Frenchmen streamed down the hill, which brought Wellington galloping up to exclaim to the 88th's commander, 'Pon my honour, Wallace, I never witnessed a more gallant charge'.[15] In the battle the allies sustained 1,250 casualties and the French 4,500.

The next day the French found a route round Wellington's left and he decided to withdraw into Portugal, but a secret plan was already in place. Masséna, thinking he had Wellington on the run, hurried after the allied armies and ran into Wellington's scorched earth policy, which unfortunately also meant suffering for the Portuguese. While rearguard actions were being fought, Wellington's main forces disappeared. Prisoners of Wellington's cavalry patrols taken by Masséna revealed the strange information that 'they were returning to the Lines', meaning the Lines of Torres Vedras where, by 10 October according to plan, Wellington's army was safely established. Not until 14 October did Masséna discover for himself the rugged mountain Lines. His own supplies and ammunition exhausted, his communications severed by guerrillas and Coimbra fallen to Colonel Nicholas Trant's Portuguese, his army starving and many sick, by mid-November he quietly slipped away to nearby Santarem where, to Wellington's amazement, he held his ground and somehow found provisions. Wellington followed, preferring not to attack but to let starvation propel Masséna to withdraw. Both armies remained in winter quarters.

Wellington described his troops in the Peninsula as 'the scum of the earth', but he also said, 'It is really wonderful that we should have made them the fine fellows they are'. He took care of his soldiers, wherever possible to see they had clothing and were properly fed and housed. To encourage a better type of recruit, he insisted the government should pay allowances for soldiers' families; British families were apt to be left to the mercy of the parish, the Irish 'on a dunghill to starve'.[16]

Many Irish recruits did not join the ranks as 'fine fellows', as Rifleman Harris confirms in his *Recollections.* So taken with the dashing appearance of the 95th Rifles, Harris volunteered for the Second Battalion. Meeting with the 95th's 'reckless and devil may care' recruiting party, he helped in bringing from Ireland to Salisbury Plain men from the Irish militia and others. Early in the morning: 'the whole lot of us . . . [were] three sheets in the wind' when they paraded before the Royal Oak at Cashel. Joined by a 92nd Highland Sergeant and a Highland piper, 'we had danced, drank, shouted and piped thirteen Irish miles between Cashel and Clonmel . . . as glorious as any soldiers in all Christendom'. When they embarked for England these 'hot-headed Paddies' got up a quarrel between Catholics and Protestants. 'They all carried immense shillelaghs in their fists which they would not quit for a moment'. At Salisbury Plain they again began their sectarian rioting, the minority Protestants once more having the worst of it. Cudgel fighting between the boys of Wicklow, Connaught, Munster and Ulster was fierce. The four officers accompanying the Irish finally got them into Andover, still fighting. When some were jailed by constables their companions tried to break down the prison gates and were only quieted when there was a 'beating-up' of the volunteer corps of the town who threatened the rioters with muskets. Before order was restored the officers had persuaded them to at least listen to a 'promise of pardon for the past'.

Within the British Army system many of the wild Irish prospered. Rifleman Harris, on one of his recruiting missions, became intimate with an Irish Sergeant Major called Adams who had been a 'croppy', a rebel in the '98 Rising, and had fought at Vinegar Hill. After his escape from the forces of the crown and spending time in the wilds of Connemara, he then decided to enlist in the Donegal Militia and from it transferred to the Irish Rifles. In Spain he became a sergeant and in the retreat to Corunna, when Sergeant Major Crosby 'failed', General 'Black Bob' Craufurd appointed Adams in his place. This able warrior furthur distinguished himself in Wellington's army at St Sebastian in 1813, taking part in the forlorn hope, and he so impressed General Thomas Graham that he was commissioned in the field. He later transferred to another regiment in Gibraltar to become its Adjutant. 'I was the only man,' recalled Harris, 'who knew Adams had been a rebel and I kept the secret faithfully till his death.'[17]

Wellington, in the custom of the time, chose his staff from family and friends, many of whom were of Irish aristocratic birth. His wife's brothers in the Peninsula served as Assistant Adjutant Generals, the Honourable Edward Pakenham to Wellington and Sir Hercules to Picton. The

Honourable William Stewart (third Marquess of Londonderry), his friend Castlereagh's half-brother, became Wellington's Adjutant-General. Two of his nieces were married to officers on his staff, one to Lord Fitzroy Somerset, his Military Secretary and future Lord Raglan of Crimea fame, the other to Lord Worcester, Fitzroy's eldest brother. Wellington would say of his 'military family' that he 'preferred ability with a title to ability without'. He was 'all for having gentlemen for officers since the British Army was what it was because it was officered by gentlemen'. Yet Wellington was not tolerant of inefficiency even in his own family; he had no hesitation in sending home his nephew William because he was incompetent and lazy.[18]

Wellington criticized many, but he could be lenient with a good commander even in a disaster like that of William Carr Beresford's, whose bad judgement at the Battle of Albuera, May 1811, contributed to the bloodbath of the 57th Foot; their losses were 428 out of 647. Over one-third Irish, they won their nickname 'The Diehards' because of this battle. A shocked Wellington saw for himself men of the 57th 'literally lying dead in their ranks, as they had stood'. Nevertheless Wellington declined to send in Beresford's dismal despatch of these casualties, which would only arouse unnecessary criticism at home. 'Write me down a victory,' Wellington is reported to have said. Indeed a victory it was – a Pyrrhic victory brought about by another Irishman, General Lowry Cole who had eagerly listened to the advice of Henry Hardinge (later Governor General of India) attached to the Portuguese forces and ordered in his 4th Division when Beresford 'lost his nerve'. Wellington, according to David Gates, 'returned the inept Beresford to his post at the head of the Portuguese military administration' (temporarily, it turned out) and General Sir Rowland Hill replaced him.[19]

Wellington's commitment to the army he led was total and this he expected of his officers, even discouraging them from going on leave. He would have been pleased with the commitment and enthusiasm of the Anglo-Irishman Major Hugh Gough of 2/87th Foot at Barossa in 1811 where he became a hero of the Peninsular War. Hugh was the son of Colonel George Gough, a prominent Limerick citizen and Commander of the Limerick Militia, under whom young Hugh served. After service with the 78th Highlanders at the Cape of Good Hope he transferred to the 87th Foot and went to the West Indies. Purchasing his majority in the newly raised 2/87th (recruited in the counties of Tipperary and Clare) this twenty-five-year-old led his regiment to the Peninsula to fight throughout Wellington's campaign. Gough, with his usual bravery, was severely wounded at Talavera, but escaped with Captain Oates, an equally brave and wounded Connaught Ranger. In February 1810 Gough and his battalion joined an Anglo-Portuguese force at Cadiz that was blockaded by the French. Barossa was the key to the route into Cadiz and there, on 5 March 1811, Major Gough led a memorable charge of the 2/87th. Shouting *Faugh-a-Ballagh! Faugh-a-Ballagh!* (Irish for clear the way) the 2/87th smashed into the second battalion of the French 8th Regiment and in a terrible bayonet fight killed or wounded over half their fighting strength. In the centre of the bloody struggle the eagle of the 8th was desperately defended by the French Colour party and the Irish cut towards it. Sergeant Patrick Masterson, a Roscommon man, snatched the pole bearing the eagle from the French and held onto it throughout the mêlée, shouting, it is said, 'Be Jabers, boys, I have the cuckoo!' For his valour Masterson was made an ensign and members of his family long served in the Faughs. Hugh Gough was given the Brevet rank of Lieutenant Colonel for his leadership at Barossa. The prized eagle was sent home and presented to the Prince Regent amidst great public acclaim for the 2/87th Foot and endless newspaper accounts appeared about Gough and his men.

Gough furthered his military reputation as a fighting Irish field commander in late December 1811 when the beseiging French broke through the fortress wall at the port of Tarifa. He volunteered to hold the breach with his regiment and during the night the defenders attempted to repair the damage. On the morning of the 31st when the French came up again they met the 87th's deadly fire, while above the din could be heard the lively drums and fifes playing 'Garryowen' requested by Gough. He and his troops repulsed them after a short fierce fight and the French melted away to the 87th's playing of 'St Patrick's Day'. Gough, cut above the eye and in the hand by flying splinters, 'modestly' told his wife in a letter:

> The scene was awfully grand; every officer and man seemed to outvie one another in acts of heroism, and never . . . can I forget their expressions and looks . . . at seeing me bleed.

The Spanish conferred on Gough the Grand Cross of the Order Of Charles III.[20] Gough, Masterson and the *Faugh-a-Ballagh* 87th had established a reputation for heroism and 5 March, Barossa Day, would long be celebrated.

Wellington and the Irish in the Advance into Spain

William Grattan in his *Adventures with the Connaught Rangers* refers to the French atrocities visited upon the Portuguese people and their land by

Masséna's starving and angry army as it withdrew to Spain in March 1811, driven out by Wellington who was now on the offensive. Masséna, on 3–5 May, attacked the village of Fuentes de Oñoro on the Spanish/Portuguese border, his aim being to relieve the Portuguese fortress of Almeida still in French hands but blockaded by Wellington. This fiercely fought battle was a very narrow victory for Wellington. In Grattan's account Colonel Wallace of the 88th, watching from high ground the battle raging below, offered his wild Connaught Rangers to Sir Edward Pakenham to clear the French 9th Light Regiment and Grenadiers out of the village. Pakenham galloped off for Wellington's approval and hurrying back called out, 'He says you may go – come along Wallace!' So ferocious was the fight that Grattan felt compelled to defend the annihilation of one group of French caught in a cul-de-sac by Rangers led by Lieutenant George Johnston: 'Mistakes of this kind will sometimes occur. . . . In the present instance every man was put to death.' For Wellington Fuentes De Oñoro was a most 'difficult' battle; he wrote to his brother William that, had Napoleon been there, they would have been defeated.[21]

Wellington sought to capture Ciudad Rodrigo in order to clear his way into Spain and on 8 January 1812 invested the town. By 19 January savage hand-to-hand fighting took place as Picton's stirring words indicate to the 88th before they fell in to storm the main breach in the walls, 'Rangers of Connaught! it is not my intention to expend any powder this evening. We'll do this business with the could [cold] iron.' The Irishmen gave a roaring cheer. Lieutenant William Mackie and twenty volunteers of the 88th led the forlorn hope of Picton's 3rd Division. After overcoming the hazards of the ditch Major General Henry MacKinnon and his aide Lieutenant Beresford of the 88th, along with many infantry, were blown up by a mine exploding beneath them. Sergeant Patrick Brazil and Privates Swan and Kelly, of the 88th, bravely captured a gun that was dangerously firing on the breach. Carrying only their bayonets, they killed the French gunners in a fierce hand-to-hand struggle. Swan was mortally wounded, his arm severed. At the lesser breach the Scottish Major General 'Black Bob' Craufurd, of the Light Division, suffered a painful death, the Anglo-Irish General Vandeleur, his Second in Command, was badly wounded and Captain George Napier, leading the stormers, lost an arm. Simultaneously Irishmen General Sir Denis Pack and Lieutenant Colonel Bryan O'Toole led a diversionary action against the south wall with two minor columns of Portuguese reinforced by the Light Company of the Dublin-raised 83rd Foot.[22] Denis Pack was the second son of the Very Rev Thomas Pack, Dean of Kilkenny, and grandson of Thomas Pack of Ballinakill, Queen's County (now Offaly). For this triumphant success Wellington received an earldom and a generous pension from the government, and the Spanish Cortes created him Duque de Ciudad Rodrigo.

After Ciudad Rodrigo had been duly sacked Wellington hurried south to take Badajoz which would give him control of both the northern and southern gateways into Spain. Speed was essential because Marshal Marmont, the younger and very competent now Duke of Ragusa, Masséna's successor, was marching west toward Ciudad Rodrigo. The assault on the recently strengthened fortress of Badajoz on 6 April 1812 was a very bloody affair. William Grattan, describing the psychology of his fellow Irishmen before going into battle, most unusual in a military memoir, noted a 'quiet but desperate calm'. As they expectantly waited all next day the men were touched in the heart by music of some of the regimental bands:

> The band of my corps, the 88th, all Irish, played several airs which exclusively belonged to their country . . . such an air as 'Savourneen Deelish' is sufficient . . . to inspire a feeling of melancholy but on an occasion like the present, it acted powerfully on the feelings of the men . . . . It was Easter Sunday.

By 9.25pm the soldiers were ready. Their ragged jackets, whiskered bronzed faces,

> but above all their self-confidence devoid of boast or bravado gave them the appearance of what they in reality were – an invincible host.[23]

Storming parties of the Light Division at the Santa Maria breach and the 4th Division at La Trinidad were launched into the horror of the battle, to be driven back. Tragically, Grattan records, the leading platoons of the gallant 4th jumped into that part of the ditch that the French had filled with water by the inundation of the Rivillas River and were seen no more: the 'bubbles that rose on the surface . . . were a terrible assurance of the struggles which these devoted soldiers . . . ineffectually made to extricate themselves'. Edward Costello, a Dubliner in 95th Rifles, finding himself in the water up to his neck was terrified and swam for the breach. Climbing from the water, as he approached the *chevaux-de-frise* (logs studded with sabre blades) he was hit and lay almost senseless among dead bodies, with screams, groans and enemy fire continuing over him. Coming to his senses much later, he found he could not stand, but was helped by men of his own Rifles and was then able to hobble into Badajoz using his rifle as a crutch.[24]

Meanwhile, with 'equal savagery', the attack by Picton's 3rd Division to take the castle, a fortification set high into the wall, had been in progress. Lieutenant James MacCarthy, a Volunteer from the 50th Regiment, in his *Recollection of the Storming of the Castle of Badajoz,* wrote that he had acted as an engineer in preparation for the attack and was amazed at Wellington's coolness under fire when he visited the trenches. Chosen to guide Picton's 3rd Division forward because of his knowledge of the ground, MacCarthy was assisting in the placement of a ladder to escalade the castle when he was hit by a ball that fractured his right thigh and he lay all night among the many wounded until moved the next day. Joseph Donaldson of the 94th (a regiment increasingly Irish), describes in his *Recollections 1856* the heroism of the attackers on the ladders, who:

> crowded them . . . many of them broke, and the poor fellows who had nearly reached the top, were precipitated a height of thirty or forty feet and were impaled on the bayonets of their comrades below . . . more who got to the top without accident, were shot on reaching the parapet, and tumbling headlong, brought down those beneath them.

Little impression was made on the castle as men, with incredible bravery, attempted to ascend while the French hurled projectiles down on them. Finally Colonel Ridge of the 5th Foot, seizing a ladder, miraculously, with his sword guarding his head, managed to stand on the ramparts; he was said to be the first man into the castle. Lieutenant William Mackie of the 88th, 'ever foremost in the fight,' writes Grattan, together with Richard Martin, a volunteer with the 88th and son of the member for Galway, succeeded in mounting ladders. Mackie soon established his men on the battlements, but Martin fell, desperately wounded. In the general rush to the ladders that now took place with terrible savagery, men of the 2/83rd Foot followed their officers up the ladders with very heavy losses. Others first up were Lieutenant Macpherson of the 45th and Sir Hercules Pakenham who scrambled in over him; both were severely wounded. Colonel Ridge and his men managed to get into the darkness of the castle where they met a French group who shot the gallant colonel.[25] The Connaught Rangers lost more than half their officers and men.

Long after the castle had been carried William Grattan was severely wounded, struck by a musket ball in the left breast while helping Major Thompson of the 74th place casks of gunpowder under the dam of the Rivillas. Violent firing delayed Grattan from reaching the camp which worried him because of his loss of blood. He was finally helped by Bray and Macgowan, two sappers of his own corps. Bray was hit in the leg when he tried to cover Grattan from enemy fire but survived to distinguish himself in the Battle of the Pyrenees.[26] Many such unsung acts of bravery and kindness are known to us only through memoirs like Grattan's. He would remain with the Colours for four years, off duty only for a few weeks after his wound at Badajoz, not going home to Ireland on leave until the spring of 1813.

Wellington, when informed of the success of 3rd and 5th Divisions in penetrating the castle, again ordered remnants of the 4th and Light Divisions into the breaches. A sickening scene awaited them at the La Trinidad and Santa Maria breaches as the young Irishman Robert Blakeney sorrowfully records: 'On looking down these breaches I recognized many old friends . . . now lying stiff in death'. It is said that on the morning after the battle Wellington wept at the sight of so many of his finest men destroyed. In Badajoz town young Blakeney was further shocked by the ensuing plundering and raping he witnessed by the totally out of control soldiery, a terrible fury shown by the worst of Wellington's erstwhile 'scum of the earth'. Crazed with drink, there was hardly an abomination of which humans are capable that was not committed, during which:

> the officers durst not interfere. The infuriated soldiery resembled rather a pack of hell-hounds vomited up from the infernal regions for the extirpation of mankind than what they were but twelve short hours previously – a well organized, brave, disciplined and obedient British Army, and burning only with impatience for what is called glory.

The orgy came to an abrupt end on the evening of the second day. Wellington, with his staff, rode into town, a gallows was set up in the square and the order given that any man found in Badajoz was to be hanged on the spot. He himself had a close call from one of his own drunken soldiers. Badajoz remained in British hands but with high cost; several regiments had lost almost half their effectives, four battalion commanders were killed and five generals were wounded, including Picton. The British Army in the Peninsula would never forget this most violent episode in the campaign to liberate the Spanish and Portuguese peoples, one that rivalled the worst atrocities of the Thirty Years' War.

Lieutenant Robert Blakeney was only a spectator of the horrors at Badajoz where he assisted generally in the trenches while awaiting transfer as Captain to the 36th Foot, a regiment not in the battle. But he was almost killed in the town trying to protect some women. Blakeney was born in County Galway to an Irish family granted land in the time of Elizabeth I. In 1804, at the age of fifteen, Robert Blakeney, 'gentleman', was appointed to an ensigncy in 28th Foot. He was full of admiration for his old regiment and for generals like Sir John Moore and the 'the great Wellington himself; and, above all, [he records] the indomitable valour of the British soldier . . . who is so often Irish'. Blakeney survived the war and died in 1858.[27]

The Irish and the French Retreat to Northern Spain and France

The way was now open for Wellington to continue his Spanish offensive of 1812 and in June he was on his way to Salamanca with a reinforced army. By 21 July both armies, the French led by Marshal Marmont, were marching parallel to each other south of Salamanca their commanders looking for some weakness to exploit. On 22 July Wellington suddenly spotted a gap between two of the French formations and Grattan's version of an often-told story about Wellington in this war is how he rode up to Sir Edward Pakenham and briefly gave his orders: 'Edward, move on with the 3rd Division – take the heights in your front – and drive everything before you.' Packenham led his 3rd Division towards the heights supported by Portuguese cavalry and General Le Marchant's heavy brigade in reserve.

Grattan's Connaught Rangers were brigaded under Colonel Wallace in the front line of Pakenham's 3rd Division with the 45th and the 74th Foot, a Highland regiment that at this time had twice as many Irish as Scots in its ranks; Pack's Portuguese and the Irish 83rd and 94th were in reserve. In the late afternoon Pakenham led them over a nearly two- mile approach, then through concealing dips and folds towards the heights, against fire from French batteries and *tirailleurs*. The battle began when the Portuguese Dragoons charged the flank of General Thomiére's French Division and Pakenham's Infantry arrived and attacked the French formation. In Grattan's account the Infantry were nearly stopped when the entire French division ran forward to meet them; a torrent of bullets brought down almost all of Wallace's front rank and more than half his officers. He quickly rallied his shattered brigade and led them towards the hill again, to the astonishment of the French who wavered, mesmerized, their musketry fire sporadic and badly aimed until one French Colonel ran out and shot Major Murphy dead in front of his regiment; he had been a popular officer of the 88th. The sight of his dead body being dragged by his horse, his foot caught in the stirrups, was too much for the Connaught Rangers. They asked to be 'let forward' and Pakenham, seeing that the right moment had arrived, called to Wallace, 'Let them loose'. With a bloodcurdling yell, such was the impetuous charge of 1,500 indomitable

British soldiers fighting in a line only two deep, that the mighty French force fell apart. In this charge of bayonets casualties were severe but, Grattan recounts, Pakenham was now about to be attacked again when, Thomières dead and his regiments shattered, General Macune called up a fresh brigade who angrily turned on their opponents. Help was at hand. In the confusion and smoke of battle Wallace's astounded regiments heard the tramping of horses' feet behind and, on the order, opened their line for General John Le Marchant's heavy dragoons who thundered through in a charge that brought excited praise from the normally reserved Wellington. When Le Marchant's excited squadrons continued their charge in a deadly fight against further French battalions, he was killed and the French fled: 'hundreds of beings, frightfully disfigured . . . black with dust . . . covered with sabre cuts and blood – threw themselves amongst us for safety. Not a man was bayoneted – not one even molested or plundered.' Grattan writes warmly of his 'invincible old 3rd Division . . . [who] surpassed themselves' in gallant behaviour to the undeserving French.[28] The Battle of Salamanca was won but not before General Sir Lowry Cole of the 4th Division was severely wounded and his men in flight because of the failure of General Sir Denis Pack and his Portuguese to storm the rocky heights. Later in the evening Wellington saved the day when he sent in the 6th Division.

Wellington's skill in directing this victory at Salamanca over Marmont brought him universal acclaim. The French General Foy magnanimously conceded that Lord Wellington's reputation came 'almost to the level of that of Marlborough'.[29] Wellington entered Madrid to a tumultuous welcome on 12 August and the Irish among his soldiers must have been pleased to hear the crowd's shouted greetings *Vivi Ilandos*, as well as *Vivi los Angoles*. The Spanish appointed Wellington Generalissimo of their forces and the Prince Regent, following on, created him a marquess with £100,000 from Parliament.

The strain of Wellington's command was beginning to show and his siege and attack on Burgos was one of his few failures and greatly criticized, for which he took full blame but blaming too his officers' deficiencies. With news that the French were gathering in strength to regain Madrid, by the last week of October Wellington had to withdraw his army back to Ciudad Rodrigo and the Portuguese border to go into winter quarters, closely followed by the French. On the retreat the troops were in utmost misery, in the rain without shelter of any sort, half the men and officers without shoes, their uniforms in rags after two years' service, and suffering from ague. Who seemed to bear privation best, according to Grattan, were the Irish infantry: 'The Connaught Rangers . . . never lost their gaiety. Without shoes they fancied themselves "at home" . . . Without food they were nearly at home, and without a good coat to their backs equally so!'[30] Grattan considered that by the time the army was back in cantonment in Portugal, by late November every battalion was reduced to half its original strength; disease and hunger attacked all. The one encouraging news was that Napoleon had suffered his great defeat at Moscow.

His army recovered and enjoying the novelty of tents, in May 1813 Wellington began his advance to the Pyrenees thrusting forward at a staggering rate over rough terrain and by mid-June he was threatening both Vitoria and Bilbao. On 21 June he began the Battle of Vitoria with Edward Pakenham acting as his Adjutant General, for Picton had returned from sick leave to command the 3rd Division again. While Wellington struck with his main body, Hugh Gough on the left, leading his 2/87th supported by the 2/83rd and 94th, advanced uphill in a charge on the village of Hermandad that cracked the French line. His regiment had severe casualties, 254 out of a strength of 637, including valuable officers like Captain Frederick Vandeleur, who died of his wounds. As the French fell back their retreat became a rout and the pursuing army found themselves in the midst of a great confusion of King Joseph's baggage caravan laden with treasure and carriages of officials, courtiers and women, wives and prostitutes alike. King Joseph barely escaped before the 18th Hussars arrived to begin the Peninsular war sport of '*le pillage*', which allowed most of the French to get away. Captain Arthur Kennedy of the 18th, writing to his mother in Belfast, mentioned only an inkling of the vast riches left behind, monies, jewels, watches, precious plate. Gough of the 2/87th wrote: 'Some of my fellows had made fortunes'.[31] Irish Rifleman Edward Costello of the 95th claimed he loaded a mule with £1,000 of gold and silver dubloons and brought it safely back to camp after warning off with his rifle would-be sharers.[32] The 2/27th acquired a circular silver gilt stand looted from King Joseph's baggage and said to have originally belonged to the royal family of Spain. Included in the 'trophies' was Marshal Jourdan's baton, which was given to Wellington by the 2/87th and the 18th Hussars, both of whom had 'acquired part of it somehow'. The Prince Regent so rejoiced to receive it from Wellington (no equivalent existed in the British Army) along with the Colour of the 4/100th French Regiment that the 87th had captured that he raised Wellington to the rank of field-marshal.

What follows demonstrates how much Wellington's commanders relied on his guidance. In late July Marshal Soult advanced through the mountains to Pamplona and was almost successful. Wellington was at San Sebastian when General Sir Lowry Cole, left on his own and anxious not to be cut off, against orders by Wellington to hold on, retired his 4th Division from above Pamplona to another ridge at nearby Sorauren.

There, with Picton and his 3rd Division in support, Cole was in danger of being attacked by Soult's larger force arriving nearby. When Wellington heard of the looming crisis he immediately raced south alone and arrived just in time. At the bridge of Sorauren he dismounted and, while Soult's cavalry could be seen entering the village, he quickly wrote out a new directive to warn Sir Edward Packenham, whose 6th Division was approaching, of Soult's presence. Fitzroy Somerset dashed off with it while Wellington galloped up the hill to take charge of the battle; he had had a narrow escape. His troops cheered that austere silhouette sitting spare and trim on his thoroughbred horse *Copenhagen*, wearing his inconspicuous dark grey overcoat, Hessian boots and cocked hat. He always brought confidence, respect and universal trust, if not love. Sir Lowry Cole recovered and the 'heroic stand' of his division on Cole's Ridge (named in his honour) in the fierce fighting of 28–30 July in the mountainous terrain of Sorauren assured Wellington a victory in this first battle of the Pyrenees, as did the arrival of Pakenham's 6th. In these battles Wellington admitted his troops 'had never behaved so well', and he included the Portuguese and the Spanish.[33]

At San Sebastian at the end of August Wellington finally achieved success in a last assault. Looting was almost as vicious as at Badajoz and he was criticized (wrongly, as it turned out) in both Spanish and Irish newspapers for instigating the burning of the city.

7 October was a momentous day when Wellington invaded France, his army crossing the River Bidassoa to engage again Marshal Soult who had built up fortifications on the Nivelle and Nive Rivers. In these bleak Pyrenees mountains where in November violent rain, snow and hailstorms never ceased, the Irish continued to perform bravely. Hugh Gough suffered a severe hip wound when his 2/87th attacked two French redoubts on the Nivelle and lost very heavily; out of 386, 216 became casualties. Wellington himself was painfully wounded by a spent bullet in February after the Battle of Orthez while riding about, as was his custom. Indomitable, he soon recovered.

Unsure of Napoleon's situation in Europe, Wellington cautiously pursued the French who arrived at Toulouse by 26 March where he ordered an attack for Easter Sunday, 10 April 1814. As the last battle of the Peninsular War it proved to be one of the fiercest, another 'close run thing' with many casualties. Beresford's 4th and 6th Divisions were soon bogged down in flooded fields and this affected the Spanish Division, which attacked prematurely. Picton failed miserably in leadership of his 3rd Division when he turned a feint ordered by Wellington into an all-out attack that sustained unnecessary casualties, perhaps hoping 'to gain just a little more glory for himself and his division before the French finally collapsed',[34] which they did, quietly withdrawing from Toulouse on the night of 11 April 1814. The following day, while host to a banquet there, Wellington received a despatch confirming that Napoleon had abdicated. As the great Duke of Wellington (created Duke May 1814) he would return to meet Napoleon at Waterloo. Meanwhile the Irish in the British Army were already involved in another theatre of war, the vast land of North America.

The Irish and the Defence of Canada in the War of 1812

During and after the American War of Independence some 70,000 Loyalist refugees had fled to Canada to continue to live under the Crown. For those remaining in the breakaway thirteen American colonies the second Treaty of Paris of 1783 had not settled all their grievances. Britain's war with France had brought a Royal Navy blockade of trade with Europe that affected the Americans and 'provoked instant war fever across the United States'. Many Americans decided there would be no lasting peace until all North America was included in their republic. 'Official grievances' might have centred on freedom of the seas infringed by Britain, but, as Canadian historian Desmond Morton puts it, 'It was the border states that wanted war . . . Seizing Canada would avenge British-inspired Indian wars and provide rich rewards in fertile real estate'.[35] The United States declared war on Britain in June 1812. The British, however, saw the ensuing North American war of 1812–14 as an annoying distraction from the fierce and deadly struggle in the Iberian Peninsula, and both British and American histories tend to gloss over it. For Canadians it was a struggle for survival in which the young and loosely knit country heroically fought off invasion attempts by Americans.

The defence of British North America was by the regulars serving in the British Army, although Canadian Militia did take part. One of these regulars was the British-born General Sir Isaac Brock, the Administrator and Commander of the forces in Upper Canada, who became a legendary hero in Canadian history and in the British Army as one who foiled Americans in their plans to capture Canada in 1812. In October 1812 he defeated the American bungled invasion at the Battle of Queenston Heights, but he was killed.

Brock was important in the life of a literate Irishman, James FitzGibbon, a Catholic born in Ireland in 1780 at Glin on the south shore of the River Shannon. In the threatened French invasion of Ireland (1795–1796) FitzGibbon, along with his father and his brother, enrolled in the local yeomanry; by now the local priest raised no objection to the FitzGibbons taking the oaths of allegiance and abjuration. James FitzGibbon, to his surprise, found that members of the Devon and Cornwall Fencibles billeted in his home were not at all as 'beastly' as local folklore portrayed the English. This persuaded him to join, in 1798, the Tarbert Fencibles who were sent to England while the regular army was in Holland. Questioning himself as to whether he was a 'coward' through avoiding regular service, FitzGibbon decided to transfer to the 49th Foot, then under the command of Lieutenant Colonel Isaac Brock. His adventures under Brock began in Holland where he was taken prisoner and subsequently released as part of a prisoner exchange. Brock, impressed with FitzGibbon's literacy (thanks to a classical education from a schoolmaster father), obtained for his favourite Sergeant Major an ensign's commission from the Duke of York. In 1802 FitzGibbon went to Quebec with the 49th Foot as acting adjutant of the regiment, becoming along the way a Protestant and a prominent Mason. He mentions in passing how difficult it was in ambush situations to control the 'impetuosity' of the many Irish in the 49th Foot.

FitzGibbon achieved fame through an action that involved Laura Secord, the American-born wife of a militiaman, a veteran of the Battle of Queenston Heights. She has passed into legend as a Canadian heroine and today has a popular brand of chocolate named after her. When her house in the Niagara district was requisitioned by Americans she overheard American officers discussing a sortie across the frontier and valiantly decided to warn the British. Driving a cow before her to conceal her errand (a questionable detail), she passed through American lines and made her way through dense bush to reach the British. On the way she was captured by Indians and persuaded them to take her to the nearest officer who happened to be FitzGibbon. Meanwhile, the raiding party of over five hundred Americans was surprised by a large body of Mohawks and Caughnawagas who, hidden in the woods, terrified the Americans with their war cries and kept firing on them for three hours. One report claimed that fifty-six Americans were killed and their Commander wounded. When FitzGibbon arrived with a company of his 49th Regiment, they were only too pleased to surrender to him rather than to the Indians. FitzGibbon's account, written later, is very modest: 'The only share I claim is taking advantage of a favourable moment to offer them protection from the tomahawk and the scalping knife'. Legend, however, has given the victory to this mere Lieutenant and ex-ranker and the Beaver Dam triumph, as it was known, brought FitzGibbon a place in Canadian history. FitzGibbon gained no military advancement until he obtained command of a company by transferring to the Glengarry Fencibles in January 1814, having had to sell his commission in the British Army. This regiment was disbanded and from then on we find FitzGibbon commanding as colonel of militia regiments at York (later Toronto). During these years he was appointed both Adjutant General and Assistant Auditor General of Militia in Upper Canada, grand-sounding titles with low pay. A man of strong physique, FitzGibbon loved soldiering and often regretted his removal into 'a colonial regiment'.

This hero of Beaver Dam again made a name for himself when, in command of the Militia, he organized government resistance in the Rebellion of Upper Canada in 1837. It was thanks to his initiative, when Lieutenant Governor Francis Bond Head 'dithered', that the rebels were routed and fled after an 'almost bloodless encounter'. His services in the Militia and various civil capacities were finally recognized, and later, on retiring for ill-health reasons, he received a small pension from the government. Thanks to the patronage of members of the aristocracy interested in Canada and in FitzGibbon personally, he ended his career as a Military Knight of Windsor, where he died at eighty-three.[36]

Joseph Grant, Brevet Lieutenant Colonel in the 41st Foot, was already enjoying good relations with the Indians when Brock and FitzGibbon arrived in British North America. He was another of the regulars in the British Army who garrisoned Canada in the early nineteenth century. From Kilmurry near Cork and born in 1762, he was the youngest son of an Irish gentry family. He had twice served in the West Indies and in the summer of 1800 Grant, his wife Isabella and infant son, along with his favourite hunting dog, sailed for Canada to rejoin his regiment, there since 1799. He found Canada 'a healthy though quiet backwater'. By 1802 he was the commanding officer at Fort St George in the sparsely settled Niagara Peninsula. From there he moved to Fort Malden, near Amherstberg, opposite Detroit, the major post on the western frontier of the British colony, where he remained until his departure from British North America in 1809. The Shawnee Chief Tecumseh, the 'Wellington' of the Indians, rose to power while Grant was there with his young family and the Irishman became his friend. He also corresponded with Joseph Brant, the Mohawk Chief, about the sale of Indian lands. In appreciation of his friendship when he was leaving Amherstberg, a group of chiefs honoured Grant in a farewell ceremony of goodwill. Many of the Indian artefacts Grant collected are today in the collection of the Royal Dublin Society.[37]

At the end of the Peninsular War Horse Guards sent veteran troops from Wellington's army to Canada where the Canadian Militia and a scanty force of British Army regulars had not been able to contain American incursions along the Quebec border. In mid-August 1814 some 16,000 arrived from Bordeaux; Irish among them were the 1st and 3rd 27th Foot and two battalions of the 88th. The short time these Irish regiments were in North America was one of 'rest and recreation' compared to the Peninsular campaign and casualties were few. The Inniskillings were part of a force organized by Lieutenant General Sir George Prevost, appointed in 1811 Governor in Chief and Commander of all his Majesty's forces in British North America. Prevost was the son of a Swiss Protestant career soldier in the British Army. When war broke out with France George achieved a distinguished reputation in the West Indies as Lieutenant Colonel of the 3rd/60th (Royal Americans). A strict disciplinarian, Prevost criticized the Inniskillings immediately on their arrival in Canada for failing to abide by 'dress' regulations, which had been of minor concern to Wellington. While probably well deserved, his criticism was tactless and ill-timed and these Peninsular veterans were deeply offended. The 1st and 3rd Inniskillings, participating on 11 September in Prevost's campaign around Plattsburg on Lake Champlain, confirmed their lack of faith in his military ability, which is most unsympathetically described in the Inniskillings' History. A flotilla on the lake, under the experienced Captain George Downie, was ordered to destroy vastly superior American vessels. Everything went wrong. Prevost ignored Downie's information that his large thirty-six-gun frigate was not ready and ordered Downie to attack. The cheers of the Americans soon announced victory over the British Fleet and Downie was killed. On the shore the troops were paralyzed by an 'inefficient staff' and the result was disastrous, even though Prevost had the larger number of troops. He made a hasty retreat towards Montreal, despite his officers' objections abandoning the sick and wounded, and many stores fell into American hands. The veterans were humiliated. More disgrace followed in a mass desertion, so angry were the soldiers at Prevost's behaviour. Inniskilling losses were two killed and twenty-five wounded.[38]

Wellington criticized Prevost for 'going to war about trifles with the general officers I sent him'; yet, writing to his former Quartermaster General, Major General Sir George Murray, now in Canada, he supported Prevost's course of action:

> Whether Sir George Prevost was right or wrong in his decision of Lake Champlain is more than I can tell; but of this I am very certain, he must equally have retired to Kingston [he meant Montreal] after our fleet was beaten and I am inclined to believe he was right.

Prevost's biographer adds: 'Had one of Wellington's senior subordinates been sent to command Prevost's troops . . . the story of Plattsburg could have had a different ending'.[39] As for Prevost's soldiers deserting, it was always a problem for the British Army in Canada.

The Connaught Rangers, also serving under Prevost, had only nine rank and file wounded. In Connaught Ranger memory the Regiment's stay in Canada was idyllic – skating and sliding on the ice of the St Lawrence River, the officers having a particularly pleasant time when they were wined and dined in places like Three Rivers. The Regiment took great pride in not losing a single man through desertion when inducements were so common in North America. In an inspection in the spring of 1815 the Connaught Rangers had on parade 58 English, 16 Scots and 738 Irish.

If the Irish in the Connaught Rangers could look back fondly on their 1814–1815 tour of duty in British North America, the 100th HRH the Prince Regent's County of Dublin Regiment of Foot, raised in Ireland in 1804, experienced both disaster and success. On its way to Canada the following year on 21 October one of the transports foundered off Newfoundland and three companies of this new regiment, one hundred and ninety-two officers and men, were drowned. Two other companies were wrecked off Cape Breton Island, but sustained no casualties, joining the regiment at Quebec in June 1806. Moving about on garrison duty until May 1813, the 100th had the misfortune to take part in Sir George Prevost's attack launched on an American garrison at Sackett's Harbour, Lake Ontario, where the British lost over one quarter of its attacking force. Another attack, however, on Fort Niagara across the Niagara River on the American shore under the overall command of Lieutenant Colonel John Murray, a former Commanding Officer of the 100th Regiment, was 'a brilliant success'. On the bitterly cold night of 18–19 December 1813 nine companies of the 100th Foot were involved; five under Lieutenant Colonel Hamilton were the main element in this attack, along with companies of 2/41st Foot, Royal Scots, Royal Artillery and Indians. Canadian Militia navigated boats across the river and the 'forlorn hope' consisted of the 100th's Lieutenant Dawson and Sergeant Spearman who was 'a man of stupendous physical strength', along with twenty picked men from the Canadian troops. Spearman was ordered to attack the American sentry at the drawbridge, whereupon Dawson led the storming party into the fort. Meanwhile Major Davis of the 100th led his company against the southern tower. The Americans soon sought safety in flight. By dawn the fort was in British hands; the drummers of the 100th made their way to the top of the main building and played 'The British Grenadiers'. The British flag, which was to fly until the end of the war, was raised and, despite the cold:

> the lighthearted Irish soldiers of the 100th were dancing on the flat roof of the barracks to the lively strains of St. Patrick's Day . . . The capture of Fort Niagara, which was almost entirely a

100th's achievement, was perhaps the most brilliantly successful action of the war. It deprived the Americans of one of their strongest positions.[40]

Bad luck again befell the 100th. A force of some 1,500 British regulars, including the 100th Foot, 300 Militia and Indians, took part in the 5 July 1814 bloody Battle of Chippewa (Ontario) under the command of Major General Phineas Riall. This thirty-eight-year-old Irishman was Commander of all troops west of Kingston when he arrived in Canada in November 1813 with Quebec-born Lieutenant General Gordon Drummond, who had returned from England as Administrator of Upper Canada. Drummond had seen active service in the British Army and had been in command in southern Ireland, but Riall had battle experience only in the West Indies. At Chippewa Riall did not know that the American forces overwhelmingly outnumbered the British until the 100th Foot and the Royal Scots were ordered to make a precipitate charge that was broken up by American superior musketry and artillery fire, forcing him to withdraw. Riall's force suffered over five hundred casualties. The commanding officers of both the 100th and the Royal Scots were wounded and the 100th's losses were so severe that 'it practically ceased to play an active part in the remainder of the war'.[41]

After defeat at the Chippewa River Drummond decided to make a stand on high ground at Lundy's Lane where for five hours on 25 July, a mile from the famous Niagara Falls, a battle raged that was one of the fiercest land actions of the war. Riall, again in command of part of the British forces, was severely wounded early in the battle and captured while being moved to the rear by his stretcher bearers who strayed into the American lines. Repeated attacks by the Americans were met with perfect steadiness by the Irish 2/89th (raised only in 1804 for the Napoleonic wars) and detachments of the Royal Scots and the 41st Foot. It was the Americans who broke off the engagement, withdrawing to take refuge in Fort Erie. After a battle that was at best an 'honourable draw', the exhausted British did not pursue, but lay down to rest among their 900 casualties. Drummond, himself wounded, testified in his Orders that the lion's share of the fighting fell to the 2/89th. In the War of 1812 clearly it was regular troops, both Canadian and British, who did most of the the fighting.[42]

When Horse Guards decided in 1814 to send a British invasion force to the American coast there was no doubt that the Anglo-Irishman Major General Robert Ross would acquit himself well as commander of a small army of 2,400, increased in Bermuda en route to 4,200. He is not well known in this war and is usually only briefly referred to by military historians, although he played a significant role in its last stages. From a minor gentry family in Rostrevor, County Down, Ross was born in Dublin, son of Major David Ross and nephew of the Earl of Charlemont. A talented young man and a graduate of Trinity College Dublin, he spoke French and Spanish and had a long service of solid accomplishment in his army career, chiefly spent with the 20th Foot. With the 20th at Corunna under Sir John Moore he won his second gold medal; in the Peninsular battles he had been prominent as a brigade commander in General Lowry Cole's 4th Division and was seriously wounded at the Battle of Orthez. With Ross in North America was Colonel (later General Sir) Arthur Brooke of the 44th Foot, and his younger brother Francis, commander of the 4th Foot, sons of a famous Anglo-Irish military family from Colebrooke, Co. Fermanagh. It is from Arthur's diary that many details of the expedition are known.

Ross and his army was landed at Chesapeake Bay in August 1814 by the Royal Navy with orders to destroy a flotilla of marauding American gun boats sheltering in the Patuxent River. Trapped by the British, their commander, Commodore Joshua Barney, burned his boats and headed for Washington. Although Ross's objective was already achieved, he decided to continue to Washington. On the way, at Bladensburg, the last defendable position on the road to the Capitol, he was confronted on 24 August by a large hastily assembled force of American Militia under Major General Winder, along with Barney's sailors and their naval guns. The latter fought bravely before surrendering to Ross and the Militia fled to bring news of the battle to Washington, but made no effort to defend the city. Ross's casualties were severe, many dying of excessive heat and exhaustion. With his advance party of officers Ross entered Washington, as alarmed to find the city largely unprotected as were the citizens to see him and his British troops. He had hoped for a truce, but when he was fired on, a narrow escape for him, he ordered that Washington's government buildings be put to the torch. The Capitol was one of the first buildings to be burned. At the White House Ross discovered that President James Madison had fled to Virginia, leaving a celebration meal on the table intended for the expected conquering Americans, which Ross's group immediately consumed with many a toast to their own arrival. They then proceeded to burn the building, undoubtedly in retaliation for the American burning of York in Canada in the previous year. The burning of Washington, carried out by an Irishman, was a spectacular and dramatic event that to this day receives scant attention from proud Americans; the newspapers of the day, of course, roundly criticized this 'barbarous' act of war. The following evening the British expedition marched silently out of the city and returned to the Patuxent River. On 30 August the army embarked on the fleet awaiting at Benedict.

In an ill-judged plan to attack Baltimore, now heavily fortified, Ross was killed by an American sniper outside the city on 12 September. Colonel Arthur Brooke then took command, but, without naval cooperation, the British forces had to withdraw. Ross was buried in the churchyard of St Paul's Anglican Church, Halifax, where his body was taken along with the wounded. A national memorial to him was erected in St Paul's Cathedral, London, another in Cork, and in the church at Rostrevor. Through a petition by Mrs Ross the title of Ross of Bladensburg, unique among official distinctions of commoner families, was awarded and used by Ross's family and descendants.[43]

The young Irish officer, George de Lacy Evans, of Moig, County Limerick, was one of the naval and military commanders who urged the attack on Baltimore. Ironically, Ross hesitated, but eventually agreed to it. Evans, who was to have a very distinguished career in the British Army, was of the de Lacy family who came to England with William the Conqueror and had provided generals and field marshals for the Austrian, Russian and Spanish armies. As third son of a minor branch of the family George had early decided on a military career and, after joining the army in India as a volunteer, was appointed Ensign in 1807 in the very Irish 22nd Foot. Within a year bravery in the field brought him promotion to Lieutenant. He served in Mauritius, Persia and India and by 1812 had transferred to the 3rd Dragoons then serving in the Peninsula, for him an 'exhilarating experience'. Fighting in the principal battles of 1813 and 1814, he distinguished himself in cavalry charges at Vitoria and in the Pyrenees battles. Twice wounded at Toulouse, he had two horses shot from under him. When Robert Ross organized his American expedition Evans, who despite his bravery had been passed over for promotion (slow everywhere at this time), was pleased to be appointed Deputy Assistant Quartermaster General. Displaying his native élan, he had reconnoitred Washington and volunteered to lead a night attack on the city, which Ross approved after he had been fired on. Zealous with ambition after Washington, Evans was part of the attempt to seize New Orleans in January 1815 under Major General Sir Edward Pakenham who arrived to replace Ross. Like Wellington, Pakenham had not wanted to fight in this war and the poor site already chosen for the battle at New Orleans was later greatly criticized by Wellington. In the attack of 8 January 1815 Pakenham was mortally wounded, sad because the peace treaty of Ghent between America and Britain had already been signed. Although a skilled commander, it is said that Pakenham's impatience in not waiting for reinforcements contributed to his death. Evans, who handled the retreat after the British defeat, was also seriously wounded again. He would be mentioned in despatches from America five times.[44]

The Irish and Waterloo

> Were you at Waterloo?
> I have been at Waterloo.
> Tis no matter what you do,
> If you've been at Waterloo.
> *United Service Gazette* 30 April 1842

The year 1815 brought the Duke of Wellington to Waterloo, his last battle, and to world fame. When the British government and the Congress of Vienna learned of Napoleon's arrival in France after his escape from Elba and of the support he quickly gathered from able leaders like Marshal Ney, the European powers knew they must act. At the end of March Wellington was recalled from his diplomatic duties in Vienna and appointed Commander-in-Chief of the British and Dutch-Belgian forces in Flanders, a truly allied army. Although his British Army would not include as many battle-hardened Peninsular War veterans as he would have wished, in fact he would have some twelve thousand veterans. He was disappointed when command of his cavalry was given to Lord Uxbridge who had never served under him but who, as Lord Henry Paget, had been brilliant under Moore at Corunna. Fortunately Wellington secured the services of men like Sir William De Lancey as his Deputy Quartermaster General, an American he had known since boyhood and a Peninsular veteran knighted for his services in Spain. George de Lacy Evans, back from the North American expedition and awarded a Majority, was his Deputy Assistant Quartermaster General. He also had other trusted Irish generals from Peninsular days like Pack, Ponsonby and Vandeleur, as well as the Welshman Picton, whom he asked for and who was 'still eager for a little more distinction . . . but was by no means anxious to serve under any other British or continental general'.[45] Many of Wellington's continental troops were mercenaries, some had fought in Bonaparte's earlier campaigns, many others were mere boys who had never fired a shot. Wellington said of the Belgian officers in his army, 'I would not trust one of them out of my sight'. The only two designated Irish units Wellington could call upon were the1/27th Foot and the 6th Inniskilling Dragoons. Other regiments like the 28th Foot, 'the Slashers' and the 52nd Foot, 'the Light Bobs', were filled with Irish, now an accepted part of the British Army.

At the Duchess of Richmond's famous ball in Brussels on 15 June Wellington admitted, in his own famous words, that he was 'humbugged' by Bonaparte's swift advance into Belgium. Attacks on Prussian outposts around Charleroi were real, not feints. Early on 16 June Wellington brought his army to Quatre Bras crossroads, where, he had learned,

Marshal Ney was heading on Napoleon's orders. Wellington wanted the crucial crossroads held in order to keep the road to Ligny open, where his Prussian Allies under the seventy-four-year-old Marshal Blücher were fighting the French some six to eight miles to the south-east. He then rode off to confer personally with Blücher at Ligny. That morning Marshal Ney and General Honoré Reille were tardy in attacking at Quatre Bras unnerved by Wellington's reputation for his skilled use of reverse slopes to conceal his army. Ney finally launched an assault and badly mauled regiments like Wellington's Own, the very Irish 33rd Foot, who fled instead of forming a square after someone shouted, 'The cavalry are coming!'. By mid-afternoon Wellington returned from Ligny and took over his scattered forces who began arriving from Brussels in the nick of time. Picton's 5th Division was ready and time and again, when French cavalry hurled themselves at his squares, he could be heard roaring out encouragement to them, '28th – remember Egypt!', and they held. Grapeshot broke three of Picton's ribs and Wellington had a close call. The Battle of Quatre Bras resulted in a draw and when word came to Wellington that Marshal Blücher and his Prussians had been badly defeated at Ligny and had to retire north to Wavre, he too was forced to withdraw. This he did to the Ridge of Mont St Jean near the village of Waterloo south of Brussels, a site he had already reconnoitred the previous year as a possible battleground. However, it was only the reassurance of Blücher's help, received in the dawn of 18 June (the day of battle), that decided him to stand and fight at Waterloo. At the Ridge Sir William de Lancey established the battle line where the army could shelter on the reverse slope. Including outlying hamlets and the Bois de Paris, the field of Waterloo was about six square miles, a small area for nearly 200,000 people to fight in.[46]

On that Sunday, 18 June 1815, Wellington and Napoleon faced each other for the first time in battle, although throughout the Peninsular War Wellington knew that the absent Napoleon had guided his marshals. Now, as he said to Baron von Müffling, the Prussian Liaison officer, Napoleon will see what a 'sepoy general' can do. From early morning Wellington, clad in his sober civilian clothes enlivened only by the four cockades of Britain, Spain, Portugal and the Netherlands in his cocked hat, rode about everywhere on his horse Copenhagen, ignoring danger, encouraging, giving orders, sometimes sheltering in regimental squares, and putting heart into all who saw his familiar figure. At other times he was seen at his command post under the famous elm tree at the crossroads above La Haye Sainté.

An Irish Sergeant, James Graham, played an heroic role when, just before noon, General Reille with four 'splendid regiments of veterans' attacked the Château de Hougoumont, the outpost on the west of the British line, in a devastating action that lasted all day. Light Companies of Scots and Coldstream Guards held on and eventually two complete French infantry divisions were drawn in against this strongpoint in what became almost a separate battle from the rest of the field. The French at one moment forced their way into the courtyard but with a herculean effort Colonel James Macdonnell, a massive Highlander of 2nd Coldstream Guards, and his Irish Quartermaster Sergeant Graham managed by sheer physical strength to shut the great gate and not one Frenchman survived inside. Wellington later wrote that 'The success of the battle of Waterloo depended on closing of the gates'. Graham would be known as 'the man who shut the gates at Hougoumont' and Macdonnell gallantly said that his award should be equally shared with Graham. In 1906 the Coldstream Guards erected a memorial to Graham in Kilmainham Royal Hospital Dublin that was later removed to his parish church at Clones, County Monaghan.[47] Kilmainham, completed in 1684, had been built by Charles II as an asylum and refuge for the disabled and retired veterans of his army. A fine classical building, it still stands.

Around 1.00 p.m. a barrage of Napoleon's guns pounded the ridge, followed immediately by the great attack on Wellington's left centre by General Count D'Erlon's formidable corps of three unwieldy massed infantry columns. A brigade of Dutch-Belgians took such a pounding that, with their officers gone, they turned and ran. But Picton's 5th Division, sheltering behind the ridge, was poised to spring up. In a magnificent counter-attack his Commanders, General Sir Denis Pack and General Sir James Kempt, both Peninsular veterans, rushed forward shouting encouragement to their brigades. Picton, leading the front line of Kempt's Brigade, bellowed 'Charge!' to his Scotsmen and was shot in the head through his famous top hat. It looked as if Wellington's line might be overwhelmed. At this critical moment Lord Uxbridge ordered the heavy cavalry, drawn up on the reverse slope, to charge over the ridge. The Royal Household Brigade of Life Guards, King's Dragoon Guards and Blues was led by Lord Edward Somerset; Major General Sir William Ponsonby was Commander of Union Brigade, so called because it represented regiments of Ireland – 6th Inniskilling Dragoons, Scotland – 2nd Royal North British Dragoons known as Scots Greys because of their grey horses, and England – the Royals. Wellington personally led forward the Life Guards. In the Marquess of Anglesey's account, as the two brigades intermingled they 'swept the demoralized enemy into the valley, some 3,000 prisoners and two Eagles were taken. Lord Uxbridge, who himself led in 'the thundering enthusiasm of the charge', was in no position to deal with the débâcle that followed. 'Wildly excited by their success scattered squadrons of cavalry regiments' kept going right up to and into the enemy's guns. But 'retribution for rashness was at hand'. French infantry soon fired on them and they were attacked by two regiments of *cuirrassiers*, while Jacquinot's *lanciers* descended upon the Scots Greys to the east.[48] Lady Butler's painting, *Scotland Forever* (Leeds City Art Galleries), captures the Greys' mad advance, one of her few paintings to show soldiers in action and one of her best-known works.

The heavy brigades had virtually put out of action a French Infantry Corps, part of its artillery and a cavalry brigade, but at a high cost. Sir William Ponsonby was stabbed to death, Major George de Lacy Evans, now acting as his ADC, suffered a sabre wound from eye to mouth and Captain Edward Kelly of the Life Guards, wounded in the leg, had three horses shot from under him before he fell. The Inniskillings lost half their strength lying dead or wounded on the battlefield. Lord Uxbridge has been blamed for leading the attack himself. As he confessed later, if he had stayed behind to direct the charge he would have seen that the heavy brigade had gone too far and could have sent in the nearest light cavalry. In fact two squadrons of 12th Light Dragoons of Sir John Ormsby Vandeleur's 4th Brigade went forward on their own to give some protection to the exhausted cavalry on their return, and in this action Sir Frederick Ponsonby, colonel of the 12th and second cousin to Sir William Ponsonby, fell desperately wounded by French sabres and was presumed dead. Robbed, ridden over, his was a miraculous escape for he lay on the battlefield some eighteen hours, eventually saved by a British soldier who stood guard over him until morning.[49] The Ponsonbys, of the family of the Earl of Bessborough in the Irish peerage, were an English family in Ireland descended from a colonel of a regiment of cavalry who accompanied Cromwell to Ireland and received grants of land.

The crisis of the battle came about 7:00 p.m. when Napoleon finally committed the infantry of his formidable Imperial Guard, some fifteen thousand men in two separate columns each with a front of sixty to eighty men, and led them himself for a short distance before Ney took over. Ney's guns pounded the Ridge where Wellington personally rallied young Brunswickers whose flight to the rear was checked by Vandeleur's cavalry. Through the smoke, not stopped by the Allied gunners, came the densely packed columns of the Imperial Guard, huge men in their tall bearskin hats who had terrorized Europe with the mesmerizing sound of the relentless beat of their drums. The major column saw no infantry ahead as they came to within some sixty yards of the crest when, turning to the Commander of the hidden 1st Foot Guards, Wellington's voice rang out above the din: 'Now Maitland! Now is your time!', and a few seconds later 'Up Guards! Make ready! Fire!' Suddenly, from behind the crest hundreds of redcoats rose up as if out of the ground and poured a torrent of fire into the front ranks of Napoleon's invincible Guard and, together with a British battery, brought down 300 in the French front ranks in less than a minute. While the Guard struggled to reform, the 52nd Foot, under Colonel Colborne, a regiment of at least 50 per cent Irish also concealed on the ridge, marched forward in orderly ranks and in another remarkable manoeuvre wheeled, turned and attacked the Guard's flank, pouring in volley after volley. They did not wait for the bayonet charge: 'The Guard is retreating' was heard everywhere. In the smoke, noise and chaos of the battle disbelief was felt by all, not least by the watching French. It was about this time that an aide brought to Wellington news that the long-awaited Prussians under Marshal Blücher had arrived; their vedettes had earlier been spotted by Wellington when some miles away. Indeed, from 4.00 p.m. the Prussians in General Count von Bülow's corps had been fiercely fighting on Napoleon's now beleagured right flank and rear at Plançenoit. Wellington took off his hat and waved it; everyone who could see him understood. The army swarmed down onto the field led by Vandeleur's light cavalry amidst great cheering.[50]

'One British regiment did not join in the advance but remained quietly on the ridge. This was the 27th Foot. They lay dead to a man in their square.' So writes Elizabeth Longford. In the words of Captain John Kincaid of the 95th Rifles, he had never 'yet heard of a battle in which everybody was killed', but this was the impression made upon him when he surveyed the centre of the British line in the last stage of the Battle of Waterloo. The words of Lady Longford and Captain Kincaid suggest total destruction of the 27th. As historian John Keegan observes, the Inniskillings are recorded as sustaining casualties of 450 of 750 officers and men, killed and wounded in their four hours on the ridge when they withstood the surging mass of cavalry, deadly musketry fire of French skirmishers, and especially the tornado of cannon shot as they stood motionless in their square. Their Light Company skirmishing to the Regiment's front rather than standing still escaped this cannonading ordeal. When orders came for the general advance the surviving Inniskillings in 'Lambert's Brigade . . . pressed down the slope towards La Haye Sainte where the 27th are said to have made many prisoners'. They also pushed on as far as La Belle Alliance, the farm that had been Napoleon's headquarters, and there 'were ordered to halt and bivouack for the night'. At roll call the exhausted remnant of the Inniskillings knew 'that on the other side of the valley the greater part of the Battalion lay piled in heaps of dead and wounded on the ground at the crossroads which their square had held so indomitably'. The 27th lost more men and officers than any other infantry battalion that day. In regimental tradition a captured

French general is said to have commented: 'I have seen Russian, Prussian and French bravery, but anything to equal the stubborn bravery of the regiment with castles I never before witnessed.' Wellington recognized the importance of the Inniskilling heroism and in later years whenever the regiment was referred to would exclaim, 'Ah, they saved the centre of my line at Waterloo'. At about 9.00pm Wellington met Blücher near La Belle Alliance to acknowledge the victory and, his army exhausted, he consented to give the final pursuit of Napoleon's Army to the Prussians. In the excitement after the battle, speaking of its near success and moments of crisis, it is recorded that Wellington burst out, 'I don't think it would have been done if I had not been there'. The Battle of Waterloo was indeed 'a near run thing'. Later, writing to his brother William, he admitted, 'It was the most desperate business I ever was in,' and in rare praise of his British Infantry he adds, 'I never saw the Infantry behave so well.'[51]

As an example of Wellington's 'hard-heartedness' his critics cite the famous Waterloo story of Lord Uxbridge, whose leg was smashed by one of the last French cannon shots while seated on his horse beside Wellington, who, it is said, paid scant attention and, supporting Uxbridge in his saddle until help arrived, then rode off. The needs of war were obviously paramount. After the battle Wellington paid a personal visit to the wounded William Verner of the 7th Hussars, a native of Armagh, Northern Ireland, and a veteran of Corunna, and issued to him the challenging comment, 'You are not nearly so bad as you think'. This brusque comment was enough to get the terribly wounded Verner back on his feet within a month; he, however, attributed his recovery to the recuperative powers of Guinness porter![52] Wellington also called on his dying friend and Quartermaster General William de Lancey, who had also been struck down while talking to Wellington and was lying in a hovel at Mont St Jean attended by his young wife. Wellington commiserated with him, then hurried off to his troops. 'Poor fellow,' he recalled much later, 'I had no time to be sorry. I went on with the army and never saw him again.' But Wellington mourned his death and all 'such brave men,'[53] and it is recorded that he wept when the long list of casualties was read out to him. Lady Butler recounts how her father told her Wellington's 'memorable words' on the loss of so many of his friends: 'A defeat is the only thing sadder than a victory'.[54]

For the common Irish soldiers, Wellington as a member of a Palesman family, had been taught from childhood to feel all the reserve of his ascendancy class when it came to the peasantry, and he was never personally sentimental about the men in the ranks. Nor were the Irish any more sentimental about their gifted yet aloof military commander in whom they put such trust. George Bell of the 34th Foot, the Border Regiment, records how the 'Patlanders', who formed a large part of the regiment, expressed this trust with inimitable humour. An exchange between two of the Irish was overheard as they approached Toulouse at the end of the war in 1814:

> 'How the divil are we to get over that big sthrame av a river to leather them vagabones out o'that,' says Paddy Muldoon. 'O niver mind,' says another old cripple who lost an eye on the Nive, 'that countryman av yours wid the long nose will show you the way when he's riddy.'[55]

In Wellington's address to the House of Lords at the passing of Catholic Emancipation in 1829 he admitted publicly his understanding of and gratitude for his Catholic Irish soldiers during his several campaigns:

> Of the troops which our gracious Sovereign did me the honour to entrust to my command . . . at least one-half were Roman Catholics . . . . without Catholic blood and Catholic valour, no victory could ever have been obtained . . . it is mainly to the Irish Catholics that we all owe our preeminence in our military career . . . I glory, my lords, in the name of Ireland . . . united with the rest of my kindred in the grateful task of closing the wounds which seven centuries of misgovernment have inflicted upon that unfortunate land.[56]

Tribute-giving of this order, however politically motivated, was not typical for Wellington; more often was his understated remark of how his soldiers got him out of a scrape more than once. Wellington, writes Elizabeth Longford, 'was deeply and emotionally committed to Ireland. The strength of this feeling was shown by the amount of time he gave throughout his life to research and writing on possible solutions for her problems.'[57]

CHAPTER FOUR

The Irish, The British Army and
The Early Victorians

I must confess I love to be on service with the Irish.

John Shipp *The Path of Glory*,
London, 1969, p. 115

Wellington's Legacy

Wellington's continuing and extraordinary ascendancy over the army in the years following Waterloo could not be accounted for, writes Sir John Fortescue. He deliberately seemed to alienate any affectionate feeling of either officers or men towards him, and his reluctance to discuss his years as a military leader disappointed would-be historians. Perhaps it was to protect his privacy that Wellington tried to close the door on his martial years, but this was not possible for him. When the Duke of York died in 1827 Wellington was immediately appointed Commander-in-Chief of the army, resigning twice for political reasons until, in 1842, he was reappointed Commander-in-Chief for life. Even when he was Prime Minister, (two short years, from 1828) he was constantly appealed to on military matters, unfortunate because he was never a military innovator, except, it might be said, for his reverse slopes tactic. In his declining years he still thought in conservative terms of a military era that was long past.

The majority of the Irish who had served so long and so valiantly under 'the Duke' found there was intense resentment by the privileged classes when it came to paying for the Army of Occupation in France, which by 1817 was being reduced. There was much grumbling by homecoming soldiers competing for employment, officers demanding half-pay, or men seeking a pension, yet an enthusiastic British public subscribed a half million pounds for the army at Waterloo; grants were distributed to disabled officers and men, widows and orphans received annuities. Life was hard for those who left the army at this time, when, following the end of hostilities, both England and Ireland suffered from economic recession. The experience of Dubliner Edward Costello of the 95th Rifles is but one example. A Sergeant in the Peninsula, he took part in the storming of both Ciudad Rodrigo and Badajoz, suffering multiple wounds. He married a French girl during his time in the Army of Occupation but they nearly starved on the sixpence a day given to him as a pension when he returned to England in 1818. Reduced to begging for help, he was assisted by Wellington's brother, the Reverend Gerald Wellesley, a brother Mason, and others, but at the cost of great humiliation and deprivation.[1] Costello managed to become an officer in the British Volunteer Legion which served in the Carlist wars in Spain in the 1830s, led by another Irishman, Sir George De Lacy Evans. At 84 Costello ended his life as a Yeoman Warder of the Tower of London.

Many Irish were still in the British Army which garrisoned the far-flung empire. When reductions of the army began after Waterloo it was said that Wellington, in order to keep a strong army, 'hid' regiments abroad to preserve them from the economists at home. When famous fighting Irish units were disbanded, like Sir Hugh Gough's 2/87th, many of the veterans volunteered and were transferred to their first battalion in India. The pattern of regimental service was evolving that would ensure that most Irish recruits would spend a major part of their years of service overseas, so that in 1827 the government was very embarrassed when numbers of troops in the country were so low that the Duke of York could not be given the military funeral befitting a field marshal.[2] Even with reductions of the army, a substantial number of Irish remained in the service and in 1830, when the Irish represented only about one-third of the United Kingdom population, more Irish than English were in the British Army. The Connors family, remarkably, maintained a tradition of one hundred years in the 87th Royal Irish Fusiliers. When Patrick Connors enlisted in the Regiment in 1839 he had followed his grandfather and father. His son was Colour Sergeant J. Connors who served in the South African War, followed by *his* son Captain J. G. Connors, who served as Quartermaster in the Regiment, dying at Malta in 1938, and he had a son serving in the Faughs.

Throughout the nineteenth century the Royal Hibernian Military School in Dublin provided the army with a steady flow of boy recruits. As well as enlisting in Irish regiments Irishmen enlisted in certain English and Scots regiments that became Irish preserves, for example regiments like the 94th and the 2/74th Highlanders were favoured by the Irish, as were the English 2nd/10th Lincolnshire and 1st/16th Bedfordshire. The 43rd, 67th and 33rd Foot were filled with Irish.[3] The Irish did not at this time dominate in cavalry units in the way they did in the infantry.

The question is often asked why anyone would continue to serve in the British Army during this period, an army where at any time a unit might be less than 50 per cent in strength because of crime, desertion and sickness. Life in the ranks was brutal, the last refuge of the 'reckless and degraded' who were pariahs in nineteenth century society and acted accordingly. Army punishment was savage, but it was consistent with the age when the death penalty was permitted for well over 200 crimes, even at the time of Waterloo.[4] Wellington upheld flogging, believing that the system which had brought victory over the French could still turn the worst of recruits into professional soldiers. Both he and the Duke of York believed that the only control of a violent and mutinous volunteer army would come through a fear of the cat-o'-nine tails. Wellington had few illusions about the moral character of most recruits as he wrote in 1829, 'The man who enlists into the British army is, in general, the most drunken and probably the worst man of the trade or profession to which he belongs, or of the village or town in which he lives'.[5] He viewed the army as a 'huge and extravagant reformatory', its inmates saved by corporal discipline on the one hand and 'precepts' established by old soldiers on the other. However, by 1844 Wellington realized that the days of flogging were numbered. Public pressure and ideas of 'liberation and philanthropy' inevitably led to a reduction in how many lashes could be ordered. In 1867 flogging in peacetime was abolished and, as a wartime punishment, it was limited to twenty-five lashes from 1879 until the Army Discipline Act of 1881 totally abolished it. Major depots increasingly had military prisons where the treadmill and solitary confinement replaced flogging. Despite evidence that army life was so harsh, thousands of young Irishman enlisted in the first half of the nineteenth century. Often it would have been because of desperate poverty. For the ever-increasing population of Ireland, hunger, apart from major famines, was a continuing problem of the cotter* class. At least in the army one was assured of a roof over one's head and regular if unappetizing meals.

Each recruit, of course, had his own tale about why he enlisted. J. M. MacMullen in his *Camp and Barrack Room or The British Army as it is* of 1846, records that it was his love of travel and adventure that persuaded him to leave clerical work in Dublin for a military career. Most recruits were very young men and it is likely that a life of dull conformity, particularly in the countryside or the village, produced a claustrophobic longing to escape into a wider world. For the young and healthy Irishman the most readily available means to that world was the British Army.

James O'Malley of Galway has told how, as a boy, he was entranced

---

* Tenants, virtually serfs, occupying cottages in return for labour.

with 'splendid, well-proportioned, brave-looking soldiers, gaily dressed' marching with their bands in the city. When he enlisted in the 17th Foot he recalled how the Recruiting Sergeant, plying them with drink, told would-be recruits of the glories of Waterloo. Tailoring his account to suit their Irish sensibilities, he had Major General Sir James Kempt as 'one of the Lords of Colde of Inneskillen, one of the bravest men who ever wore a sword'. Kempt was in fact Scots/English, not Irish, and commanded a brigade at Waterloo not, as the Recruiting Sergeant said, the heroic 27th at the crossroads. From 1852 O'Malley found himself in the 17th's almost entirely Irish grenadier company.[6]

Another Irish recruit in the 17th Foot was Thomas Faughnan from County Leitrim near the River Shannon, who enlisted in 1847. His family had been devastated by the famine: 'all my near relatives in Leitrim were either dead or had emigrated to America'. He told with pride how the Regiment marched from Dublin to Castlebar to the admiration of the country people. A Roman Catholic, he had no difficulty over worship as the battalion band paraded the men to chapel. He rejoiced in the size of his Captain, a six-foot-four-inches-tall Limerick man called John Croker, as well as another giant recruit from the Claddagh named Paddy Belton. Faughnan did not appreciate changing barracks every ten months, but was greatly impressed by Richmond Barracks in Dublin when he was chosen to go to London for the parade at the time of Wellington's death. Among the picked men, although he was five feet eleven inches tall, he was 'the smallest man of the party'.[7]

The British Army in Ireland in 'Aid of the Civil Power'

Some of Faughnan's duties in Ireland were neither to his nor his fellow soldiers' liking, such as supporting the magistrate who read the Riot Act in the Castlebar election of 1850. These duties, as in the eighteenth century, were a reflection of the need to use the army to control social unrest that was also rampant throughout the nineteenth century.

In the early decades of the century fear of the mob in their various factions was most evident in Ireland. With the reduction of the army after the French war there was fear that returning soldiers as well as demobilized militia would make almost a 'standing army of the disaffected', allying themselves with those thousands who lived on the verge of starvation. By 1813 the army had ensured that half the Militia in Ireland was English, while the Irish Militia served on the mainland to 'civilize' them. The soldiers had a difficult time in the midst of this anarchy; in mid-February 1822 wives of soldiers in the Rifle Brigade were raped in front of their children and soldiers were encouraged to desert and join the rebels. The regular soldiers bore the brunt of these uneasy years. A particularly trying time for the army was the 1831–38 Tithe War in Ireland when troops were used in the collection of unpaid tithes, for them a most unpleasant and unpopular duty. By 1836, to meet this situation, the Irish Constabulary, formed from 1822 as Ireland's first country-wide police force, had to be reorganized and this was done on regimental lines; most senior officers were ex-military men, and constables lived in barracks and engaged in military drill.

The 'faction' fighting at times seemed merely recreational and the British Army was never happy when summoned by the Constabulary to help contain it. At a great faction fight in County Kerry part of the 69th Regiment from Tralee under Captain Richard Hooper remained spectators. As he told an enquiry, 'I saw no favourable opportunity of intervening to quell the riot'. Captain Hooper's discretion was probably justified; it would have been difficult for the army to have escaped the charge of taking sides if any armed intervention had been attempted. The British Army could often do little more than watch the battling and perhaps wonder if these local champions might be persuaded to take the King's shilling, as the Irish poet and songwriter Percy French suggests for his 'Cornelius Burke':

> When first I took up arms, 'twas a faction-fight in Clare;
> The Burkes they all were there and faith they did their share!
> My father said, "Cornelius, you've a mighty martial air –
> I think that you were cut out for a soldier!"[8]

Social tensions also continued to engage Irish troops in the north of Ireland and abroad. When Daniel O'Connell, the champion of Catholic Emancipation, prepared to speak in Protestant Belfast on 2 January 1841 the Inniskilling Dragoons were brought from Dundalk, and even artillery pieces were prepared for any action.[9] In 1843 the 87th Foot, (Royal Irish Fusiliers from 1827) had the unhappy task of curbing civil disturbances in Leeds, England, and in Scotland, where workers rioted over the wretched working conditions in coal mines and iron works. Many of the dissidents were the equally robust Irish Navigators (Navvies), driven out of Ireland by the famines to find work on the railway. There were complaints that some Irish in the ranks were being 'contaminated' by their countrymen on the railroads and because of this between 1844 and 1845 there were seventy-two courts-martial and forty-six desertions in the 87th.[10]

The often mindless feuding mentality that characterized faction fighting could also find expression between regiments as in *Belts* from Rudyard Kipling's Barrack-Room Ballads:

> There was a row in Silver Street that's near to Dublin Quay,
> Between an Irish Regiment an' English cavalree . . .

He caught the flavour of such rioting, which was a perennial problem in the British Army of the nineteenth century, in a line from another verse:
The English were too drunk to know, the Irish didn't care . . . [11]

The Irish and the Early Victorians in India

With this background of a whole society convulsed by political and social upheaval it is not surprising that young Irishmen would have been enticed to enlist with stories of adventure and valour in far-off lands, and India was the place where military action was to be found. The younger sons of impoverished Anglo-Irish Protestant gentry could attend the East India Company's military seminary at Addiscombe, England, that opened in 1809, and then serve in 'John Company's' huge army. Nearly 250,000 white and native soldiers made it larger than any European army except that of Russia. The smaller Imperial forces tended to look down upon this 'mercenary' army in India, its ranks filled with sepoys (Indian soldiers), while its European officers included serious-minded middle-class careerists. From the early nineteenth century the Irish made up nearly half the recruits for the European regiments in John Company's army and recruitment was helped when the East India Company opened recruitment offices in Ireland.[12] The Irish were often also a majority in the Crown regiments serving in India. A famous Irishman at this time, Colonel Rollo Gillespie, became a folk hero in India and Ireland and in the British military world an exemplar of Irish military prowess.

Rollo Gillespie came from a Scots family who supported the Stuarts and had been forced to flee to County Down, where he was born in January 1766. His wealthy father paid handsomely for the young Gillespie to become a Cornet in the 3rd Horse and soon he was the object of public attention. Slim-bodied, short-statured and delicately featured, this young man's fiery temper involved him in a duel with the brother of Sir Jonah Barrington, a public figure of the age. Barrington was killed and Gillespie fled to Scotland, but later was 'honourably acquitted' after a much-publicized trial. In 1794 he was again in the public eye after a feat of derring-do that involved swimming ashore from a naval vessel at Port-au-Prince, San Domingo to demand surrender from the French Governor. On San Domingo, a band of marauders burst into his house to be met by the little man in his night attire who killed six of them outright and chased off the other two, suffering only a head wound from which he quickly recovered.

Gillespie, a natural leader of men, by 1805 had made his way to India to take command of the 19th Light Dragoons at Arcot. Fourteen miles away at Vellore was a fort garrisoned by four companies of the 69th Foot, and three battalions of Madras infantry who were very agitated because General Sir John Craddock, obtuse Commander of Madras forces, deeply offended the native troops' religious beliefs by issuing new regulations: 'a new pattern of turban, prohibition of caste marks on the face, and the shaving off of beards'. Followers of Tippu, Sultan of Mysore, encouraged the sepoys' anxieties and, as unrest began, Craddock considered cancelling the new regulations. Lord William Bentinck, Governor of Madras, feared the British losing face if the commander of the Madras Army climbed down and no changes were made. The result was that, on the night of 10 July 1806, the sepoys at Vellore mutinied. European sentries were shot, British soldiers in the hospital murdered and soldiers of the 69th were shot in their barracks as they slept. A remnant managed to fight their way to a redoubt they established on the ramparts surrounding the inner gate of the fort. An officer of the 69th, who was outside the fort, rushed to Arcot for help. On the way he met Lieutenant Colonel Rollo Gillespie out for a morning canter, and within fifteen minutes Gillespie led the 19th Light Dragoons galloping towards Vellore, followed by horse artillery and the 7th Madras Native Cavalry. Reaching the gate ramparts, he was pulled up by rope and joined the 69th remnant. It seemed hopeless until his galloper guns arrived and, on his order, blew in an entrance. The cavalry poured into the fort and in a sharp engagement some three hundred and fifty mutineers were killed. Those captured, after trial, were either blown away by guns, shot by muskets, hanged or transported, and the mutinous regiments were disbanded. This, writes Anglesey, is 'one of the few examples of . . . swift and courageous action nipping mutiny in the bud'.

In 1807 Gillespie transferred to the 8th Royal Irish Light Dragoons, then stationed at Cawnpore. In 1814 he took part in the invasion of Nepal to punish some Gurkhas who, after subduing the hill country, continued to engage in Indian frontier disputes with the British who controlled the low country of Nepal. Overall direction of this campaign was under the Irish Lord Moira who had combined the offices of Governor General and Commander-in-Chief in Bengal. He formally declared war on the Gurkhas in November. Two columns (of four) were led by Major General Gillespie, the hero of Vellore, and Sir David Ochterlony, the American-born Major General of 'conspicuous ability', popularly known by his Irish troops as 'Ould Maloney'. In an attempt to take a Gurkha hill fort at Kalunga on 31 October Gillespie, with the cry 'Now for the honour of Down', led the dismounted 8th Royal Irish Light Dragoons and others in an attack that was repulsed. It was one wildly brave feat too many and Gillespie was killed. His friend and fellow Ulsterman Charles Kennedy of the artillery carried his body away, escorted by the Royal Irish. A statue of this Irish hero was erected in St Paul's Cathedral and several years later on 24 June 1845 a monument to the 'saviour of Vellore' was unveiled in the Square in Comber, his home in County Down. A small obelisk to him still stands in Kalunga. The late Victorian patriot poet Henry Newbolt celebrated Gillespie's daring action in his *Gillespie*:

> They've kept the tale a hundred years,
> They'll keep the tale a hundred more:
> Riding at dawn, riding alone,
> Gillespie came to false Vellore.

Contemporary critics judged Gillespie mentally unstable; he had received head wounds in earlier battles and it was said that 'his mind was unsettled by alcohol and megalomania', but it was his 'intense desire for glory' that was his undoing.[13] An interesting result of this costly little war was that, when Ochterlony brought it to an end in 1816, the British were given the right to recruit among the Gurkhas whose fighting qualities they greatly admired and still do.

The notable John Shipp, who had none of the social connections of Rollo Gillespie, is important for us because of his chequered career in the British Army and for his insights into the Irish he served with in the Nepalese War which he recorded in his memoirs. At age twelve, his mother dead and his English soldier father on foreign postings, Shipp, aided by parish officers, joined the 22nd Foot, thus escaping the dreary existence of an English parish workhouse. In the Mahratta War of 1804–1805 he led a forlorn hope with such courage that he was given an ensigncy in the 65th Foot, followed by a lieutenancy in the 76th. Unable to afford the expenses of an officer's life, when he returned home with his regiment he sold out. Military life, however, proved preferable to civilian and he enlisted once more, in the cavalry, which brought him to India again and to the rank of Sergeant. In 1815 he was given another commission, a rare phenomenon in the army, this time in the Irish 87th Foot, the Faughs. Arriving at Dinapore Shipp found his new regimental station deserted except for an old half-drunken Irishwoman, Judy Flanagan, who, after questioning him did he 'really belong to the old Fogaboloughs?' told him that 'the old Fogs' had been gone for three days, 'to fight against Paul' [the Nepalese]. Catching up with the Regiment he was delighted that all the officers including the commander received him kindly: 'This generous welcome . . . I did not in the least expect . . . Officers promoted from the

ranks are generally received with some caution and perhaps a little prejudice, but there was nothing like that with this distinguished Regiment'.
The march of the 87th, the only Crown Regiment with Shipp's part of the
force, was arduous and dangerous and it brought from Shipp his often-
quoted praise of the Irish in the 87th:

> There is a promptness to obey, a hilarity, a cheerful obedience,
> and a willingness to act, which I have rarely met with in any other
> body of men . . . a generosity of spirit I have never known . . .
> They were willing to share their last drop, and last crust with a
> comrade; and would go to any lengths to oblige, or cover up, for
> one another. There was a unity among them that excelled
> anything I have ever met and for fighting they were absolute
> demons. . . . They are said to be too impetuous . . . but that is a
> fault on the right side, and has gained England many a victory.[14]

Shipp would serve thirty-two years in India and his memoir, written years
afterwards, is one of the few first-hand accounts of the 87th in these early
years.

In India even the men in the ranks, whether in Royal or John Company
regiments, by all accounts regarded themselves as 'sahibs', for thus were
they addressed by Indian servants and menials, although they had been
recruited from the lowest of unskilled labourers and were sometimes
called 'a new low caste in caste-ridden India'. They were still warriors,
representative of a master race who regarded no Indians except the
Gurkhas as their equals in military terms. Normally the ordinary soldier
met only low caste sweepers, bhisties (water carriers) and other barrack-
servants, who exempted him from usual fatigues. He lived segregated in a
cantonment, the local Indian community and Indian barracks being out-
of-bounds to him. A soldier could spend a dozen years in the subcontinent
and return home completely ignorant of Indian culture, the only legacy of
his years of service a smattering of Hindustani words and phrases. When
discipline broke down soldiers could go without their pay. Captain Albert
Hervey, serving in a sepoy regiment in John Company's Madras Army,
writes of a Royal regiment in the late 1830s he saw passing through Vellore
that was badly organized, 'for the main body . . . the column en route
presented a very soldier-like appearance'. But what astonished Hervey was
a long line of soldiers following as stragglers, some inebriated, and accompanied by wives and children all in a pitiable state. Some soldiers
approached Hervey to sell him their 'ammunition boots'; one of them, an
Irishman named Terence O'Brien, told him it was to buy breakfast for his
wife and children who accompanied him. After talking to him Hervey went

out of his way to feed and help this soldier and his family and was thanked profusely by Mrs. O'Brien in her Irish brogue 'that rendered her language perfectly unintelligible'. Some Irish rankers in India in the pre-mutiny days undoubtedly suffered from the regimental lack of discipline that Hervey bemoans. Yet service in 'the Shiny' had its compensations; food was generally plentiful and, as Maurice Moriarty, an Irish-speaking NCO from Dingle in the 29th Regiment, wrote home to his parents in the 1840s, 'extras such as fowl, eggs, sweetmeats and fruit . . . are not beyond the means of any soldier in India'. It is not surprising many soldiers chose to stay in India, transferring to another unit when their own returned home.[15]

Irishmen were prominent in the First Afghan War of 1839–42. The British had always been concerned that Russians and Persians might interfere in Afghan affairs. To prevent any military incursion the chief political adviser and envoy to Afghanistan, the Ulsterman Sir William Macnaghten, persuaded the Governor General, Lord Auckland, to overthrow the current amir Dost Muhammad, who was friendly to the Russians, and establish a puppet ruler Shah Shuja, who was unpopular with his own people. This called for a British invasion of Afghanistan and a pointless war followed. The army was not happy about the campaign, which called for vulnerable lines of communication through the passes held by wild Ghilzais. The commander of the 'Army of the Indus' (formed in 1838) was General Sir John Keane from Waterford, who captured Kabul in August 1839. He complained that he had had no political briefing that would suggest the intense resistance of the Afghans as he and his army advanced on Kabul through difficult mountain countryside, 'full of robbers, plunderers and murderers, brought up to it from their youth'. The Afghans were not pleased to see Shah Shuja installed in Kabul as Keane and his officers had been led to believe. Keane returned to India leaving a garrison to support Macnaghten.

Clearly the Afghans despised their British rulers. A rising was led by Dost Muhammad's son, Akbar Khan, in which officers were openly insulted and troops constantly risked having their throats cut on sentry duty. Small attacks took place around the army's camp and it was soon realized that the smooth-bore muskets of the army were no match for the long-barrelled rifles of the Afghans who were, it was said, 'perhaps the best marksmen in the world'. When Macnaghten was murdered on his way to a conference it was agreed to retreat to India and on 6 January 1842 the Kabul force headed for Jellalabad, a strong British post about sixty miles east. The worst disaster to date in British military history followed. Some 16,000 people, including British and Indian troops, wives, children and many camp-followers, were slaughtered or died of cold in the snow of the mountain passes. Surgeon William Brydon in the Bengal army was allowed to escape, so the garrison at Jellalabad would know the fate of the Kabul force. A few others, including wives and children, struggled through later, some having been taken prisoner.[16] In both the subcontinent and in England the shock was immense.

After the massacre of the Kabul force the Jellalabad garrison won fame by defeating the attacking Afghan army of Akbar Khan in April 1842, in which the heroism of the 13th Foot earned the Regiment its title 'Prince Albert's Light Infantry' and the attention of J.M. MacMullen, that educated, literate Irish recruit in search of adventure. He enlisted in the 13th, then considered a very Irish regiment; in the first decade of the nineteenth century it had contained 80 English, 6 Scots, 2 foreigners and 485 Irish. Perhaps more important to him was that the 13th was already in India when he joined it. In his memoir MacMullen records his observations of the life of Irish soldiers serving in the ranks on the Afghan frontier at this time. On St Patrick's Day 1844 his fellow Irish recruits demonstrated for him their sheer love of fighting in a brawl that took place in Sukkur camp, reminiscent of the faction fighting in Ireland. The drunken combatants, who at home would have shouted for 'Whitefeet or Blackfeet, Shanavast or Corovat', now fell upon one another defending causes such as 'Repeal of the Union and Father Mathew'. MacMullen marvelled at such a 'strange ebullition of national feeling, thousands of miles from home in a frontier station of the British Empire in the East'. He accepted the mayhem as part of the Irish character: 'an Irishman is an Irishman the world over', and those same men could be seen drinking together amicably in a few hours. In the ten months he spent in Sukkur camp half the fifty people who died did so because of excessive drinking compounded by sunstroke. MacMullen was a shrewd judge of his fellow Irishmen's failings, not least of which was their tendency to nurse grievances, which were readily passed on: 'Paddy . . . is a faithful chronicler of insults, personal and national'. They excitedly received any copy of Dublin's *Freeman* or *Nation* newspapers that came their way, but their bent for politics, which represented their intelligence and education, showed how liberal were the Irish soldiers when removed from 'the noxious influences of Jesuitical charlatism'. Although the Irish were 'more vindictive and revengeful than either the English or the Scotch' and were not easily disciplined, with good officers they readily responded to a good word and kind treatment.

MacMullen's experience as an orderly room clerk, where he was harassed by an adjutant who had 'taken a scunner' against him, was not a happy one. When the regiment returned to England in 1845 MacMullen felt he was again badly treated when, among his complaints, a private was promoted over his head. Although he had felt at home in the military and among the veterans of the 13th, he applied for his discharge. The colonel tried to dissuade him, but, dissatisfied with the army, MacMullen purchased his release, aided by friends in Dublin. In India more than four hundred of his fellow soldiers in the ranks had volunteered to stay when his regiment returned home and received a bounty for doing so. Some of them joined the 86th, the Royal County Down Regiment, popularly known as the 'Irish Giants' from the stature of the men. To the credit of their much respected Irish Commander Sir Michael Creagh, flogging was virtually unknown among them.[17]

In the first half of the nineteenth century two British Army officers would further the cause of the British Empire in India. Major General Sir Charles Napier's victories would result in annexation of the Sind (Scinde) in 1843. Major General Sir Hugh Gough's conquest of the Sikhs would result in British annexation of the Punjab in 1849. Both territories are now provinces of modern Pakistan.

Charles Napier's father, Colonel the Honourable George Napier, reputed to be the strongest and handsomest man in the army, was the penniless son of the fifth Lord Napier, partly Irish through his mother. Charles's mother, Sarah Lennox, was the daughter of the Irish Earl Cadogan, one of Marlborough's staff officers. He and his siblings grew up in genteel poverty at the village of Celbridge, County Kildare, amidst affluent Anglo-Irish relations: his Aunt Emily Lennox at nearby Carton House was the wife of the Irish Lord James Kildare and his Aunt Louisa Lennox, at nearby Castletown House, was the wife of the Irish Thomas Conolly, heir and grand-nephew of William Conolly, Speaker of the Irish House of Commons. Charles's 'attitudes to subject peoples were conditioned . . . by his memories of Ireland' and he always would refer to comparisons with Ireland.[18] Charles and two of his brothers, William and George, were taught military engineering, swordsmanship and a sense of duty and honour by their father, who greatly influenced them. All three would become Generals in the British Army, William becoming the noted historian of the Peninsular War. At twelve Charles was commissioned in the 33rd Foot, commanded by Lieutenant Colonel Arthur Wesley, whom he greatly admired. He served in the Peninsular War and briefly in the War of 1812. From 1822 he happily spent several years as Resident of the Greek Island of Cephalonia.

When nearly sixty Napier accepted, in 1841, command in the Bombay Presidency, along the way having been promoted Major General. In August 1842 he was ordered by Lord Ellenborough, the new Governor General, to command troops in the Baluchi province of Sind, then a British protectorate. New stringent treaties demanded by Ellenborough with the amirs, tribal rulers of Sind, provoked conflict and, when Baluchi warriors stormed the British Residency at Hyderabad in January 1843, Napier decided it was time to take up the sword. A great believer in the British Empire, he wrote in his journal: 'We have no right to seize Scinde, yet we shall do so'. Napier's views were 'merely reflecting the beliefs of his age, for most Victorians were convinced that the benefits of British rule justified all interference with existing rights'. In February, at Miani, Napier achieved a bloody defeat of the Baluchi Army. In this battle the Irish Lieutenant Colonel John Lysacht Pennefather, colourful son of a Tipperary parson, led his 22nd Foot 'composed entirely of Irishmen' and the only Crown regiment in the battle. Though greatly outnumbered, the British force of Sind, its centre formed by the 'high-blooded fierce impetuous soldiers' of the 22nd Foot, together with irregular cavalry and native infantry, met the gorgeously clad Baluchis with the bayonet and sent them back in a bloody encounter. In the three-hour fight Pennefather was seriously wounded; the British lost under 250 killed and wounded, the Baluchis an estimated 5,000. Like General Sir Eyre Coote sixty years earlier in India, Napier broke with tradition and in his despatches mentioned by name NCOs and other rank heroes, both Indian and British. His final victory against the Baluchis was at Dubba near Hyderabad on 24 March 1843 and Sind was annexed. His success prompted *Punch* to credit Napier with the clever but apocryphal message 'Peccavi' (I have sinned). Appointed as Sind's first Governor, this small eccentric man ruled as a paternal autocrat. He was 'concerned as always for the welfare of the common people of the country', and made of Sind 'a territory quite different from those governed by the civilians of John Company'. He soon, however, quarreled with the Company's officers and, because of this, along with his own and his family's poor health, he resigned and returned to England as a hero.[19]

Major General Hugh Gough, as a Major in 1809, led the 2/87th Foot in the famous charge at Barossa. At the end of the Peninsular War he spent the next several years in his native Munster on half-pay as a magistrate, accepting in 1837 the Mysore Divisional Command in the Madras Army. Three years later he led a British expeditionary force to China where, in the Opium Wars, he was successful in surrounding Canton, occupying Shanghai in 1842 and advancing to the important city of Nanking, which capitulated. Gough returned to India and was appointed Commander-in-Chief, which actually meant only Bengal.

His first campaign on arrival in India, aged 64, was the Gwalior War of December 1843 against Mahratta princes in Gwalior who were secretly negotiating with the Sikhs of the Punjab. Both these fierce peoples had large armies that were always a threat to the British and Lord Ellenborough took the initiative to protect British interests and ordered an army to be assembled. Gough was successful at Maharajpore; a separate Mahratta force was defeated at Punniar by General Grey. This forty-eight-hour conflict which resulted in the conquest of Gwalior was not given much public attention by home newspapers more concerned with the Corn Law struggles and trial of the Irish Daniel O'Connell for 'seditious conspiracy'. The severe fighting, however, 'by our brave and valorous troops' was reported in the *Illustrated London News* of 9 March 1844.

Gough's name is chiefly connected with the Sikhs, 'the last of the warrior peoples of India unsubdued by the British'. Since the death of Ranjit Singh (1839) friction between the British and the Sikhs of the Punjab increased, as did internal disorder in the Punjab. The British, watching warily, began to organize an army. When the Sikh Army, known as the Khalsa, well trained by foreign mercenaries especially in the use of artillery, crossed the Sutlej River into British-ruled territory in December 1845 and invested Ferozepore, a typical mud village, Gough immediately arrived with his army and defeated them at Mudki on 18 December. After Gough's victory the new Governor General, Sir Henry Hardinge, a Peninsular veteran and Guards officer, offered to serve as Gough's Second-in-Command, a most unusual situation. But just before the 21 December Battle of Ferozeshah Hardinge, as Governor General, forbade Gough to attack without waiting for Major General Sir John Littler and his division. Their disagreement caused delay, but Gough had to obey. Historian Donald Featherstone points out that 'never before had such powers been exercised by any Governor General in the field'. Gough did not mention this in his despatch.

In this bitterly contested battle many Irish in the First Bengal European Regiment were casualties when their charge was halted by the Sikhs whose surprising and devastating use of landmines scattered men in every direction. Many were burnt and mutilated. The Regimental Colour was found under the body of Ensign Moxon by Ensign P. R. Innes who, 'in spite of severe fire, gallantly recovered and brought the Colour back in safety, the men of the Regiment hailing its restoration with shouts of joy'. It hangs on the walls of Winchester Cathedral where the blood of Ensign Moxon may still be seen. Always in the midst of fighting in this battle was the white-haired Gough, riding out in his white coat to 'draw the enemy's fire away from his soldiers', a gesture that 'epitomized the concept of gentlemanly chivalry'. He could be heard urging his troops in his racy Irish brogue to use the bayonet, to him the 'prince of weapons'.[20] Ferozeshah was a British victory, but the high cost for the British was some 2,400 casualties, for the Sikhs an estimated 5,000. Gough's victory against the Sikhs at the Battle of Sobraon in early February 1846 ended the war, but the press questioned his appalling casualties. He had, however, won this First

Sikh War, was awarded a Baronetcy and granted a pension of £2,000 from both the House of Commons and the East India Company

The Sikhs wanted revenge and the murder by them of an English officer and a civil servant on 20 April 1848 was seen as the signal for a general uprising in the Punjab. After an unnecessary and unwise cavalry charge with casualties at Ramnagar in November Gough was informed by Governor General Lord Dalhousie that he would be glad of a victory. Gough advanced at once and the Battle of Chillianwalla on 13 January 1849 was another bloody affair. Both sides attacked simultaneously; it was a draw rather than a victory. Some believed that the Sikhs, knowing Gough's pugnacity, had 'got the old man's Irish out' and deliberately provoked him so that he attacked using tired troops. Gough was saved, as always, by the discipline and bravery of his troops. A large number of the casualties would have been Irish, for this was the time when 'regimental rolls began to resemble Irish parish registers and the march of the British Empire in India was milestoned by graves bearing Irish names'. The huge casualty list so shocked authorities in Britain that it was reported that Wellington, who had earlier praised Gough, now told Sir Charles Napier that one of them had to go to India and take over the post of Commander-in-Chief.[21] *Punch* called for Gough's immediate dismissal. Before Napier arrived as the new Commander-in-Chief in May 1849, Gough had brought this Second Sikh War to an end with an overwhelming victory at Gujrat in February, using fresh troops, superior artillery and cavalry to surprise the enemy when their battle line disintegrated. The Sikhs surrendered and the Punjab was annexed to British India. Queen Victoria 'acquired' the magnificent Koh-i-noor diamond as a token of Sikh surrender, and Gough and the men in the ranks did well out of prize money. Gujrat brought Britain's new Irish hero a viscountancy and another large pension. Napier wittily expressed his view of Gough, admiring him as a person but criticizing his generalship, for their careers had overlapped in India where they had amicably quarreled over the treatment of rebels:

> Everyone who knows Lord Gough must love the brave old warrior who is all honour and nobleness of heart and . . . were his military genius as great as his heart, the duke (Wellington) would be nothing in comparison.

In England *Punch* 'outrageously glorified him . . . . When Lord Gough met with a reverse, *Punch* set him down for an incompetent octogenarian; now that he has been fortunate *Punch* believes him to be a gallant veteran'.[22] In 1862, already retired, Gough was made a Field Marshal and died seven years later in his ninetieth year, one of the greatest of the 'sepoy generals'.

Always courageous, Paddy Gough's gift of communicating his love of battle to his troops and his concern for their welfare inspired great loyalty, and never was he defeated in battle. The Sikhs had intense respect for this 'fighting general'. It may have been that Gough's often-derided 'Tipperary tactics' did much to persuade the Sikhs, like the Gurkhas before them, to become supporters of the British Army in the years preceding the crisis of the Indian Mutiny. The British welcomed them with their 'ready-made stock of pugnacity waiting to be harnessed'. The Pathans and the Sikhs were a proud warlike people: 'like the Irish . . . they would fight each other if there was no one else to fight. It was quicker and easier to make them into soldiers'.[23]

Irish military leadership would not to pass away with the deaths of men like Wellington, Napier and Gough; Garnet Wolseley and Frederick Roberts would dominate the rest of the nineteenth century. Wolseley, born in Dublin in 1833, was the son of a retired and impecunious army officer from a family of soldiers who could look back to Colonel (later General) William Wolseley, who had fought beside King William in the Battle of the Boyne in 1690. Garnet's father died when he was very young, leaving only a small pension for his family, so that Garnet's mother appealed to Wellington who eventually appointed him ensign without purchase in the 12th Foot, a rare occurrence at that time. Without family resources, Garnet saw martial valour as the only way for advancement, along with his own ardent wish to succeed. So, desiring action, young Wolseley transferred to 80th Foot, already engaged in the Second Burma War, where, in 1853, he was seriously wounded. He had his first exhilarating experience of battle and was promoted to Lieutenant. Wolseley's first encounters with the Irish military undoubtedly influenced his ability to grasp quickly the need for flexibility with Irish soldiers when it came to discipline. As a callow Subaltern at the Rangoon base he paraded three 18th Royal Irish recruits before their commander Brevet Lieutenant Colonel John Grattan CB, an old and amusing Irishman. Grattan had been taken prisoner in the China War of 1841–42, carried about in a cage for the amusement of those who had never before seen a European. These young defaulters, untrained high-spirited boys, had refused to obey a zealous young Wolseley in the way he ordered. He expected them to face rigorous punishment; instead, to his astonishment, he encountered a kind of 'family' discipline. After listening to Wolseley's charges the old colonel suddenly erupted, calling them 'limbs of Satan' and, after a volley of oaths, literally kicked them out of the orderly room, shouting, 'Get out ye blackguards', then he collapsed in laughter. Enlightened, Wolseley retired from this experience convinced that there was a need in the army for Irish soldiers to have Irish officers over them and consequently be better able to deal with them than strangers can.[24]

The other great Irish Victorian soldier was Frederick Sleigh Roberts. Born at Cawnpore in 1832, he was the son of Lieutenant Colonel (later General Sir) Abraham Roberts from Waterford, who commanded the 1st Bengal European Regiment in the East India Company's army and later commanded a brigade in the First Afghan War (1839–42). After Eton and Sandhurst and then training at Addiscombe, the Company's school in England, young gunner Second Lieutenant Frederick Roberts went to India commissioned in the Bengal Artillery. Uncomplicated, brave and direct, this young man made good use of his early years as Aide de Camp to his father at Peshawar on the North West Frontier and then as a battery officer in the Bengal Horse Artillery which was 'largely composed of Irishmen'. Barely five feet three inches tall and with only one seeing eye, 'Little Bobs', when he joined his battery at Peshawar, admitted that its Irishmen 'could have lifted me up with one hand'. Roberts and Wolseley would both have experience on the Quartermaster General's staff at the time of the Indian Mutiny and this service was undoubtedly useful when they were later involved in army reform. In pursuing reforms Roberts would avoid making enemies in a way that Wolseley did not.

By the time of the Crimean War army reforms were badly needed and the consequences of the deficiencies encountered there continued to challenge the army throughout the nineteenth century. New ways of thinking as represented by Wolseley and Roberts took a long time to influence the army that Wellington had dominated for so long. A brilliant strategist and masterful technician, Wellington had earned a memorable place in the British Army. His soldiers remembered that he never threw armies away and he gave to them all the belief that they were led by 'officers and gentlemen'. Perhaps, as Elizabeth Longford observes, he 'tended to over-value the "gentlemanly" side of an officer's education compared with the technical'. A former master of detail and foresight, as Commander-in-Chief he refused to countenance any change in the Army's system of purchase that would continue to protect commanding officers like Lord Cardigan who contributed to the Light Brigade's disaster in the Crimea. But 'within the officer class [he] believed in promotion by merit. He had appointed a Colonel Sale over the heads of various generals to the colonelcy of his old regiment, the 33rd Foot.' Wellington did not sufficiently resist a parsimonious government that eliminated resources like the Royal Waggon Train that were so needed in the Crimea and did little to modernize in any way an army still fighting with Napoleonic-era weapons. It was that said the British Army would have been blessed had

Wellington retired well before his death in 1852 taking many of his generals with him; as his descendant, the 7th Duke of Wellington, astutely writes:

> The incompetence shown during the Crimean War is often, with some justification, laid at his door. No man should ever cling to a job when he is too old, and no one will ever tell him when that moment arrives.[25]

CHAPTER FIVE

The Irish in the Crimea

It was the indignation aroused in Britain by the state of
affairs revealed through Russell's despatches that saved
the army from annihilation through sheer neglect.

Nicolas Bentley, Introduction to
Russell's Despatches From the Crimea
London, 1970

The British Army, the Irish and the Crimea

The large number of Irish in the British Army from the early nineteenth
century reflected an astonishing Irish birth rate of thirty per thousand of
population. On the eve of the great famine of 1845–48 the population was
more than eight million and almost half a million more Irish were to be
found in cities like London, Liverpool, Manchester and Glasgow. In the
decade 1845–55 more than two million left Ireland permanently, most of
them travelling in family units.[1] Unfortunately for the British Army
recruiting of the huge male population of the Irish countryside began to
dry up. For the restless Irish youth who wanted to break out of his claustrophobic, insular and disease-ridden society the adventure call of the
army, that 'heroic option', was much less attractive when he could move
with his family to share with them a new life in the new world.

Along with the need for troops to meet the colonial commitment was the
army's continuing need to maintain law and order during the social disturbances of the time. Resentment of this role of the military was widespread
and had led to a growing recruitment problem. Nor was this antagonism
restricted to Ireland. The Scottish Highlands were always a major source of
recruits for the British Army, but at the time of the Crimean War the infamous 'Highland Clearances' were under way. People were evicted from
the land to make way for more profitable sheep and troops were used for
police work to facilitate these evictions. Such was the bitter resentment that:

When Lord Macdonald sought to persuade his tenants to join the
78th Regiment (the Ross-shire Buffs) he was told to send his deer,
his roes, his rams, dogs, shepherds, and gamekeepers to fight the
Russians.[2]

When the Crimean War began in 1854 the British government considered
it had no alternative but to support the Turks and the French to stop
Russian ambitions in the eastern Mediterranean. Even before the army
left Britain it was obvious to the military establishment that recruits, arma-
ments and stores were all in short supply in putting regiments on a war
footing. Battalions, though well enough trained for war in colonial and
overseas commitments as in India, had no experience of manoeuvring in
larger formations. Only in the previous year was a large military exercise
held in England and, in an age when officers knew only barrack-square
drill, competent field generals were scarce. Because of the reductions in
the army after Waterloo, neither was there any system to fill rapidly the
ranks of many regiments that were considerably under strength. Drafts of
experienced soldiers were moved to make ready the first 25,000 men for
the Crimea, but reinforcement units were filled with raw recruits, mobs
of half-trained frightened boys with only a cadre of experienced soldiers
among them. It was a national embarrassment when by mid-1855 the
British Army was only a quarter of the size of the French force. During
the war the problem of obtaining reinforcements for the army reached
crisis proportions. As sickness and battle casualties depleted the ranks of
the allied armies, the British joined in the prevailing panic to use
mercenaries and Polish, Swiss and German legions fought alongside
British, French, Turks and Sardinians. For the first time since Waterloo
the British Army was fighting against another European army.

In command in the Crimea was Wellington's successor as the army's
Commander-in-Chief, the one-armed sixty-six-year-old patrician Lord
Raglan. Urbane, tactful, conciliatory and very hard working, he was so
much a man of the Peninsular War, where he lost his arm, that he in-
variably spoke of 'the French' when he meant the enemy. Only after a
series of stinging articles in *The Times* was he seen more frequently among
his troops. Surrounding him was a staff generally judged to be incompetent except for the occasional general like Sir Richard Airey, the
Quartermaster General, and the experienced Limerick man, the sixty-
year-old Sir George de Lacy Evans who commanded the 2nd Division.[3]

Although exact numbers of Irish serving in the Crimean War are not
known, recent research estimates that forty per cent were from Ireland.
They served not only in Irish but also in British regiments, a practice
known from the Peninsular War. Two examples among many are the 23rd

Royal Welch Fusiliers who were 'almost to a man' from Ireland, and the 33rd Duke of Wellington's Own, long known as an Irish regiment. In the cavalry Irish were in the 11th Hussars and 17th Lancers who took part in the famous charge of the Light Brigade. In Ireland there was intense interest in this war generated by the presence of so many Irish who sent home to family and friends many accounts and letters that were published in Irish newspapers.[4]

When the call to arms came, Queen Victoria was much impressed by the bronzed and soldierly 18th Foot, The Royal Irish Regiment, just back from India and Burma. There, the climate had taken such a heavy toll that, when only four hundred of them were fit for active service, volunteers were invited from the 51st and 94th Foot and, thus reinforced, the Royal Irish were delighted to be sent to the Crimea.[5] Similarly, on mobilization of the 8th Royal Irish Hussars their band had to be broken up to make up numbers in the ranks. When rumours of war became fact in their headquarters at Dorchester, the 8th were acclaimed as heroes in its streets while citizens and 'wild drunken Irishmen' alike celebrated the orders for the Crimea.[6]

Disaster hit the cavalry even before they arrived in the Crimea. A proposal was made that the cavalry regiments might ride across country to Marseilles for embarkation, but Lieutenant Colonel Edward Hodge of the 4th Royal Irish Dragoon Guards opposed the plan because discipline was so lax that men would succumb to drink along the way. The cavalry sailed for the Bosphorus, but the *Europa* carrying the commanding officer of the 6th Inniskilling Dragoons, Colonel Willoughby Moore, and his headquarters, caught fire two hundred miles off Plymouth. Moore, his Veterinary Surgeon Kelly, sixteen men, equipment, baggage and all the horses were lost.[7] Cholera completed the decimation of the cavalry units encamped at Devna, a very swampy place in Bulgaria, and by the time they moved to the Crimea all regiments were much reduced in numbers.

The despatches of William Howard Russell, an Irishman employed by *The Times* in 1854 as virtually the first war correspondent, shocked the nation by showing how much in need of reform was an army that had been taken for granted as one of the finest in Europe. As the war progressed Russell became the greatest thorn in the side of the Horse Guards Establishment. Of humble birth in County Dublin, over the years he managed to combine intermittent journalism with reading law and from 1841 reporting for *The Times*. In 1850 he was called to the English bar and four years later was sent to the Crimea by his newspaper. Scorned by many as a 'vulgar low Irishman' and an 'Apostate Catholic', he was nevertheless an affable individual of great personal charm and considerable courage who had no difficulty in finding informants about the failings in the army. Feared for his pen and his tenacity and with the knowledge that his outspoken Crimean despatches were feeding a public fascinated with the war, he was reckoned to be someone it was worthwhile to cultivate. The 'redoubtable and sharp-sighted' Russell had much to say about the horrors of cholera when it struck the army's Varna/Devna assembly camp and how an old Turkish barracks filled with lice, fleas and rats was converted into a hospital/morgue. The facts spoke for themselves, but his reports were seen as showing up the army's inadequacies in dealing with cholera and the unnecessary hardships the soldiers suffered and this did not make him welcome by Lord Raglan and the authorities. Russell was with the army from the time it embarked at Southampton in February 1854 until the proclamation of peace two years later; he lived with the army and knew at first hand of what he wrote. His famous despatches from the scene revealing the government's mishandling of Crimean affairs have been credited with bringing about the resignation of Lord Aberdeen's Cabinet. More important to Russell was that 'the British soldier ceased to be an isolated and helpless victim of departmental incompetence and ministerial indifference'.[8]

Garnet Wolseley, now a Lieutenant in 90th Light Infantry, on his arrival in the Crimea soon saw the staff officers as deplorable: if any had been privates 'he was sure their colonels would never have entertained the notion of promoting them to corporal'.[9] Another critic of the army in the Crimea, particularly of the medical services, was the energetic and famous Florence Nightingale who established her celebrated hospitals at Scutari where, within six months of her arrival, she brought order out of chaos and the hospital death rate fell drastically. One of her nurses paid tribute to the humour of the Irish patients, their 'quick feeling and ready wit'.[10] The Irish Sisters Of Mercy, who witnessed the shocking medical services, formed a particular attachment to the Irish 89th Foot. Among them was Isabella Croke, whose brother was the very political Thomas Croke, Catholic Archbishop of Cashel. Croke was one of those prelates who worked with the papal delegate and Archbishop of Dublin, Paul Cullen, to extend Roman Catholic pastoral care to the large number of Irish soldiers in the British Army.

The failure in leadership in this war was most clearly revealed in the cavalry. Leading the Heavy Brigade was the fifty-five-year-old the Honourable James Scarlett, who inspired confidence but had seen no active service. The Light Brigade was led by the fifty-seven-year-old Lord Cardigan, a vain snob who also had never seen active service. Commander of the Cavalry Division was the Irish Lord Lucan, Cardigan's hated brother-in-law, aged fifty-four, also with little military experience but a great deal of arrogance, which had made him hated by his Irish tenants around

Castlebar, County Mayo. As for the opinion of the troops, in the words of Major William Forrest of the 4th Dragoon Guards: 'We all agree that two greater muffs than Lucan and Cardigan could not be. We call Lucan the cautious ass and Cardigan the dangerous ass.'[11]

The cavalry had moments of both glory and disaster. When a huge Russian force moved towards the British camp at Balaclava on 25 October 1854, the first opposition the Russians encountered and were turned away from was the two-deep red-clad line of the 93rd Highlanders, whose brave stand William Howard Russell called 'that thin red streak tipped with a line of steel' to become in army history 'the thin red line'. The Russians were then hit by the Heavy Brigade, squadrons of the 5th Dragoon Guards leading, the 6th Inniskilling Dragoons, Scots Greys and 4th Dragoon Guards following, that crashed into the centre of the advancing Russian cavalry. Within eight minutes of savage fighting the Russians broke and the guns of a troop of Royal Horse Artillery coming up prevented them from rallying. The Light Brigade, which was only five hundred yards away, did not intervene: when an impatient Captain William Morris in the 17th Lancers, a veteran of the Sikh wars, begged Cardigan to charge the Russians, he was told that Lucan's orders were that the Light Brigade was to stay put.[12] When the Light Brigade did move that day it was to disaster. 'Someone had blundered'.

At the centre of the controversy over responsibility for the disaster was the excitable figure of Captain Louis Edward Nolan. From an old County Carlow family, Louis' Irish grandfather, Babington Nolan, had served in the 13th Light Dragoons. His father, an Infantry Captain in the 70th Foot, was in Upper Canada where Louis was born in 1818. After a chequered career, Louis senior eventually found a position as an unofficial British Vice Consul at Milan where he raised his three sons and obtained commissions for his son Louis Edward, first in the Austrian Imperial Hussars and then in the British 15th Hussars. With this regiment Louis went to India. After sick leave in England he returned to India four years later as riding master of his Regiment, becoming known as a superb rider. As Aide de Camp to the C-in-C Madras during the Second Sikh War Nolan ended his regimental life. In the Crimea he was Sir Richard Airey's Aide de Camp, by then having published two well-received books on cavalry training and tactics. Nolan, believing in 'the superiority of light over heavy cavalry', had nothing but contempt for both Lucan and Cardigan, who he vociferously criticized for what he thought was the shameful inactivity of the Light Brigade in the Crimea so far. Unfortunately Nolan was seen by his contemporaries as an arrogant prig. Personal animosities therefore played their part in the subsequent tragedy of the Light Brigade.

After the attack of the Heavy Brigade Russians could be seen attempting to carry away from the Causeway Heights and redoubts guns they had captured in the morning. Lord Raglan, on the Heights, immediately sent down Captain Nolan with a written order to Lord Lucan below 'to advance rapidly to the front, follow the enemy and to try to prevent the enemy carrying away the guns'. As Nolan was about to gallop down the steep hill, Raglan called out a verbal order: 'Tell Lord Lucan the cavalry is to attack immediately'. On reading the order a perplexed Lucan later claimed that he could see neither enemy nor guns. A previous order to him to recover the Heights seems not to have enlightened him. When Lucan queried the obviously impatient Nolan, 'Attack sir? What guns sir?' he, maintained Lucan, 'pointing at the guns more than a mile and a quarter away at the western end of the North Valley . . . replied in a most disrespectful . . . manner, "There my lord, is your enemy, there are your guns".' These famous words precipitated Lucan's order to Lord Cardigan and the Light Brigade to advance into the 'Valley of Death'. Cardigan protested, but had to obey. When Cardigan's brigade advanced Nolan dashed out in front shrieking and wildly gesticulating, but in the noise of the guns he was not heard and he was killed immediately by a shell splinter. What he was trying to say will never be known. He *may* have been trying 'to change the direction of the Light Brigade's advance'.

The Brigade rode on through a gauntlet of fire from Russian artillery and of musketry from both Heights. Lucan was slightly wounded as he led two regiments of the Heavy Brigade forward to support the Light Cavalry, but casualties caused him to call a halt. Lord Cardigan breached the Russian battery at the end of the valley, but, wounded, isolated and attacked by two Cossacks, he turned and rode back alone, for which he was later criticized. It is reported that he rode again towards the enemy to look for remnants of his Brigade and met the few remaining 8th Royal Irish Hussars to return with them. They would never forget the things they had seen: 'Sergeant Riley of the 8th riding with his eyes fixed and staring, his face as rigid and white as a flagstone, dead in his saddle.' The Brigade's total loss, Anglesey estimates, was 245 of the 661 believed to have been in the charge killed or wounded, and forty-five officers and men taken prisoner.

The controversy over the roles played by Lucan, Cardigan and Nolan continued for many years. History has attached some blame to Cardigan, but in Lord Anglesey's opinion Lord Lucan should be held accountable. If he had 'remained calm, set aside his contempt for the Commander of the Forces' and his feuding with Cardigan, and had applied his 'undoubted intelligence' to Raglan's acknowledged unclear orders, 'he would not have gone far wrong'. Moreover, 'he did not ask for the help of the French cavalry. He made no use of his horse artillery'.[13]

The following day the Russians launched a minor offensive called 'little Inkerman' against Sir George de Lacy Evans' 2nd Division, which was turned back. During the engagement he had managed his troops ably, but later, weakened by recurrent diarrhoea and diabetes, fell from his horse which partially rolled on him. Utterly prostrated, he retired to a hospital ship at Balaclava and gave divisional command to his Brigade Commander, General John Lysaght Pennefather. Returning home, Evans was hailed by *The Times* of 12 December 1854 as a model of 'truest heroism and finest chivalry'. On 23 January the same paper praised this Irish officer who had advanced by merit in the field rather than patronage as 'one of the best officers in the army' and went on to review his military career. Note was also made of his work as a radical Member of Parliament promoting the welfare of the rank and file. Evans's 'good press' was undoubtedly helped by the friendship he had developed with his fellow-countryman William Howard Russell. After the war the *Morning Post* of 9 March 1857 hailed him as a 'Crimean hero of the first rank'.

Major General Pennefather is remembered as 'the soldiers' soldier'. Known to swear tremendous oaths in the heat of battle, he was both famous and loved in the British Army for his fearless and inspiring leadership. At the bloody Battle of Inkerman on 5 November 1854 Pennefather, as Commander of 2nd Division, was in the centre of the fray in what was described as a 'soldiers' battle', fought without much direction from Raglan and his staff. When it looked as if the Russian infantry might be retreating, Pennefather stoutly maintained that he could follow up and 'lick them to the devil' if reinforced. His words were translated by a pleased Lord Raglan for General Canrobert, a French Divisional Commander, who exclaimed: '*Ah! quel brave garcon! quel brave homme! quel bon general*'. Pennefather summed up this battle in his rich and expressive vocabulary, 'I tell you, we gave 'em a hell of a towelling.'[14] The following month Pennefather suffered a life-threatening attack of cholera and, after an attack of dysentery in the spring, was sent home to recover. He ended his army days as Honourary Colonel of his old 22nd Foot, and then as Governor of the Chelsea Hospital, the London refuge for soldiers where he died in 1872.

Following Inkerman the army settled down to a prolonged siege of Sebastopol during the terrible Crimean winter of 1854–55, a time when the rambunctious young Garnet Wolseley, eagerly seeking action, was twice severely wounded, losing the sight of one eye. For his work in the trenches he was mentioned in despatches, awarded the French Legion of Honour, the Turkish Medjidie and promoted Captain. By spring the British forces had only 11,000 fit for combat with 23,000 sick or wounded. Reinforcements began to arrive in December. The service companies of the 89th Foot, 783 strong, left Cork for Gibraltar in April 1854, not arriving at Balaclava until 17 December, thus missing the hard battles at Alma, Balaclava and Inkerman, but they experienced the full misery of the Crimean winter. When they entered the trenches for the siege of Sebastopol within their first fortnight forty-five men died of cholera, including their Brevet Major the Honourable Charles Daly, who had been with the regiment twenty years. Chaos prevailed throughout the army with matters like food supply determined by where a unit was stationed; the cavalry and the Highland Brigade fared much better than the infantry on the Heights because they were nearer Balaclava, the source of supplies. Officers generally lived well compared to their men. Surely Captain Brigstock of the 4th Dragoon Guards surpassed them all: 'Wearying of the war [he] sold out in disgust and by auction disposed of no fewer than 197 pots of preserved meat and more than a dozen hampers of food'.[15]

Major General Sir William Eyre, son of Vice Admiral Sir George Eyre, was, like Pennefather, a fighting general, and was wounded when his brigade was engaged on 18 June 1855 in an abortive attack on the Redan, a formidable fortification at Sebastopol. Before the attack Eyre whipped up the enthusiasm of the 18th Royal Irish, addressing them in Erse and telling them that he hoped their exploits would 'make every Irish cabin ring'. At dawn volunteer sharp-shooters from the 18th Foot were part of Eyre's advance guard that surprised the Russians in a cemetery in the suburbs of Sebastopol, capturing it. William Howard Russell reports that companies of the 18th then rushed out of the cemetery and managed to reach and occupy some outlying houses where parties from Eyre's other regiments joined them. Russian guns were only able to destroy the upper storeys of the houses so that a vigorous return fire was possible, to which the Russians retaliated, killing many. Meanwhile a strange hiatus occurred in the midst of battle:

> Officers and men sat about drinking coffee which the women [in the houses] were induced to make. . . . The Irishmen were quick to unearth a store of wine and cherry brandy and many were soon reeling about . . . pirouetting in bonnets and shawls regardless of the firing. . . . Once when two Irishmen quarrelled over some booty a ring was formed in the open and they fought it out with bare fists.

General Eyre, now wounded, his communications cut off, did not hear immediately of the collapse of the British attack on the Redan and his men had to hold on all day despite mounting casualties. All conquests except the cemetery, held with severe casualties, were abandoned and it was the 'opinion of everyone who fought and watched that day that they had been disgracefully managed'.[16]

Thomas Faughnan records how his 17th Foot took part in a disastrous attack on the Redan against well-prepared Russians. In the advance of the storming parties he was shot through the arm, fracturing the bone, and his 'noble' Captain John Croker from Limerick, of the Grenadier company, fell shot in the head. Faughnan later composed a long poem in heroic style to commemorate his death and the battle, the final verse of which reads:

> But few escaped of the forlorn band,
> Of that chivarlic company Croker did command;
> But those who did stuck by their leader still,
> And laid his corpse to rest on Cathcart's Hill.[17]

The Connaught Rangers were delighted to hear they were to be included in another assault on the Redan on 8 September, the last phase of the siege of Sebastopol: 'Our fellows,' writes Captain Steevens of the 88th, 'with their natural Irish vivacity gave vent to their feelings in hearty cheers and yells' to the great alarm of a visiting staff officer. The Rangers were led to their trenches by Lieutenant Colonel G. V. Maxwell from County Derry, who had taken over from their much loved Lieutenant Colonel Horatio Shirley, a Commander who never hesitated to congratulate his men. An Irishman from Carrickmacross, County Monaghan, Shirley had gone to the 88th from the Rifle Brigade in 1833 and he always chose to lead from the front. At the Battle of the Alma, September 1854, a Russian bullet lodged in the prayer book he carried in his revolver holster. Now, as Brigade Commander, Shirley was still in the forefront in this Redan assault, but was disabled almost immediately when round shot drove stones and dust into his face blinding him so that he had to be led away with tears running down his cheeks. As the 88th were hurrying past him to the attack, a voice was heard to bawl out, 'Don't cry General dear but stop there, fure we're going to take the place for ye'! In fact the British attack was 'an inglorious conclusion to the siege', as Denis Judd writes. At the ditch of the Turks' defences there were only three scaling ladders and the Connaught Rangers found themselves among the crowded mass of officers and men of all regiments jammed together in the salient, all the time fired on by the Russians on the flanks. The British had to retreat to their trenches through another gauntlet of fire. Total Connaught Ranger losses were Captain Grogan and thirty rank and file killed and Lieutenant Colonel Maxwell and eight officers severely wounded. A brave young Irishman at the Redan, much lauded by the *Cork Examiner* as 'Redan Massey', was eighteen-year-old Lieutenant William Massey, a young Dubliner in the 19th Foot. One of the first to enter the defensive ditch, exposed to Russian fire he suffered a broken thigh, yet he exhorted fellow wounded to be brave before the enemy.[18] After the French took the Malakoff (a Sebastopol redoubt) at noon, the Russians' positions were untenable in the other defences and they withdrew during the night-blowing up forts, arsenals and docks. Sebastopol was abandoned and the war was ended.

Of the 21,327 British fatalities only 2,255 were killed by enemy action, 1,847 died of wounds and a shocking 17,225 from disease, including Lord Raglan. As William Howard Russell's despatches reveal of the British base at Balaclava, 'words could not describe its filth, its horrors, its hospitals, its burials, its dead and dying Turks . . . or its decay'. Clearly reforms were needed in the British Army.[19]

After the Crimean War many Irish were among the first winners of the Victoria Cross instituted by Queen Victoria to recognize publicly individual acts of exceptional bravery regardless of rank. The first investiture was at Hyde Park, London, 26 June 1857. Captain Thomas Esmonde from County Waterford, of the 18th Royal Irish Regiment, won his award for bringing in wounded during the attack on the Redan in June 1855. In a most unusual action he daringly extinguished a lethal fireball that would have betrayed his working party's position. Other Irish winners were in British regiments, such as Sergeant (later Major General Sir) Luke O'Connor of County Roscommon, in the 23rd Welch Fusiliers, the first Victoria Cross awarded in the army. Badly wounded on the Alma in September 1854, he continued to carry the Regimental Colours to the end of the action though urged to go to the rear. He recovered to participate in the attack on the Redan a year later where he was shot through both thighs and won the award for both actions as well as a commission. Brevet Lieutenant Colonel (later General) Francis Maude from Armagh, in the Buffs (3rd Foot), led a ladder party in the Redan assault in September 1855. Fighting alongside him was Private Joseph Connors of Listowel, also 3rd Foot, whose prowess in hand-to-hand combat also brought him the Victoria Cross. Quartermaster Sergeant John Farrell of Dublin in the 17th Lancers won his award for helping to rescue a fellow Lancer after the charge of the Light Brigade, in which his own horse was killed under him and he was wounded. At Inkerman Lieutenant (later General) Mark Walker of County Westmeath distinguished himself in front of his regiment encouraging his comrades to advance against two Russian battalions. Private John Byrne of Kilkenny, 68th Regiment, at Inkerman brought in a wounded soldier under fire and later bravely engaged in hand-to-hand combat.[20] Sergeant John Park of Londonderry and Alexander Wright of Ballymena, both in 77th Foot, were recognized for their valour at the Alma, Inkerman and the taking of the Russian Rifle pits. Sergeant (later Lieutenant) Ambrose Madden from Cork, 41st Regiment, bravely led a party at Inkerman that captured one Russian officer and fourteen privates, three by Madden personally.

In Dublin on 22 October 1856 a great banquet was given at the Customs House to honour the Crimean veterans now garrisoned in Ireland. The public subscription appeal brought in £1,000 beyond expenses; clearly the Irish population recognized these returned veterans as the popular heroes of the day.

CHAPTER SIX

The Irish and India
From the Mid-Nineteenth Century

My name is O'Kelly, I've heard the Revelly
From Birr to Bareilly, from Leeds to Lahore,
Hong-Kong and Peshawur,
Lucknow and Etawah,
And fifty-five more all endin'in 'pore'.

R. Kipling, 'Shillin' a Day',
Barrack Room Ballads

The Great Imperial Crisis: The Irish and the Indian Mutiny of 1857

It was very common for military men rather than civilians to govern parts of the far-flung British Empire. In India there was frequent combining of civilian and military roles and two outstanding examples are Ulstermen Henry Lawrence and John Nicholson. The limited career possibilities for the sons of Ulster's gentry and professional families undoubtedly contributed to the presence of so many northern Irishmen as administrators in the nascent civilian government of newly acquired Indian territories.

The five Lawrence brothers are one example of an Ulster family whose sons found careers in India. They were sons of a tough army colonel in India, whose family were descended from Scots planters who settled in Ulster in the reign of James I, a sturdy lot who 'kept the Sabbath and anything else they could lay their hands on'. After attending the strictly disciplined Foyle College in Derry run by their clergyman uncle, all five brothers would distinguish themselves in the Mutiny. After Addiscombe, the East India Company's military college in England, and a commission in the Bengal Artillery Henry was Resident in besieged Lucknow, John was chief commissioner in the Punjab and Captain Richard Lawrence was

Commissioner of Police at Lahore. George and Alexander had begun their careers in the Indian Cavalry; George was one of the staff officers who, kept as a hostage by the Afghans after Sir William Macnaghten, the British Resident at Kabul, was murdered,was later released, becoming Deputy Commissioner at Peshawar and a Major General.

The huge new province of the Punjab, annexed by the British, was administered by a group of officers referred to as 'the picked men of India', civil servants trained at Haileybury (the Company's college in England for administrative posts) or soldiers of the Bengal Army seconded for civilian duties. More than half were from Ulster or Scotland and all were strong Protestants. In a three-man board of administration set up by Lord Dalhousie, the Governor General, Sir Henry Lawrence as senior was its President. As a soldier in the Bengal Artillery, Lawrence was responsible for all military, political and diplomatic business; Sir John Lawrence, practical and shrewd, was in charge of finance and land revenue, and Sir Robert Montgomery, their school friend from Ulster days who would become grandfather of the future Field Marshal Bernard Montgomery, was in charge of law and order, roads, communications and education. Henry Lawrence's sense of passionate purpose and strict work ethic left a legacy that was dominant in the Punjab for years. He joined his young men in daily prayer and meditation, but his earnestness was not appreciated by Lord Dalhousie who found him tiresome. Moreover, Henry strongly disapproved of Dalhousie's policies of annexation of the Punjab; in his view 'the Punjab should remain a buffer state against the turbulent Pathans of the North-West frontier'. Henry also quarrelled with his brother John, who was always pro-annexation. Such were these tensions that Henry, posted to Rajputana as agent, ousted he felt from the Punjab, ill, dispirited and depressed by the death of his wife, decided he had to resign. He was about to go home when the imperious Lord Dalhousie was replaced by Lord Canning, also of Irish ancestry, and Henry gladly accepted his offer of the position of Chief Commissioner of Oudh. Recently promoted Brigadier General with full military powers, he arrived at Lucknow as Resident on 20 March 1857.[1] It was to cost him his life.

The Indian Mutiny, sometimes called the Sepoys' Revolt, began 10 May 1857 at Meerut, Bengal, and although it was chiefly confined to the army in Bengal it has been looked on as a momentous event in Indian history and one with repercussions for the whole British Army. Its origins have been attributed to the refusal of the sepoys to accept cartridges for the recently introduced muzzle-loading Enfield rifle, which had to be bitten off before loading and which, it was said, were greased with the fat of pigs, an offence to Muslims, and that of cows, holy to Hindus. This led to rumours that the British planned to pollute and then christianize the whole sepoy army. Although orders had been issued for a new loading drill where fingers instead of teeth could be used to open cartridges, they arrived too late. The Ulsterman John Nicholson attributed the origin of the Mutiny to 'neither greased cartridges, the annexation of Oudh, nor the paucity of European officers . . . For years I have watched the army and felt sure they only wanted their opportunity to try their strength with us.' In short, the sepoys of Bengal had lost confidence in their British leaders.[2] Indeed Sita Ram, a loyal soldier of the Raj in the Bengal Army from 1812 for forty-eight years, who wrote about the Indian military scene in the first decades of the century, believed that the British officers in the Company's Army of an earlier generation, many speaking Indian languages, communicated with their men in a more familiar manner than those in later years. Geoffrey Moorhouse, who quotes from Ram's memoirs, writes that 'The blunder over the greased cartridges would have been much less likely in 1812 than in 1857'.[3]

When panic spread at the news of the Mutiny, Sir John Lawrence, as Chief Commissioner of the Punjab, began a severe and immediate policy of disarming some 2,500 men of the native regiments; in many places he did not hesitate to have sepoys executed. He was greatly helped by a Movable Column he had recently formed to head off trouble in the Punjab, recruited from 'irregulars' and the fierce hill tribes. Captain John Nicholson, who had suggested the Column's formation, was now its Commander, promoted to Brigadier General, a leap which annoyed many senior officers.[4] These punitive actions saved the Punjab and were approved by many Crown officers. Irish regiments in the British Army stationed at Peshawar, such as the 87th Royal Irish Fusiliers and 27th Inniskillings, were active in rounding up rebels and witnessing the execution of sepoys when they were blown away from guns. Captain James Bailie of the 87th wrote to his father, 'It was a horrible sight . . . but a very satisfactory one'. He also records how his regiment shot nearly 200 of the wretched 51st Native Infantry when they tried to grab arms and escape from Peshawar.[5]

After the initial uprising at Meerut the rebels headed for the imperial city of Delhi and, with Company soldiers of the 3rd Light Cavalry, plundered and massacred the population. The city was no longer in British hands and the Delhi Field Force set up a camp on the exposed Delhi Ridge. Fortunately the resolute Sir John Lawrence decided to risk sending troops to Delhi and Captain Henry Daly was ordered to take down to the Ridge some 153 sabres and 349 rifles of the elite Corps of Guides, tough horsemen and infantry from the Punjab recruited in 1846 from the disbanded Sikh regiments and every warlike tribe. They set out from Mardan on 12 May on a forced march of 580 miles accomplished in twenty-six days mostly at night, 'a feat . . . unrivalled in the history of mounted troops' and at the hottest season of the year. The story of their tumultuous arrival at the camp on the Ridge says a lot about Daly's leadership qualities. When asked by a staff officer how soon he and his greatly admired Guides could be ready for action, Daly cheerfully replied, 'In half an hour', and that same afternoon his men helped drive off an attack from Delhi. All summer the rebels attacked the small British camp on the Ridge. Daly was seriously wounded when he led the second of two desperate charges and managed to save some guns. Always concerned for those he commanded, he seems to have been appreciated equally by his superiors and his men, and as a fluent speaker of Hindustani, Maratha and Gujrati he could be heard encouraging them in their own language.

Captain Henry Dermot Daly's Irish family was from County Galway. One of the heroes of the Mutiny he was born in India in 1823, the son of the Lieutenant Colonel of 4th Light Dragoons. Commissioned at nineteen as an Ensign in the 1st Bombay European regiment, he became its Adjutant in 1846 and distinguished himself in the 2nd Sikh war at Moltena and Gujrat. Three years later he raised the 1st Punjab Cavalry with whom he fought in several minor campaigns on the frontier in the early 1850s and is remembered as a brilliant 'irregular' cavalry leader. In 1856 he raised and commanded the 1st Oudh Irregular Cavalry, but very shortly after that transferred as Second in Command to the Corps of Guides.[6]

Meanwhile Major General Sir Hugh Wheeler, the sixty-seven-year-old Irish-born commander of the Cawnpore Division with a long distinguished career in India, felt all was well. However, from mid-May he sensed trouble was brewing in Cawnpore but by 3 June, although there was still excitement and unrest in the city, he felt his position was secure enough to send some men of the British 32nd Foot to Henry Lawrence in Lucknow. Two days later, on 5 June, the attack began and the subsequent massacre at Cawnpore when Nana Sahib, the arrogant son of a Mahratta monarch, disgruntled with the British Government for not paying him his deceased father's pension which had terminated at his death, agreed to lead his own men and mutinous native troops in rebellion, supported by the rabble of the town. Whenever rumours of an imminent uprising spread throughout the colony, civilian families fled to the hospital/barracks complex, an ill-chosen site, its entrenchment walls not finished and its exposed position difficult to defend. One possible reason for this choice may have been that Wheeler had not really believed the sepoys would mutiny.

Now crowded into the entrenchment were over 900, of whom 400 were women and children, only 300 combatants, many of them invalids, 100 civilians and a few loyal native officers and sepoys. There were muskets and ammunition, but only a few light guns. Conditions soon became nightmarish. Attacks by mutineers continued until 24 June when Wheeler, urged by Captain Moore, an Irish officer of the 32nd Foot, agreed to surrender and accept Nana Sahib's treaty: those not connected with Lord Dalhousie's government and willing to lay down their arms would receive safe passage down the Ganges to Allahabad, giving up money, stores and guns, boats to be provided for the wounded, women and children. Wheeler trusted Nana Sahib who was of the same caste as his own wife. A terrible massacre followed at the river bank. 'No sooner were we in the boats,' records Lieutenant Delafosse of the Royal Artillery, 'than . . . [hidden] guns . . . opened on us.' Boats burst into flames, many victims were burnt, others bayoneted and a witness saw General Wheeler cut down by a sword blow. 'When the firing ceased, the men were separated from the women and children and were all shot.' About 125 women and children were pulled out of the river and brought to a house owned by Nana Sahib. Joined by other captives, some 200 of them were then crammed into a few rooms and kept as hostages where many died of dysentery and cholera. In mid-July, as the British Army under Brigadier General Henry Havelock approached to relieve Cawnpore, all these hostages were massacred and their bodies thrown down a well, some while still living. On Havelock's arrival the terrible atrocities were revealed. Lieutenant Delafosse, Lieutenant Thomson of the Native Infantry and two Irish privates, both wounded and naked, were the only survivors of a group of officers and men who had been fighting off sepoys on the shore so that a group stranded in their boat could escape. When they returned to the river the boat was gone and they were left to make their way on foot along the river's edge towards Allahabad, still fending off rebels until they reached the protection of a local rajah. Delafosse lost his reason for a time but recovered; he eventually joined the 101st Royal Bengal Fusiliers and rose to command the Regiment.[7]

Besieged also by rebels in June was Lucknow, one of the few places in Oudh still under British control. Described by William Howard Russell as a 'vision of palaces', Lucknow's siege caught British public attention. On news of the outbreaks, from mid-May Henry Lawrence as Resident and Commander had the Residency and compound strongly reinforced to defend the many Europeans who sought shelter with his 1,700-man garrison. Lawrence was killed in early July by a shell which burst into his room as he lay resting. His body was quickly buried in the Residency graveyard beneath his own epitaph: 'Here Lies Henry Lawrence, Who Tried to Do His Duty'. He was held in such esteem that the four soldiers of the 32nd Foot who carried his pall kissed his forehead in farewell. Lawrence had appointed as his successor Major Banks of the Lucknow

Division, and command of the Lucknow troops was entrusted to John Eardley Wilmot Inglis, grandson of the Donegal-born Anglican Bishop of Nova Scotia, Charles Inglis. With the 32nd Foot since 1833, John Inglis was a Brevet Lieutenant Colonel after engagements in the Sikh Wars and would be commended for his direction of the prolonged siege of the Residency in which many suffered greatly.

Before Lucknow was relieved, the rebel-held city of Delhi finally fell to Crown and Company regiments after the stern thirty-four-year-old, black-bearded, six-foot-two John Nicholson brought his 4,200-strong Movable Column down from the Punjab to the Delhi Ridge, fighting mutineers along the way. On 14 August he led it into camp amidst the cheers of the army and music of the band. His tremendous reputation as 'the pacificator of the Punjab' had preceded him and he was welcomed as someone who would inject life and hope into the dispirited troops. With little official position, it was his leadership that the Field Force on the Ridge was prepared to follow, a strange phenomenon wrote Daly some years later when he had become General Sir Henry Daly:

> Only those who remember the too frequent attitudes of superiority adopted by the officers of the Queen's service towards those in that of 'John Company' will realize how great the tribute to a dominating personality was the fact that [these same officers] . . . should have been willing to serve under this regimental Captain in the Company's service, this General by grace of God, who had ridden into camp like a king.

The Victorians made much of this 'Lion of the Punjab' who could show mercy, yet did not hesitate to use the 'blowing away by cannon' to control mutinous sepoys and who thought all mutineers should be hanged regardless of whether they could be proved guilty of atrocities. There was a hard, vengeful side to Nicholson, indeed to many of these dedicated soldiers, but their Victorian manly sensibilities were inflamed by news of the atrocities against women at Cawnpore, which Captain Garnet Wolseley with the 90th Foot saw for himself and 'ached for revenge'.[8]

John Nicholson became a legend in India before he was thirty. His Protestant ancestry dates to 17th century Ulster where two Nicholsons were killed in the Siege of Derry. His father, a Quaker, studied at Trinity College Dublin, became a doctor and successfully practiced in Dublin where he brought his Presbyterian bride, Clara Hogg of Lisburn, Ulster. John, the second of seven children, was born in 1822 in Dublin. Dr Nicholson died when John was only nine, leaving his mother to raise her family in straitened circumstances, until her brother James Hogg invited them to live in Lisburn. Hogg, a successful lawyer in Calcutta, had made a fortune in the East India Company and was now a director of the Company in London. He sent John to the Royal School at Dungannon until he was sixteen when he obtained a cadetship for him in the Bengal Native Infantry. John's younger brothers would follow him to India – a fine example of how service in the East India Company's army appealed to young Irishmen of limited prospects. But this was not without cost. Alexander was killed in the Khyber Pass by Afghans. Charles would have his arm amputated after the Battle of Delhi and William's mysterious death in the Bombay Army in 1849 was never explained.

In India Nicholson had been a protége of Henry Lawrence, with whom he had a very close friendship and under whom he served in 1847 when Henry was resident at Lahore, part of a group of young men who proclaimed Christianity as the only truth. As a soldier/administrator he was in turn Deputy Commissioner for Rawalpindi, Bannu and Peshawar, where he brought such order that there was a minimum of crime, and where he dispensed his own, if sometimes ruthless, justice. In the 2nd Sikh War in the Punjab Nicholson also served on General Sir Hugh Gough's staff and was always outspoken and highly critical of Gough's tactics and strategy, especially of the disastrous Chilianwala battle. Nicholson became arrogant, haughty, a passionately sincere charismatic figure who evoked love, admiration, fear and envy as a leader, seen by detractors as a bully, by admirers as a hero. There is a story about him that after Gough's Battle of Gujrat, in February 1849, Nicholson with his Pathan irregulars vigorously pursued Sikhs until they surrendered. He then released Sikh prisoners on his own volition, his mercy and courage so subdued them that they began a new 'creed' of revering 'Nikalseyn', deifying him as another incarnation of their God Brahmin, which greatly annoyed him.[9]

Nicholson was in overall command of the storming of Delhi and carefully prepared his officers; on 14 September the assault of four columns went in. After a British cannonade, personally leading the first column near the Kashmir Gate, he 'was the first to ascend the breach meeting a storm of bullets'. He 'drove mutineers from the wall and followed by his men he captured house after house', followed closely by the second column under Colonel William Jones of the 61st Foot. When the Kashmir Gate was blown in by sappers of the 52nd Foot, Colonel Campbell's third column advanced through smoke and flying debris. Among those pouring into the city and down the narrow streets was Nicholson's brother, Lieutenant Charles Nicholson, commanding sepoys. Nicholson's first column and Colonel Jones's second should by now have captured the Kabul Gate to let in Major Charles Reid and his fourth column who were to attack mutineers in the Kishangani suburbs outside the Kabul and Lahore gates and then enter the city. But Reid's force was in trouble when he encountered fierce fighting and he and many others were wounded. Kashmiris under Captain Richard Lawrence (one of the famous Lawrence brothers) broke in disorder under the heavy fire and were only saved by cavalry. When Nicholson's troops beyond the Kabul Gate were halted by rebel fire confusion reigned. In a rage, not knowing of Reid's delay but aware that everything was about to go wrong, Nicholson took command of the stalled advance and hurled the 1st European Bengal Fusiliers down a narrow lane towards the Lahore gate. Only four could march abreast and they were open to frontal artillery fire from the Burn bastion, a stronghold along the way, and terrible musket fire from houses on either side. The many Irish in the 1st Bengal Fusiliers had already suffered casualties and Captain Greville of the Regiment proposed instead to break into the houses and take the sepoys in the rear. Nicholson should have realized that progress was only possible by this means, but he would not agree and, calling excitedly to the demoralized Fusiliers to continue the charge, he went down the lane and was mortally wounded. An order to the Fusiliers to retire to the Kabul Gate was given by one of their officers, a move seen to be 'not only justifiable but well judged and right. The passage of this lane should never have been attempted.'[10] As to why a great leader should be so faulty in his judgement, Nicholson's biographer, Hesketh Pearson, has suggested that 'the hours of strenuous exertion under a brazen sky which exhausted other men excited him' and in this wildly enthusiastic frame of mind he charged brandishing his sword and, typically, expected others to follow.

Young Lieutenant Frederick Roberts found his fellow countryman, the hero of Delhi, lying on a doohlie beside the road at the Kashmir Gate, left there by bearers who had run off to plunder. Roberts, as a staff officer, had been sent by General Wilson to report on the progress of the day's attack. Nicholson could only tell him, 'I am dying . . . '. 'The sight of that great man lying helpless and on the point of death,' wrote Roberts many years later, 'was almost more than I could bear . . . to lose Nicholson seemed to me at that moment to lose everything.' To Roberts, Nicholson 'was the beau ideal of a soldier and a gentleman'. He had him taken to the field hospital by soldiers of the 61st Foot where he died nine days later, having learned that Delhi had fallen to the British after great slaughter. John Lawrence, with whom Nicholson had often disagreed, said in tribute this success could not have happened without John Nicholson. His recently raised Multani Horse, desolated by his death, wept at his funeral and a few days later when ordered to march somewhere they refused: 'They owed no allegiance to the English government . . . they had come down to protect and save Nicholson, and to loot Delhi'. A memorial to John Nicholson is in the Cathedral in Lisburn, which Lord Roberts visited in 1903 and, a few years, later Field Marshal Wilson unveiled a statue to Nicholson in Lisburn's market square.[11]

The heroism of the attackers at Delhi was reported in great detail in the *Illustrated London News* of 21 November 1857, with much praise for Nicholson and the 1st European Bengal Fusiliers. The bravery of two Irishmen in that regiment at the Kabul gate was recognized by two VCs won by Sergeant J. McGuire from Enniskillen and Drummer Miles Ryan from Londonderry, who threw burning boxes of ammunition over the parapet, thus saving many lives. Other Irishmen in English regiments were also awarded VCs, such as Bugler Hawthorne from Londonderry in 52nd Foot who, in the action at the Kashmir Gate, saved a wounded officer of the Engineers.

At Lucknow the first breakthrough to the beleaguered garrison occurred on 25 September when a small force appeared, led by Sir Henry Havelock and Sir James Outram, both with long experience in India. Some thousand troops advanced through the narrow streets subjected to fierce and in-cessant fire from mutineers and General Havelock was badly wounded. Colonel James George Neill, at the head of the 1st Madras Fusiliers, 'Neill's Blue Caps', died, shot through the head in the last street leading to the Residency. Despite heavy casualties, they continued the advance and were the first troops to enter the Residency.[12] Largely an Irish regi-ment, their nickname 'Blue Caps' came from their headgear, a forage cap covered with blue cloth having a curtain and peak. Neill, a Scot, was a Cromwellian Puritan and, like Nicholson, another 'God fearing man . . . Stern and hard-swearing, strong and masterful . . . but he was also loved . . . by his personal staff.[13]

Sir James Outram's little army was not strong enough to conduct the garrison out of Lucknow. His added forces along with existing shortages of food and other supplies were causing even greater misery in the Residency, although finding the supplies Henry Lawrence had hidden did help. The number of wounded increased from frequent sorties against enemy gun emplacements and from snipers in the surrounding houses so that medical supplies were seriously depleted. The Union Jack continued to fly defiantly above the Residency, yet everyone knew that unless further relief arrived disaster loomed. At the end of October news got through to the garrison that another relieving force under General Sir Colin Campbell, the new Commander-in-Chief in India, was building up its strength. The problem was how to ensure the army would not be bogged down in the labyrinth of streets before it got to the Residency.

The way into Lucknow was finally shown to Campbell by another hero of the Indian Mutiny, the Irishman Thomas Henry Kavanagh from Mullingar in Westmeath. He was a low-paid civilian clerk at Lucknow with fourteen children and much in debt, who found during the siege that he possessed remarkable martial gifts, volunteering to serve with Cornish miners of the 32nd Foot who were busy in a sustained counter-offensive as the mutineers tried to tunnel beneath the Residency to plant mines. Soon General Outram was referring to him as 'the assistant field engineer', as Kavanagh and others blew in rebel tunnels and even engaged in pistol fights in candle-lit darkness. In November Kavanagh volunteered to reach Campbell's force and to guide it on the best route to the Residency, yet he knew that if captured, his would not be a quick death. Kavanagh was tall, blond and strongly built and Outram doubted whether his disguise as a northern freebooter, achieved with the use of oil and lamp-black and remnants of Indian clothing from the garrison, would get him through the Indian lines. It did, and with the aid of an heroic Indian guide, Kavanagh swam the river and bluffed his way through enemy lines until he met a British picket. Eight days later he led the relieving force towards the Residency. For his deed on 9 November T. H. Kavanagh was awarded the first civilian Victoria Cross and afterwards shared the details of his exploits in his 1860 book *How I Won the Victoria Cross*.[14]

On Kavanagh's advice Campbell brought his army, not through the centre of the city as Outram and Havelock had done, but across country from the south-east to cross the canal north and advance to the Residency through the area of palaces and their gardens. Many casualties were sustained along the route especially by the Gaelic-speaking 93rd Highlanders; in sharp fights with the rebels Campbell lost ten per cent of his army. Captain Garnet Wolseley was at this final relief of the Lucknow Residency. On 16 November, after the Sikander Bagh Palace was captured in a fierce fight by Highlanders and Sikhs, he had the unpleasant task of burying some 2,000 mutineers. The next day he was ordered by Sir Colin to lead a storming party against the Khoorsheyd Munzil (Happy Palace), one of two remaining to be taken before the relieving force could get through to the Residency. Wolseley was to keep his men under cover while he returned with information about the palace's defences, but, if he could take it, 'he should do so by all means'. This and Campbell's promised recommendation for a VC was enough for the ambitious young Wolseley. After the guns of the Naval Brigade battered the walls, Wolseley was the first to scramble over them to find sepoys escaping through the courtyard. At the sound of the bugle his supporting companies came up: 'his own sober Saxons . . . murderous looking Sikhs, and reckless, daredevil Irishmen of the 53rd . . . flushing . . . luckless sepoys'.

Wolseley did not stop here, however, for he decided to deny Campbell's 'pet Hielandmen', whom everyone knew he favoured, the honour of the final breakthrough to the Residency. So, on his own initiative, Wolseley proceeded under fire to the nearby Motee Mahul (Palace of Pearls) the last obstacle in front of the advancing force. His men hacked out a small hole in the palace's thick wall and one by one they crawled through into the courtyard. While they were chasing rebels there was a loud explosion and through the smoke and rubble poured Captain Tingling and his company of Wolseley's own 90th Foot from the Lucknow garrison who had mined the wall to assist the relieving force. It was a dramatic meeting between Wolseley and Tingling. Wolseley had the honour to be the first of Sir Colin's army to reach the garrison. Campbell was none too pleased with his initiative.[15]

Not until 16 March 1858 did Campbell, with a large army, recapture Lucknow city from the rebels, a time when 'soldiers again went mad' reported William Howard Russell for *The Times*. 'In an orgy of plundering . . . Drunk with excitement they smashed everything they could lay their hands on.' Such looting was very reminiscent of Badajoz in the Peninsular War. In April Russell was nearly killed by Rohilla ghazis, fanatical Muslims, caught up in an attack on one of Campbell's columns that was attempting to clear the left bank of the Ganges. Russell, already ill, fainted and fell from his horse and the ghazis 'thundered over him leaving him untouched except for bruises'.[16]

In the Mutiny campaign Frederick Roberts, as a Staff Officer, had been slightly wounded and mentioned in despatches several times. In January 1858 he was attached to a column sent to search out rebels and at the village of Khodagunge he won the Victoria Cross for hand-to-hand combat with mutineers, an astonishing feat given his small stature and only one seeing eye. While following retreating rebels Roberts saw two sepoys escaping with a standard; he dashed at them and wrenched the standard away, cutting one down. On the same day in a similar incident he rescued a Sowar, slaying his opponent with a single blow of his sword. There were many young Irishmen like Roberts who welcomed the many 'little wars' of the nineteenth century as a chance where they might win glory and honour, not only for their own name, but also for the British Empire. Two others were the Gough brothers.

Lieutenant Hugh Henry Gough of the 1st European Light Cavalry, during the advance on Lucknow in November 1857 with Sir Colin Campbell's relieving army, became fast friends with Roberts, joining him in a dangerous ride to bring up ammunition. In that same month Hugh was in the first of two actions where his gallantry led to the award of the Victoria Cross. On 12 November, outside Lucknow, he attacked the defenders of two guns capturing the cannon and later, on 25 February

1858 near Jellalabad, he displayed courage and resource in capturing more guns and engaging in several single combats. His brother, Major Charles Gough of the 5th Bengal European Cavalry, won his award for four dashing exploits culminating when he saved his own brother's life at Kurkowdah on 15 August 1857 and, on 23 February 1858 at Meangunge, he saved a brother officer's life at great risk to himself.[17] The Goughs were from another remarkable Anglo-Irish military family, the great-nephews of the 87th Foot's Major Hugh Gough of Peninsular War fame who captured the French Eagle at Barossa. Charles's son, Johnny, in the Rifle Brigade, won the VC in 1903, unusual for father and son, or for brothers, to win the VC.

After the fall of Lucknow Captain Garnet Wolseley was appointed Deputy Assistant Quartermaster General in Sir Hope Grant's Lucknow Field Force, another of several columns hunting down scattered rebels. He replaced his future rival Frederick Roberts who returned to Ireland on sick leave. Wolseley's Brevet Majority followed and in due course his Brevet Lieutenant Colonelcy, all without purchase and greatly appreciated since Campbell's promised recommendation for a VC did not materialize. Then again, in 1860, as Hope Grant's Deputy Assistant Quartermaster General Wolseley participated in storming the Taku Forts in China. Extended home leave followed, most of it spent in Ireland.

The White Mutiny – Amalgamation of the British Army and East India Company Regiments

After the Indian Mutiny, in late 1858, the governance of India was transferred to the British Crown, ending the long rule of the Honourable East India Company. A Viceroy replaced the Governor General and European troops in the Company's service were transferred to the British Army by a Royal Proclamation of November 1858. The distinction between Royal troops and the Company's European troops was now to disappear and the British Army serving in India was to form part of the Imperial British Army whose units would take turns in garrisoning India. Among the Irish rank and file, and indeed among all John Company's European regiments, a crisis arose when the Crown took over. Troops protested through memorials and petitions in what became known as 'the White Mutiny', claiming that it was not fair to move them about as they had not joined the Queen's army. Soldiers made demands that they should be given their discharge, or at least a bounty for a new enlistment under the Crown. At a ceremonial parade celebrating the Queen's birthday the Madras Fusiliers refused to cheer her. Other acts of insubordination occurred and Lord Canning, fearing the contagion would spread, agreed to let those who wanted their discharge return to Britain, their travel home to be free. Of the 16,000 Europeans (most of them Irish) who received the offer 10,116 took their discharge, and a little over a quarter of these reenlisted at home. It has been argued that the high numbers of those leaving the service represented 'raw lads . . . landed in India and immediately . . . put to severe regimental training in the hottest part of the year'.[18]

In the process of transferring, the old John Company European Bengal, Bombay and Madras Fusilier battalions became numbered Royal Fusilier battalions in the British Army, the 101st to 104th. The 3rd Madras and 3rd Bombay European regiments, both raised in 1854, became the Crown's 108th and 109th Infantry regiments respectively. In 1881 a further reorganization took place; old regimental numbers were discontinued and an Irish territorial designation was assigned. The 101st and 104th became 1st and 2nd battalions Royal Munster Fusiliers; the 102nd and 103rd became 1st and 2nd Royal Dublin Fusiliers. The 108th Madras, Irish from its beginning, was linked to the existing 27th Inniskilling Fusiliers and the 109th Bombay to the Leinster Regiment. All these were based in Ireland with their own depots. For the sepoys or Indian soldiers of John Company's armies, a separate Indian army was established in which the only Europeans would be officers. Until Indian independence the British Army in India and the Indian Army were under the umbrella of the Crown and many Irish continued to serve in both.

Roberts in India

Roberts's actions in winning the VC in January 1858 were followed by a bout of ill health and he accepted medical home leave and with £500 prize money and a distinguished reputation for bravery returned to Waterford where his family had close links with that city. His great-grandfather had designed many of the city's major buildings, including the Protestant and Catholic Cathedrals; his grandfather was a well-known local clergyman and his father had been in the Waterford Militia before joining the East India Company's Army. Roberts spent much time in Waterford as a boy and in 1859, in Waterford's St Patrick's Church, he married Miss Nora Bews, daughter of a retired Black Watch officer. Roberts and his bride sailed for India where he would serve until nearly the end of the century[19], gaining promotion through a series of staff appointments leading to Quartermaster General in Bengal.

The Second Afghan War (1878–80) gave Roberts his first field command when in the spring of 1878 he was appointed Commander the Punjab Frontier Force. He was the man on the spot when trouble arose in November with Afghanistan, the wild land between British India and Russia that both nations had always desired to influence. The ruler, Sher Ali, ignored British warnings against allying himself with the Russians whose forces were then on Ali's northern borders and had agents operating in Kabul. The result was the British plan to invade Afghanistan. Roberts, appointed a very young Major General in December, advanced from India leading his column, the Kurram Field Force, against the Pathans and cleverly misled them at the Peiwar Kotal pass to win the first victory of the war on 2 December. Sher Ali fled. The Afghans, under Sher Ali's son Yakub Khan, then seemed to agree to a peace treaty to end the war and accepted Major Sir Louis Cavagnari, a British political officer, as Resident in Kabul. Roberts was a hero in India and Britain, congratulations were sent from the Queen and the Viceroy and he was knighted. He had barely time to settle in Simla, the army's mountain headquarters, when news came that a rebel mob had stormed the British Residency at Kabul and slaughtered the entire garrison, including Major Cavagnari and his military staff. Roberts was immediately ordered to assemble an army, now named the Kabul Field Force, and to march against Kabul in the interests of justice or as some said, retribution. He led his Field Force through treacherous mountain terrain, engaging the Afghans in minor encounters until, in a sharp fight at the Charasia Ridge near Kabul, he defeated them. There, on 6 October 1879, Major George Stuart White of 92nd Gordon Highlanders won the Victoria Cross. This Anglo-Irishman, born at Ballymena, County Antrim, was called 'one of the bravest men and an Irish gentleman to boot'; his citation records that he led an attack in person on a fortified hill. His men being exhausted, he took a rifle and himself shot the leader of the enemy. The act so intimidated the rest that they fled and the position was won.

Roberts ably took Kabul, but he knew the British were not welcome in Afghanistan. Restless Afghan tribes were still menacing and Roberts was forced to take over and strengthen a fortified camp at Sherpur outside the city, a fortuitous move for in late December he was attacked by Afghans, who greatly outnumbered him. Fortunately he was reinforced by a Brigade under Charles Gough VC, his old friend and now a brigadier. During a terribly hard winter Roberts established his authority in Kabul and hanged forty-nine tribesmen who were found guilty of the massacre at the British Residency, quite certain it was his duty to do so. He was promoted to the local rank of Lieutenant General.

Fame awaited Roberts. In June 1880 Ayub Khan, Yakub's brother, claimed the throne at Kandahar and in July the Afghans achieved a crushing defeat over a British brigade at nearby Maiwand. Ayub then headed for Kandahar where General James Primrose's garrison was soon put under siege. When news came of the Maiwand disaster, Roberts was ordered to relieve Primrose and on 9 August began his celebrated march from Kabul to Kandahar, some three hundred miles over mountainous country accomplished in just three weeks, a feat that caught public attention, as did its catchy name. On his arrival he was none too pleased to find that General Primrose's force was more 'demoralized' than decimated, and 'never even hoisted the Union Jack until the relieving force was close at hand'. To Roberts there had been no real danger, nor was Kandahar in a weak position with its fifteen-foot-thick and thirty-foot-high walls and many guns. Roberts was furious. He had already learned from Primrose that Ayub Khan had lifted the siege of Kandahar and was entrenched nearby. With his men still exhausted from the excessive daytime heat, cold nights and sore feet, Roberts, ill with fever, nevertheless lost no time and attacked this clever Afghan's camp the following day, 1 September, capturing all his guns. Ayub Khan and his bodyguard fled in a cloud of dust. When the 92nd Highlanders and the Gurkhas deployed for a charge, Major George White contributed to his VC in another brave action. Under heavy fire he led the final charge against a strong enemy position of two guns, rode straight to within a few yards of them, dashed forward and secured one. Roberts's losses in this Battle of Kandahar that ended the war were not considered heavy for such an important victory. The armies now departed from Afghanistan for India and the rule of the county was left to the pro-British Abdur Rahman.[20]

When Roberts returned to England on well-earned sick leave he was greeted as a national hero. The *Waterford News* of 4 February 1881 praised the march and his 'brilliant victory', and also noted that, 'although there were no Irish regiments on the march, Irish soldiers served in the British regiments which participated'. The obviously nationalist writer of the newspaper could not help adding, 'The son of the abused Celt did the work and again the "Sassenach" gets the profit and the glory'. In this case, Roberts, at least, got 'the profit and the glory'. Showered with honours, he received an honourary degree from Oxford, swords of honour from Eton and the City of London, and the handsome sum of £12,500 and a GCB. He and his wife were also guests of the Queen at Windsor. Already a Major General, he was disappointed that he had not received a promotion, as had the celebrated Major General Garnet Wolseley who had been in the public eye again since his Zulu campaign and had received twice as much money as Roberts. These two Irish heroes were now constantly before the British public through the press, their rivalry, as Roberts's biographer David James suggests, chiefly carried out by their respective very loyal staffs. Other historians have taken a stronger view and see their 'feud' as splitting the Victorian Army into two factions: Wolseley's 'African' Ring against Roberts's 'Indian' Ring. Like other men of ability, both had their critics. In 1892 Roberts was raised to the peerage as Baron Roberts of Kandahar. Rudyard Kipling celebrates the diminutive Roberts as the soldiers' hero, venerated by his troops as Wolseley never would be:

> 'E's the man that done us well,
> An' we'll follow 'im to 'ell –
> Won't we Bobs?[21]

In 1881 Roberts was appointed commander of the Madras Army. From 1885 until 1893, when he left India for the last time, he was Commander-in-Chief, which meant of the Bengal Army with 'supervisory powers over the other two presidencies' of Madras and Bombay. Philip Mason, the noted historian of the Indian Army, gives an interesting assessment of Roberts's legacy in India. He had 'vastly increased the efficiency of the Indian army' and 'set a pattern for the British officer in India for eighty years'. He was loved by both British and Indians, but although he had greatly admired the soldierly qualities of the Gurkhas, Sikhs, Dogras, Rajputs and Pathans and looked on them as valued friends, he wrote: 'Native officers . . . can never take the place of British officers . . . Eastern races, however brave and accustomed to war, do not possess the qualities that go to make good leaders of men.' Roberts, in Philip Mason's view, 'was a practical man and his views were those of his own generation and not of eighty years later. . . . But his virtues lent them weight'.[22]

On Roberts's return to Ireland in 1893 Waterford conferred on him the freedom of the City. At the ceremony the mayor boasted that 'our country has given many brilliant generals and gallant soldiers to the British Army', and Roberts graciously replied that he was 'proud of being an Irishman'.[23] He was promoted Field Marshal in 1895 and appointed as Commander-in-Chief in Ireland. But 'Old soldiers never die!' as the saying goes, and when the Anglo-Boer War brought defeats for the British Army Roberts could not refrain from offering his services to the government and he was accepted.

Troops returning to Ireland brought with them tales of fighting on the North-West Frontier and India became part of the folk consciousness of the Irish people. The India-Irish connection appears in the third verse of *The Rose of Tralee*, which became a popular Irish folk song:

> In the far fields of India 'neath war's dreadful thunder
> Her smile and her countenance were solace to me,
> But the cruel hand of death has now torn us asunder
> And I'm lonely tonight for the Rose of Tralee.

Promoted by the Irish newspaper the *Nation*, it was written by William Pembroke Mulchinock of Tralee, a writer who had been on the North-West Frontier during the Sikh Wars of the 1840s.[24]

O'Moore Creagh, one of the Irish Junker class, had, like Roberts, long service in India. He was a member of an Irish Catholic landed gentry family from County Clare, as he said an Irish-Gaelic family. Five ancestors had served with the 'Wild Geese' under Count de Lally, the French General of Irish descent, when he was forced to surrender to Eyre Coote at Pondicherry in 1761. Some Creaghs returned to Ireland, became Protestant and held estates in Counties Clare and Limerick, serving also in the military. Creagh's father had been Post Captain in the Royal Navy. His mother was a daughter of The O'Moore of Cloghan Castle in King's County. He never had doubts about following a military career and in 1866, after the RMC and purchasing his commission, he was gazetted ensign in the 95th Foot which was stationed in India.

In 1879 in the Second Afghan War marauding tribes on the North-West Frontier were very restless, bent on mischief among themselves and often harassing British lines of communication in the border area. Captain Creagh was involved in a typical incident. In charge of a detachment of some 100 men of his Merwara Battalion, whose patois he was one of the few officers to understand, he was ordered to protect the small village of Kam Dakka on the Kabul River from hostile Mohmands whom the villagers claimed were gathering to attack them. Creagh arrived and set up his defensive position on the banks of the river. The villagers on the Frontier, however, were not always to be trusted and when the Mohmands duly attacked they, as Creagh had suspected, were aided by the villagers. Greatly outnumbered, he held them off for several hours in a heavy fight that included bayonet charges. His ammunition failing, Creagh found himself in a tight corner when General Maude, his Divisional Commander, who had won his VC in the Crimea, heard of his plight and sent reinforcements. Creagh supported with the bayonet the sudden cavalry charge of the 10th Bengal Lancers across his front and the Mohmands retreated in haste pursued by the Lancers. Some Mohmands remained in the hills maintaining their fire. No proper advance of the reinforcements was ordered by their Commanding Officer who was not familiar with the ground and his reinforcements had arrived piecemeal. His artillery merely shelled the tribesmen from high ground and they attacked again. To his disgust, Creagh was then ordered to the high ground and with great difficulty brought his approximately thirty killed and wounded to prevent them from being mutilated. Then, instead of finishing off the enemy, which Creagh proposed, the entire force was ordered to retire on Dakka, continually harassed by Mohmands. For his actions Creagh won the Victoria Cross; he himself recommended several of his detachment for the Indian Order of Merit.

Several years later, when he was in command of a 2nd Baluchi Battalion, Creagh had companies of Pathans under him and, observing these hardy warriors, he made a comparison between them and the Irish:

> The Pathans are, like my own countrymen, impulsive, easily excited. . . . Like my countrymen, the Pathan has a strict sense of honour of his own, and in both races the sense of honour differs markedly from that found amongst the English.

And, Creagh adds, 'It is very necessary that British officers who are serving with Pathans should be familiar with this code of honour and treat them in accordance with it'.[25] After forty-eight years in India this Irish Victorian hero finished his career as Commander-in-Chief of the Indian Army 1909–14, succeeding Lord Kitchener.

Most members of the British Army served in India sooner or later, and for those Irish who enlisted for adventure the opportunity for fighting was readily to be found on the North-West Frontier in innumerable campaigns, battles and forays against Pathans, Afridis and many other tribes. When the Chitral Relief Force of 1895 was mobilizing at Nowshera to relieve the garrison at Chitral in the remote area north of Peshawar against tribal attacks, the intrepid Irishman Lieutenant Colonel Philip (Micky) Doyne of the 4th Royal Irish Dragoon Guards was greatly disappointed that his regiment was not included. The amusing story from J. M. Brereton's *4th/7th Royal Dragoon Guards* of how Colonel Doyne included himself in the expedition shows all the ingenuity of the Irish soldier and his love of fighting. At the same time it is a comment on what distinguishes 'an officer and a gentleman'.

In 1892 Micky Doyne had brought the 4th Royal Irish Dragoon Guards from Ireland to Rawalpindi, the 'Aldershot' of Northern India, where they were to remain for the unusually long period of eight years. Aged forty-two, he had seen twenty-seven years service with never a shot fired in anger. So, taking leave on the pretext of going 'for the shooting' (not quite untruthful) and without badges of rank, he made his way by the mail train to Nowshera where the 2nd King's Own Scottish Borderers were forming up for the attack. Bent on 'death or glory' and employing his 'Irish guile', he managed secretly to join in the attack with the 2nd Scottish as a private soldier. In fact Brigadier General Bindon Blood seems to have been aware of Doyne's presence in this regiment and there is a fine story of how Blood, in order to prevent his Staff Officer, Major George Younghusband, from recognizing 'a friend' in the ranks marching with the Regiment, diverted his attention by an astonishing eulogy on the beauties of the landscape. Doyne fought bravely 'with great gallantry and was one of the foremost in carrying the Malakand Pass with the bayonet', emerging from the battle unscathed. Afterwards this mad Irishman 'discharged' himself from the 2nd Scottish and began to make his way back to Rawalpindi. At Nowshera he shocked a major in the Guides whose tent was invaded by an apparently drunken, unkempt private who, in a thick Irish brogue, asked for whisky. The Major was about to send him off when the Irish voice was heard to speak in a 'conspiratorial' tone: 'It's all right, old boy. I'm Colonel Micky Doyne of the 4th DGs'. Whereupon the two officers spent a very jovial time together until Doyne left to catch a train that would return him in time to resume his command.

News of this exploit soon reached HQ at Simla where it was felt that, although Doyne's initiative and enthusiasm were secretly admired, he had to be shown that he had engaged in 'conduct to the prejudice of good order and military discipline'. For a Commanding Officer to absent himself on false pretences and pose as a Private demanded that 'Authority could only take a strictly official view of the matter'. Some leniency prevailed and there was no court martial, but:

> When Doyne applied for an extension of command in March 1896, he was politely refused and advised to retire on half-pay. Thus, the 4th Dragoon Guards and the Army lost a fine officer and a gallant soldier who, but for officialdom might well have achieved high rank and honours.[26]

Micky Doyne never saw Ireland again. After purchasing land near Ambala to raise polo ponies, he died of illness in 1898.

The great popularizer of the soldier in India was the India-born Rudyard Kipling who, as a journalist at Lahore from 1882, often encountered British 'Tommies' in the police court. The soldiers he knew best were the English and the Irish. During his school days at Westward Ho in England, on the school staff were the Irishman Kearney and the Londoner Sergeant James Schofield, the school's drill sergeant who, it is thought, influenced Kipling's characters Mulvaney and Ortheris in his stories in *Soldiers Three*.[27] Terence Mulvaney, the intelligent, talkative and often drunken Irishman from Port Arlington, tells most of the stories of the exploits of his friends and they and the *Barrack Room Ballads* are representative of the old long-service army in India. Kipling gave to his contemporaries a rare picture of the military way of life of the ordinary soldier, showing how their comradeship gets them through the often tedious days of soldiers' lives. The regiment was their home and there they stayed despite cholera-stricken camps, bloody skirmishes and often bad leadership, sometimes assailed by bouts of misery and depression, as Mulvaney bursts out in his rhetorical question:

> Mary, Mother av Mercy fwhat the divil possist us to take an' kape this melancolious counthry? Anser me that Sorr.

In order to get his fellow soldiers, the London slum boy Ortheris and the Yorkshireman Learoyd, through the prostrating heat of one stifling June night, Mulvaney launches into a story called *With the Main Guard* about the very Irish Black Tyrones sent to help Mulvaney's regiment 'to tache the Paythans' a lesson. The Black Tyrones was Mulvaney's first regiment, probably a militia unit: 'Faynians an' rebils to the heart av their marrow was they, an' so they fought for the Widdy [Queen Victoria] bether than most being contrairy – Oirish'. In Mulvaney's humorous telling of the bloody action a close 'family' connection emerges. Out of harm's way in the battle a Tyrone sergeant is found 'sittin on a little orfcer bhoy' of the regiment who was struggling and crying to return to lead his men against the Pathans in a proper fight, not just throwing stones. The boy's father, it seems, was the landlord of the sergeant's mother in Clonmel, and feeling very responsible the sergeant desperately asks, 'Will I go back to *his* mother an' tell her I've let him throw himself away?'[28]

As late as the 1930s in the Irish Free State among the slum-dwellers of Limerick memories persisted of what was seen as an exciting and heroic life in the British Army in far-away exotic India. Frank McCourt in his autobiographical *Angela's Ashes* describes the fantasizing of the 'biggest and oldest boy in his class' at school:

> He can't wait to grow up and be fourteen so that he can run away and pass for seventeen and join the English army and go to India where its nice and warm and he'll live in a tent with a dark girl with the red dot on her forehead and he'll be lying there eating figs, that's what they eat in India, figs, and she'll cook the curry day and night and plonk on a ukulele and when he has enough money he'll send for the whole family and they'll all live in the tent.[29]

CHAPTER SEVEN

The Irish and the Late Nineteenth Century
Small Wars

The average soldier played out his role as an unsung hero dying well in a small war somewhere in a climate and terrain that was frighteningly alien.

Donald Featherstone
Victorian Colonial Warfare, Africa
London, 1993, Introduction, page 9

THE IRISH IN THE GREAT LONE LANDS OF NORTH AMERICA

Wolseley and The Red River Expedition

While India was claiming the attention of the Irish in the British Army, they were also no strangers to fighting in North America. The British Government sent troops to Canada shortly after the American Civil War began in 1861, prompted by an incident between a Union warship and a British Royal Mail steamer from which two Confederate envoys were removed. By the time Garnet Wolseley arrived in Nova Scotia the threat of war had eased. Proceeding to British Army headquarters at Montreal, where his duties as Acting Deputy Quartermaster General were not onerous, in 1862 he took leave to visit the southern United States to obtain a first-hand impression of the fighting. He met the Confederate Commander Robert E. Lee, whom he greatly admired, and discussed the war with him. On his return to Montreal he wrote a popular account of his journeys that was published in *Blackwood's Magazine* of January 1863 wherein he recommended that England should side with the Confederacy, although the institution of slavery was not favoured.

Canada was too quiet for this ambitious warrior until after the Civil War there once more appeared a threat to British North America, that posed by the Irish Fenian Brotherhood who made bellicose statements about an invasion. It was the American wing of the Irish Republican Brotherhood (IRB), a secret society founded in March 1858 in Ireland dedicated to establishing an independent Irish Republic. By 1866 American Civil War veterans were gathering in filibuster bands on Canada's straggling and ill-defined frontier. Lieutenant Colonel J. O'Neill, born in County Monaghan, a former Union Army cavalry officer, managed to cross the Niagara frontier with 800 Irish Americans and won a skirmish on 2 June at the Battle of Ridgeway against British forces and local Canadian Militia before retiring to the USA. Wolseley was promptly sent from Montreal, but arrived only in time to see the Fenians in their large scow apprehended by the Americans before they reached the American shore. They were soon paroled and let go.[1] Wolseley saw no action, but was assigned to train mixed brigades of regulars and militia. His experiences in Burma, the Crimea, in the Indian Mutiny and his many wounds made him a great favourite with the troops. In September 1867, after leave in Ireland, he was recalled to Canada as Deputy Quartermaster General. The next year he returned briefly to Ireland to marry the beautiful and clever Miss Louise Erskine. During this time he attracted official notice on the publication of his highly successful *The Soldier's Pocket Book for Field Service* in 1869, 'the first book of its kind to prepare soldiers for war and duties in the field'. His wide-ranging commentary offended civilians when he advised soldiers 'to despise those in civil life'. He criticized the conduct of the British officer: 'It was not enough for an officer to be a master of drill . . . he must have some knowledge of how men were to live as well as die.' He also denounced the phrase 'officer and a gentleman', the simple word 'soldier' was sufficient. Wolseley's abiding interest was in creating a better and more modern army and this brought criticism and enemies. Always outspoken, he also offended the press, suggesting they were an annoyance to the military. He was soon seen as arrogant, someone who did not try to hide his intellectual superiority.[2]

In the early summer of 1870 Wolseley, already in Canada, was the man to lead a military force to restore order in the crown colony of Assiniboia, as the well-settled Red River Valley country in Manitoba was called. Two years earlier the Canadian Government, worried about American western expansion, resolved to purchase the Hudson's Bay Company's territorial rights to the huge area of land west and north from the border of Ontario to the Pacific and Arctic oceans. The inhabitants of Assiniboia were not consulted in this transfer, and the Métis (people of mixed French and Indian blood) could foresee the destruction of their traditional seigneurial system of land holdings and the end of the buffalo. A revolt to protect settlers' rights broke out led by Métis under their leader Louis Riel. He created his own provisional government and, hoping to negotiate with the Canadian Government, seized Fort Garry, the Hudson's Bay Company post and Assiniboia administrative centre (now the City of Winnipeg), and imprisoned a few settlers who objected to his authority. When one of the raiders, an 'Orangeman from Ontario' in a party to release Riel's prisoners, was executed, every Orangeman and Protestant voter was outraged and pressed the governments at Ottawa and Westminster for military action.[3]

The Red River Expedition, the last British military expedition in North America, was also Colonel Wolseley's first independent command and to it he brought his very thorough organizational skills where no detail was too small for an expedition that would have to carry its own supplies over long distances. His 1,200-strong force consisted mostly of Canadian Militia, Imperial troops of the elite 1st/60th Rifles, a battery of Royal Field Artillery, a detachment of Royal Engineers, a portion of army service and hospital corps and a group of Imperial staff officers. They travelled some 1,200 miles by train, steamer and specially built boats manned by skilled Canadian Voyageurs and soldiers, across lakes and rivers with their dangerous portages, and marched through vast wilderness finally to the prairie. Not a man was lost thanks to Wolseley's superb planning.

Among the officers were three who would be long associated with Wolseley and known as Wolseley's 'Ring', talented young men he felt he could trust chosen from the many who besieged him with applications. The Irishman Lieutenant William Butler of 69th Foot later wrote:

> Everybody wanted to go on this expedition . . . a 'beyond' into which steam power did not enter, where there were no roads, where there were still real live Indians.[4]

He and Lieutenant Hugh McCalmont, also Irish, were very honoured to be chosen to serve under Wolseley, seen as 'the rising star of the British Army'. The Englishman Lieutenant Redvers Buller of the 60th Rifles was the third would-be Ring officer.

William Francis Butler, a poor Irishman from Tipperary of little formal education, was to become one of the most literate figures of the Victorian era and a soldier of distinction. Born in 1838 at Ballyslateen, he was the seventh child of Richard Butler, an impecunious small land holder who was descended from the Catholic branch of the younger son of the 9th Earl of Ormonde and who seemingly had not suffered under the Penal Laws. Peninsular War tales he heard from local veterans decided William to choose the army as a profession, but there was no money for such a poor Irish Catholic lad and he received his commission only through the influence of a distant relative, General Sir Richard Doherty, in Sir

Richard's old Regiment the 69th Foot. Like Wolseley, Butler could not expect advancement through the purchase system, but he was a young man of great intelligence and imagination, strikingly handsome, over six feet tall with a superb physique. He saw service in Burma and India but no action. While home on leave in Ireland in 1870 he read of the Red River Expeditionary force assembling and immediately sent off his famous telegram to Wolseley: 'Remember me. Butler, 69th Foot.' Not waiting for a reply he left Ireland and caught up with Wolseley in Toronto, only to find there was no job for him. Ever resourceful and determined, he suggested that Wolseley might need information on what was happening with the Americans, particularly the Fenians. Wolseley agreed that he needed an intelligence officer, later even claiming that the idea was his own. In an earlier interview in 1868, in Montreal, he claimed he had recognized Butler's 'all round intellectual superiority'. Now Lieutenant Butler was 'just the man I wanted to go round through the United States to the Red River . . . finding out how matters really stood there.'[5] Butler started for Lake Superior the next day on his 'roving commission'.

In his *Autobiography* (p. 113) Butler describes Wolseley at this time in prose that justifies his own reputation as a writer:

> A man in the prime of manhood, somewhat under middle height . . . exceedingly sharp penetrating blue eyes, from one of which the bursting of a shell in the trenches of Sebastopol had extinguished sight without in the least lessening the fire that shot through it from what was the best and most brilliant brain I ever met in the British army. He was possessed of a courage equal to his brain power.

Lieutenant Hugh McCalmont joined the expedition in an equally enterprising way. Unlike Butler, he came from a well-to-do and solidly Protestant Anglo-Irish family. His father, a wealthy Ulsterman, lived the life of a country gentleman at Abbeylands near Belfast. His mother was the daughter of James Martin of Ross near Oughterard on the fringes of Connemara, while his wife, Rose, was the daughter of Lord Clanmorris of County Galway. The family was well able to purchase a commission for Hugh in the 9th Lancers. Hugh loved army life and when he too read of the Red River Expedition he managed to obtain leave from the Lancers and hurried across the Atlantic at his own expense hoping to join it. Luck was with him. A fortuitous meeting with Mrs Wolseley on a steamer crossing Lake Superior to meet her husband at Fort William may have helped and they became great friends. Wolseley was at first reluctant to take on any 'volunteer' as McCalmont surely was, even with a letter from

Sir Hope Grant, his distinguished Commanding Officer of the Lancers. The matter of his participation was settled when Wolseley learned that McCalmont 'knew about boats', having been a 'wet bob' at Eton.[6]

While Wolseley's expedition struggled across the country through thick forests and swamps, over rocks and rivers, Butler accomplished his roving commission travelling south, then west, then north-west up the Red River, by train, stage coach, steamer and horseback. He was told that 'the American frontier opinion' did not expect the expedition would ever get out of the bush. His greatest enemies were the hordes of mosquitoes with which he battled all the way. This trip gave Butler a great opportunity to exercise his own initiative, which was to go on to Fort Garry, undoubtedly driven by curiosity to meet Riel. The meeting was most unsatisfactory. Butler was not impressed with Riel, nor with his haughty demeanour. He had failed to see Riel as a zealous, single-minded leader of a cause that was lost. This was unfortunate, for later Butler would be known for his sympathy for the underdog, and in fact he later admitted that Riel's cause in many ways was just.

Butler learned that Wolseley's force would be welcomed at Fort Garry by both French and English settlers who were in fear of an Indian uprising. Armed with this information, he set out to meet Wolseley and the Red River Expedition travelling for some twelve days south and east by canoe down rivers and across lakes with his Indian and half-breed paddlers through some 400 miles of rough and wild country. After many portages and changes of canoes, he heard from Indians that 'a great army of white braves had been sighted'. Just above Fort Frances near the border of today's provinces of Manitoba and Ontario, where the waters of Rainy Lake spill into the Rainy River, Butler went ashore above the rapids. It was not long before he saw a large canoe approaching propelled by eight Iroquois paddlers and carrying a British officer whose voice rang out: 'Where on earth have *you* dropped from? ' It was Wolseley. Butler saluted: 'Fort Garry Sir', he said. 'Twelve days out'.[7] The meeting of these two Irishmen in the wilds of Canada would take its place in the annals of the British Empire, the British Army and Canadian history. Wolseley's force eventually reached Fort Garry, which the soldiers in fighting formation approached cautiously only to find the gates wide open and the fort empty except for the Hudson's Bay Company factor. The Union Jack again flew over the fort, replacing the Métis flag, a *fleur-de-lis* and a shamrock on a white background symbolizing Métis and Fenian unity. The troops of the Red River Expedition had hoped for a fight; what they found was a bloodless campaign, except having been bitten raw by mosquitoes and black flies, but not a shot fired. Frustrated, the little army went mad, not looting as in the Peninsula and India, but drinking. Early in September 1870

Wolseley and the Imperial troops departed, their 'mission of peace', to use Wolseley's own phrase in the proclamation he issued, had been accomplished.

Wolseley was a hero in Canada after his Red River success and honours were heaped on him. He was fêted at a banquet in Montreal and the Hudson's Bay fort at the north-west corner of Lake of the Woods was named Fort Wolseley, but he was peeved that the Canadian Government did not appoint him Lieutenant Governor of the new province of Manitoba.[8] Home in England, he found he was only a minor hero, his success in Canada overshadowed in the newspapers by the Franco-Prussian War. The government was grateful, however, and he was given a knighthood, but to his disappointment he was out on half-pay. He kept busy writing articles on the Red River Expedition, highly critical of the Canadian Government and always written anonymously, but as everyone knew who the author was his name was kept before the public.

William Butler's Roving Commission

Meanwhile the adventurous Lieutenant William Butler was about to create a name for himself in Canadian history. When the Imperial troops departed for England in the autumn of 1870 Butler remained behind, reluctant to leave the west where the frontier life, vast open spaces and solitude continued to fascinate and appeal to his 'brooding Celtic spirit'. Fortunately he was offered, by the newly installed Lieutenant Governor Archibald of Manitoba, another roving commission for the Canadian Government who would be administering lands formerly the preserve of the Hudson's Bay Company. He was

> to explore the conditions under which the Indians, half-breeds and a few whites were living in the country . . . and recommend to the Government of Canada the best way . . . to ensure the establishment of the rule of law in the North-West Territories well in advance of settlement.

Butler joyfully accepted. Still on leave from his regiment, the opportunity to see more of this vast land and learn for himself of the Indian tribes for whom he had developed a romantic sympathy in his boyhood after reading the novels of James Fenimore Cooper, was a dream come true. For some four months Butler travelled just under 4,000 miles through an almost empty land, by horseback, dog sled and snowshoes, sleeping beside many a campfire in bitter cold as well as at Hudson's Bay posts and mission houses. On his return, among the recommendations he submitted in his report to the Government of Canada was one for a special police force, which was formed two years later to 'become the best known body of law enforcement officers in the world – the North West Mounted Police',[9] later the Royal Canadian Mounted Police. Butler's enthusiastic and personal response to the Canadian north-west is captured in two books he wrote and published, *The Great Lone Land* of 1872 and *The Wild North Land* of 1873 that are still read whenever the story of the settling of the Canadian west is told.

The Irish in Early Nineteenth Century Africa

Turning now to Africa we find that since the early days of Imperialist expansion the many Irish in the British Army who served at 'the sharp end' did not always wisely judge the fighting prowess of their enemies, white or black. Early in 1824 Sir Charles McCarthy, 'a stately, bearded, pig-headed Irishman', Governor in Chief of the British settlement on the West Coast of Africa, decided to put down Ashanti warriors who had dared to attack British soldiers manning British coastal forts and raid tribes under British protection. With only a small force of British troops, native levies and a band playing, he incautiously advanced into the jungle to be wiped out in a battle against a large body of Ashantis. McCarthy's head was cut off and his skull was preserved as a fetish, used as a drinking mug at royal feasts at Kumasi.[10]

Another too confident soldier was Captain Thomas Charlton Smith of the 27th Foot (Inniskillings). An experienced officer who had served at Waterloo and had long African experience, he had to be rescued with his small force in South Africa when, in 1842, he attacked Boers (farmers) who, meeting British regulars for the first time, carried the day. This conflict arose when Zulus continued attacking the Natal Boers and stealing their cattle. Aggressive Boers retaliated by threatening to attack the Anapondu tribe whose territory, lying on the boundary of Natal, was under British protection. Smith was sent from the Fish River area by Governor Napier with companies of Inniskillings, Cape Mounted Rifles, Royal Engineers and Artillery to act as commander of Port Natal (modern Durban) in the Colony which had been established and proclaimed by the Boers in the 1830s as a rudimentary form of republic. He was to make the Boers understand that, although they professed to have founded a republic, they were still British subjects:

> He was expected to overawe several hundred Boers – hunters from their earliest youth. . . . and to enforce the <u>Pax Britannica</u> between them and the Zulus.

After marching 260 miles through wilderness Smith set up his camp near the town and harbour. He soon decided to lead a party of Inniskillings with a few artillerymen in a surprise night attack on 23 May, hoping to strike the first blow against Boers who, he learned, were gathering 'up country'. Despite his past war experience, he burdened himself with guns drawn by slow moving bullocks that had to be urged on with yells and curses, breaking necessary silence and the element of surprise. Loss of guns and extensive casualties who had to be left behind forced him to retreat to his camp where nevertheless he withstood a siege of nearly four weeks. With the loss of provisions, starvation was very close and reinforcements were needed.

News of their predicament was brought to Grahamstown by Richard King, a colonist who volunteered to ride through a wilderness alive with wild beasts and swam some 200 rivers in his ten-day 600-mile dash for help. A detachment of 100 Inniskillings under Captain G. A. Durnford arrived on the schooner *Conch*. With the 25th Regiment, who had also arrived by sea, Durnford scoured the bush and the Boers abandoned their siege. Captain Smith was made a Brevet Major for maintaining the post, hemmed in as he was with his wounded and without supplies, and the grateful British settlers presented him with a sword of honour.[11] In 1843 Natal was formally annexed to Great Britain with the result that many of the Boers continued their trek into the Transvaal and the Orange River Colony.

Of the 27th Foot who fought at Port Natal, most came from the islands of Lough Erne in Northern Ireland. Very Irish, 'it was only under peculiar circumstances that the 27th would enlist an Englishman at that date'. The Inniskillings were renowned for their physical size and, among other pioneering tasks, they helped to build the Anglican Cathedral in Durban. They played an important role in Natal.

Captain Durnford came from a military family whose name would become well known in Natal, Point Durnford being named after them. The 27th in later years also supplied a Governor in Natal, the gallant and eccentric Colonel Sir John MacLean, one of the Regiment's most famous Field Commanders. A Scot, MacLean had served in the Royal Scots and the Gordons, but had been a passionately 'honourary Irishman' from the time he joined the 27th in 1804. He had commanded the third battalion, 'the Young Inniskillings', in the Peninsular War where Wellington had shown faith in his military capabilities. By 1825 he was Major General and, on the death Sir Lowry Cole, was appointed to the colonelcy. Universally loved for his eccentricities, one anecdote showed his deep faith in the capabilities of his Regiment, but little acquaintance with the Bible. When he was dying in Natal in 1847 he was visited by a clergyman who read the story of the crucifixion of Jesus to the old colonel:

> At the conclusion of the reading Colonel MacLean said, 'Is that true, sir?', and upon the clergyman, greatly shocked, assuring him that it was true . . . Colonel MacLean directed him to read it again. He did so. The colonel laid for some time in silence, and then said, 'You assure me this is all true?' 'Oh, yes, your Excellency.' Colonel MacLean was again silent for some time, when he burst out with, 'Well, sir, by Jove! I should like to have been there with the light company of the Twenty-Seventh, and they would have never done it!'[12]

The Irish in the Ashanti War of 1873

In 1873 a new colonial war in Africa would bring Sir Garnet Wolseley to public acclaim. Before that happened, the assertive Wolseley, who never hesitated to curb his Irish tongue, was given the opportunity to do something more directly about his abiding interest in British Army reform. In 1871 he was appointed Assistant Adjutant General of the British Army and brought into the War 'Office by Edward Cardwell, the Secretary of State for War, who in the 1860s had begun to initiate sweeping reforms that would totally alter the army and be forever associated with his name. The Duke of Cambridge, cousin of the Queen and the very conservative Commander-in-Chief of the Army, was a formidable opponent and in his eyes the studious Wolseley was no more than an upstart, 'a radical Cardwellite'. In fairness, it should be noted that in his own way the Duke was also working for the welfare of the soldier. William Butler saw Wolseley as a 'thinking' soldier, 'a breed rare' among the higher-grade officers with whom Butler associated. It is not surprising that Wolseley passionately supported that most controversial bill, the abolition of purchase. Both he and Butler were unusual in entering the Army 'by way of a favour and rise to the rank of lieutenant-colonel through merit not cash'.[13] Wolseley also supported the short-service plan for soldiers that Roberts, his fellow Irishman and rival, was against. General Robert E. Lee's Civil War Confederate Army had shown Wolseley that, if properly trained, short-service men could be great soldiers. Education for the soldier was another subject dear to his heart. Keen and knowledgeable, he found favour among young officers and in the eyes of the public, but was labelled a revolutionary by the Court and the older conservative officers at Horse Guards.

When trouble arose on the Gold Coast of Africa in 1873, again with the

Ashantis, Wolseley, through Cardwell's influence, was appointed to command the military expedition against these powerful and fierce warriors in what was called the Second Ashanti War. An inland tribe, the Ashanti were continuing to raid their peaceful neighbours the coastal tribes, who were under British protection. With a large army, the Ashanti King Kofi Karikari had dared to invade the British Protectorate, disrupt lucrative British trade and, more important, threaten British prestige. Wolseley now with the local rank of Major General, at forty the youngest in the army, saw his command 'as a crusade' to bring King Kofi to terms and to restore Imperial stability on the Gold Coast. He gathered together his Ring, superior young men to be known as 'the Ashanti Ring', among them Captains Butler and McCalmont. Butler, still in the west of Canada, by chance read a newspaper report of Wolseley's force for the Gold Coast now gathering in London and sent off another of his arresting telegrams: 'Remember Butler. Will sail by first steamer'.[14] He joined Wolseley's headquarters at Cape Coast Castle in late October 1873. The brilliant Lieutenant Colonel George Pomeroy Colley, a newcomer to Wolseley's Ring, was a Protestant Anglo-Irishman born in Dublin to an old Kilkenny family dating back to the fifteenth century. He was an officer of great promise, a keen scholar who had passed out top of his form at Sandhurst and had graduated from the Staff College with the highest marks ever achieved.

The Gladstone Government had been reluctant to incur the expense of sending an army, moreover the Duke of Cambridge objected to sending white soldiers to the Gold Coast, a country known as the white man's grave because of its pestilential climate. Butler astutely describes (in his *Autobiography*, p. 148) Wolseley's unique situation:

> A general and some 30 – 40 officers . . . had landed on the most pestilential shore in the world for the avowed object of driving back a horde of 40,000 splendidly disciplined African savages who had invaded British territory. All the hopes founded upon the idea that the native races who lived under our protection in the forest lying between the sea and the River Prah – Fantis, Assims, Abras, and others – would rally under English leadership to do battle against their hereditary enemies the Ashantis has proved entirely fallacious.

Butler's words proved only too true, as Wolseley found when he and his officers tried to rally native tribes to fight. With a small force of British marines, sailors, 2nd West Indians and Hausas, Wolseley succeeded in a small victory against the Ashantis at a place called Esaman, a few miles west of Cape Coast Castle. His success was largely due to his own vigour and that of his staff officers as they threw themselves into the short-lived fight, but he soon realized the coastal tribes were none too eager to fight England's war. If Wolseley was to subdue King Kofi, 'a man of remarkable ability for an uneducated barbarian',[15] in his capital at Kumasi, he would need from England those first-rate regular battalions he had requested be held in readiness and now he pressured the War Office for them.

In the meantime, to offset the poor performance of the coastal tribes, early in November Wolseley told William Butler to go to the Kingdom of Akim in the north-east to seek the support of the chiefs whose warriors were considered the best fighters of the Gold Coast, longtime enemies of the Ashantis. It was said that if 'anyone could win the Akims to the English cause it was this fast-talking Irish raconteur'.[16] With his Akims Butler was to attack the flank of King Kofi's Ashanti army as it withdrew across the Prah River into their own territory. Like his Red River assignment, this independent command particularly appealed to Butler, but after three months in the jungle he was almost a beaten man, yet he would not give up. He had exhorted, bullied, cajoled and bribed his Akim chiefs and their warriors, who were more interested in drinking the rum he provided than in fighting Ashantis, until, at a place called Akina deep in Ashanti territory to where he had managed to harry them, Butler sadly watched his Akim warriors do an about-face and quietly leave. The day before Wolseley's decisive Battle of Amoaful the Akims had learned of Ashantis in the jungle ahead – it was time to go home.[17] Butler had underestimated their shrewdness and intelligence, a most humiliating failure; moreover, he had constantly battled fever. When he finally emerged from the jungle and returned to the coast he could barely walk, struck down by a virulent fever that left him emaciated and delirious for a long time. Brought onto the hospital ship he was pronounced dead, until an attendant recognized life signs. Butler lay in Netley Military Hospital in England for two months.

Around the end of the year some four thousand troops began arriving. Immediately Wolseley put Colley in charge of the transport, where he proved invaluable, scurrying about the country to find enough native carriers to carry the necessary food and ammunition. 'He brought order out of chaos,'[18] Wolseley would say later. During November Wolseley, very ill with fever and dysentery, languished in a hospital ship where he was attended to with great devotion by young Lieutenant (afterwards Major General Sir) Frederick Maurice who became his friend and biographer. As feared, disease became rampant. Captain McCalmont had already been invalided home to England with fever.

By late December Wolseley was on his way to Ashantiland heading for the boundary of the Prah River some seventy miles from the coast, his meticulous planning again in evidence. His troops, clad in uniforms of grey homespun he himself had designed, carried booklets carefully outlining all the hazards of disease and jungle warfare and marched on a road through the jungle built by Major Robert Home's engineers that boasted clean water and way stations for the sick. Wolseley's force crossed the Prah into Ashanti territory with great spirit, for delay was fatal in that climate, Ashantis confronting them all along the dense jungle route to the accompaniment of their drums and war songs, which struck terror into the hearts of all, especially the native levies. Had the poor bullets of the Ashanti been more effective, as Donald Featherstone points out, 'the expedition would very quickly have been without officers and reduced to minimal numbers'. Wolseley was successful in the fierce Battle of Amoaful where the Black Watch, bravely leading the attack, had the heaviest casualties. Their own Scots war cry and shrill swirl of the bagpipes rivalled anything the Ashantis produced.

To direct this battle Wolseley had set up his headquarters at the nearby village of Egginassie and when the Ashantis attacked at close range his 'calm, proud air' was reported by H. M. Stanley, the haughty explorer-journalist of the *New York Herald*. This war was extensively covered by journalists, some armed, and although Wolseley was no lover of war correspondents, at this battle he grudgingly admired how Stanley coolly kept firing at the encroaching Ashantis with great determination and skill. Within striking distance of Kumasi, his communication and supply lines severely harassed by Ashantis, Wolseley decided to make a dash for the capital and, four days later, on 4 February, riding a mule he entered the city with a Rifles escort. He was received ceremoniously by the Black Watch who were drawn up in the large market square by Brigadier General Alison who had advanced to take the city without a shot being fired.[19] King Kofi, his court and his army, had fled with most of the treasure and valuables. The arrival at Kumasi was an anticlimax to Wolseley's campaign but an incredible experience for his troops to see an African stronghold, the domain of a great African king. Wolseley's work was not finished, empowered as he was to seek a peace settlement with the king. Ultimatums through messengers were continually ignored until, after repeated warnings, Wolseley's engineers blew up King Kofi's great palace and put the torch to that barbarous city, where just hearing of the too-visible evidence of human sacrifice had greatly sickened Wolseley. Along the return route to the coast King Kofi's envoys caught up with Wolseley at a place called Fomana and there a peace treaty was signed in which Kofi agreed to Wolseley's terms, together with enough gold to mark his submission. Wolseley had redeemed British prestige.

Returning to England, he was celebrated as a national hero and promoted to full Major General. The Queen relented in her disapproval of her popular general, reviewed his little army at Windsor and invested him with the Order of St Michael and St George, and Knight Commander of the Bath (KCB). He received the thanks of Parliament and £25,000, as well as honorary degrees at Oxford. The term 'All Sir Garnet' was now on everybody's lips when referring to something well done – as the Ashanti Campaign surely was. This war had made Wolseley's reputation, undoubtedly aided by the penny papers, for he had been in the public eye since the beginning and now the press lionized him.

Captain Butler was not overlooked. He was promoted to Major, given a CB and was honoured to have the Queen visit him at Netley Hospital. The *Illustrated London News* of 4 April 1874 commended the Duke of Cambridge for his 'express mention' of Captain Butler in the House of Lords, a sure sign that 'Headquarters of our noble Army . . . appreciated Captain Butler . . . . We have been more inclined to dwell upon the case of this officer,' the paper continues, ' because the home staying and reading English public is indebted to him . . . for two delightful books *The Great Lone Land* and *The Wild North Land*, which we hope will not be his last narrative of adventurous travel.' But it was Wolseley's appraisal of him in his despatches that pleased Butler most:

> Captain Butler has not failed, but most successfully achieved the very object which I had in view when detaching him for the work he so cheerfully and skilfully undertook. He has effected a most important diversion in favour of the main body and has detained . . . one of the most powerful chiefs.[20]

Wolseley as Governor in Natal – 1875

A hero like Wolseley could not expect to remain unemployed for long in this century of the expanding British Empire. In February 1875, as the man of the hour, he was appointed to take temporary military and civil command in Natal as Governor and Chief Administrator, an appointment not to his liking as a soldier, but one he accepted when promised he would serve in South Africa only six months and that his military career would not be affected. When tensions arose between white colonists and black natives in Natal the Colonial Secretary Lord Carnarvon saw an opportunity to change Natal's constitution that could then lead to a confederation of Natal and Cape Colony and the two Boer republics of the Orange Free State and the Transvaal under a unified British Government. In this Wolseley wholeheartedly concurred, but the colonists had other ideas. For one thing the Natal government had only recently passed a resolution to bring in responsible government. In addition the Natal Legislative Assembly had passed certain repressive measures against natives, policies anathema to the Colonial Office. It was a delicate situation in which force was not to be used.

Heading again for South Africa with Wolseley was his staff drawn from the clever members of his Ring. Allowed to choose only four officers he did so from those who had been with him on the Gold Coast: two Irishmen, Colonel George Pomeroy Colley whom Wolseley always admired and Major William Butler. This time it was Butler, in County Kerry, where he was recuperating from his Ashanti fever, who received the telegram from Wolseley: 'Come at once and be ready to start with me for South Africa on Thursday'. Along with Major Henry Brackenbury and Captain Lord Gifford they charmed the citizens of Natal and were quickly nicknamed 'the brilliant staff'.[21]

In reforming the Natal administration Wolseley immediately gained control of the Executive Council by appointing his Ring officers, astutely giving sitting members leave of absence with full pay. To gain control of the larger Legislative Council Wolseley employed all his diplomatic skills and charm, hosting lavish parties, balls and entertainments at Government House, Pietermaritzburg, that quite dazzled the citizens. An amusing but unexpected result of this mad social whirl, much to Wolseley's annoyance, was that the wives and daughters found his officers irresistible and they responded, particularly Brackenbury and Gifford, who embarked on innumerable love-affairs. Butler does not seem to have been so smitten or at least he was more discreet. It is said that Wolseley himself was not oblivious to the charms of a pretty woman. However much he disliked such diplomatic and social manoeuvring, he was good at it, and the Legislative Councillors, overawed by his tremendous energy and drive, agreed to accept most of his reform programme which virtually amounted to reducing their longstanding 'Constitutional privileges'. Wolseley undoubtedly held strong imperialist views, but he also thought that the colonists could not govern themselves. In the Assembly a curious incident took place when Colley, about to speak in support of Wolseley's Bill to modify the Natal Constitution, seemed to demonstrate misgivings about it: he hesitated, stammered and could not go on, a painful experience for all to see. John Robinson of the *Natal Mercury* suggests an explanation: Colley 'being a high-minded Irishman with a strong sense of justice, the task of depriving a people of their political rights was "so repugnant to his instincts" that he found it impossible to perform his duty'.[22]

Butler also had misgivings. He was relieved when Wolseley, having set up a government, sent him and Colley to sound out the Boers on the idea of confederation, Colley to the Transvaal and later Butler to the Orange Free State. For Butler, a withdrawal into the wilderness as he had done in Canada was not only a rejuvenating experience, it was also an opportunity to be separated from Wolseley for a time. Although they admired each other always in public, they were quite apart in temperament and thought. Both career soldiers, these two Irishmen espoused different views of Empire and Imperialism, which can be seen in their attitudes towards the treatment of the native peoples, especially the Zulus. While Wolseley advocated annexation of Zululand and approved the Boer method of controlling Zulus by 'reducing them to manageable proportions', Butler thought 'the Zulus should be left to themselves'. It has been suggested that perhaps Butler's sympathy for the black man derived from his boyhood in Ireland, having witnessed peasant evictions by British authorities. A complex man, Butler went so far as to say he considered 'the white man's treatment of the South African native a crime against humanity'.[23]

Wolseley's six-month term finished and he left South Africa at the end of August 1875, glad to go. He had warned Lord Carnarvon that 'Natal was the weakest and most dangerous point in the Empire . . . with a powerful Zulu nation on its frontier'. If annexation of Zululand had taken place then, before King Cetshwayo could organize his army, in Joseph Lehmann's view, the ensuing disastrous war might have been avoided. Did Wolseley's policy of 1875 advocating annexation influence the British government to make decisions that resulted in the invasion of Zululand four years later?

The Irish in the Zulu War, 1879 – Disaster at Islandhlwana

A handful of Irishmen were prominent in the Zulu War that followed and two would win the Victoria Cross. This war, it was said, was provoked by the expansionist and Imperialist policies of Sir Bartle Frere, Governor of Cape Colony and High Commissioner for Native Affairs in South Africa. After the British annexed the Transvaal in 1877 they inherited the Boer border disputes with the Zulus, prompting Frere to prepare to annex Zululand. To justify an invasion Frere gave King Cetshwayo impossible ultimatums, among them that he should disband his Zulu army. To this he could not agree; he could not persuade his people to change the military caste system that Zulu society was built upon. When nothing was heard from Cetshwayo, on 11 January 1879 General Lord Chelmsford, Commander of Imperial Forces in South Africa, crossed the Buffalo River into Zululand at Rorke's Drift with his third or central column, determined to subdue the Zulus. His plan was to converge on Zululand from different points with four columns and push through to Ulundi,

Cetshwayo's capital, much as Wolseley had done at Kumasi in the Ashanti War.

Rorke's Drift was built by an Irishman named James Rorke, one of the early settlers in Natal; his father, an uncle and a cousin had served in the ranks of an Irish regiment that landed in 1821 at Mossel Bay, Cape Colony. As a civilian James served in the commissariat in the Seventh Kaffir War in 1846 and then found himself in Durban. Now married, he went inland and in 1849 acquired a large farm on the Natal side of the Buffalo River where he built a house and storehouse for his trading activities with the Zulus with whom he got along very well. At the same time he made a proper ford at the river which became known as Rorke's Drift. The farm and buildings were then taken over by a Swedish Missionary, the Reverend Otto Witt, who turned the storehouse into a stone chapel and added to Rorke's cattle pen a stout rectangular wall of breast-high stone.[24] Chelmsford comandeered these buildings as a hospital and supply base when planning his invasion. From his house Rorke had a view of the Nqutu Range in Zululand some ten miles away and one mountain in particular stood out, isolated and of an unusual shape resembling a great crouching sphinx. The Zulus called it Isandhlwana. It and Rorke's Drift, the sites of the first two battles of the Zulu War, became famous in South Africa and Britain.

By 21 January Major Cornelius Francis Clery had laid out a camp in the shadow of the steep rocky hill of Isandhlwana for Colonel Richard Glynn's third column. Clery, Glynn's principal staff officer, was born in Dublin, the son of an Irish wine merchant. A graduate of Sandhurst and the Staff College, he had been a professor of tactics, producing the book *Minor Tactics,* which was used by the British Army for years. A bachelor and a dandy described as 'a queer-looking bloke with a puzzle beard and blue whiskers', he was 'more of a student of war than a warrior', always on staff.[25] Clery was one of a handful of Imperial officers to survive the slaughter at Islandhlwana.

Colonel Anthony William Durnford was not so fortunate. His uncle was that Captain G. A. Durnford of the 27th Foot who in 1842 had landed reinforcements for the beleaguered Captain Smith at Port Natal. Durnford was born in Ireland into a British Army family who had several members in service. After attending the Royal Military Academy at Woolwich he was gazetted Second Lieutenant in the Royal Engineers in which his father, a Captain, later became Major General. His brother Edward, a retired Colonel, had been a captain in the Royal Marine Artillery. Anthony Durnford saw service in Ceylon as Assistant Commissioner of Roads and Civil Engineer, followed by various postings in Malta, England and Gibraltar. His was a somewhat unfulfilled career and he arrived in Cape Town 'a forty-one year old captain who had never seen active service'. His majority soon followed and he was posted to Natal where he was unfortunately involved in a military blunder connected with the Langalibalele rebellion in the Bushman's River Pass affair. He fought bravely and acquitted himself well, losing the use of an arm, but he gained a reputation for being reckless and impulsive, and his criticism of all but three Natal Volunteers (who had been killed) at Bushman's River Pass brought strong condemnation of him in Natal society that would have repercussions in the future. Retaining his standing in the army, he was promoted Lieutenant Colonel and appointed Assistant Colonial Engineer at Pietermaritzburg in Natal.[26] Durnford has a unique place at Isandhlwana: it was upon him that most blame was laid for that great disaster.

Soon after Lord Chelmsford arrived in Natal to gather his forces Durnford proposed to him that he himself raise some 7,000 Natal Kaffirs with European officers and NCOs. Chelmsford, very pleased, originally appointed Durnford to overall command of the second column, but Chelmsford's staff objected that Durnford was too young to command such a large force, and when he demonstrated his too independent-minded spirit he was reprimanded by Chelmsford and his force was broken up. He was ordered to join Colonel Glynn's third column encamped at Rorke's Drift with the Natal Native Horse (NNH) of about 250 men, and three companies of the 1/1st Natal Native Contingent (NNC) and the small Rocket Battery. Durnford's 'chagrin' at losing his independent command can be imagined; he was a good soldier and more-over he understood and sympathized with his Natal Kaffirs, many of whom knew him from his time in Natal.

The Ulsterman George Hamilton-Browne was *not* so sympathetic to the native contingent. Known as 'Maori Browne' from his service in the Maori wars of the 1860s, if anyone fitted the description of a tough Irish mercenary, it was Hamilton-Browne. A hard-bitten soldier of fortune, he had served as a driver in the Royal Horse Artillery, in the Papal Zouaves, and had commanded irregular soldiers in the Kaffir War. Now he was appointed to command 1st Battalion of Rupert Lonsdale's 3rd Regiment of the NNC, and 'he ruined it'. Like Durnford, he had experi-ence in bush warfare, but unlike him Hamilton-Browne had 'little use for his sixty non-commissioned officers and absolutely none for the 1,200 natives under his command whom he consistently referred to as "niggers"'.[27] He survived the Battle of Isandhlwana out of pure good fortune only because he and his battalion, sent out to search for Zulus, were not in the camp on that fatal day, 22 January.

After that terrible defeat at Islandhlwana Queen Victoria spoke for an appalled British nation when she exclaimed in her diary: 'How this could happen we cannot yet imagine'. How 'savages' could have out-manoeuvred General Lord Chelmsford and 'trampled to death' Imperial troops, veteran soldiers, was a question needing an answer. Leading Zulu chief Mehlokazulu answered the question after the war: 'If the English had stuck together more than they did they would have beaten us . . . we were all astonished at the way they fought'.[28] Lord Chelmsford's forces were indeed divided. When Durnford, still encamped near Rorke's Drift, was ordered to bring his troops to the camp at Islandhlwana his instruc-tions included information that Chelmsford would be moving out to attack some Zulus about ten miles away. Chelmsford duly left with part of his force, alerted by Major Dartnell, sent out on patrol, who requested reinforcements, thinking he had located the main Zulu impi. The camp at Isandhlwana was left unfortified, not even laagered, and for this Chelmsford was later greatly criticized. His defence was that the camp was only a temporary one, his aim was to search out quickly the Zulu army and attack it. His orders to Brevet Lieutenant Colonel Henry Pulleine of the 1/24th Foot were to remain in the camp and defend it, but Durnford's orders were vague as to what he should do on his arrival at the camp mid-morning. As an officer senior in rank to Pulleine, did Durnford therefore inherit Colonel Pulleine's order to stay in the camp? Military historians have argued this point ever since. Ian Knight considers Durnford felt he was there to support Chelmsford's force, not to reinforce Pulleine, and Donald Morris thinks Durnford 'plainly felt that if Pulleine remained in the camp with his original force, the spirit of the General's orders would be met'.

When Durnford and his forces rode out to look for Chelmsford, left in the camp under Pulleine, according to Ian Knight, were six companies of his 24th Foot, largely a Welsh regiment, four companies of the 3rd NNC, a hundred mounted men of detachments of South Africans and about a hundred soldiers left behind by Chelmsford, in all some 1,700, of whom 800 were white, 900 black. Isandhlwana was a traumatic event for the old Imperial 24th Foot, as it was for the Zulus when they discovered, with awe, that the 24th's regimental badge, a recumbent sphinx, eerily repli-cated the shape of the hill of Isandhlwana where they were slaughtered. Before Durnford set out he sent ahead troopers under Lieutenants Raw and Roberts of the NNH to scout the plateau. Raw's men spotted a few Zulus driving cattle up a slope who then disappeared. Following in pursuit, one trooper suddenly came to the edge of a wide deep ravine and nearly fell in. To his amazement he saw, seated on the floor of the ravine and all up the rising sides, over 20,000 Zulus. In a campaign that has gripped the imagination there was probably a no more electrifying moment: the main Zulu impi had been found. The Zulus understood what the sight of that lone trooper meant and 'the entire host lumbered to its feet . . . and started to clamber out of the ravine as the horseman, shouting the alarm, turned and fled down towards his companions'.[29] From a distance Captain George Shepstone, son of the Minister of Native Affairs in Natal and on Durnford's staff, seeing the fleeing horseman followed by black figures on the run, understood what was happening. He ordered that Durnford be found while he raced to bring the news to Isandhlwana camp where, breathlessly, he informed Colonel Pulleine, who already had reports of Zulus on the plain. Pulleine sounded the alarm, but he seems not to have realized that the huge Zulu army was heading for his camp and, instead of grouping the camp's defenders into a tight mass on favourable ground, he scattered them around the area even more. By 2.30pm the fearful fighting was over and no one who remained in camp was left alive.

Durnford, far out on the plain and still searching for Lord Chelmsford, had just received word from Trooper Whitelaw of the oncoming impi. He glanced up to the rim of the plateau and saw a black mass of Zulus on the heights, and as he watched they swept down onto the plain. Durnford quickly turned back, Zulus were already between his mounted men and the left of the camp, and with his native horsemen he rode hard for a big donga (a ditch or watercourse some twenty yards wide and three to four feet deep) where he dismounted, deciding to make a stand against the Zulu horde. Some Newcastle Mounted Riflemen joined him there. It is reported that Durnford, his useless arm tucked into his tunic, was laughing and encouraging his men to fire as he strode up and down the donga. Ammunition soon ran out, which seemed to have happened everywhere in this battle, and Durnford sent riders back to get what they could, but not finding their own ammunition wagon appealed to the quartermasters of the 24th Foot, who, it was said, jealously guarding their supplies, would not share them out. Durnford then ordered his Natal Native Horse to fall back towards the camp and they joined the rest of the mounted men in the mouth of the saddle, but it was impossible to form 'a solid position beneath the mountain' where scattered groups tried to make a stand. Durnford excused his men of the NNH, who had fought well, and they began to retreat on the road to Rorke's Drift. Durnford was last seen 'in front of the saddle' where, with some seventy men who still had ammunition, he made a final hopeless stand. A Zulu who was there remembered 'the tall figure that cried "Fire" time and again'. Finally, ammunition gone, they had to resort to the bayonet until, overwhelmed by a strong Zulu charge, they all died. Durnford's body was found later in May on that field of ghastly mutilated bodies identified by his 'long drooping moustache' by Captain Theophilus Shepstone. Archibald Forbes, the renowned war correspondent of the *Daily News* also there, writes: 'Durnford had died hard, a central figure of a knot of brave men who had fought it out around their chief to the bitter end'.[30]

Near Durnford's body was that of another Irishman, the Honourable Standish William Prendergast Vereker, third son of Viscount Gort in the Irish peerage and only twenty-five years old. As a third son young Vereker had been at loose ends for a career and in time tried his luck in South Africa. He gained experience in the British Army as a trooper in the Frontier Light Horse in Wolseley's campaign against Sekukuni in the Transvaal. After this he was offered and accepted a commission in the 3rd Regiment of the NNC at the time Durnford was given command of the 1st Regiment, and this brought him to the Battle of Isandhlwana. After fighting with Lieutenant Raw's mounted natives through the carnage of the upper camp they started to leave, but a dismounted Natal Kaffir rushed at Vereker and claimed the horse he was riding as his; in the mêlée his horse was grabbed by Raw to replace Vereker's lost mount. Vereker courteously dismounted and handed the horse over to the Kaffir, an act that cost him his life.[31]

Hamilton-Browne, who survived that dreadful day, had the dubious honour of being 'the only man to witness the attack on the camp from the plain'. When he heard guns firing and saw Zulus advancing in large numbers who were between himself and the camp, he realized that the fighting was now in the camp itself. He repeatedly sent messages back to the elusive Lord Chelmsford, but when he happened to meet him on the latter's way back to see for himself, Hamilton-Browne's warning that the camp was lost was still not believed, so 'little regard' had Chelmsford for this Irish mercenary.[32]

Only some fifty-five Europeans and perhaps three hundred Natal Kaffirs survived, scattered throughout the countryside. Such was the slaughter that many brave deeds could not be verified, but later two Victoria Crosses were awarded posthumously to the Anglo-Irishman Lieutenant Nevill Josiah Aylmer Coghill and Lieutenant and Adjutant Teignmouth Melvill, both of the 1st/24th Foot. They lost their lives attempting to save the Queen's Colour of the regiment, that important symbol, together with the Regimental Colour, of the allegiance soldiers give to their regiment and to their country. Also recognized in Coghill's award was his heroic attempt to save his brother officer's life.

Nevill Coghill was the son of Sir Joscelyn Coghill, Bart. of Drumcondra, County Dublin, and Castletownshend, County Cork, a talented Anglo-Irish family of scholars, churchmen and military men. His grandfather was an admiral, an uncle was in the Buffs, and his cousin was Edith Somerville of the famous Anglo-Irish writing team of Somerville and Ross. At the time of the battle Coghill was acting as an extra ADC and mounted staff officer to Colonel Glynn. Earlier in January he had severely wrenched his knee when his horse slipped and he could barely stand, but he would not leave his duties to be hospitalized at Rorke's Drift, an example of the calibre of those officers. To Melvill, in the last hours when the battle raged all around the tents in the camp at Isandhlwana, was entrusted the Queen's Colour of the 1st/24th by Colonel Pulleine who ordered him to take it away to a place of safety. Melvill rode out with the awkwardly encased Colour over his saddle and joined the streaming refugees who were heading for the Buffalo River which would take them into Natal. Hotly pursued by Zulus, Coghill joined him, barely remaining mounted because of his knee. One nineteenth century dramatic painting celebrating their bravery pictures their wild ride through a group of attacking Zulus. Coghill managed to reach and cross the river; his blue patrol jacket may have deterred Zulu fire as Cetshwayo, it is said, told his Zulus to aim particularly at red-jacketed soldiers. Melvill, in his red tunic, was continually harassed by Zulus who crowded him on every side. Exhausted and hampered by the heavy case of the Colour, he got into the river, but his horse sank immediately. Still carrying the Colour, he was swept down the rough stream bouncing against rocks. Lieutenant Higginson, adjutant of the 2nd/3rd NNC, also in the river, tried to help but could not. Coghill, already on the Natal shore, saw that Melvill was in trouble, struggling with the Queen's Colour, and turned his horse back to the river only to have it shot by a Zulu and he himself thrown into the water. Nevertheless, he plunged forward, despite his injured leg, and hauled Melvill to shore, but the latter had been unable to retain his hold on the Colour and it swept away downstream. They then struggled up the slope supporting each other, Coghill walking with difficulty. Zulus soon caught up with them as they sheltered against a large rock where they were killed. Coghill could have escaped, but refused to leave a fellow officer in distress, nor could he not try to rescue the Queen's Colour. Later in February a scouting party sent out to search for bodies found Coghill and Melvill near Fugitive's Drift, and there where they died the Reverend George Smith, Chaplain from Rorke's Drift, read a burial service.

The *Gazette* of 2 May 1879 stated that Lieutenants Coghill and Melvill would have been recommended for the Victoria Cross had they survived. There was no authority for posthumous awards of the VC in 1879. When the regulations changed in 1907, the first posthumously awarded VCs were presented to the families of these two officers. Sir Bartle Frere, in whose service Coghill had been an aide, erected a large stone cross and tablet where the two soldiers died,[33] and a memorial window to Lieutenant

1. Ulster Protestant paramilitary mural in Belfast exploiting the Cuchulainn myth. *Courtesy of Professor Keith Jeffrey, University of Ulster.* A similar mural was seen by the author in Belfast.

2. Brigadier General the Hon Robert Monckton, who was with Wolfe at Quebec in 1759. *Engraving by Miller after Thomas Hudson; National Archives of Canada/C-046681.*

3. Lieutenant Colonel Sir Guy Carleton, Wolfe's QMG at Quebec. *Engraving by Ritchie, Alexander Hay/National Archives of Canada/C-006150.*

4. Lieutenant General Sir Eyre Coote con-
solidated British control over southern
India in the 18th century.
British Library, India Office, London.

5. Arthur Wellesley, 1st Duke of Wellington,
Commander-in-Chief of the Allied
Armies in the Peninsular War.
Illustrated London News Picture Library.

6. James FitzGibbon, former Lieutenant of
the 49th Foot and hero of Beaver Dam
in the War of 1812, in old age.
National Archives of Canada/C-105846.

7. British Army Barracks at Fermoy, typical of barracks throughout Ireland.

W.A. Fitzgerald photograph/Author's Collection.

8. Major General Sir Hugh Gough, conqueror of the Punjab.

National Army Museum.

9. Major General Sir Charles Napier, conqueror of Sind, in India in the 1840s.

National Army Museum.

10. *(above left)* General Sir
    George de Lacy Evans,
    commanded the 2nd
    Division in the Crimea.
    National Army Museum.

11. *(above)* Captain Louis
    Edward Nolan, 15th
    Hussars.
    *Illustrated London News
    Picture Library.*

12. *(left)* Corporal Thomas
    Faughnan, 17th Foot.
    *Illustration from his auto-
    biography 1882.*

13. William Howard Russell, *Times* Correspondent in the Crimea.

Victoria and Albert Museum.

14. Brigadier General Henry Lawrence, Resident at Lucknow, Indian Mutiny, 1857. *John Young Collection.*

16. Lieutenant Nevill Coghill, VC (posthumous) 24th Foot, Isandhlwana, South Africa, 1879. *John Young Collection.*

15. Thomas Henry Kavanagh, VC, a civilian clerk, hero at Lucknow, Indian Mutiny. *Victoria and Albert Museum.*

17. Surgeon Major James Reynolds, VC, Rorke's Drift, South Africa.
    John Young Collection.

18. General Sir Garnet Wolseley, Supreme Commander in South Africa after Isandhlwana. *James Ashfield: National Archives of Canada/C009993.*

19. General Sir William Butler, Commander-in-Chief of the British Army just prior to the Anglo-Boer War. *National Archives of Canada/C-021287.*

20. Brigadier General Fitzroy Hart, Commander 5th (Irish) Brigade, Anglo-Boer War. *John Young Collection.*

21. Lieutenant General Cornelius Francis Clery, Commander 2nd Infantry Division, Anglo-Boer War. *John Young Collection.*

22. Field Marshal Lord Roberts, VC, Commander of the British Army in South Africa from 1900. *By kind permission of the Royal Munster Fusiliers Regimental Association.*

23. (*above left*) Lieutenant General Sir Thomas Kelly-Kenny, Commander, 6th (Infantry) Division, Anglo-Boer War.
By kind permission of the Queen's Royal Surrey Regiment Museum.

24. (*above*) Field Marshal Sir John French, Commander of the British Expeditionary Force 1914.
John Young Collection.

25. (*left:*) Lieutenant General Sir Bryan Mahon, Commander 10th (Irish) Division.
From Bryan Cooper's *The Tenth (Irish) Divison in Gallipoli (1918)*.

26. Lance Corporal Michael O'Leary, VC, 1st Battalion Irish Guards, Cuinchy, France
1915. *Painting by Lady Butler, courtesy of the Irish Guards.*

27. *(above left:)* Major Paul Charrier, 2nd Royal Munster Fusiliers, killed in the Retreat from Mons 1914.
    By kind permission of the Royal Munster Fusiliers Regimental Association.

28. *(above:)* Corporal William Cosgrove, VC, 1st Royal Muster Fusiliers, Gallipoli 1915.
    By kind permission of the Royal Munster Fusiliers Association.

29. *(left:)* Lieutenant (later Captain) Henry Desmond O'Hara, DSO, 1st Royal Dublin Fusiliers, killed Gallipoli 1915. From *Our Heroes, Mons to the Somme, 1916,* see also *The Irish Sword, Vol. XVIII, #73, 1992.*

30. Temporary Lieutenant Joseph Bagnall Lee, 6th Royal Munster Fusiliers, killed at Gallipoli 1915. *By kind permission of his grand-nephew Michael Lee.*

31. Private William McFadzean, VC, 14th Royal Irish Rifles, killed 1 July 1916, on the Somme. *By kind permission of his nephew Billy McFadzean.*

32. Lieutenant Tom Kettle of the 9th Royal Dublin Fusiliers, pictured on the far right as a young man with the Malahide cricket team. Charlie Adams, the tall young man on the far left, became a 2nd Lieutenant in the Royal Dublin Fusiliers and was taken prisoner in 1916. Unlike Tom, he survived the war.

Photo by kind permission of Norman Adams, c/o The Royal Dublin Fusiliers Association.

33. Lieutenant Colonel F. Percy Crozier, Commanding Officer of the 9th Royal Irish Rifles 1916, from his *Impressions and Recollections (1930).*

34. Lieutenant John Vincent Holland won his VC at Guillemont in France in 1916 while serving with the 7th Battalion, Prince of Wales Leinster Regiment.
Courtesy of the Leinster Regimental Association.

35. Private Thomas Hughes receives his VC from King George V. He won it at Guillemont in France in 1916 with the Connaught Rangers.
Courtesy of Mr Danny Tiernan, Connaught Rangers Regimental Association.

36. Lance Corporal Francis Ledwidge, 1st Inniskilling Fusiliers, Irish poet, killed July 1917, Ypres Salient. *By kind permission of Major (Ret'd) J.M. Dunlop, Curator, The Inniskillings Museum.*

37. Captain Willie Redmond, MP, 6th Royal Irish Regiment, killed at Messines in 1917.

38. Regimental
    Sergeant Major
    John Ring, 2nd
    Royal Munster
    Fusiliers.
    *By kind
    permission of the
    Royal Munster
    Fusiliers
    Association.*

39. General Sir
    Hubert
    Gough,
    Commander
    Fifth Army.
    *Imperial War
    Museum.*

Coghill and his father, Sir Joscelyn Coghill, Bart., can be seen in the Parish Church of St Barrahane, Castletownshend, County Cork. To end the story, the tattered Queen's Colour of the 1st/24th was found at the same time as the bodies of Melvill and Coghill, discovered in a shallow part of the river. In a very emotional formal ceremony it was returned to Colonel Glynn at Helpmakaar (near Rorke's Drift).

Durnford, only too quickly, was made the scapegoat for the disaster at Isandhlwana; it was claimed he left the camp and thus divided the force for its defence. The Natal Volunteers, who remembered Durnford's military blunder of a few years before and his criticism of them at that time, also blamed him. He was already a controversial figure in Natal colonial society, where, despite his long estrangement from his wife in England, his reputation was not helped by his liaison with Frances Colenso, daughter of the famous Bishop Colenso of Natal, nor by the Bishop's sympathy for native Africans which coincided with Durnford's own.[34] Frances Colenso sought help from Durnford's brother Edward and together they devoted their efforts to clearing his name. A Court of Enquiry produced no opinion.

The Defence of Rorke's Drift

> It is something to be able to know that the prowess of Waterloo and of Inkerman is still present in the race . . . .
>
> *The Natal Witness*, Pietermaritzburg,
> 28 January 1879

The magnificent defence of Rorke's Drift is one of the British Army's great epic actions. Occurring over the night of 22/23 January, immediately after the disaster at Isandhlwana, the heroic stand of so few did much to redeem the earlier defeat and eleven VCs were won, the most for any single battle in British military history. One was awarded to an Irishman, the thirty-five-year-old Surgeon-Major James Henry Reynolds born at Kingstown, County Dublin. Educated at Trinity College, Reynolds entered the Army Medical Corps as an Assistant Surgeon, then was promoted to Surgeon after service in India. At Rorke's Drift he was in charge of the little makeshift hospital housing thirty-three patients. His VC citation recounts how he gave constant attention to the wounded when under fire, and his bravery when he voluntarily conveyed ammunition to the defenders of the hospital exposing himself to cross-fire. At one point he dragged James Dalton, the brave Acting Assistant Commissary Officer, out of the line to dress his wounds. Mentioned in despatches was James Dunn, a twenty-six-year-old Irishman and Senior Commissariat Officer at Rorke's Drift, who had already gained experience on the Cape frontier and in the Transvaal.[35]

By mid-afternoon of 22 January news began to come in that the camp at Isandhlwana had been annihilated and that some four thousand Zulus were advancing on the run towards Rorke's Drift. This group was under Cetshwayo's 'aggressive' brother Dabulamanzi, who, not having been at Isandhlwana, now appeared in Natal against Cetshwayo's orders wanting a share of the action and possibly glory, not to mention loot. Immediately Lieutenant James Chard of the Royal Engineers took command as senior officer and, together with Lieutenant Gonville Bromhead of 'B' Company of the 2/24th Foot, hastily organized primitive defences, loop-holing the commissariat and hospital and connecting the buildings by constructing walls of mealie bags and biscuit boxes. The small garrison of some one hundred and thirty-nine men of all ranks included Bromhead's 'B' Company, three civilians as commissariat officers, the surgeon and the missionary, the Reverend George Smith. Even the patients in the hospital were issued with rifles and some manned the barricades. For twelve hours wave after wave of nearly four thousand ferocious and brave Zulus relentlessly attacked them. In the early morning hours, as the garrison watched fearfully, Zulus appeared again but amazingly they soon disappeared: so many Zulus had been killed, wounded or were exhausted, and as one historian astutely observes, all were hungry! Fifteen of the garrison had been killed, two were dying, twelve badly wounded and the rest had minor injuries.[36]

Wolseley was in Cyprus as soldier/administrator and First High Commissioner, an unsatisfactory assignment of less than a year, when in February 1879 news came of General Lord Chelmsford's invasion into Zululand and the defeat of the British Army at Isandhlwana. He immediately wrote to the Duke of Cambridge tentatively voicing his concern to be where the action was: 'as I know the people and the country well, I think I might be of use', a rather diffident tone considering how keen he was to be sent to South Africa. The Duke was hardly the best person to write to in light of how Wolseley had upset both the Duke and the conservatives at Horse Guards over army reforms. Back in England Wolseley learned that, over the Duke's objections, he was appointed Supreme Commander of Her Majesty's Forces in South Africa and High Commissioner for South-East Africa with the local rank of general. Lord Chelmsford was to remain as Second in Command. Queen Victoria also objected to his appointment, favouring Lord Chelmsford over this pushy radical. Prime Minister Disraeli, it is said, tried to mollify her: 'It is quite true that Wolseley is an egotist and a braggart. So was Nelson . . . Men of action . . . when eminently successful in early life are generally boastful and full of themselves.' The British public, however, applauded Wolseley's appointment. Their popular hero would retrieve the honour of the British Army and the phrase 'All Sir Garnet' was still heard everywhere. Indeed *Punch* went further and compared Wolseley to that other great Irishman, Wellesley (Duke of Wellington):

> When Wolseley's mentioned Wellesley's brought to mind;
> Two men, two names, of answerable kind:
> Call to the front, like Wellesley, good at need,
> Go, Wolseley, and like Wellesley, greatly speed.[37]

Wolseley in South Africa, 1879

Wolseley reached Durban at the end of June 1879, a good five months after the British Army's defeat at Isandhlwana and the heroic stand at Rorke's Drift. His presence was thoroughly resented by Lord Chelmsford, who, with a much larger army, was proceeding a second time against the Zulus and was only a few miles from their capital of Ulundi, determined to redeem his military reputation and without the interference of his new commander. He ignored Wolseley's orders, feigning ignorance that he had been demoted and as usual sent in his reports to the War Office in London. On 4 July, at Ulundi, Chelmsford defeated the Zulus who hopelessly but bravely fought against the British square. In thirty minutes the battle was over and Cetshwayo fled. Chelmsford ordered Ulundi burned, then immediately retired and departed for the coast to sail for home, rightly claiming he had received no directives from Wolseley as to what to do after a victory. Wolseley heard the news of the victory of Ulundi not from Lord Chelmsford but from Archibald Forbes, the war correspondent for the *Daily News*. Nevertheless he wired his congratulations to Chelmsford and when they briefly met on Chelmford's way to the coast there were no hard words,[38] but Wolseley understood very well that a conservative officer like Lord Chelmsford was not interested in new tactics or weaponry, so it is not surprising that his military opinion was that Chelmsford should not command troops in action again.

A distinguished Anglo-Irishman with Lord Chelmsford's force was Captain Lord William de la Poer Beresford. He was the third son of the 4th Marquess of Waterford, the aristocratic Irish family who gave members to the Protestant Church and the British forces. Although born in Northern Ireland in the quaint village of Mullaghbrach where his father was a Church of Ireland rector until assuming his title, Lord William always thought of Curraghmore, the imposing family seat in Waterford, as home. He was commissioned in the 9th Lancers where a contemporary was Hugh McCalmont of Wolseley's Ring and the two young men became noted racing sportsmen, common in their Anglo-Irish world. Hearing of the Zulu War, Captain Lord William took leave from his duties as ADC to the Viceroy in India and joined Colonel Redvers Buller as his staff officer. Buller was in command of all mounted volunteers in South Africa. On 3 July, before the Battle of Ulundi, Beresford won the VC in the midst of a sudden Zulu attack when he rescued Sergeant Fitzmaurice of the lst/24th Foot, who was serving as mounted infantry. Beresford, seeing Fitzmaurice wounded, dazed and fallen from his wounded horse, rode forward and with great difficulty, as Fitzmaurice was a huge man, pulled him up on his own horse and together with Sergeant Edmund O'Toole of the Frontier Light Horse who had come to their aid, they beat off with sabre and carbine a large group of charging Zulus. Alternately firing and retreating, they managed to get to the camp at the river. The next day in an action in keeping with his sporting spirit, Beresford gained his long-standing title 'Ulundi Beresford' when, in a race among Buller's officers to be first man into Ulundi, he galloped ahead, jumped a thorn barricade that protected Cetshwayo's big kraal and landed among the huts.[39]

It remained for Wolseley to attend to the mopping-up and capture of King Cetshwayo who, at the end of August after a long chase when many tired patrols had been sent out repeatedly, was finally cornered and captured. Wolseley's important captive was not the cruel-looking savage that was expected as head of his ferocious Zulu army, but a tall muscular man of great dignity with an intelligent face. Wolseley treated him as an outlaw rather than as a deposed king, and ignored then harangued him for his sins before he sent him to jail in Cape Town. This was contrary to what the *Illustrated London News* of 20 September expected: 'We trust he will be kindly and honourably treated as prisoner of war (or prisoner of state) for he is neither a rebel nor in any way a criminal, and has bravely defended his own country as he had a right to do against a foreign invasion.'

William Butler was also in total sympathy with King Cetshwayo's plight, to be expected considering his views. On hearing of the Zulu War, Butler had offered his services in South Africa and was appointed Quartermaster General in February 1879 and then as Assistant Adjutant General at Durban. Before leaving Natal he heard that Cetshwayo, imprisoned in Cape Town, was longing for the green rush mats he was used to sleeping on all his life. Butler personally brought some to him by ship. 'The once great king wept at sight of the rushes. "Say to him he has brought sleep to me," he told the interpreter . . . Butler was close to tears too. "It was the same as putting a bit of green sod into the cage of a lark," he said.'[40] This is but another example of Wolseley's and Butler's differing views of the treatment of native peoples. The Zulu War was not popular in England and when King Cetshwayo was brought there he was received not only with delighted curiosity by admiring crowds, but also with kindness by the Queen.

Wolseley as High Commissioner had then to proceed with the pacification of Zululand, not a task he enjoyed, nor, some think, one he was fitted for. His settlement of dividing Zululand into thirteen chieftaincies to be under British suzerainty and the very loose control of a Resident was disastrous, however much the settlement was seen by some to be a 'Zululand for the Zulus'. Major General Sir F. Maurice would later kindly write that Wolseley at this time 'seemed out of touch with his subject and out of sympathy with his surroundings'. What Wolseley needed, writes Maurice, was the invaluable assistance of Colonel George Pomeroy Colley, the Anglo-Irishman on whom Wolseley had greatly relied in his Ashanti campaign. But Colley was in India as Lord Lytton's military adviser, needed at the time of the death of Sir Louis Cavagnari in Kabul, and Wolseley had reluctantly authorized him to go.[41]

Wolseley still had to deal with the restless Boers who were unreconciled to the annexation of the Transvaal and again pressing for independence. A strong hand was needed to emphasize the Imperial directives and halt the Boer drift into open rebellion and in September 1879 Wolseley as High Commissioner proceeded to the Transvaal. But first he organized a Transvaal Field Force for a punitive expedition to subdue Chief Sekukuni and his warring Bapedi tribe in the north-west Transvaal who were defiantly raiding and massacring Boer and Briton alike. It was a little campaign that gave Wolseley the opportunity to redress his disappointment in not having more direct involvement to end the Zulu War. Sekukuni's mountain stronghold was successfully taken at the end of November in a hard fight in which several of Wolseley's officers were casualties, including Maurice, who 'continued to dash up the mountain with a bullet in him'. The Queen and the government were extremely pleased and sent congratulatory telegrams to Wolseley. The rebellious Boers were impressed with his success with Sekukuni. Wolseley reiterated to them that annexation of the Transvaal was 'irrevocable', and by April 1880 the more moderate of the Boers convinced the hot-heads that open rebellion was not feasible at this time. The presence of Wolseley's redcoats and their own lack of ammunition were undoubtedly factors: Wait until the High Commissioner and his redcoats went home was the advice given by a Boer newspaper.[42] Their turn to revolt would come.

Wolseley returned to England in May, again greeted as a hero by the press and the public who had been constantly informed of his achievements by many lively accounts in the penny papers. He was 'Our Only General' and in the Gilbert & Sullivan musical *Pirates of Penzance* he became for them 'the very model of a modern Major General', a tune everyone was soon singing. Wolseley himself took great delight in this. He was pleased with his successes in South Africa: had he not rescued the honour of the British Empire, captured two native kings, and brought peace to the Transvaal ? This last accomplishment was not to last, but in the meantime he was 'master of the small war' and at the height of his popularity. He had received no government honours for his services in Cyprus or South Africa. Hoping for a peerage, he was instead gazetted the Grand Cross of the Order of the Bath (GCB). Before leaving South Africa he had learned he would be appointed Quartermaster General, a post that would allow him to continue with army reforms, albeit accompanied by the constant struggle with the Duke of Cambridge and the War Office. Wolseley helped to bring about important changes in the army in the territorial system and the abolition of flogging and improvements in pay, food and housing. The conservatives continued to look on him as a radical, which he was not. Rather he was 'a modernizing force in an age where such influences were all too rare' and, as General Sir Evelyn Wood, who had himself introduced reforms when he commanded the army's training centre at Aldershot said, Wolseley 'did more to improve the fighting efficiency of the army than any soldier I have met'. This included encouraging officers to study their profession and to read; his own love of reading, he claimed, came from his Irish mother.[43]

The First Anglo-Boer War – The Battle of Majuba Hill – 1881 and Sir George Colley

> He needs no tears who in the van
> And forefront of the fight
> Met death as should a gentleman
> Upon Majuba's height.
>
> Lines on General Sir George Colley's death
> Cloete, Stuart, *Against These Three*,
> Boston, 1945, p. 131

When Wolseley returned home, on his recommendation the Anglo-Irishman Major General Sir George Pomeroy Colley, his esteemed friend and one of the most gifted of his 'Ring', was appointed as Governor of Natal, High Commissioner for South-East Africa and Commander-in-Chief of the army. Seemingly 'the epitome of the successful professional general', Colley's death at Majuba Hill on the Natal-Transvaal border on 27 February 1881, together with the defeat of the British Army, shocked the British public. He and his well-trained regulars of Imperial regiments underestimated the enemy and were defeated by a few raggle-taggle Boers and mostly farm boys at that.

The Boers had not been reconciled to Wolseley's proclamation; they merely bided their time until 16 December when, at Paardekraal near Pretoria, they declared the independence of the Transvaal as a republic. Four days later they openly defied troops of the British Army when Lieutenant Colonel Philip Anstruther with some 250 men of the 94th Foot (shortly to become 2nd Battalion Connaught Rangers), with their band playing unconcernedly, approached Bronkhorstspruit on their way to Pretoria. A horseman rode up with a message to Anstruther to surrender immediately: the Transvaal was now a republic and the movement of foreign troops was forbidden. He refused the ultimatum and the Boers, firing from concealed positions, killed or wounded all the officers and about two out of three non-commissioned officers and men. Irish soldiers thus experienced the first shots of the Transvaal or First Anglo-Boer War. This first clash between Boer and Briton demonstrated what Colley and the British Army would have to contend with.

Soon Boers were besieging British garrisons throughout the Transvaal. Colley began to gather a Natal Field Force to relieve them, a mixed bag of troops about eleven hundred strong, companies of young and short-service soldiers with many seasoned veterans, six guns, but very weak in mounted troops. With this force he decided to confront the Boers, who, in a bold move, invaded Natal and established a defensive position at Laing's Nek. On 23 January 1881, from near Laing's Nek, Colley attacked with supreme confidence and was thoroughly defeated. In successive small engagements he suffered losses and his little army became bogged down.

In late February 1881 Colley decided to capture Majuba Hill, a key topographical feature that he had noted the Boers used as a daytime observation post from which they withdrew at night to their laagers below. Colley at forty-six had never held an independent command and, theoretician that he was, he neglected mapping and had not sufficient information about the summit or 'dead ground' on the slopes.[44] He also had not informed his officers of his plans. His was a puzzling failure of command that has caused much speculation. On the night of 26 February Colley led his mixed force of some six hundred on a difficult night climb up the steep south side to the top of Majuba Hill to what he thought was an impregnable eyrie. His soldiers, exhausted from carrying heavy packs, were told only to keep absolute silence. In the dark some units became hopelessly lost. At the top he found a plateau perhaps half a mile around with a hollow in the centre where he established a small field hospital. Some men were deployed around the perimeter, but no defensive entrenchments were thrown up. In the cold dawn Colley's soldiers rather too confidently surveyed the Boer positions below, some Highlanders shouting insults at them. By 7.00am a group of Boers began a slow ascent up the easier north side, others fired from below. Little damage was done during the early hours and so little regard had Colley for the fighting Boers, even when warned repeatedly of their threatening approach by Lieutenant Hamilton of the 92nd Gordon Highlanders that, exhausted, he went to sleep. When more and more Boers appeared to pour in close-range fire and then withdraw, confusion reigned among the troops and Hamilton requested a charge: 'We will wait until the Boers advance on us,' he was told, 'then give them a volley and charge.' Instead, Colley's forces were routed in disorder and panic and he was killed with a bullet in his head. The battle was over in very few hours and veterans and newspapermen were in headlong flight down the mountainside. Some said Colley died trying to rally the men and was the last to die, others that he was waving a white handkerchief in surrender, while one rumour was that Colley had killed himself. Speculations about Colley's death abounded; was he over-confident or had he 'actually lost touch with reality' as the historian Michael Barthorp suggests.[45] Clearly this gentle and intelligent Irishman had badly misjudged the capability of the Boers; he would not be the last British Army soldier to do so. He was, however, held responsible for this disaster. Yet he was a brave man, if foolhardy; earlier in February at the Ingogo River he had personally led a small force against a group of Boers in a battle from which he only narrowly escaped.

The Queen, as did Butler and Wolseley, deeply lamented both the defeat and the death of 'poor Sir George Colley', a man, it was said by his soldiers, 'too nice for generalship'. In the peace settlement that followed Butler 'approved Gladstone's recognition of Boer independence [in the Transvaal] . . . probably the only professional soldier in England to do so'.[46]

Wolseley, the Irish, and the Revolt in Egypt – 1882

Wolseley, in London as Adjutant General of the Army, was delighted when appointed to command a British Expeditionary Force to Egypt in 1882 to quell a popular rebellion in the Egyptian Army under Colonel Ahmed Arabi, a fellah, a man of the people. There had been no question of whom to put in command. Briefly, the background to this situation was that the extravagant Khedive Ismail, nominally a vassal of Turkey, had over the years almost bankrupted his country through borrowing and spending to modernize Egypt. Britain, France and Turkey stepped in and in 1879 deposed him in favour of his son, the pliable Tewfik, that their interests might be protected, especially the important Suez Canal that had been in British hands since 1875. Arabi became spokesman and champion for the growing resentments of the Egyptian population against the collaborator Tewfik and the flood of foreigners in their country, and especially for the Egyptian Army whose soldiers suffered under miserable conditions. Tewfik had to go. He was driven out of Cairo and Arabi, with his cry of 'Egypt for the Egyptians', became virtual dictator. Arabi's popular revolt brought him into direct conflict with England and military intervention followed.

Soldiers in Wolseley's Ring, including Lieutenant Colonel William Butler, were, like his chief, only too eager for action again. There was a lingering doubt in Butler's mind that in this war he was campaigning 'not for a worthy cause, but for the bankers of Europe'. He realistically decided that 'the soldier of today must be content with what he can get'.[47] Many young men petitioned Wolseley for positions in the force he was gathering and two he could not refuse were Arthur, Duke of Connaught, the Queen's favourite son, and George, the Duke of Cambridge's son. Their presence in his army proved fortuitous, since both returned home with glowing accounts of Wolseley's skill in command.

By mid-August 1882 Wolseley's army landed at Alexandria, which had already been bombarded by the navy. In less than a month Wolseley, with masterly direction, accomplished a resounding victory at Tel-el-Kebir, the fortified Egyptian Army camp on the Sweetwater Canal about forty miles north-east of Cairo. For the benefit of newspaper correspondents and, of course, the Egyptians, Wolseley's plan involved a feint attack to Aboukir Bay that was followed by a night passage down the Suez Canal (foolishly left unguarded by Arabi) to land at Port Said, rather than proceeding up the Nile Valley to Cairo as Napoleon had done. By 20 August 'Wolseley was in possession of all the important points on the canal with his army based at Ismailia, only twenty-five miles east of Tel-el-Kebir'.[48]

Wolseley launched his army from Kassassin, one of the largest ever mounted by the British at one time, in another surprise, a night march across six miles of featureless desert with nothing to steer by but the stars, a task entrusted to a naval officer. It was a remarkable feat for some twenty thousand troops, achieved in amazing silence except for a drunken Scot who had to be silenced with chloroform. The army attacked at dawn on 13 September and surprised the Egyptians in a short, sharp battle that was over in thirty-five minutes. The Highlanders led, to the sound of their bagpipes, and the leading companies of Royal Irish Regiment under

Colonel Gregorie closed upon the firing line and 'with wild yells' drove before them with the bayonet the Egyptians who fell back to a second line of works in good order. Although enfiladed from a redoubt on their left, the Royal Irish drove the Egyptians from this second line until they themselves were halted to reform their ranks. Gradually the Marines and the 1st Battalion Royal Irish Fusiliers were successful on their front and the Egyptians retired in disorder. Lieutenant Wilbraham of the Faughs records how he and his 'B' company routed Egyptians from near a five-gun battery. In pursuit of an Arab, who turned on him, Wilbraham tripped over his scabbard but his life was saved by Kelly, his company's right-hand man, who bayoneted the Arab who was about to club him with his rifle, 'much to my relief', writes Wilbraham.[49]

After the battle Wolseley and his staff reached the stone bridge at Tel-el-Kebir over the Sweetwater Canal, cheered by Gordon and Cameron Highlanders. There he dismounted and dictated the order for the pursuit of the retreating Egyptians and his despatch for England that announced his victory. Lieutenant Colonel Butler's view was that 'the Battle of Tel-el-Kebir was neither glorious nor necessary'. He told his wife that 'to beat these poor felaheen soldiers was not a matter of exultation . . . the capture of Arabi's earthwork had been like going through brown paper'.[50] Among Wolseley's officers it seemed he alone saluted these 'humble felaheen' of the Egyptian Army and did his best to have Arabi's death sentence commuted.

Cairo was captured and before he left Egypt Wolseley was decorated by the reinstated Khedive Tewfik with the Sultan's highest award, the Grand Cross of Osmanieh. Despite Butler's reservations, the Battle of Tel-el-Kebir was very popular with the British public. Great crowds met Wolseley on his return to London and he was later warmly greeted by the Queen and the Duke of Cambridge, thanks to the presence of their sons in his army. He was given £30,000, promoted to full general and made a baron, Lord Wolseley of Cairo. Wolseley was at the height of his career and ready for another 'small war'. Two years later he was again the obvious choice to head what was called The Gordon Relief Expedition, one of the most unusual of the British Army's little wars.

The Irish and the Gordon Relief Expedition – 1884

In the Egyptian-conquered Sudan in the early 1880s a Muslim holy man, the long-awaited 'Mahdi', Mohammed Ahmed, announced himself a prophet and led a revolt of the Arabs against their Egyptian oppressors. Dervishes, or 'poor men', joined the Mahdi in a holy war and set the Sudan in flames. To put down the revolt the Khedive of Egypt appointed Colonel

Hicks Pasha, an Englishman and former Indian Army officer, to lead the Egyptian Army against the rebels with the result that, in November 1883, some ten thousand Egyptian troops were annihilated at El Obeid, south of Khartoum, the capital of the Sudan. 'The entire Sudan above Khartoum was now in Arab hands,' and Britain and Egypt agreed to evacuate the scattered Egyptian soldiers and civilians, thus leaving the Sudan to the Arabs. But who would lead them ? Clearly, without British intervention the outlook for the foreign population of the Sudan would be grim. Public pressure in England mounted that something should be done and in January 1884 the government sent General Charles (Chinese) Gordon to Khartoum with vague directives to restore order in some sort of peace treaty with the Mahdi and to supervise the evacuation. Armed force was to be avoided but, as the writer Lytton Strachey claims, Gordon 'was in favour . . . of vigorous military action', albeit he agreed to accept the government's policy. Gordon arrived in Khartoum as Governor General in February. He 'kept his word to the British government and evacuated widows, wives, children, and men who would not be pressed into . . . his Civilian Volunteer Defence Force'. An escape route, Butler claimed, could have been kept open for Gordon himself,[51] but it soon became evident that Gordon did not intend to leave Khartoum. In March the Mahdi's forces cut the lines of communication to London and Cairo and invested the city. Gordon would hold on and remain in Khartoum for nearly a year inspiring the small garrison and the city's people. It has been suggested that Gordon's behaviour could have been a kind of moral blackmail to involve the British government more directly in the Sudan. Certainly this was Prime Minister Gladstone's view, who, forced by public opinion, reluctantly in August 1884 authorized a military operation to relieve Khartoum and rescue Gordon.

William Butler told Lady Butler this was 'the very first war in the Victorian era in which the object was entirely worthy'. To Butler, Gordon was 'the bravest and noblest soldier of our time' and he compared his courage to that of General James Wolfe. Wolseley was also a friend and admirer of Gordon, one of the few he would say 'who came up to my estimate of the Christian hero'.[52] Indeed, Gordon's reputation, his brave character and heroic stand dominated the expedition, even giving it his name, admired as he was by the British from the Queen down. His sometimes wildly vacillating journal shows his mystical and unshakeable religious faith, for Gordon, though an eminent soldier, was not an ordinary man. Already a legend in the British Army, paradoxically his fame was mostly in the service of foreign governments. He had led the 'ever victorious army' of the Imperial Chinese government against the Taiping rebels and had served with distinction as the Khedive Ismail's Governor of Equatoria in the southernmost region of the Sudan, and again as Governor General of all Sudan in Khartoum.

An extraordinary idea Wolseley pushed after discussions with his trusted Ring members, one based on his and Butler's experience in the Canadian wilds, was to have boats used to transport the main army and supplies up the Nile River rather than marching across the desert from Suakim on the Red Sea to Berber. He got his way, despite strong criticism by experts in London of this Nile route. Butler, with Colonel Alleyne of the Royal Engineers, was ordered to investigate and have constructed eight hundred boats like those used in the Red River Expedition known as 'Whalers' and manned by Canadian 'Voyageurs'. Sanctioned by the Canadian government, men enlisted as civilians not soldiers. 'Voyageur', however, embraced a wide range of recruits, few with knowledge of boats and not what Wolseley or Butler envisioned: lumberjacks from Ottawa, young business and professional men from Winnipeg. At Wadi Halfa Butler recognized one man from his Red River days, William Prince, Chief of the Swampy Indians from Lake Winnipeg: 'he had been the best Indian in my canoe'.[53] All answered the call for the adventure of a lifetime. Butler's and Alleyne's enthusiasm was such that, to the surprise of the scheme's detractors, within a month of the eight hundred whalers being ordered, four hundred had been built in England and shipped to Egypt. In addition there were steamers from Thomas Cook and Sons and to command them with a naval contingent Wolseley appointed the enthusiastic Anglo-Irish Captain Lord Charles Beresford, RN, one of the most flamboyant sailors of the Victorian age and brother of Lord William 'Ulundi' Beresford, VC. Lord Charles had captured the public's attention in a daredevil action in Alexandria in 1882 in that campaign under Wolseley when, during the bombardment of the city, he ran his gunboat *Condor* right under the nose of the Egyptian batteries.

Wolseley instituted another bold idea, his Camel Corps to be known as the Desert Column as against the River Column and used in emergency circumstances. Consisting mostly of detachments from all the well-known and prestigious Guards and cavalry regiments, including the 5th Royal Irish Lancers, it was facetiously dubbed 'the Camelry', or as Butler would acidly comment, 'London society on camels'. Hugh McCalmont was appointed Second in Command of the Light Camel Corps, not first as he had hoped, but as he would write in his memoirs he 'had to make the best of it'.

Wolseley's orders were to rescue Gordon and Colonel John Stewart of the 11th Hussars, who had accompanied Gordon. It was a campaign that did not run smoothly for he encountered tensions and jealousies at Wadi Halfa among his Ring, now fifteen years older than when they had first come together. His criticism was centred on the delays of the boats and on his Chief of Staff Redvers Buller for not organizing sufficient coal for the steamers or enough supplies for the expedition and he wondered why he had appointed him. Buller, in fact, did not think Gordon worth all the expense; he particularly despised the use of the whalers as a means of transportation and this brought him into conflict with Butler. For his part Butler became inflamed by what he saw as the misuse of 'his whalers'. Living abstemiously himself he was impatient with Egyptian Army officials and British officers commanding Egyptian units who thought nothing of commandeering the boats to transport their own personal and question-ably necessary supplies. He bombarded his colleagues with communiqués requesting greater speed and was undoubtedly too outspoken. To Butler it seemed that the most important aim of the River Column was being lost sight of, which was to get the troops to Khartoum with all possible speed to rescue Gordon. If Wolseley showed the impetuosity of the Irish, so too did Butler, and Wolseley had to chastise him, forbidding him to command the whalers beyond the Third Cataract. Butler was deeply humiliated. Wolseley found Butler to be a brilliant but irritating officer: 'too much an individualist to be a good team man'. Yet in his campaign journal he would later write of Butler: 'He has "Paddy's" faults in an ordinary degree, but he has all his good qualities, talents and virtues to overflowing . . . . He makes me very angry at times but I always like him.'[54]

To speed up the boats Wolseley cleverly instituted a prize of £100 to whatever battalion should travel the Nile from Sarras to Debbeh in the shortest time, the winners to be given pride of place in the advance to Khartoum. The 1st Battalion, Royal Irish Regiment won the prize and Wolseley's congratulatory note to Lieutenant Colonel Hugh Shaw, VC, expressed his pleasure: 'Being an Irishman myself it is very gratifying to feel that my small prize has been carried off by my own countrymen'. The regimental historian describes how the Royal Irish infantrymen, who had never handled an oar in their lives,

> worked like galley slaves . . . in burning and daily increasing heat they rowed and poled, and hauled the boats by ropes through the easier portions of the rapids. In the more difficult places it became necessary to lighten the whalers . . . and to transport the cargo across the rocks.[55]

Time was running out. Wolseley received Gordon's last message at the end of December, 'Khartoum all right.14.12.84, C. G. Gordon', but an ominous verbal message also sent was that he was besieged on three sides and that Wolseley 'should come quickly'. Immediately Wolseley decided to send the Desert Column (Camel Corps) under Brigadier General Sir Herbert Stewart, one of his most trusted officers, to cut across the desert from Korti to Metemmeh on the Nile, shortening the route by some two hundred miles. At Metemmeh Captain Lord Charles Beresford and his fifty-seven-strong naval brigade accompanying the Column were to man Gordon's steamers anchored there and then 'dash' the ninety-six miles to Khartoum.

At the end of December the Desert Column was on its way, presenting a grand spectacle. By 16 January 1885 Arabs could be seen in the distance, clearly intending to block the way to the much-needed wells at Abu Klea and to the Nile. The Irishman Major John French was sent forward with a patrol of his 19th Hussars, the only horsemen with the Column, to probe the Arab force in front of the wells. French, accompanied by a corporal, barely escaped capture; he had to relinquish a prisoner he had seized and bolted back to the Column.[56] The next day the Column moved slowly forward in square towards the wells and there occurred what Winston Churchill called 'the most savage and bloody action ever fought in the Sudan by British troops'. The Dervishes' ferocious attack made history when they 'broke the British square', an event immortalized by Kipling in his poem 'Fuzzy-Wuzzy' (last verse):

> So 'ere's *to* you, Fuzzy-Wuzzy, at your 'ome in the Soudan;
> You're a pore benighted 'eathen but a first-class fightin' man;
> An' 'ere's *to* you Fuzzy-Wuzzy, with your 'ayrick 'ead of 'air -
> You big black boundin' beggar – for you broke a British square![57]

Captain Lord Beresford was on one side of the square with his blue-clad sailors when their Gardner gun jammed and his life was miraculously saved only because he leaped underneath it.[58] The square quickly rallied, the gap was filled and the battle was soon over. Dervish bodies were piled both in and outside the square and the Desert Column's losses for such a small force were heavy: 18 officers and 150 men killed or wounded. The next day General Stewart received a mortal wound and died a month later, a very great loss to both Wolseley personally and to the Column.

Against Wolseley's orders Colonel Sir Charles Wilson, who took over command of the Desert Column, waited three days at Metemmeh before setting out for Khartoum in Gordon's manned and armoured steamers. As Gordon's biographer, Roy MacGregor Hastie, points out 'a senior naval officer had been sent with the column together with a cadre of sailors', and asks. 'Why did he wait for three days ?' The steamers were ready. He meant, of course, Captain Lord Charles Beresford. The answer was that Sir Charles Wilson was in command but Beresford was 'laid low in hospital with a painful boil on his bottom' and his naval brigade needed to be reorganized after casualties on the march . Confusion, if not bungling, attended this crucial time. Wilson later justified his delay by claiming that he had to reconnoitre the river for suspected Mahdist attacks and then to repair and refuel the ships. Finally, on 24 January Wilson set sail for Khartoum in two steamers with some two hundred Sudanese soldiers and twenty red-coated soldiers of Royal Sussex Regiment deliberately in full view because Gordon had written that red coats would intimidate the Mahdists, which, amidst increasing rifle fire and shelling, did not happen. When Wilson arrived in sight of the besieged city on 28 January no flag flew from Gordon's wrecked palace and there was no sign of Gordon. Khartoum had fallen. Wilson had arrived too late. From Khartoum he immediately turned back towards Metemmeh, the steamers were soon wrecked by Mahdist fire and he was rescued only by the bravery of the 'now recovered Beresford' who, in the *Safieh*, made his own 'epic voyage' up the Nile, despite fire from shore batteries and a burst boiler. The words 'too late' echoed around the world, taken up by newspapers, and Wilson was blamed and made the scapegoat for the failure of the entire expedition.[59]

Wolseley, on hearing of Gordon's death, spoke of this 'as the saddest day of his life'. He had set out on this noble enterprise to rescue Gordon with such high hopes and his sense of failure was acute. For the first time in his career he had experienced failure as a commander and this he firmly believed marked a turn in his fortunes. In a way it did, for this was his last command in the field. Wolseley was blamed for not moving his forces faster and also for dividing them. His wrath and that of the British public fell chiefly on Prime Minister Gladstone for not authorizing the Gordon Expedition sooner. With Gordon's death the Expedition lost its purpose and could leave the Sudan.

Withdrawal was a slow business, as Butler found when he assisted the retreat down the Nile, but he was again in Wolseley's favour because of his efficiency. He then accepted command of the new Egyptian frontier, now at Wadi Halfa, with the temporary rank of Brigadier General beginning in September 1885. For four months Butler did his job with few troops, defending the railway line and outposts against the Arabs who were still operating hit and run raids. When reinforcements arrived he also demonstrated skill and good planning in directing a brigade in a battle at Ginniss in December under General Sir Frederick Stevenson, Commander-in-Chief of the British Army in Egypt, who adopted Butler's plan. The Arabs were driven back and 'it was Butler who organized the cavalry pursuit'. In July 1886 Butler was invalided home, exhausted by hard work, heat and frustration. His lack of tact in continuing to send communiqués to the War Office begging for supplies for his isolated soldiers had not made him popular, and on his return from sick leave he was placed on half-pay. Later that year his rank of Brigadier General was finally confirmed and, although still on half-pay, he was given a KCB.[60]

Wolseley returned home depressed by his failure, mollified when the government raised him in the peerage to the rank of viscount and made him a Knight of St Patrick. His spirits soon revived and he was again vigorously caught up in army reform at the War Office, loudly complaining about poor weaponry and the army's seniority system. He refused a command in India, but accepted command of the forces in Ireland, a not very onerous posting. He had mixed feelings about Ireland, as do many who leave then return, and what he saw as the 'disloyalty' of his fellow Irishmen distressed him. The Home Rule question, always a thorny issue in Ireland, to Wolseley the Imperialist was anathema. He and Lady Wolseley managed to enjoy themselves and hosted lavish parties in their handsome apartments in the historic Royal Hospital Kilmainham, Dublin, headquarters of the Commander-in-Chief of the Army in Ireland. In 1894 he was made Field Marshal and a year later he succeeded the Duke of Cambridge as Commander-in-Chief of the British Army, a position he had coveted. Alas, the position had been drastically changed, its significance greatly reduced. Wolseley found that military affairs were in the hands of a civilian administration under the Anglo-Irish Lord Lansdowne, Secretary for War, while he, the soldier, was without any real control. At the same time 'Our Only General's' popular reputation was being eclipsed by Roberts and Kitchener, the 'new public idols', and the Anglo-Boer War looming on the horizon would set the stage for their further exploits.

CHAPTER EIGHT

The Irish in the Second Anglo-Boer War

'Three Cheers for Krooger'

An Inniskilling Fusilier,
History of Royal Inniskilling Fusiliers,
London 1934, p. 382

Irishmen in the British Army were more than pleased to hear in 1899 that war had erupted in South Africa, for it offered another chance for action. A soldier of the 1st Inniskilling Fusiliers summed up the feelings of all ranks when, as his battalion was entraining at Mullingar that autumn, he called out, 'Three cheers for Krooger!' When asked why he wanted to cheer our enemy the man replied, 'Sure if it hadn't been for that old divil there would niver have been any fighting at all'! In Ireland, despite anti-British, pro-Boer demonstrations, the army reports for the Dublin area show that the years of the Boer War (1899–1902) furnished the highest number of Irish recruits to the British army, higher even than 'loyal Belfast'. About thirty thousand Irishmen are thought to have served against the Boers.[1]

Paul Kruger was the indomitable seventy-four-year-old president of the Transvaal and an important Boer in South Africa. Trouble had been brewing since gold had been discovered in the 1880s in the Transvaal and on the Witwatersrand of Johannesburg, a wealth that gave political 'substance' to the Boer vision of a united South Africa, but which also in part led to British aspirations that the two Boer republics, the Transvaal and the Orange Free State, should be joined in a united South Africa under the Crown. Britain's Imperialist aims were ably expressed by Sir Alfred Milner, appointed in 1897 as Governor of Cape Colony and High Commissioner for South Africa. Paul Kruger stood in his path. Boer and Briton were on a collision course, both committed to their nationalist aspirations of a united South Africa, one under the Vierkleur, the other under the Union Jack.

Their bitter clash centred chiefly on the position of the 'Uitlanders', or foreigners, who had flooded into the Transvaal because of the gold-mines. Many of these newcomers, among them both English and Irish, were merely gold-seekers and, together with the big corporations and business people of Europe, their values were soon at variance with the sober, God-fearing Boer farmers and small tradespeople. Those Uitlanders who were prepared to settle in the country petitioned frequently for a fair place in Transvaal society, especially for the unconditional franchise that the Boers denied them. (Boers demanded fourteen years' residence, but were willing in 1899 to reduce the time of waiting.) For Paul Kruger, deeply religious and, the grand old man of the Voortrekkers of 1838, there was more at stake than granting the franchise to the Uitlanders. This was Boer sovereignty, their very freedom as more Uitlanders arrived in the Transvaal to outnumber them. At the Bloemfontein Conference, held from 31 May to 5 June 1899, Milner pressed Kruger for reforms he knew could not be accepted and, predictably, an emotional Kruger refused.

General Sir William Butler, whom Milner called 'that brilliant but impossible Irishman', also played his part. He was in South Africa, undoubtedly on Wolseley's recommendation, as Commander-in-Chief of the British Army, appointed December 1898, and as acting High Commissioner during Milner's three-month leave of absence in England. Butler had been reluctant to accept these appointments, for he correctly suspected that there would be trouble in South Africa. He saw the Johannesburg Uitlanders particularly as 'probably the most corrupt, immoral and untruthful assemblage of beings at present in the world'.[2] For him the most suspect and perhaps ruthless Uitlander of them all was the Englishman Cecil Rhodes, the diamond king of Kimberley, who was committed to a united Africa under the British flag.

During this period Milner had been urging Butler to prepare his forces for war and Butler, as requested by the War Office, dutifully inspected the 'defences of the British colonies in South Africa'. But in his report he advocated a strictly defensive policy. Having just published a biography of General Sir George Colley at Majuba, he realized the capabilities of the Boers. His increasingly anti-war sentiments, his sympathies for the Boers, as well as his hostility to Uitlanders, ensured that his was a most anomalous position – a soldier urging peace while his diplomat/politician counterpart, the Imperialist Milner, urged war. Happily, the War Office inadvertently provided a way out of this dilemma. In a communiqué asking him simply for information about army supplies and 'any observations', they got back more than they expected, an opinion that as a soldier he had no business to express: 'I believe that war between the white races . . . would be the greatest calamity that ever occurred in South Africa'.

This was too much and gave Milner the chance to press openly for his replacement. Butler resigned as Commander-in-Chief on 4 July 1899 and his resignation was reluctantly accepted by the government on 9 August. Butler's words were written, he said to Milner in an interview, 'in the highest interests of the British Empire and for the honour of Her Majesty's Army', but he had put his army career in jeopardy, including his hopes for an independent command. The often-voiced question, weren't all Irish Catholics supporting the Boers?, was answered by Butler's biographer Edward McCourt: 'He was not opposed to British policy in South Africa or anywhere else because he was an Irishman and a Catholic, but because he was an impulsive humanitarian hostile to the men of any nation who oppressed and exploited their fellows'. Butler, more than others in the British Government or in the British Army at this time, seems to have realized that disaster awaited South Africa in the event of war, and this Milner, to be fair, recognized: 'His merit was,' Sir Alfred said, 'that he knew the size of the job.' Ironically, in the end his views were defended by Lord Esher who also admired Milner. Years later, after Butler's death, when writing to King Edward VII Esher realized 'that much of the advice Butler gave has since proved correct', and adds, 'His Irish blood may possibly influence his temper and political judgement, but leaves his military capacity untouched'.[3] Butler returned to England in September a month before the war broke out, very much criticized by the London Press for his 'pro-Boer' sympathies. He was, however, not in total disgrace with the army and the War Office offered him (on Wolseley's recommendation) the home command of the Western District with headquarters at Devonport.

By September the Boers were ready for war. There had been overtures of peace by moderates on both sides, but the momentum for war was too strong. On 9 August Kruger had been manoeuvred to issue his own ultimatum that 'all British troops on the frontiers be withdrawn, and that those on their way to South Africa be sent back'. The British government rejected it. A previously reluctant Orange Free State rallied to Kruger's side and on 11 October 1899 the great Anglo-Boer War began.

Wolseley had recognized the Boers as 'a stiff-necked and hardy people' and during the summer of 1899 he believed that a very large force would be needed in any struggle against them. Except for a small increase of forces, both the Secretary for War, Lord Lansdowne, and the government ignored Wolseley's recommendations for reinforcements to be ready to augment the army, objecting chiefly to the cost. Although the army was not well prepared initially, as the war progressed Wolseley was finally successful in sending to South Africa a force of some 267,000 'with its full complement of artillery and cavalry'.[4]

Many Irish were in prominent positions in South Africa from the beginning of the war. The General Officer Commanding British forces in Natal in 1899 was Lieutenant General Sir George White VC, an Ulsterman from County Antrim. White had had an unusual career. After Sandhurst and service in India, promotion was so slow that after twenty-seven years' service he was still only a Major in the Gordon Highlanders in which rank we met him in 1879, aged forty-four, winning the VC under General Roberts in the Second Afghan War. At that time he was made a CB and promoted to Brevet Lieutenant Colonel. From then on his rise was swift; he was made a Major General ten years later and in 1893 was appointed Commander-in-Chief in India, succeeding Roberts, followed by an appointment as Quartermaster General at the War Office.

This war would be a real test of leadership for men like White. Brave men, they had prospered in their careers chiefly by fighting poorly armed natives in the many little engagements throughout the Empire. They were not prepared when pitted against these highly-motivated white Boer opponents who wore no uniforms, were often shabbily dressed, but were well-mounted, excellent horsemen and with modern weapons were soon to be considered the best shots in the world. Not having seen military action for some time it came as a great shock, to Sir George when, at the end of October 1899, only a short time after the minor successes of the Battles of Talana Hill and Elandslaagte, he found himself and his forces under siege at Ladysmith.

When the Boers invaded Natal the 1st Royal Irish Fusiliers and the 2nd Royal Dublin Fusiliers were immediately involved in the Battle at Talana Hill, the first real engagement of the war. Talana was one of two kopjes near the little coal-mining town of Dundee, about forty miles north of Ladysmith, where Major General Sir William Penn Symons was in command of 4,000 men. White, in overall command in Ladysmith, had 8,000. On rumours of Boers advancing, White, not quite sure of the Boers strength and uneasy about splitting his forces, rather tentatively suggested that Symons join him in Ladysmith, but Symons refused, confident that his British Army regulars could hold Dundee against any Boers, whom he saw 'as simple farmers'. During the night of 19 October Boer scouts stumbled on a picket of Royal Dublin Fusiliers under Lieutenant Cecil Grimshaw who wisely retired and sent word back to the main camp at Dundee. The Irish Fusiliers knew nothing of this and half an hour after the usual 'stand to arms' at 5.00 am, shells suddenly fell among their tents. Then a soldier looked up to see Boers lining the heights of Talana Hill; under cover of night they had climbed up and were now ready for action. Quickly, British artillery opened fire and the Battle of Talana Hill was on. The Dublin and Irish Fusiliers, supported by a battalion of the Royal Rifle

Corps, began an advance up the difficult and steep hill, but 'the Boers on the hill-top were able to pick off almost everyone who showed himself . . . Courage and persistence told at last, assisted by the British artillery', which unfortunately shelled its own men. The Boers were driven off the crest and streamed across the plain below, but there was no cavalry pursuit and, after being allowed to remove their wounded and bury their dead, they could disperse and reform in safety. The battle was counted a victory and the Dublins were singled out and celebrated back in England in a ditty that began 'Bravo the Dublin Fusiliers'.[5] Casualties were heavy among the two Irish battalions and General Penn Symons, impatient to see the hill himself, was mortally wounded.

Two days later that controversial and lively cavalryman Major General Sir John French came into prominence at the Battle of Elandslaagte. The only son of a retired naval officer, he was raised by six sisters when both his parents died young. Although born in England where his branch of the family had lived since the eighteenth century, French always considered himself an Irishman, tracing his lineage from fourteenth-century Norman settlers in Wexford. His Irish heritage, of which he was so proud, gave French a continued interest in Ireland's problems and the firm conviction that it also gave him 'a special understanding' of them. In fact one sister became a noted and committed Irish Nationalist. After two years in the navy as a cadet and midshipman, French opted for the cavalry because of his love of horses, entering the army by way of the militia and hard study. Duly gazetted in the 8th Queen's Royal Irish Hussars, he soon transferred to the 19th Hussars, possibly because the 8th were too expensive. For his service in the Gordon Relief Expedition he was promoted to Lieutenant Colonel.

After commanding 1 Cavalry Brigade at Aldershot, in late September 1899 Major-General French was on his way to South Africa to command the cavalry, a vague mission in a war that was inevitable but had not yet begun. On arrival he was ordered by the War Office to take temporary command of a cavalry brigade in Natal and on 20 October reached Ladysmith where Sir George White was in command. In Ladysmith he immediately heard a report from captured Boers that they had cut the railway line and seized a supply train at Elandslaagte. French was ordered to investigate and found Boers there. The next day White, buoyed by news of the Talana victory, sent him 'to clear the neighbourhood of Elandslaagte of the enemy and to cover the reconstruction of the railway and telegraph lines'. Early on 21 October French's force of five squadrons of Imperial Light Horse, a Natal Field Battery and companies of Manchesters (infantry) manning an armoured train and escorting Royal Engineers in another left Ladysmith. The line was repaired and French drove some Boers out of the station buildings, who retired to prepared entrenchments on a nearby kopje and proceeded to fire on French with their accurate artillery. To attack them he called for reinforcements and received from Ladysmith the rest of the Manchesters, Devonshires and Gordon Highlanders and field artillery, with a squadron of the 5th Royal Irish Lancers in escort. The 5th Dragoon Guards were already probing Boer strength. On their arrival French immediately conferred with Colonel Ian Hamilton, a survivor of Majuba eighteen years before, who now commanded the infantry. It was 'French's show', as Sir George White said to him when he arrived to watch the short-lived battle. In a desperate fight when storming the kopje, aided by a thunderstorm, Hamilton rallied the Manchesters and Gordons who finally seized the crest to the cries of 'Majuba! Majuba!'[6]

Waiting for the retreating Boers were French's cavalry, hidden on the flank under Major St. John Gore of the 5th Dragoon Guards, who was, as French told him, to have 'the honour of commanding the first real cavalry charge since the Crimea'. Gore received orders from Major Haig 'to pursue with *vigour* when you see Boers beginning to fall back . . . press the enemy *with the lance* if you can'. This they did in the evening of that day, charging the fleeing Boers and using their lances relentlessly. Lance Corporal Kelly of the 5th Lancers was said to have 'speared two of the fleeing Boers riding on one pony with one thrust of his lance'. Irish Lancer Private Thomas Doolan, writing to his mother, described the pursuit and attack: 'As soon as the Boers saw the lances they threw up their rifles and ammo in the air and cried "Friends" but it was no go.' The Boers who got away harboured a hatred of the cavalry ever after, especially for the 5th Irish Lancers. The lance to the Boers was like 'a long-handled assegai . . . . barbarous . . . not to be used by civilized men'.[7] The minor Battles of Elandslaagte and Talana Hill were the only successes of the British Army in that autumn of defeats.

White decided that Elandslaagte was not worth holding and French and his cavalry retired to Ladysmith. With Boers threatening the area, the Royal Irish and Dublin Fusiliers and the Dundee garrison, now under Major General Yule, also retired and, after marching mostly by night sixty miles in deep mud and miserable weather, they struggled exhausted into Ladysmith. Regrettably some wounded were left behind, as well as many stores. By 29 October Ladysmith, the third largest town in the colony and an important rail junction of the Natal Orange Free State and Transvaal lines, bulged with some 13,000 troops and a refugee population. Boers could be seen gathering in the surrounding hills and making obvious preparations to attack from gun emplacements, notably with their formidable ninety-four pounder 'Long Tom'. French's cavalry patrols confirmed this and were engaged in several skirmishes. It has been suggested that White could have fallen back to make a fighting retreat to the south of the Tugela [River] and there make a stand. He decided instead to remain in Ladysmith, hoping to mount a blow before Transvaalers could be joined by Free State Boers to encircle the town. It was not a wise decision and historians have suggested reasons for it. The idea of retreat in the British Army was bad for morale and to be avoided if possible, but above all White was supremely confident that Boers were no match for his British Army regulars.

White planned to strike north of Ladysmith, hoping to close the pass of Nicholson's Nek to Boer reinforcements from the north. He devised a three-pronged attack, dividing his forces and involving night marches. In the darkness before dawn on 30 October the Royal Dublin Fusiliers, in an infantry brigade with the Leicesters, 1st and 2nd 60th Regiment and the Liverpools under Lieutenant Colonel Geoffrey Grimwood, marched to storm Long Hill and Pepworth Hill, about five miles north and north-east of the town. Ian Hamilton's brigade, Devonshires, Manchesters and Gordons, followed, General White himself leading his own 'dear old 92nd' (Gordons). White's plans fell apart. The Boers could not be found at Long Hill; they had changed position as was their custom and worked round behind Grimwood to send a veritable storm of fire against his brigade. French's cavalry, which was supposed to be in support on the right, ended up in a wrong position. He and his men hastily dismounted to help Grimwood. Everywhere troops were pinned down. It was hopeless and by late morning White decided to order a withdrawal, which took place in what was described as 'extreme confusion', although eyewitnesses observed it was more like panic, except for the Royal Artillery who covered the retreat.[8] The Boers could have charged but did not.

Worse was yet to come and the Irish particularly suffered humiliation. Returning to Ladysmith General White heard of the disaster that befell Lieutenant Colonel Frank Carleton, whom he had sent out with his column that same night to march to Nicholson's Nek from where he could attack Boers in the rear and block any retreat. Under Carleton were over 1,000 men of his own Royal Irish Fusiliers and the Gloucester Regiment, a mountain battery with mules carrying small guns, and inexperienced men leading about one hundred pack mules with extra ammunition. Carleton never got to Nicholson's Nek. Leaving before midnight, he realized by around 2:00am that it was impossible to reach the pass by morning light and he decided to spend the night on the adjacent Tchrengula Hill. There in the darkness on the steep slope without proper guides the mules stampeded, crashed down on the Gloucesters and ran off with the spare ammunition. Some Gloucesters, thinking that the fleeing mules were Boers charging, ran down in panic shouting 'Boer cavalry !'; others ended up in Ladysmith with the mules.

The Faughs reached the crest where the Boers, alerted by all the noise and uproar, were ready for them in the early morning light with accurate fire and, as Marcus Cunliffe records, 'However closely they sought cover among the boulders men were hit, the Boer fire grew ever more intense, but . . . we never saw Boers within range except single men as they doubled from cover to cover', all the time closing in on the Irish. In such a situation any action turns into confusion and one such was when someone in a detached group, not a Faugh they stoutly maintained, raised a white flag. Carleton acquiesced. Seeing men from the main column streaming back into Ladysmith, he, with no guns, ammunition or any means to signal for help as his heliograph was on a runaway mule, had to order a ceasefire. It was a bitter moment for brave men. The Royal Irish Fusiliers were furious at having to lay down their arms and many kept on firing; officers broke their swords in anger. Soon they were encircled and rounded up by the Boers who took over 1,000 prisoners by train to Pretoria, including 13 officers and 480 men of the Faughs. One bright note which the Faughs' historian records was that the Boers allowed many of the wounded to return to Ladysmith as sick prisoners were a nuisance.[9] By 2 November the Boers had cut the railway line to the south and the siege of Ladysmith began.

White never recovered from this humiliating defeat. His 'great blow' against the Boers at Nicholson's Nek came to be known as 'Mournful Monday' by the London press and 'Little Majuba' by the Boers. His decision to remain in Ladysmith undoubtedly tied up his Natal Field Force, but on the other hand it also kept Boer forces north of the Tugela busy for a long time, allowing a breathing space and time for troops to arrive from England. White took all responsibility for the disaster, but criticism continued: if only he had sent away his three cavalry regiments and his Intelligence officers before the Boers completely closed in. In fact Major General French got away. When he received a welcome telegram ordering him to Cape Town to take command of the Cavalry Division, French persuaded railway officials to ready a train and he, with Major Douglas Haig, his Chief Staff Officer, his staff, some servants and horses managed to get out on the last train. These two future field marshals and Commanders-in-Chief of the British Army in the First World War crouched on the floor of the railway carriage in a most undignified manner amidst the hail of Boer bullets, expecting at any moment to be captured. 'It was a close thing,' writes Holmes, French's biographer.

Irishmen in the British Army fighting against other Irishmen was no new thing and indeed, in the relief of Ladysmith in February 1900, there were two brothers from Longford on opposite sides. Corporal James Flynn was fighting with the Royal Inniskilling Fusiliers, while his brother Michael was in John MacBride's pro-Boer Irish Brigade . Both were casualties. The Brigade's green flag, 'gold fringed with a harp in the centre inscribed "Our Land – Our People – Our Language" could be seen waving over the Irish Brigade camp among the Boers besieging Ladysmith.' Already in South Africa MacBride, born in County Mayo, helped to form the Irish Brigade and took charge when the commander, the American 'Colonel' John Fillimore Blake, was wounded. Mainly Irish-American volunteers were born in Ireland or of Irish descent, many were also Irish Uitlanders from the Transvaal. Robert Kee, a writer on Irish nationalism, claims that these Irishmen, compared to Irishmen in the British Army, played an 'insignificant' part in the war. Their group only lasted for a year, from September 1899 to September 1900, and numbered around 300 men altogether, although the United Irishmen claimed 1,000 to 1,700. Even so, it was not a 'brigade' in the usual military sense. However, they gave Nationalists at home in Ireland who opposed the Boer War the satisfaction that militant Ireland was making a stand against the British. MacBride 'personally seems to have fought with gallantry'. In Ireland he would achieve a certain fame when he married the beautiful Maud Gonne, the Irish Nationalist revolutionary, and would become more famous when he fought in the Easter Rising in Dublin in 1916 and was subsequently shot by the British.[10]

Major Alex Godley of the 1st Royal Dublin Fusiliers and Captain Charles Fitzclarence of the Royal Fusiliers were two Irishmen at Mafeking when this little isolated town on the border of the northern Cape and the Transvaal came under siege in mid-October 1899 by Boers who tore up the railway and telegraph lines. Godley had been in the middle of a staff course at Camberley when rumours of troubles with the Boers were rife. Like so many, he very much wanted to go to South Africa. With the help of Colonel the Honourable George Gough, an old hunting friend and now private secretary to Wolseley, Godley and Fitzclarence, on loan from their units, served as Special Service officers under Lieutenant Colonel Robert Baden-Powell. Commander of the 5th Dragoon Guards, Baden-Powell had been ordered by Wolsley in July 1899 to raise two irregular mounted infantry regiments, a Rhodesian corps and a Bechuanaland Protectorate Regiment. They were to divert Boer commandos on the western frontier of the Transvaal and Orange Free States in the event of hostilities. For its defence the town had only these irregular troops, the Town Guard, the police, a railway detachment and a Cape Boy Contingent, in all numbering some 1,200. An attack on Mafeking was inevitable; it had important rail connections, but for Boers it had strong symbolic importance as the birthplace of the disastrous Jameson Raid of January 1896 into the Transvaal. Sanctioned by Cecil Rhodes to provoke Uitlanders into action, it was said to be 'the real declaration of war', a warning that Boers would eventually have to fight.

In the subsequent siege of Mafeking Godley acted as Baden-Powell's right-hand man and adjutant of the Bechuanaland Protectorate Regiment, while Fitzclarence was in charge of 'B' Squadron of the same regiment. Godley was from an Anglo-Irish military family. His father was Lieutenant Colonel of the 56th Foot, youngest son of John Godley of Killegar, County Leitrim. An uncle was a major in the Dublin Fusiliers through whose influence Alex was gazetted to the 1st battalion. Another uncle was in the 28th Foot and a great-uncle was Admiral James Bird. After Sandhurst Godley was stationed in Ireland with his regiment for several years where he enjoyed the life of the Westmeath polo-playing, fox-hunting gentry; this, along with his family background, admirably suited him to being a Mounted Infantry officer. In 1894 he took a course in mounted infantry at Aldershot, two years later becoming adjutant of the Mounted Infantry regiment there. Godley was no stranger to Africa; in 1896 he was the adjutant of a Special Service Battalion of Mounted Infantry sent to Africa by Wolseley for the Mashonaland Campaign, a battalion whose Irish company included members of Royal Irish Regiment, Royal Irish and Royal Dublin Fusiliers. For his services in Mashonaland Godley was awarded a brevet majority, but disappointed that he had not seen a fight.

Captain Charles Fitzclarence was also from an Anglo-Irish family, from Bishops Court, County Kildare, who claimed to be descended from William IV and the actress Mrs Jordan. There is an amusing story about Fitzclarence when, in a quieter period after the relief of Mafeking, he and Godley, while riding about the country around Rustenberg, called in at a farm house for coffee where they met a fine-looking old Boer who drew their attention to portraits of the Royal family. He said his name was Rex and that he was a direct descendant of George IV, whereupon Fitzclarence immediately claimed a 'cousinship' with him, referring to his own ancestors.[11] Godley and Fitclarence were handsome young men whose military experience and social standing added greatly to the morale of this little colonial town.

Mafeking, however, was made famous by the presence of the exuberant, clever, joke-playing Baden-Powell, founder in 1908 of the Boy Scout movement. B. P., as he was usually called, was quite unlike the worried Sir George White in similar circumstances in Ladysmith. Baden-Powell's cheery messages to the outside world downplaying siege conditions inflicted by the 'heartless Boers' were heard as British pluck personified in the face of adversity. Although Mafeking was never a serious target for the Boers, casualties from enemy shelling and raids on enemy lines were 'proportionately much heavier than in the sieges of Kimberly and Ladysmith', and the Mafeking siege, as Thomas Pakenham writes, was longer, producing a cumulative strain.[12] In October Captain Fitzclarence won a VC, praised by Baden-Powell for his 'extraordinary spirit and fearlessness' when he led his men in a successful night raid that caught some Boers by surprise in a large isolated trench. Fitzclarence had been the first to leap into the fray and in the hand-to-hand bayonet encounter was slightly wounded. Emerson Neilly of the *Pall Mall Gazette*, one of the many correspondents in Mafeking, unfortunately reported afterwards that 'the trench had been held mostly by young boys', but he adds: 'If any shame attends to the killing of youngsters it must rest on the shoulders of those fathers who brought them there'.[13] It was certainly common Boer practice to use the very young and the very old as soldiers.

Fitzclarence was again involved in a raid ordered by Baden-Powell on 26 December, henceforth known as Black Boxing Day. This overly ambitious raid to capture Game Tree Hill, a fort in Boer hands some two miles to the north that Baden-Powell thought was only in the process of being strengthened, was a complete failure due to poor reconnaissance. Fitzclarence, commanding one of two squadrons of the Protectorate Regiment, found the Boer fort to be a sand-bagged blockhouse some ten feet high with loop-holed walls. When Godley, flying a white flag, took out the armoured train he found fifty casualties, twenty-four killed and Fitzclarence among the wounded, a large number for this small garrison.[14]

Kimberley in northern Cape Colony was not militarily important but was already world-famous as the site of the De Beers Diamond Mines, which were controlled by the equally famous Cecil Rhodes, the Boers' arch enemy. Just before the outbreak of the war Rhodes hurried to Kimberley, 'his town', the place where he had made his first fortune and where his autocratic ways soon showed that he considered himself the *de facto* leader, superseding the authority of the commanding officer and the mayor. Lieutenant Colonel Robert Kekewich of the 1st North Lancashire Fusiliers, an unassuming forty-five-year-old Victorian soldier, was in overall command of the regular troops already in Kimberley and some eleven hundred in local volunteer forces. He proclaimed a state of siege and martial law on 14 October when, as he was talking to army head-quarters in Cape Town, the line was cut by the Boers who could be seen on the horizon.

The siege of Kimberley was unusual because of the struggle between the British Army represented by Kekewich and Cecil Rhodes, who had no use for the military. Major W.A. O'Meara, Royal Engineers, Intelligence Officer during the Kimberley siege, writes that Rhodes's main complaint about Kekewich was that 'as a soldier Kekewich could not and would not aid and abet Rhodes to force the hand of the superior military authorities' to rescue the town, and he records how Rhodes lashed out at Kekewich and the army:

> Your damned soldiers are so loyal to one authority that I verily believe if God Almighty even was in a fix you would refuse to get him out of it should the doing so interfere with your damned military situation.[15]

In his defence of Kekewich O'Meara asked, 'Was ever another British commander in a more trying position ?' Mafeking, Kimberley and Ladysmith would not be relieved until after Lord Roberts arrived in South Africa to take over the British Army. In the vanguard of each relieving force would be an Irishman.

By November British Army troops were pouring into South Africa. In October the 2nd Royal Irish Rifles began to mobilize and out of 704 Rifles reservists summoned only nine failed to put in an appearance. They left Belfast amidst scenes of wildest enthusiasm, arriving in Cape Town on 13 November. Less than a month later they suffered grievously in their first action at Stormberg Junction in the eastern Cape, in the Drakensberg Range, the first of the disastrous battles experienced by the British Army during December of 1899. The Rifles, together with the Northumberland Fusiliers, Mounted Infantry, some Cape police, Royal Field Artillery and Royal Engineers were under the command of General Sir William Gatacre who decided to surprise and recapture strategic Stormberg from the Boers. Surprise them he did, but not in the way he intended. Gatacre was a martinet known as General 'Backacher' because of his passion for physical exercise and his lack of sympathy for any sign of fatigue in his troops. This, it was said, contributed to the coming disaster, together with bad luck, bad judgement, poor reconnaissance and misunderstanding by guides and by the General himself. To encourage his Rifles, already tired because of poor train arrangements by Gatacre's staff, at 9.15pm Lieutenant Colonel Henry Eager addressed his men before they set out from Moltena on a night march of some ten miles: 'The battalion represents the North of Ireland which is watching you. I know I have not to ask you to do your duty.'

When daylight came the column, undoubtedly lost, was still marching in fours into the Boer-occupied valley, passing the hill they could have climbed to dominate Boer camps below. Seeing the danger, Colonel Eager ventured to suggest detaching a half company as advance guard, but General Gatacre brusquely rejected it. The surprised Boers opened fire from the heights to which they had rushed on seeing the column approach. In an endeavour to clear a detached kopje on the left Colonel Eager and his men were shelled by their own field artillery who, in the still uncertain light, had mistaken the Rifles for the enemy. Eager was the first to be hit and later died of his wounds, other officers and riflemen were severely wounded. Those lying under the cliffs ready to advance were driven back down the slope harassed by their own guns, others were subjected to fierce fire from invisible Boers and Gatacre ordered a retirement. In the meantime some six hundred of the Fusiliers and Irish Rifles remained on their hill tenaciously keeping up the fight with the Boers expecting a flank attack to be ordered. No orders came, they were forgotten and left to their fate; 634 unwounded officers and men were taken prisoners by the Boers. The disaster was not discovered until Moltena was reached; Gatacre and his bad staff work were blamed for this calamity. When the General later addressed the Irish Rifles to explain the reason for this failure, 'probably the men did not understand his explanation; but they did understand full well that they had been repulsed though they had hardly been engaged'. Yet they cheered him and begged to be taken back to Stormberg for another attempt! Gatacre was subsequently sacked.[16]

The dashing Irishman Major General Arthur Fitzroy Hart came into prominence in the opening Battle of Colenso on 15 December, commanding his 5th Irish Brigade of 2nd Dublin, 1st Inniskilling Fusiliers, 1st Connaught Rangers and 55th Border Regiment (also very Irish). They were part of the large army under General Sir Redvers Buller VC, whose aim was to relieve the beleaguered town of Ladysmith. The fiery Hart, after some thirty-five years in the army, was seen as a haughty man brimming with self-confidence. The son of a depot major at Templemore who became a Lieutenant General, young Hart was educated in a 'conventional middle-class manner' at Cheltenham and Sandhurst, joining the army in 1864. He saw service in the Ashanti and Zulu Wars, the 1881 First Boer War and the Egyptian War of 1882 where he was Wolseley's Deputy Assistant Adjutant General. This led to his promotion to Major-General and command of the Irish Brigade in South Africa. His haughtiness may have been encouraged by his early marriage to the heiress May Synnot, daughter of a wealthy landowner of Armagh, whereby Hart became connected with the landed interest.[17] After serving under Wolseley, Hart does not seem to have absorbed any of Wolseley's new ideas and continued to believe in tactics associated with the Crimea forty-five years earlier. When he led his Irish Brigade of seasoned soldiers and eager reservists to the Tugela River to open the battle that morning, 'He had already put them through a parade ground drill as he had every morning for a fortnight, then, still as if drilling . . . marched them forward in quarter column and close order'. The Boers, entrenched in the kopjes above the swiftly-flowing river, were well placed to cover the drifts (fords) that led across it. It was a sad day for the Irish.

Hart, ordered by Buller to cross Bridle Drift, could not find it. Distrusting his map indicating the drift a short distance to the west, he chose to follow his native guide who spoke no English and vaguely pointed east towards the river, then bolted at the first shot. Hart did not send scouts ahead and he also ignored the warning sent to him by Colonel Burn-Murdoch of the 1st Dragoons of the Boers across the river. In broad daylight Hart marched his Irishmen massed together across a coverless veldt of a flat salient that formed a big U-shaped loop of the river. They were a perfect target for the unseen Boers on the heights, whose accurate fire burst upon them from all sides. It was a death trap. Within forty minutes some four hundred men were mown down. Undoubtedly brave, Hart, known as *Coeur de Leon* and General 'No-Bobs' because he never ducked under fire, recklessly dashed about in the midst of this chaos, ignoring bullets and spurring on his brave Irishmen, who would not yield as long as he with 'unquenched ardour' kept them there. In the ensuing confusion some Dublin Fusiliers actually rushed into the river, only to drown with their heavy equipment because the river had been dammed by the Boers and was eight feet deep, not two as had been expected. A few managed to swim back.[18] Casualties in Dublin Fusiliers and Connaught Rangers were particularly heavy and Hart's brigade had the severest losses of the troops engaged. 'The daring and bravery of the Irish Brigade is beyond description,' writes Private Tucker of the Rifle Brigade who were nearby and had also received many shells:

> I have only one fault to find with the Irish but perhaps it is a good one – they are too reckless as regards taking cover. They expose themselves too much and thus more lives are lost than is necessary. In fighting an enemy like the Boer, in his native cover, this is madness.[19]

When, later, despite their casualties and ordered by General Buller to retire, the Irishmen did so under protest. The first attempt to relieve Ladysmith had failed.

As with the Colours, saving guns was always considered an honourable achievement demanding the highest recognition. Buller, horrified by Hart's defeat, ordered a rescue of the twelve field and eight naval guns that had been abandoned by Colonel Charles Long, commander of Royal Field Artillery. Volunteers were requested and one of them was Lieutenant the Honourable Frederick Roberts of the 60th Rifles, the only son of General

Lord Roberts, Commander-in-Chief in Ireland, and acting at this time as ADC to Lieutenant General Sir C. F. Clery, commander of 2nd Infantry Division. Clery is that eccentric Anglo-Irishman who had laid out the camp at Islandhlwana twenty years before. Frederick lost his life in this action and was awarded the VC posthumously. The space young Roberts and others had to cross to reach the guns was swept with shell and rifle fire and 'Lord Roberts's son was shot as we were going up' recounts Corporal George Edward Nurse (later a lieutenant), an Irishman from Enniskillen of 66th Battery Royal Field Artillery who was assisting and who also won the VC in that action. Captain Walter Congreve of the Rifle Brigade, himself wounded, brought in his friend Roberts who died the next day. Captain H.N. Schofield, another of Buller's ADCs, and Corporal Nurse managed to hook in the limbers and together they brought in two of the guns. Captain Hamilton Lyster Reed from Dublin, of 7th Battery, also won a VC in another attempt to save the guns and was wounded. A sad footnote concerns young Roberts. A charming young man, he had failed the Staff College entrance examination and it was only due to his illustrious father's embarrassed pleas to Wolseley, the army's Commander-in-Chief and Roberts Senior's 'rival', that he was considered at all. Perhaps volunteering like this was young Roberts's way of proving himself.[20]

Several Irishmen serving in the Boer War would come to high rank and prominence in the First World War and two of them were at Colenso, Lieutenant Colonel Lawrence Parsons and Major Henry Wilson. Parsons, as one of Buller's commanders of artillery, had tried to prepare the ground for Hart's brigade with his twelve guns to help Hart in his passage to the Bridle Drift; unfortunately 'some of his shells fell among Hart's leading troops'. At the end of February 1900 Parsons had the opportunity at Pieter's Hill 'to exploit Buller's revolutionary new tactic for coordinating artillery and infantry' for the first time by sending 'a creeping curtain of shell-fire' over their heads as they advanced. Lawrence Parsons came from the cadet branch of an old Anglo-Irish Protestant family from Parsonstown, King's County, related to the earls of Rosse and a descendant of Sir William Parsons who settled in Ireland in 1590. He was the only son of an 'unpractical scholar' living modestly near Birr and was close friends with his cousins at Birr Castle. A competent classical scholar himself, he chose the British Army for his profession and after Woolwich was commissioned in 1869 in the Royal Artillery. He went to India where memories of the Indian Mutiny were still very much alive and John Nicholson became his hero. His wife Florence Graves also came from a distinguished Irish family who had come to Ireland in the seventeenth century, a family of scholars, divines and military men, which included the poet Robert Graves.[21]

Major Henry Wilson was Brigade Major of Major General Neville Lyttelton's 4 Brigade whose difficulties, compared with those of General Hart's 5 Brigade, were minimal. Wilson records in a letter to his wife:

> We never got near the river and although I was under fire for 5 hours and sometimes brisk fire I can only swear to having seen 5 Boers. It's quite marvellous. I doubt our having killed 100, they remain complete masters of that side of the stream and I don't see myself how we are going to cross the river to get to Ladysmith.

Henry was from a family of Ulster Protestants whose ancestor, John Wilson in William III's suite, received a grant of land in County Antrim. Another ancestor made a fortune in the shipping business in Belfast in the eighteenth century, after which the family abandoned trade and purchased estates in Southern Ireland where Henry, in 1864, was born in County Longford. He 'maintained the character of his sturdy uncompromising Ulster forebears . . . his genial cheerful disposition derived from his southern Irish connections'. Henry went to Marlborough College, but did not do well. As a younger son of a landed Anglo-Irish family, Henry went to the army but failed in his try for Woolwich and Sandhurst. Finally, by way of the militia, 'the back door of the army', he was gazetted first to the 18th Royal Irish Regiment then transferred to the Rifle Brigade. He saw service in India and was wounded in Burma, the result of which left him with a twisted face and he became known as 'the tall ugly Irishman'.[22] He was a young man with burning ambition and later, in August 1900, he joined Lord Roberts's staff in Pretoria as Deputy Assistant Quartermaster General. He and the Field Marshal would eventually become firm friends.

Field Marshal Lord Roberts of Kandahar Arrives

> Roberts was, like so many great soldiers, an Irishman . . .
>
> Stuart Cloete, *Rags of Glory,* New York, 1963, p. 229

Roberts's arrival in South Africa was as a result of Black Week, those December battles under General Buller when highly trained soldiers in the British Army suffered humiliating defeats at the hands of the often rough Afrikaners who had also put three towns under siege. Buller, a protégé of Wolseley, was undoubtedly made a scapegoat for the army's defeats. To his credit, Buller had said when appointed to his command that he would have preferred to serve as Chief of Staff under his old mentor Wolseley as the Commander-in-Chief.[23] Lord Lansdowne became convinced that General Buller had to be replaced and by Lord Roberts, whose antipathy to Buller was not helped in that he blamed Buller for his son's death. Buller in the end was kept on to command in Natal.

And so Lord Roberts of Kandahar, another 'Sepoy general' like Wellington, was appointed at the end of 1899 as Commander-in-Chief to rescue the prestige of the British Army in South Africa. *Punch* saw a connection between Wolseley and Wellington, and Kipling also celebrates a similar connection with Roberts in his poem 'Bobs', so nicknamed by his soldiers:

> Then 'ere's to Bobs Bahadur – little Bobs,
> Bobs, Bobs,
> Pocket-Wellin'ton an' *arder* -
> Fightin Bobs, Bobs, Bobs!

In another often quoted verse of that same ballad Kipling underlines the impact of the diminutive Roberts:

> Oh 'e's little but he's wise,
> E's a terror for 'is size . . .

Roberts, as Byron Farwell notes, 'had no doubts about his own abilities',[24] and while still Commander-in-Chief in Ireland he did not hesitate to correspond with Lord Lansdowne and put himself forward as the man to command in South Africa. He was more than ready to be in the field again and even had outlined a policy towards the three besieged towns. The question can be asked why was Wolseley, who had wide experience in South Africa and 'knew the Army better than any man living' not considered for the job in South Africa? For some Victorians 'Wolseley was the greatest soldier their century had produced since Wellington', even though he had not commanded in a major war. As for Roberts, in India he was considered to be 'among the three greatest Commanders-in-Chief in the ninety years between the Mutiny and Partition, dominating the Indian military scene in the nineties'. That Lord Lansdowne, War Secretary, was a friend of Roberts might well have added to the reasons why Wolseley did not receive the appointment to command in South Africa. But paramount was Wolseley's health, which he could no longer conceal. This most capable if arrogant soldier was losing his memory, probably the beginning of Alzheimer's disease, 'a sad end to a brilliant career'. As he got worse, he did not remember having met people, which is typical of that disease; when in 1908 William Butler visited him for the last time, his old chief did not know him.[25]

Roberts landed at Cape Town in early January 1900, a company of the newly arrived Royal Irish Regiment forming a guard of honour. With him as his Chief of Staff was General Kitchener who had returned to England as the hero of the Battle of Omdurman in 1898 and elevated to the peerage as Lord Kitchener of Khartoum, recognized as the avenger of General Gordon. The diminutive Roberts and the towering Kitchener made quite a contrast, as did their characters: the genial Roberts had done much to raise the status of the private soldier in India while the reserved Kitchener was someone who barely addressed a private soldier.

Roberts, Kitchener and Wolseley were three national heroes of the nineteenth century whom Correlli Barnett sees as prime examples of the Anglo-Irish gentry, 'the nearest thing Britain ever possessed to the Prussian Junker class'. Kitchener's English parents only fitted the picture of the Anglo-Irish for twelve years, but he would later assert he was 'much more Irish than Roberts, that's why I understand them', a delusion [which] was to influence his judgement. His father was a retired Colonel from the Indian Army and purchased an estate on the Kerry-Limerick border. Colonel Kitchener had only contempt for his Irish tenantry and, an arrogant man, he never found an entré into the established Irish gentry who were his neighbours which, along with his wife's health, undoubtedly influenced him to sell his Irish estates after only a few years. As with the Junker class, Roberts and Wolseley were also the sons of soldiers; like many Anglo-Irish, all three were poorer than their English counterparts and all had advanced in their British Army careers through intelligence and merit, careers they had assiduously cultivated.[26] As Roberts's Chief-of-Staff, Kitchener was greatly resented by officers senior to him, his position virtually amounted to his being Second in Command of the British Army in South Africa, but Roberts had total trust in Kitchener and they worked well together. There was no love lost between French, commander of the Cavalry Division, and Kitchener. From the beginning of their association there were personality clashes between the 'ascetic, almost monkish Kitchener, and the ebullient, mercurial French'.[27] Nor did that other Irishman, Lieutenant General Sir Thomas Kelly-Kenny, much like Kitchener, whose overbearing ways and interference in Kelly-Kenny's 6th Infantry Division, especially at Paardeberg, greatly irritated him. Kelly-Kenny was the second oldest general in the army, the oldest being Roberts. He was 'somewhat of an Irish Nationalist, a Catholic, and a Wolseley admirer like his old friend Sir William Butler',[28] but, unlike Butler, he had little sympathy for Boers.

On his arrival Roberts immediately concentrated on the need for mounted infantry which he saw as not only essential to move about the vast country but as a necessary tactic to counter the mobility of the Boers on their swift ponies. One company from each infantry battalion was ordered to be converted into mounted infantry or MI, a process already begun in some Irish regiments. Before the Royal Irish Regiment left Ireland in September 1899 a draft of officers and men was sent to the mounted infantry course at Shorncliffe in England, and on arriving in South Africa at the end of January 1900 formed part of the 5th Mounted Infantry Regiment. The Royal Munster Fusiliers were ordered to form an MI company shortly after their arrival in Cape Town in September. After the Stormberg battle of December two companies of the 2nd Royal Irish Rifles were converted into MI and detached to join one of the many composite MI battalions being formed. Later MI colonels, under whom MI companies of the Royal Irish Rifles served, highly commended their horse management as 'exceptionally good': 'That, with the Irishman's way with a horse, was the least that could be expected.'[29]

Roberts's Great Flank March, Sir John French and the Relief of Kimberley

By 10 February Roberts had decided that Kimberley must be relieved first, largely influenced by Buller's failure to force the passage at the Tugela, and also by the growing tension between Kimberley's commander Colonel Kekewich and the ever-aggressive Rhodes who was screaming to the world to be rescued and threatening to surrender, under pressure, he said, from Kimberley's citizens. On 11 February Roberts took most of his huge army on what has been called the Great Flank March, swinging widely around the eastern flank of the Boer positions at Magersfontein in the western Orange Free State; his ultimate aim was Bloemfontein, its capital. Roberts's innovative plan was not to use the railway as the Boer leader Cronjé expected, but to march across the arid veld. Another of several deceits was that Lord Methuen was left behind to sit on the Modder River and feint a frontal attack towards the Boers at Magersfontein while Roberts's troops headed south to the little town of Ramdam which became the jumping-off point of the flank march. Major Seymour Vandeleur, Senior Transport Officer in General Kelly-Kenny's 6th Infantry Division, has recorded the impressive spectacle of Roberts's vast army on the move:

> As far as the eye could see the veldt was alive with troops. Thin clouds of dust . . . in front marked the progress of the cavalry division, . . . thicker dust clouds denoted infantry brigades toiling slowly behind; . . . thickest and blackest were raised by loaded mule waggons straining in the rear.

Vandeleur was another of those Special Service officers in South Africa. From a landed Anglo-Irish family with a long military tradition, he was very much an example of the Irish Junker class, his father was Lord Lieutenant of County Clare. The Vandeleurs, of Norman origin, settled in Ireland in the seventeenth century and seem ever to have been a race of soldiers. Of Seymour Vandeleur's five great-uncles four attained the rank of general and were conspicuous in the campaigns of their day. Among them was General Sir John Ormsby Vandeleur KCB who commanded Light Cavalry at Waterloo. After Sandhurst Seymour was commissioned in the Scots Guards in 1889 and joined their 2nd Battalion in Dublin. He was also one of those soldier-adventurers of the nineteenth century who, on four months leave of absence from his regiment, travelled to Somaliland to shoot game. More than a mere shooting trip, he travelled beyond explored country and on his own initiative mapped the whole route, having prepared himself by taking a course of lessons on the sextant, and presented on his return a map to the Royal Geographic Society. Always restless and again looking for adventure, he went to Uganda, volunteering for service with the Uganda Rifles in 1894. There too he made the first authentic map, and subsequently was elected Fellow of the Royal Geographic Society and given a DSO for his services. The army, however, chiefly claimed his loyalty. In the fighting in Egypt he was a (bimbashi) Major in the 9th Sudanese battalion and was also at Omdurman under Kitchener, spending nearly two years with the Egyptian Army. Vandeleur was then appointed by Kitchener as an Inspector in the soldier-civilian service in the 'regeneration' of the Sudan where he served under another Anglo-Irishman, Lieutenant Colonel Bryan Mahon. He and Mahon were among the first officers to leave the Sudan for the Boer War.[30]

At 3.00am on 11 February, leaving the camp south of the Modder, Lieutenant General John French led his cavalry division in a remarkable ride that greatly added to his reputation. The previous day Roberts had stressed to French and his commanders the importance of the relief of Kimberley and added – 'You are going to get the greatest chance cavalry ever had'. With the long lines of his cavalry French rode south, then east from Ramdam for fifteen miles to secure the crossings of the Riet River for the infantry at De Kiel's Drift. Such was the chaos at the crossing that not until mid-morning the next day could French continue on the second leg of his journey, heading north over some twenty-five waterless miles of flat, dry land, arriving at the Modder to cross it at Klip Drift. It was great cavalry country, but it was the hottest time of the year. At Klip Drift he had to wait for Kelly-Kenny's Infantry Division to catch up with supplies and became very impatient, as he had promised Kitchener he would be in Kimberley by 15 February. Kelly-Kenny duly arrived, but only because of an all-night forced march through rain storms and almost unbearable heat during the day. While waiting for Kelly-Kenny French, trying to assess Boer strength through his field glasses, noted Boers positioned along about ten miles of kopjes, between which ran a gap or valley with a low ridge at the end where more Boers lay in wait. French decided to run the gauntlet, to gallop up the valley right through the Boer centre that he saw as a weak part. It was a 'quick insight', as the *Times History* later called it, a 'secret French had divined' that Boer rifle fire [would] 'avail nothing against the rushing speed and sustained impetus of the wave of horsemen'. On the morning of 15 February Kelly-Kenny's men were north of the Modder and French resumed his advance. Out rode the cavalry, Boer fire opening up on them, but French used his horse artillery to good advantage and was reinforced by Kelly-Kenny's divisional artillery. To the watching infantry of 6th Division, the sight of those horsemen thundering through the heat and dust was one they would never forget, a charge the *Times History* reported that 'marks an epoch in the history of cavalry', while it praised 'the reckless daredevil confidence that carried it through'.[31] When the cavalrymen dashed onto the ridge the Boers broke and fled; some were speared and captured, others carried away the news of this amazing ride. French called a halt around Abdon's Dam where the men could get water, but such was the scarcity in the month of February that the horses received none. He and his staff then slowly rode into Kimberley only a few miles ahead, arriving about 6.30 pm that evening to a tumultuous welcome. After only minor resistance, Boers investing the town began to melt away. The four-month siege was over and the news, flashed to England, was received with great excitement. The relief of Kimberley was the first British success in months.

The *Official History* has praised French's charge as 'the most brilliant stroke of the war'. In fact it was not a cavalry charge in the accepted sense but solely to break through to Kimberly. In Thomas Pakenham's opinion it was 'a magnificent, but quite unnecessary dash to self-destruction across the veld'. The sight of so many dead and dying horses littering the veld was undoubtedly pitiful. The Marquess of Anglesey, however, defends French and his famous 'Klip Drift Charge':

> it was considered absolutely necessary to get through to Kimberley at all costs so as to prevent its supposed imminent surrender . . . that this later proved not to be at all the case does not invalidate French's decision.

There were twelve casualties among French's men. Roberts extended his grateful thanks to him, as did the Queen. French, on arrival in Kimberley, had an 'uncomfortable interview' with Lieutenant Colonel Kekewich, undoubtedly influenced by Rhodes, and when French departed two days later Kekewich discovered (without being told) that he had been replaced by Colonel Porter of the 1st Cavalry Brigade as garrison commander. This was not an edifying action on French's part and to Richard Holmes, French's biographer, it was an injustice to Kekewich.[32]

'My Brave Irish'

Meanwhile in January Major General Hart and his Irish Brigade were again in battle in Buller's campaign to take the hills north of the Tugela and clear the way to relieve Ladysmith. The Irish General C. F. Clery, now commander of 2nd Division, was ordered to conduct a frontal attack on the Tabanyama Ridge and he sent up to the west of Three Tree Hill General Hart and his Irish Brigade with batteries to support them. The Irish went forward in an inspiring attack, as the Inniskilling historian writes: 'The soldiers, burning to efface the memory of what seemed to them their unaccountable rebuff at Colenso, forced their way forward with great speed . . . whilst the enemy . . . fired . . . hotly down upon them'. Hart's men were soon in the trenches on the lower crest of Rangeworthy [Heights]. The Boers fell back to the true crest about a thousand yards northward and continued their fusillade. Then, with his usual impetuosity and confidence, Hart was about to lead a spirited attack up the exposed slope and sweep the enemy from the hill when Clery suddenly ordered a halt. After conferring with his colleague General Warren, he had decided that another such frontal attack on exposed ground could not be supported by artillery and he was concerned about casualties; the cost so far to the Irish Brigade had been 365. Two days later, on 24 January, with other troops still clinging to the southern crest, the Inniskillings remained inactive spectators of the bitter fight raging above them on the plateau of the massive Spion Kop by 10 and 11 Brigades, and longing to help. In the morning the army heard with stupefaction that Spion Kop had been evacuated during the night; a general retirement had been ordered by General Buller because of General Warren's slowness in attacking Rangeworthy Heights.

A month later the reinforced Irish Brigade were in the thick of the battles for the Tugela Heights when General Buller again tried to break through to Ladysmith by driving the Boers from a chain of steep-sided hills known as Wynn's, Hart's, Pieter's and Railway. These were slaughter grounds for the Irish, but before the battle in the afternoon of 22 February the Inniskillings had time to swim in the Tugela! Fighting was particularly savage for 5 Irish Brigade the next day when ordered to attack Hart's Hill, also called Inniskilling Hill to commemorate the gallant deeds of the Inniskillings in these battles. Hart, impatient as usual, ordered his bugler to sound the 'Charge' repeatedly, and in the hail of Boer fire Colonel Thackery of the Inniskillings fell mortally wounded, leading the battalion he loved. Many were killed and wounded as they rushed to within a few yards of the Boer trenches. Survivors had to fall back; 'there were not enough men to do the work'.[33] The remaining Inniskillings were then joined for a second attack by companies of Dublin Fusiliers and Connaught Rangers who had meanwhile been engaged on another part of the hill, suffering considerably. 'With a terrific yell the Inniskillings . . . sprang over the false crest and hurled themselves once more at the [Boer] entrenchments', Dublin Fusiliers and Connaught Rangers following. 'The Boers were not taken by surprise' and their fire was intense. The courage of the Irish so impressed them that they 'allowed a few of the Irishmen to leap unharmed into their works and then seized and disarmed them before they could use their bayonets' – a magnanimous gesture. The Irish lay prostrate on the hill all night in agony, only the wounded received water. Their officers, hoping for reinforcements, waited in vain for orders to renew the attack. Reluctantly, at about 6.00am, the order for the Irish Brigade to retire was given by Colonel Brooke of the Connaught Rangers. Casualties amounted to over 500 in less than twenty-four hours, including the colonels of the Dublins and Inniskillings who were killed. Inniskilling losses were 'the highest proportion of any regiment in the war so far'.[34]

Three days later on 27 February the Irish were again in attacks on Pieter's, Railway and Inniskilling/Hart's Hills that at last broke the stubborn Boers. Just before the advance began came the heartening news of Roberts's success at Paardeberg and of the Boer leader Cronjé's surrender. In the early afternoon the 2nd Royal Irish Fusiliers began their climb, scrambling up the rocky hillside to emerge on the flat crest and capture one of the peaks of Pieter's Hill. Two companies of Dublin Fusiliers, along with Scots Fusiliers, stormed the northern kopje of Pieter's Hill but were 'beaten back with severe casualties'. Hart's and Railway Hills were, however, in British hands and only the last peak of Pieter's remained to be taken. Much later that afternoon three companies of Royal Irish Fusiliers led by Major F. F. Hill again went forward, covered by rifle fire of Dublin Fusiliers, and 'every officer in this Faugh party became a casualty . . . . Nevertheless the Irish reached the Boer kopje and hung on there until dark, finding at midnight the enemy was gone'. The Tugela Heights were in Buller's hands, and the proud Boers pulled out, a great tide flowing northward from Ladysmith.[35]

Captain Hubert Gough and the Relief of Ladysmith

On the evening of 28 February the twenty-nine-year-old Anglo-Irish Captain Hubert Gough of the 16th Lancers rode into Ladysmith, leading an advance guard of a composite squadron of Colonial troops in Lord Dundonald's 2nd Mounted Infantry. With Ladysmith in sight Gough had asked permission to ride forward, but his cautious MI commander had dithered; it was 'too dangerous' to go on. The impatient Gough, a man of 'dash and enthusiasm' writes: 'At last I escaped with permission to proceed'. In the late afternoon a dusty and emotional Gough was greeted enthusiastically in the town by the cheering population and by Sir George White, now a visibly worn-out man both physically and emotionally. Outwardly calm, White greeted his old friend: 'Hello Hubert, how are you?'[36] They had met in the 1890s in India at Simla when White was Commander-in-Chief. The one hundred-and-eighteen-day siege of Ladysmith was over. A few days later Buller's tattered army led by Dublin Fusiliers made a formal entry into the town. Buller and White would be cheered by excited crowds in both England and South Africa.

Hubert Gough, of a distinguished Anglo-Irish military family from Limerick and Tipperary, was the son of Major (later General Sir) Charles Gough who won the VC in the Indian Mutiny. After Sandhurst Hubert was commissioned in the 16th Lancers and served in India. Released from the Staff College, he arrived in South Africa as a Special Service officer in November 1899. At Ladysmith to his great delight he met his younger brother Captain John Gough of the Rifle Brigade. 'Johnnie', as he was known, was also a graduate of Sandhurst, gazetted Second Lieutenant in the Rifle Brigade in 1892; he served in the Sudan under Kitchener and at the end of October 1899 went to South Africa. Like many others, Johnnie saw conflict between Boer and Briton as 'long overdue' and was keen to get into action. He expected to participate in 'useful fighting' at Ladysmith, but arrived only in time to cover the withdrawal of General White's army into the town. Over the months of the siege Johnnie and his Brigade had been in some sharp raids against the Boers with casualties. On the day of the relief he was still out in the hills on duty and did not know his brother had led the advance into Ladysmith until he received a message to meet him. After three years Hubert did not recognize this unfamiliar officer riding towards him on a grey pony who said, 'Hallo Hubert . . . how fat you have got!' To Hubert Johnnie seemed 'fitter and browner than any man of the garrison I had seen', yet Johnnie was only too pleased to receive food from Hubert's men.[37]

Reports of conditions in Ladysmith after the siege varied. Some saw the town and garrison as 'remarkably fit', others saw them as 'wearied and emaciated'. Drummer Barton of the 2nd Battalion, Royal Irish Fusiliers, compared the state of the soldiers in his regiment with those of the garrison, who were looking 'very poor, but clean and tidy . . . we were in rags, some of us in Civilians clothes captured in the Boer Laagers'.[38] But during the siege nearly 600 soldiers died, 59 from shrapnel wounds, the rest from disease, mostly enteric fever and dysentery. Among those invalided home was General White, a man Roberts now 'refused to employ', although he was a friend from their days in India. Buller, however, offered him command of a division, somewhat of a 'come down'. White's great mistake was 'letting himself be trapped in Ladysmith', yet after the war he was remembered for his 'endurance and courage there'. An equestrian statue of him still stands in London.

After the relief of Kimberley on 15 February Roberts's plan to advance to Bloemfontein was briefly halted when he engaged the Boer leader Cronjé in battle at Paardeberg Drift on the Modder River. Cronjé and his large force had headed eastward along the Modder, determined to prevent Roberts from reaching Bloemfontein. As Cronjé prepared to cross the river to establish a position to block Roberts General French, sent out by Kitchener, caught up with him. With only part of his cavalry, who were exhausted from a gruelling march from Kimberley and already depleted, all French could do was to keep Cronjé from escaping until Roberts's infantry arrived. Kelly-Kenny's 6th Division duly arrived, tired and hungry, pushed hard by Kitchener. Cronjé was all but surrounded. He set up a laager and dug in on the river bank against the advice of his commanders who wished him to break away before he was encircled, which he could have done. He decided to fight.

Simmering tensions over command in Roberts's army and over tactics at Paardeberg soon surfaced between Kelly-Kenny and the rigorous Kitchener, in command since Roberts was ill at Jacobsdal. Kelly-Kenny, senior commander at this time, appealed to Roberts and was asked to consider Kitchener's orders as Roberts's own. Kelly-Kenny agreed, humiliating as he felt it to be: 'After all . . . he had been fighting in China while Kitchener was still a boy.' Kelly-Kenny favoured shelling, surrounding and starving Boers into submission, a conservative approach dictated by the fact that his men were already exhausted and on short rations. Kitchener decided on a strong frontal attack to hit the Boers hard before they had time to organize and he relentlessly pursued this plan. 'Kelly-Kenny did successfully prevent his 6th Division from renewing their frontal attack from the south,' but 'failed to prevent Kitchener continuing the flank attack.' Fighting came to a standstill and there were terrible casualties. Moreover, 'senior commanders had lost their faith in Kitchener' who never informed them of his strategies for the battle.[39]

Roberts, returned from his sick bed, first thought to continue Kitchener's attack, then changed his mind and cancelled it, appalled at the number of casualties and realizing the decided reluctance of his divisional commanders to carry on as planned. There was also an immediate threat in the surrounding area from the able Christiaan De Wet who had captured a nearby kopje. Roberts hesitated, put off any decision for the present and, it was claimed, 'urged retirement to Klip Kraal Drift'.[40] Even great men, it seems, have their moments of doubt, which Kitchener never seems to have had. Roberts 'recovered', helped undoubtedly when De Wet gave up and retired, and he soon ordered a full-scale bombardment on Cronjé's laager. He denied Cronjé's appeal for a truce to bring in the wounded, which brought Cronjé's defiant refusal to surrender. Then, on learning that women and children were in the laager, Roberts offered them safe passage; Cronjé still refused. On 27 February Boers were seen raising white flags in their trenches opposite the Canadians. Cronjé had to follow suit and sent a message of surrender to Roberts who gracefully received him in his camp.[41] A most interesting photograph of the Boer War shows the surrender of the big, shambling, unkempt, heavily bearded Cronjé to the small, straight-backed khaki-clad Roberts, whose only ornament was his imposing presentation sword from his famous Kabul to Kandahar march. Cronjé, dismounted, stands beside a drooping pony that unwittingly echoes his defeat. The newspaper people and civilians present were appalled at the sight of the tattered and decrepit-looking Boers who, with weeping wives and children, emerged from the devastated laager. Major Seymour Vandeleur thought the Boers were 'a fine-looking lot of men'.

After Paardeberg the way to Bloemfontein was open to Roberts and the capital surrendered to him on 13 March without a fight, to be renamed 'Bobsfontein'. A period of rest and reorganization of the exhausted British Army followed, hampered by typhoid fever that swept through the camps. There were many conflicting accounts about the inadequacies in Bloemfontein in handling the epidemic and, as in the Crimea, the medical establishment of Roberts's Army was greatly criticized.

Forming of the Irish Guards

Severe casualties in the Irish regiments in the Battles for the Tugela in February moved Queen Victoria to telegraph to General Buller her 'deepest concern of the heavy losses sustained by my brave Irish soldiers. I desire to express . . . my admiration for [their] splendid fighting qualities'. Wolseley, writing to the Queen in March, heartily approved and 'presumed to suggest that the Queen should now order all her Irish regiments to wear the shamrock in their head-dress on . . . St. Patrick's Day'. A greater mark of appreciation was pending. Concurring with the Queen's wishes an Army order dated 1 April 1900 authorized that an Irish Regiment of Foot Guards be formed, to be designated the Irish Guards to commemorate the bravery shown by the Irish Regiments in South Africa from 1899 – 1900. Lord Roberts was chosen as the first Colonel and Lieutenant Colonel R.J. Cooper transferred from the Grenadier Guards as the first Commanding Officer. Alexander Godley, Charles Fitzclarence VC and Seymour Vandeleur DSO also transferred to the new regiment. Their only bond in the early days was that all were Irish and all were intensely conscious of the honour shown to the whole Irish nation by the creation of their regiment. The first actual recruit was James O'Brien of Limerick. The Irish Guards did not serve as a whole unit in the Anglo-Boer War, but contributed a section to the 1st Guards Mounted Infantry Company. In a heavy action Colour Sergeant Hudson won the DCM for gallantry, the first Irish Guards non-commissioned officer to receive a medal in action.[42]

Colonel Bryan Mahon and the Relief of Mafeking

In early May Roberts and his great army were on their way to the Transvaal. Realizing that political pressure to relieve Mafeking was building, he sanctioned two relief columns to be sent. Colonel Bryan Mahon DSO, an Irish Hussar who was now a Special Service officer in South Africa, would leave the south Kimberley area with his flying column of South African mounted infantry, many of them Uitlanders from Johannesburg, colonials in the Kimberley Mounted Corps and a hundred men of the Royal Horse Artillery. Also under Mahon was a representative detachment of one hundred selected infantrymen, twenty-five each from English, Irish, Welsh and Scottish regiments. In the other column, gathering under Lieutenant Colonel H. Plumer in Rhodesia, were two hundred constables of the British South Africa police, fifty men of the Rhodesia Horse Volunteers, a four-gun battery of Royal Canadian Artillery, accompanied by one hundred dismounted men of the 3rd Queensland (Australian) Mounted Infantry. When combined, these two columns would represent all corners of the Empire, thought to be a politically expedient gesture carefully arranged by Roberts.

Mahon's feat, and that of his flying column, was to cover some two hundred and forty miles in twelve days: 'Drought and dust and sickness, not Boers, had proved their most dangerous enemies'. His men and horses were suffering greatly from water shortage, but for the most part he had out-marched Boer detachments sent to intercept him. On 14 May there had been a sharp fight when the Boers attacked and Mahon had thirty-one casualties. He and Plumer joined forces on 15 May eighteen miles from Mafeking where Mahon, as senior officer, took command of both columns and, moving parallel, they headed for Mafeking, but were attacked by the formidable Boer Commandant Koos de la Rey. Geoffrey Powell, Plumer's biographer, points out that Mahon kept a strong reserve and kept de la Rey from his flanks. The *Times History* reports that 'Plumer . . . had to fight for every yard of the way towards the town . . . Casualties were again severe'. By the next afternoon the Mafeking townspeople could see 'shells exploding in the distance . . . a dark mass of horsemen appeared' and a heliograph blinked a message: 'From Colonel Mahon's force – How are you getting on?' Baden-Powell answered simply: 'Welcome'.[43]

On the evening of 16 May Major Karri Davis with a patrol of his Imperial Light Horse, an Uitlander regiment, was the first to ride into Mafeking, surprised at the somewhat low-key reception by the first people they met. The relief force was to arrive the next morning, 'after breakfast it was said', but Mahon, worried about another Boer attack, 'thought otherwise'. At 3.30am he and Plumer, with their exhausted force, arrived in Mafeking to waken the sleeping town with the marching feet of their men and the rumble of their guns. When Baden-Powell took the salute at the official ceremony later in the day Mahon and Plumer were at his side. Behind the relief column marched the garrison, 'lean, tough scarecrows in their patched uniforms,' including Captains Godley and Fitzclarence VC, and the townspeople now responded enthusiastically. The relief of Mafeking was accomplished after seven months and the news travelled around the world. In London crowds went wild. The name on everyone's lips, however, was not Mahon's or Plumer's, 'the rescuers of Mafeking', but Baden-Powell's, whose picture appeared everywhere and in which he wears the felt campaign hat that would become known to Boy Scouts throughout the world.[44]

Colonel Bryan Mahon of Belleville, County Galway, came from an Anglo-Irish ascendancy family. First commissioned in the Connaught Rangers, he then transferred to the 8th King's Royal Irish Hussars and became their adjutant. Like Parsons and Vandeleur, Mahon was seconded to the Anglo-Egyptian Army under Kitchener to take part in the re-conquest of the Sudan and commanded a cavalry squadron with distinction at Omdurman. After Mafeking Mahon returned to the Sudan as Military Governor of Kordofan and, before retiring in 1914, he was GOC of the Lucknow Division.

The Irish Civilian Volunteers in the British Army

After 'Black Week' in December 1899 thousands of volunteers from Britain, Ireland, Canada, Australia and New Zealand signed up to fight in South Africa in a great wave of patriotism. The War Office, with some reluctance, agreed to Buller's plea after Colenso for 8,000 irregulars to be sent from England. Wolseley had always seen the need for reinforcements in South Africa, but he was astonished to hear that Lansdowne and the War Office had agreed to engage civilian volunteers. Volunteerism was a phenomenon of this war among middle and upper classes; 'gentlemen rankers', stockbrokers, journalists, dons and MPs hurried to join the new Imperial Yeomanry. One remarkable unit was the 13th Irish Battalion of the Imperial Yeomanry, largely made up of upper-class Irish civilians; 'the flashy and social show-piece of the volunteer movement', it soon was known as the 'Millionaires' Own'. In it were four companies or squadrons; one, the Duke of Cambridge's Own, raised by the Earl of Donoughmore, contained very wealthy men-about-town. Of the three other squadrons one was known as the 'Irish Hunt Contingent', officered for the most part by Irish Masters of Foxhounds; commanded by Captain the Earl of Longford, it included Lieutenant Viscount Ennismore; in its ranks were mostly Dublin men. In the other two were Ulster Protestant Unionists who included Sir John Power, the whisky baronet, the Earl of Leitrim and James Craig, the future Lord Craigavon. Many officers paid their own passage to South Africa and gave their pay to the Widows and Orphans Fund. Craig spent his ample means freely on his men and made it his business to know their troubles. He had taken a commission in the 3rd (Militia) Battalion of the Royal Irish Rifles in January of 1900 and then was seconded and served as a lieutenant with the 46th or Hunt Company, to become, briefly, a professional soldier. The 13th Battalion's commander, however, was a regular British Army infantry officer, Lieutenant Colonel Basil Edward Spragge who 'proved himself a regular ass'.[45]

The Battle at Lindley on 31 May in the Orange Free State, the very day that Roberts was entering Johannesburg, became notorious because of the social position of the 13th (Irish) Imperial Yeomanry, whose first engagement this was. Their humiliating surrender caused much rejoicing among pro-Boer Irish Nationalists at home in Ireland, a surrender stemming from confusion in communications between Lieutenant General Sir Henry Colville, Commander of the 9th Division, and Colonel Spragge who was ordered to join Colville at Lindley. Colville denied that Spragge had ever been ordered to join him and there were some who believed that the order was sent to Spragge by Boers under Piet de Wet, who hoped to lure the

13th into a trap. Whether this was true, Spragge found neither Colville nor any message for him when he arrived at Lindley, only Boers, and he was in danger of being trapped. Instead of making a fighting retreat to Kroonstad, Spragge took up a defensive position to the north of Lindley and sent a message to Colville asking to be rescued, a message Colville did receive but decided not to do anything about as he was already harassed by the enemy. Spragge then waited to be rescued. The Boers, on hearing of the plight of 'so many politically and socially important gentlemen', hurried to attack them. The 13th Irish made a gallant stand, holding out for four days, and, except for an unfortunate incident when a white flag was raised by 'a quite irresponsible, inexperienced person, a Corporal Jacques', they might well have held out for another twenty-four hours to be rescued by Lord Methuen, who arrived just a little too late. After bitter fighting, some three hundred and ninety of the 13th Yeomanry had to surrender and were marched into captivity, among them Spragge, Lords Ennismore, Leitrim and Donoughmore, along with James Craig. Their casualties before surrender were eighty-three all ranks killed, wounded and taken prisoner; Sir John Power, the whisky baronet, was killed and Lord Longford was severely wounded. After the battle the Boers congratulated them, saying, as Trooper Fitzgibbon records, 'Well done! You fought well, right well!'[46]

Craig's eardrum was pierced at Lindley by a splinter from an exploding gun. The Boers attended to him and, when they were unable to help him, generously sent him across the border into Portuguese territory for medical treatment. From Lorenço Marques he made his way to Durban. 'While there he was gazetted to be Deputy Assistant Director of the Imperial Military Railways because of his organizing ability'. He bought a model railway on which he practised signalling and did his job so well it was said 'a column never had to wait long for a train'. Later in June 1901 Craig was invalided home with dysentery, but with improved health he returned to South Africa to command 'D' Squadron of the 29th Battalion of the Imperial Yeomanry, known as the Irish Horse and mainly raised in Ulster, with Lord Longford, now recovered, as its Colonel. Shortly after these reinforcements arrived in South Africa the war ended and Craig's career as a soldier was finished.[47]

Erskine Childers was another volunteer, a committee clerk in the House of Commons, an Anglo-Irish gentleman ranker without any military experience. He arrived in South Africa in February 1900 as a driver and stableman with the Honourable Artillery Company (HAC), one of the most prestigious and ancient of the British volunteer units and now called to active duty. They trained throughout the spring of 1900 and were becoming very impatient at the lack of action, although assured by Roberts that 'there was plenty more work to be done'. In June a delighted Childers learned that his battery was to be part of the escort of a convoy sent to relieve and resupply Lindley where the 13th (Irish) Battalion of the Imperial Yeomanry had come to grief. Boers were seen swarming around the town, now in British hands. The 26th was an unforgettable day for Childers and the HAC's first action: 'The convoy and its escort came to a crest that ended in an abrupt typically flat-topped kopje . . . bristling with Boer riflemen . . . the HAC Battery was to engage it frontally . . . under intense rifle fire the guns were unlimbered . . . the range of the hostile kopje quickly found' and Childers enthusiastically noted: 'Our shrapnel are bursting beautifully over the Boer lines'. The next day Childers experienced shell fire which did little damage and 'the convoy lumbered into Lindley'.

Erskine Childers, a law graduate from Cambridge University, was a talented writer who published his experiences in South Africa: *In the Ranks of the C.I.V.* (City of London Imperial Volunteers), 1900 and *The H.A.C. in South Africa* in 1903. He was from an influential upper middle-class family with ruling class connections: a cousin, Hugh Childers, would in due course be Secretary of War, First Lord of the Admiralty, Chancellor of the Exchequer and finally Home Secretary. Erskine was born in London where his father Robert's short life was spent as a distinguished civil servant and scholar. His Anglo-Irish heritage came from his mother, Anna Henrietta Barton, who came from the Anglo-Irish Protestant Bartons of County Wicklow in Southern Ireland. Erskine's parents died when he was young and he and his siblings were raised in Ireland by his uncle, Charles Barton, a popular squire who served as County Wicklow's High Sheriff. It was in his home that Childers developed his passionate concern for Ireland that would eventually lead him to take the path of the revolutionary in Ireland's struggle for independence.[48]

On 31 May 1900 Johannesburg surrendered. Roberts agreed to Boer terms that street fighting was to be avoided because of potential damage to women, children and property, while the Boers promised that the gold mines would not be destroyed. Another important condition was that Boers must be allowed to withdraw their army intact, a negotiation seen, in Pakenham's opinion, as Roberts's gravest 'strategic mistake'. After surrendering Johannesburg, despairing Boers retreated to Pretoria and soon, among themselves, even the 'unyielding' President Kruger began discussing a general surrender. After ordering the Pretoria forts dismantled, he fled east to Machadodorp with most of his government, towards the Portuguese frontier, abandoning their beloved Pretoria. Confusion reigned and looting in the city began.

Then a change of heart occurred among the Transvaalers, spurred on, it is said, by the assurance of President Stein of the Orange Free State never to surrender and reinforced in part by news of the capture at Lindley, by Piet de Wet, of those important Irish gentlemen, the volunteers of the 13th Imperial Yeomanry. The Transvaalers decided to fight on. Meanwhile word came to Roberts of peace proposals by Louis Botha and of an agreement to give up Pretoria without a fight. Both, it turned out, were Botha's strategies to gain time to regroup his forces. On 5 June, when Roberts triumphantly entered Pretoria unopposed, a sense of victory was lacking, even if it was the culmination of a great march from Bloemfontein to Pretoria. There he waited patiently for the surrender of Botha's army, which, it became apparent, was not forthcoming. Roberts, realizing his mistake, renewed battle with the Boers who began to harass his now reduced army around Pretoria. The Battle of Diamond Hill, on 11–12 June, was such that both sides claimed victory. However, Brandwater Basin in the Orange Free State, in July, was for the Boers a decisive defeat when the largest number of prisoners were taken since Paardeberg. By August Roberts's army was joined by Buller's Natal forces and they were ready to 'disperse or destroy the last of the Transvaal army'.[49]

In this campaign the 1st Inniskillings were more than pleased to be included by General Buller after their new Commanding Officer, Lieutenant Colonel Payne, DSO, requested more action. On 27 August they participated in the Battle of Belfast or Bergendal, 'the last set piece battle of any size in the war', which occurred on the Delagoa Bay railway line, important for Boers as it led to the outside world. Using Buller's plan, Roberts directed the combined operations. Buller discovered a weak point in the centre of Botha's line near a place called Bergendal farm, where a large kopje topped by immense boulders was almost a natural fortress, but isolated and jutting out like a salient, not easily defended. Allotted to it were Botha's best troops, some sixty to seventy-five men of Johannesburg police known as 'Zarps', fierce men, 'the epitome of the brutal Boer'. The Inniskillings found them 'a magnificent-looking lot of big men with huge beards . . . the finest men and best shots in the Boer army'. It was a violent little battle for the attacking infantry. A tremendous bombardment by Buller's artillery preceded the attack, in which the surviving Zarps amazingly stood firm and opened accurate fire on the advancing infantry, the Rifle Brigade supported by the Devonshires, and the Inniskillings supported by the Gordons, who had to cross open and broken ground. An Inniskilling officer reported how he and his company narrowly escaped death in the final charge up and over the kopje: 'All our guns . . . on seeing us charge fired as hard as they could . . . all pouring over our heads from behind . . . we had to stop and lie down twice'. Both Roberts and Buller were watching when Buller, noticing the men fix bayonets, stopped 'our Long Toms which were so far back they could not see us. As it was, a 94 lb. shell burst about thirty yards in front of the right of our lot'.[50] It was a near thing. The Inniskillings' casualties were seventeen slightly wounded, but the Rifle Brigade and the Zarps suffered greatly. The Boer force, however, got away. The victory allowed Roberts to annex the Transvaal.

Roberts then announced that the war was 'practically' over and made plans to go home, delegating command to Kitchener, who only had to 'mop up'. Roberts was wrong, but so were many others. Like Wolseley as High Commissioner after the Zulu War of 1879, Roberts did not seem to recognize the strength of Boer political aspirations. Losing capitals was not important to them; their governments simply took to the bush and the high veld; some thirty thousand Boers were still at large, tough, able, determined, proud to be called 'bitter-enders'. In a guerrilla war of roving commandos, they would astonish and infuriate the British Army for nearly two more years.

Roberts could look back with some pride on his achievements of less than a year; the besieged towns had been relieved, capitals taken, Boer leaders scattered. But, thinks David James, Roberts's biographer, had he left the country with a signed peace settlement or had he achieved total defeat of the Boers, many of the criticisms against him, especially over the destruction of farms, would never have been made.[51] At the beginning of his campaign Roberts had given the impression of being too lenient with the Boers and the prevailing view of him was that he possessed 'great kindliness and consideration'. A hardening of his policy towards Boer women and children was seen towards the end of his time in South Africa.[52] Roberts had viewed the farm-burning measure as a military one. Boers were frequently cutting the railway lines, disrupting and derailing trains carrying needed supplies; why should he (Roberts) not keep them from these supplies, starve these marauding commandos and their families and thus hasten the end of the war ? Many soldiers favoured this policy, for example those Anglo-Irishmen Hubert and Johnnie Gough, as did many of the British public.

Despite his mistakes, Roberts has been seen as a competent and energetic commander. In January 1901 he returned to England to a hero's welcome. He was raised to the rank of Earl, of Kandahar, Pretoria and Waterford, made a Knight of the Garter, the first since Wellington to receive it, and awarded by Parliament £100,000, a tangible appreciation of his services. He was also appointed Commander-in-Chief of the British Army, Wolseley's old job, in which his efforts at reform were as curtailed as Wolseley's had been.

Kitchener Takes Over – The Irish in the Guerrilla War

Kitchener soon realized that the war was far from over; he would be pitted against vigorous younger Boer leaders. He even more ruthlessly carried out Roberts's farm-burning practice and in Afrikaner memory he was the creator of the concentration camps where thousands of Boer women and children died of disease and deprivation. It was not a time for heroes, yet the Irish continued to perform individual acts of bravery. Private John Barry from Kilkenny, a regular in the 1st Royal Irish Regiment who had seen service in India, won his VC and lost his life at Monument Hill near Belfast, 7/8 January 1901. In a surprise Boer night attack Barry, who was nearest to a Maxim gun, picked up a pick-axe lying near it and forced his way to the gun through the Boers who tried to stop him; he had just time to smash the breech before he was literally swept down by a hail of bullets.[53]

A few months later Seymour Vandeleur, another brave Irishman, lost his life in a Boer attack. He was a type of whom it was said, 'Men of his stamp do not die in their beds'. In April 1900, after his service under General Kelly-Kenny, Vandeleur was offered another post as Senior Transport officer to Major General Hutton, the recently appointed Commander of 1 Mounted Infantry Brigade. Like Godley at Shorncliffe, Vandeleur had been very proud to be one of the first officers to be trained in the newly formed Mounted Infantry course at Aldershot in 1891. Then, in November 1900, came an offer from Lord Kitchener of the command of 2nd Mounted Infantry Battalion, an independent command no ambitious soldier could refuse. By January 1901 Vandeleur was engaged in safe-guarding convoys marching to and from Rustenberg, north-west of Pretoria, through country infested by De la Rey's commandos. On one reconnoitering foray Vandeleur, severely wounded, was rescued by his reliable Sergeant Major. After hospitalization in Johannesburg, he was met by his father in Cape Town and brought to Ireland to convalesce, such were the privileges of the Anglo-Irish. While there he read in the *Honours Gazette* of his promotion to Lieutenant Colonel. His wound forgotten, he insisted, after a Medical Board, on returning to South Africa and in August 1901 he was given command of a column of Mounted Infantry, Kitchener's Fighting Scouts, four field guns and a half battalion of infantry, another independent but much larger command to be proud of. Directed to join the column at Nylstroom just north of Pretoria to get acquainted with the force before the outgoing commander left, tragically Vandeleur never arrived. He left Pretoria late at night by a train of three open trucks and one ordinary corridor coach, in which were two ladies with children and Major Beatson. An escort of NCOs and men were in the armoured trucks next to the engine. Besides baggage and stores was £20,000 cash, the pay of the troops in the northern district. The train was ambushed just beyond Waterval North by the notorious train-wrecker Jack Hindon, ironically another Irishman, and a party of Boers. A dynamite mine under the rails exploded beneath the engine and musket fire was poured into the train. Both ladies were wounded and, as Vandeleur sprang to the door of the coach to take command, he was shot at close range by a Boer. Twenty-five NCOs and men and five civilians were casualties as the wreckers proceeded to loot and burn the train. It was an action right out of an American 'wild west' film. Vandeleur's body was recovered and buried with full honours in the English Church in Pretoria.

Vandeleur's biographer laments that 'he did not fall in the fair field of battle . . . but was the victim of a pitiful highway robbery, murdered in cold blood without the chance of reprisal by a dastardly scoundrel who wrecked trains for loot'. These are surely the chivalrous sentiments of another age. Yet, as Farrar-Hockley would also write of the Gough family, Hubert and Johnnie, such precepts as honour, duty, courage and glory, in short 'principles of chivalry in war', were still observed by Victorian society. Colonel F. I. Maxse claimed that one purpose of writing his biography was 'to afford to Vandeleur's countrymen a glimpse of what is being done by hundreds of [such] picked officers who are the real builders . . . of our Empire'.[54]

In these last months of guerrilla warfare the impetuosity of the dashing Anglo-Irish Commander Lieutenant Colonel Hubert Gough resulted in an action both tragic and comic at Blood River Poort on 17 September 1901. Ever since Ladysmith Gough had trained his men vigorously and gained a reputation for daring escapades in the field. Now he was commanding one of four columns sent by Kitchener to block the way into Natal of Louis Botha, known through intelligence reports to be in the neighbourhood with some seven hundred men. Among Gough's 'composite troops' were some Royal Irish Fusiliers who, bored with blockhouse duty, had volunteered to serve as Mounted Infantry. Whether Gough was ignorant of the size of Botha's force is not clear, but, delighted when he saw about 200 Boers at a farmhouse in the distance, he attacked, not waiting to scout the ground, assuming this was all of Botha's force. It was too great a chance for a cavalryman to miss. In a furious thousand-yard gallop, his battery of guns racing behind, Gough led three of his four companies over the skyline and across open country. Boer sentries gave the alarm and from a gorge hidden by rock walls of the Blood River Poort 500 of Botha's main force suddenly appeared and 'almost at once began to envelop him'. The 200 men

Gough had seen were only a detachment of Botha's larger column. In less than twenty minutes nine officers and thirty-eight men were wounded. Gough and 235 men, along with two guns, valuable ponies, rifles and ammunition, were captured. After a bizarre adventure where he tried unsuccessfully to hide in a huge ant hole, Gough was discovered, but managed later to escape in the darkness. News of his humiliating and disastrous experience soon spread rapidly in South Africa, a story not to be ignored by the press. Gough himself was very shaken by it, questioning whether he was simply 'carried away by the excitement of taking a challenge offered by the enemy'. Kitchener's secretary sent him a telegram: 'Lord Kitchener . . . is sure you had done your best . . . . he had not lost confidence in you'.[55]

Lieutenant General Sir John French's talents as a cavalryman were perfectly suited to the free-ranging cavalry tactics needed in rounding up Boer guerrillas from May 1901 to May 1902. In command of columns in the eastern Transvaal and in Cape Colony, he had no difficulty in adhering to Kitchener's reminder of 'the necessity of *severity* in dealing with captured rebels'.[56] Commanders of Kitchener's mobile columns were so successful that the Boers bitterly surrendered in April and the peace treaty was signed finally at Vereeniging in the Transvaal on 31 May 1902.

In 1903 Dublin welcomed home the 2nd Battalion, Royal Dublin Fusiliers, and hosted a grand dinner and reception. The *Irish Times* of 14 November described the arrival of the 'Old Toughs' and paid tribute to these 'hardy, wiry warriors, they looked thoroughly capable of accomplishing the daring and courageous deeds which have covered the Dublin Fusiliers with special glory'. A few years later a Memorial Arch was erected at a corner of St Stephen's Green in the centre of Dublin to honour the memory of the officers and men who served in the British Army in the South African War. It was dedicated on 19 August 1907 by his Royal Highness Duke of Connaught, Commander-in-Chief, in a stirring ceremony with dignitaries and and old soldiers present. Inscribed on its surfaces are the principal actions in which the Royal Dublin Fusiliers were engaged: Talana, Colenso, Tugela Heights, Hart's Hill, Ladysmith and Laing's Nek. The Irish Nationalists' bitter taunt of 'Traitors' Gate', with which it was pilloried because of Irish soldiers' allegiance to the British Army, did not destroy the monument's significance for the relatives of Dublin Fusiliers and other regiments. As Nora Robertson writes of these sturdy Irish heroes:

> Their British allegiance was part of the queer mix-up of those days. Those who knew them best realised what good Irishmen

they were. . . . They joined for many . . . reasons but they were with their pals and when it came to a fight they behaved as gallantly as Irishmen always do.

Fortunately for the survival of 'Traitors' Gate', with the passage of time 'most people have forgotten what it signifies'.[57]

CHAPTER NINE

The Irish in the Great War
1914 – 1915

The stoutest men from hill, valley and town were pressing into the British army, and long columns of armed Irishmen, singing Ireland's latest love-song, *It's a Long Way to Tipperary*, went swinging . . . down to the quays to the ships waiting to bring them to a poppy-mobbed grave in Flanders.

Sean O'Casey, *Drums Under the Windows*,
London, 1945, pp. 315–316

The Irish in the British Army Prior to the First World War

Once the excitement of the Anglo-Boer War subsided the British knew they would have difficulty maintaining their small volunteer army to garrison the United Kingdom and to maintain troops in India and throughout the Empire. In numbers the British Army paled in significance compared to those of the Prussians, Russians and the French. Recruits were hard to find when the Industrial Revolution offered employment and there were improved conditions for agricultural labourers. The decade before the First World War shows a decline of Irish-born soldiers in the British Army, falling to 9.4 per cent in 1913, but historians agree that this level closely matched the percentage of Irish in the population in the British Isles. Scholars caution that the proportion of soldiers of Irish extraction was greater than statistics indicate. The Irish Nationalists' anti-recruitment campaign against enlistment in the British Army continued after the Boer War and caused some concern to the Irish administration at Dublin Castle. Yet Lieutenant Colonel H. N. Jourdain of the Connaught Rangers in his *Ranging Memories* records that 1911 was his best year for recruiting for the Rangers throughout Connaught, when he achieved 'the highest and largest number that had ever been recruited in any one year at Galway'.

Jourdain himself had been inspired to join the Connaught Rangers after reading of their Peninsular War exploits by the 19th century Irish novelist Charles Lever. Jourdain's Huguenot family fled Europe after the Edict of Nantes (1685); one branch went to Ireland, his own went to England where several entered the British Army. After Sandhurst Jourdain was successfully gazetted to the Rangers' 1st Battalion for a career of over thirty years. He little realized he would be the last Commanding Officer of the Connaught Rangers and the regiment's historian.[1]

Enlisting in the British Army in this period were John and Denis Lucy, two young Irishmen from County Cork, sons of a cattle farmer and an excellent example of William Butler's sturdy 'Irish peasant stock'. Denis would lose his life early but John survived both World Wars and his valuable book *There's a Devil in The Drum* (1938) is a rare look at his experiences as a young Irish Private training in peacetime in an Irish regiment and then in the grim early battles of 1914. John rose to officer rank in his own regiment. When asked why he enlisted he had always replied, 'For me pound', that is – his daily ration of army bread, but he and his brother:

> were tired of fathers, of advice from relations. . . . The soft accents and slow movements of the small farmers who swarmed in the streets of our dull southern Irish town . . . filled us with loathing. Blow the lot. . . . . we were full of life and the spirit of adventure . . . . We got adventure. We enlisted.

They took the King's shilling and swore to serve and protect him for a period of seven years with the colours and five in the reserves. But, writes Lucy:

> We swore with some national qualms of conscience. As a sop to our feelings we chose an Irish regiment . . . one stationed far away at the other end of Ireland.

This was the 2nd Royal Irish Rifles and at their depot, 'the Ulster town' which was in fact Belfast, harsh training turned them into soldiers and, for John, it was the worst six months of his life. They studied hard. Their education was already above that of their comrades, though they had had to go to the army school. They sought promotion even though it meant to 'lose caste and numerous friends'. In early 1914 they were both promoted to Lance Corporals and when war broke out John, at twenty, was a full Corporal, Denis was nineteen and each was in command of a section of eight men. With pride in arms came pride in their regiment. At their

Salisbury Plain station John knew his regiment was well-trained and 'most spectacular when turned out', but what impressed him was the Royal Munster Fusiliers on their church parade 'who showed the professional Irish soldier at his best in all the panoply of 1914'.[2]

The Irish and the Curragh Mutiny

While Denis and John were being initiated into their new life in arms, in March 1914 occurred the Curragh Mutiny, an 'incident' in which some Irish in the British Army were placed in a difficult position that almost caused a split in the army. The problem, one from the 1880s, centred around the Home Rule Bill for Ireland, a move to transfer rule from the Parliament at Westminster to Dublin, and trouble flared at the possible passing of a third Home Rule Bill promoted by the Liberal Government and due to come into force in 1914. The Protestant Unionists in Ulster were always vehemently against Home Rule: to them 'Home Rule meant Rome Rule' because of the strength of the Roman Catholic Church and passions always ran high. From January 1913 Ulster Volunteers, under the leadership of Sir Edward Carson MP, had been forming to protest against imposition of Home Rule and at the end of December 1913 in southern Ireland a similar organization, the Irish Volunteers, inspired by the Ulster Volunteers, was formed under Professor Eoin MacNeill with the opposite intent, 'to ensure the implementation of Home Rule'. Both volunteer organizations were already armed and the possibility of open conflict between the two or between the British Army and one or both of them was a very real problem for the British Government in early 1914.

A distraught Liberal Government considered different options and finally chose a course of action that looked as if the government would assert its authority and impose Home Rule in Ireland. The navy would bring reinforcements to Northern Ireland to control any possible disorder, while it was rumoured that 3 Cavalry Brigade of the 5th Royal Irish Lancers, the 16th Lancers and the 4th Queen's Own Hussars stationed at the Curragh Camp just west of Dublin under General Sir Hubert Gough might be ordered to Northern Ireland to quell any Volunteer/Unionist threats. A directive from the War Office brought much confusion: officers of the brigade, if domiciled in Ulster, were given a choice to either serve or be exempt from any order that would actively engage them against Ulster. Other officers, if they refused, would be dismissed from the service. Troops were really only to bolster Ulster depots to keep the peace, but the message was received as an ultimatum and fifty-eight officers at the Curragh Camp decided to resign rather than move against Ulster and their fellow Irishmen. The Mutiny at the Curragh was no mutiny in the strict sense; Gough and his officers had merely been asked to make a choice; no orders were disobeyed, yet the effect was the same. The crisis sent shock waves throughout the army, traditionally thought to be detached from politics, as there was much sympathy and support for Protestant Ulster/Unionist thinking among the officer class,[3] not only among the Anglo-Irish. In fact 'domiciled in Ulster' only applied to five of fifty-eight officers involved.

In London Gough communicated his officers' decision to resign to General Sir Henry Wilson, Director of Military Operations at the War Office from 1910. He also informed his brother Johnnie who was Brigadier General, General Staff at the Aldershot Command, who felt he too should offer to resign. The retired elderly Lord Roberts, a committed Unionist, had his say; indeed Prime Minister Asquith and others believed the old Field Marshal was personally responsible for the 'mutinous talk' in the army. Roberts seems to have been much concerned that the strain on the army might be too great for it to recover, so he was prepared 'to declare the Home Rule Bill illegal and unconstitutional'. The result was that Westminster backed down and Hubert Gough was welcomed back to the Curragh from London and reinstated in his command. He could tell his officers they would not be used to enforce Home Rule in Ulster. The Army Council, in their 'historic document', also assured Gough and his officers in Ireland that 'the incident . . . in regard to their resignations had been due to a misunderstanding'.[4] Roy Foster, an eminent present-day Irish historian, claims that this document was 'enforced on an inept War Secretary' by 'the political assumptions and prejudices of a few high ranking officers'.[5] The Adjutant General, Lieutenant General Sir John Spencer Ewart, certainly lumped Hubert and Johnnie Gough and Sir Henry Wilson together as 'three bigoted Irish Protestants', and they were indeed at the centre of this crisis.[6] Hubert's concern was not so much Ulster as the position the army was put in; he indicated that had a direct order been given he would have obeyed as a true soldier.[7]

Sir John French, now Chief of the Imperial General Staff (CIGS), was also in the middle of this commotion. Although he took great care to remain politically colourless, he was encouraged to resign because he had signed the government's embarrassing retraction statement. He thought his career in the army was finished, sincerely doubting he would remain Commander-in-Chief designate of the British Expeditionary Force if England went to war with Germany. After the Curragh Incident he was seen as 'a political general', but, as his biographer observes, 'it was because he was politically naive that he got into such difficulties'.[8] His fears were not realized. It is clear that since the Boer War the Anglo-Irish had risen to high rank and, as the Curragh Incident showed, the leadership of the British Army was remarkably in their hands.

The 'Old Contemptibles'

It was said that the First World War burst upon an unsuspecting world with great surprise, but for more than a decade war with Germany had been expected by most thinking people. Ideas of invasion and intrigue had been appearing in gripping spy stories of current literature. For example Erskine Childers' novel *The Riddle of the Sands* as early as 1903 tells of secret German preparations for an invasion of England which two intrepid young Englishmen discovered while exploring the north coastal waters of Germany in their small yacht. From 1904 there was the growing strength of the German Navy, loudly boasted about by Kaiser Wilhelm that it would rival even the renowned British Royal Navy. This greatly alarmed European powers and the British Army command began to show a growing preoccupation with the prospect of having to assist in any European conflict. Sir John French, as CIGS in 1912, informed his three directorates that his goal was 'to get the army ready for war'. It was chiefly due to the controversial and outspoken Anglo-Irish General Sir Henry Wilson, the Director of Military Operations at the War Office and principal liaison officer with the French Army, that a British Expeditionary Force was firmly written into French mobilization plans of 1911 when and if France was attacked by Germany, and that it was ready to move to France in August 1914.[9] Wilson was the only British Army officer who seemed to have a good relationship with the French. A Francophile, he spoke the language fluently. Virtually no one else in the British high command had this facility, nor, with the exception of General Robert Nivelle, did anyone in the French High Command speak English fluently. Wilson was a tempestuous, dominating figure, seen as an intriguer rather than a commander, who loomed large in military and political affairs in the first years of the twentieth century.

Sir John French's appointment to command the British Expeditionary Force was confirmed on 30 July, despite his misgivings after the Curragh Mutiny débâcle. The British press praised his appointment and Colonel Huguet, the French military attaché in London, observed that 'it was a popular one in France: Sir John was warm and generous, easily approached, had the well-being of his men at heart and was loved by his soldiers'. French was 'a significant and controversial figure in his own right' who called forth both admiration and hate. He seems to have carried on 'vigorous and well publicized disputes with everyone'. French's biographer further claims that recent revelations about his 'irregular private life has reduced him to the status of a lecherous old Irishman'. As for his military achievement, perhaps Brian Bond's verdict on French is not too far from the truth: 'a brave fighting general who proved to be out of his professional depths'.[10] After the disastrous Loos battles of autumn 1915 there was such pressure to remove French that in December he resigned as Commander-in-Chief in France, replaced by General Sir Douglas Haig. In January 1916 French was appointed Commander-in-Chief Home Forces, a newly created post, and in February he was created Viscount French of Ypres.

Britain declared war on Germany on 4 August 1914 and immediately the British Expeditionary Force began to leave for France. In a great outpouring of patriotic spirit Irishmen everywhere, even from abroad, responded enthusiastically. One example is Private J. S. Meehan, an Irish regular and reservist in the Royal Munster Fusiliers who hurried home from Canada on the outbreak of war to join the 2nd battalion in February 1915, thus missing the ordeal at Etreux. He would fight throughout the war, was badly wounded several times and, promoted from the ranks, would retire from the army in 1919 as a Lieutenant in the Royal Irish Regiment.

All the historic regular Irish regiments in the British Army served in this war, along with three New Army Irish Divisions: the 36th (Ulster), 10th and 16th (Irish), citizen soldiers, all volunteers as there was no conscription in Ireland. Over 200,000 Irishmen participated along with an unknown but substantial number of Irish women, mainly nurses in auxiliary units: 'proportionately the greatest deployment of armed manpower in the history of Irish militarism'.[11]

The Irish people were caught up in the war excitement and everywhere demonstrated pride in their historic Irish regiments when they left Ireland. From Cork, where the Leinster Fusiliers had been very popular after a three-year stay, the 2nd Battalion's steamer left the quay on a glorious August morning amid a real Irish send off. 'All the way down the River Lee . . . crowds on the bank cheered loudly and everywhere Irish pipes were heard playing rollicking tunes.'[12] The Irish newspapers of the day contributed greatly to the general enthusiasm in reporting the departure of Irish troops. On 6 August the *Galway Express* reported that '375 1st class Reservists of the 2nd Battalion Connaught Rangers fully equipped for active service left Galway for Aldershot, England . . . their physique drew favourable comments from all spectators'. One witty Connaught Ranger was heard to say in an unmistakable Dublin accent that he promised 'to bring back three Germans on his watch chain'. The Irish made good copy for the newspapers that were soon filled with their exploits and how they sang their Irish rebel songs. *Tipperary*, then an unknown music hall song, was sung by the Connaught Rangers as they marched out of Boulogne and was 'picked up by a reporter to travel around the world as the song of the war'.[13]

For the 1st Battalion Irish Guards this was their first campaign as a full battalion since formation in 1900. Their reservists streamed in to London's Wellington Barracks from all parts of Ireland amidst great excitement. Many were members of the Royal Irish Constabulary (RIC) with whom the Irish Guards had a close connection: in November 1914 when reinforcements were first required, the government permitted only 200 men from the RIC to enlist in the Irish Guards but 'nine times that number volunteered . . . all well over six feet tall, magnificent men'. When First Battalion left for France, 98 percent were Irish and about 90 percent were Roman Catholics. The now frail Field Marshal Lord Roberts, Colonel of the Regiment, inspected the battalion in London on 11 August before its departure, his presence adding to the excitement of their war preparations. With Roberts on the parade square was the Commanding Officer Lieutenant Colonel the Honourable G. H. Morris, a career soldier who had served in South Africa, a brilliant staff officer. He had transferred from the Rifle Brigade to the Irish Guards on its formation as other Irish officers had been proud to do. Born at Spiddal, Co. Galway, into a distinguished Anglo-Irish family, he was a younger son of Lord Killanin, the famous Irish judge and humourist and Lord Chief Justice of Ireland. Morris's parents enjoyed a mixed marriage, his father was Catholic and his mother Protestant, a family background that may account for his openness. His attitude to 'politicizing' in his battalion, however, was typical of the army regulars. A revealing story is told about him after John Redmond and John Dillon, two important Irish Nationalist politicians were seen in late July 1914 walking past Wellington Barracks in London and some Irish Guardsmen, recognizing them, rushed to the railings shouting, cheering and waving their hats. Hearing of this incident Morris later spoke to the battalion about this 'remarkable, disgraceful demonstration', but he ended his remarks, probably with a twinkle in his eye: 'You are all, or nearly all, racing men and like a good bet from time to time. Back what horse you like – but keep your tips to yourself'. They got the message.

Peter Verney, an Irish Guardsman himself, writes of the 'complete absence of religious or political controversy' in the Regiment since its formation which, he adds, 'has characterized the Irish regiments for so long: It was not that they did not deeply feel the unrest in their native country – it was just that they were above it; once in uniform they felt and owed an allegiance to a higher cause'.[14] Young John Lucy, on the eve of war speaking for the Irish regulars in his 2nd Royal Irish Rifles, summed up this thinking: 'Events outside the army hardly concerned us at all.

International affairs were beyond the professional soldier. . . . Our job was to fight. We were well trained and willing to fight any foreigner, and we were delighted at the prospect of war and glory'. As Lucy and his Irish Rifles marched towards the Belgian frontier on 21 August they also wanted to be recognized as Irish soldiers:

> French poilus . . . watched us pass and they cheered us . . . ; '*Vivent les Anglais*'. For my company I gaily corrected them: '*Nous ne sommes pas Anglais, nous sommes Irlandais*'. They liked that . . . and shouted: '*Vivent les Irlandais*', and we cheered back at them: '*Vive la France*'.

The British Expeditionary Force regulars in 1914 proudly accepted the nickname 'The Old Contemptibles' which came from Kaiser's Wilhelm II's disparaging order 'to exterminate the treacherous English and walk over General French's contemptible little army'.[15] When the 'Old Contemptibles' went to war, considering the long service given to the British Army by the Irish, it should come as no surprise that the first rifle shot fired by the army on the continent in nearly a century was fired by an Irishman, Corporal E. Thomas from Tipperary. His 'C' Squadron, 4th Irish Dragoon Guards, was in action against a patrol of German Uhlans in the first contact between the BEF and First German Army at about 7.00am on 22 August 1914 at the village of Casteau some five miles from Mons. A stone memorial marks the spot. The Uhlans came leisurely down the road; then, as if they smelled a rat, they halted and turned back. Thomas remembers that Captain Hornby's 1st Troop caught up with them in the village, scattering them and some Cuirassiers with their swords. When Thomas's 4th Troop arrived in support, Hornby ordered 'dismounted action! . . . Bullets were flying past us . . . I could see a German cavalry officer some four hundred yards away . . . mounted in full view . . . I took aim, squeezed the trigger . . . he fell to the ground obviously wounded.' Thomas 'undoubtedly fired the first British shot of the war,' writes the historian of the 4th/7th Dragoon Guards, 'equally undoubtedly Captain Charles Hornby was the first man to kill a German,' for which he won a DSO. It was Thomas who became a national celebrity, when the 'first shots' story appeared in many newspapers. The son of a Captain Quartermaster in the Durham Light Infantry, Thomas enlisted as a boy trumpeter in the Royal Horse Artillery and in 1904 transferred to the 4th Irish Dragoon Guards in India as bass drummer. Rising to Corporal on the outbreak of war, he left the band to become a trooper in 'C' Squadron.[16]

An Irishman, Lieutenant Maurice James Dease, 4th Battalion, Royal

Fusiliers, won the first Victoria Cross in the war (posthumously). He was the only son of Edmund F. Dease of County Meath and heir presumptive to his uncle Colonel (later Sir) Gerald Dease, Viceregal Chamberlain in Ireland, member of an ancient family of Catholic gentry in County Westmeath. Young Dease was a career soldier and graduate of RMC Sandhurst, gazetted 2nd Lieutenant in 1910. Appointed machine-gun officer of his battalion in 1912 he was killed on 23 August 1914 at Nimy, an old industrial suburb north of Mons beside the canal where, several times wounded, he refused to leave his guns and continued firing until all his men were killed or wounded. He died of his wounds after holding at bay an estimated two battalions of German infantry.[17]

Despite the *Official History*'s claims that the BEF was the 'best equipped' Army ever sent abroad, David Ascoli observes that it lacked 'heavy artillery and high explosive shells . . . had only two machine-guns . . . to each infantry battalion; no short-range trench mortars; no close-range hand grenades; . . . all standard equipment . . . of the German Army'. Thus the BEF 'survived its early battles by a mixture of training, discipline, good humour, courage, unique musketry skill and the brilliant use of divisional artillery'. One German soldier said, 'They were . . . very exceptional soldiers'.[18] The great bravery and heavy losses of Irish regiments bear out this assessment. A large Celtic Cross still stands at the La Bascule crossroads commemorating the 2nd Royal Irish's first action in the Battle of Mons. The Irish fought against a large force from the German IX Corps pouring across the Condé Canal, and under fierce fire they assisted their 8th Infantry Brigade to retire, but at great cost. Early in the battle Captain the Honourable Fergus Forbes, commanding 'A' Company, was mortally wounded. A member of the distinguished Anglo-Irish family from Co. Longford, he was a direct descendant of Sir Arthur Forbes, Earl of Granard, founder of the Royal Irish Regiment in the seventeenth century. Three members of this family were connected with the Royal Irish in the First World War: Fergus Forbes's brother, the 8th Earl of Granard, formed and commanded the 5th Royal Irish Regiment for 10th (Irish) Division, and Lieutenant Colonel George Forbes, 1st Battalion Royal Irish, died of wounds received at St Eloi in 1915.[19]

John Lucy and his well-trained Irish Rifles were amazed at the success of their own 'apalling' rapid rifle fire in this battle. He could see how the German infantry 'withered away under it' and therefore he could not understand when a retreat was ordered: 'Marching away. . . . was not soldiering'. By his order Field Marshal Sir John French, the BEF commander, dismayed not only soldiers like John Lucy, but his commanders who claimed their troops were not broken or unfit. Contributing to French's decision to retreat was that he had not been informed when, on 24 August, General Lanrezac ordered his French Fifth Army to retire, which left the BEF dangerously exposed. In Sir John's opinion he had little choice but to retire also. He was convinced from then on, writes French's biographer Richard Holmes, 'that the French were basically un-trustworthy as Allies', which did not help Sir John in future British/French collaboration. However, it was the threat of three German Corps greatly outnumbering the BEF that pushed it on its hot, dusty, exhausting march south.[20]

The famous retreat from Mons ending in late August 1914, lasting some thirteen days and nights, was one long rearguard action that called forth innumerable brave stands and feats of heroism. One such was the rear-guard action of the 2nd Royal Munster Fusiliers at Etreux, commanded by Major Paul Charrier who had only recently relieved Lieutenant Colonel J. K. O'Meagher. Under him were also two troops of 15th Hussars and two guns of 118th Battery Royal Field Artillery. Brigadier General Maxse of 1 Guards Brigade, ordered to cover the retreat of General Haig's I Corps, gave Charrier a free hand in conducting his retirement. Fighting retreats and brave stands have always been enshrined throughout the history of warfare; one newspaper described Charrier's heroic rearguard action as 'a little Thermopylae'.

Charrier's work diary came into the hands of a German general, Dr Max Von Bahrfeldt, Commander of 19th Reserve Division, who had intended to hand it back to Major Charrier's family after the war. Some forty years later, in 1956, through official channels, his son, in fulfilling his father's wishes, had it brought to the family. Charrier's diary throughout is brisk and businesslike, befitting his long experience as a professional soldier, and a terse final entry reads: 'Morning of 27th August 1914 – mission, rear guard.' The Munsters were directed to hold on to their position until ordered or forced to retire. By noon the road to Etreux was reported clear of all transport and a little later General Maxse despatched orders to retire to all units of the rearguard. This message failed to reach Charrier and his Munsters, and by late afternoon the battalion was cut off. Charrier then went forward to organize an attack on the enemy holding the outskirts of the village, his gigantic figure made conspicuous by the green and white hackle of the Munsters he always wore on his khaki-coloured helmet. Captain H. S. Jervis, a Company Commander in the battalion, was captured by the Germans and while a prisoner of war wrote to Mrs Charrier a graphic first-hand account of the heroic action of both her husband and the Munsters:

> Eventually the Germans . . . cut us off completely, the key to their position being a loopholed house. The major personally led two

charges in a magnificent attempt to capture this. In the first of these he was wounded, but insisted upon retaining command and cheering us on. Shortly afterwards he was wounded again. . . . He heroically continued . . . till after sunset. . . . Still leading and setting an example to all, he was shot a third time and mortally. He fell in the road.

'Charrier,' Jervis writes, 'was mentally and physically one of the biggest men in the Army.' Lieutenant Thomas of the battalion, badly wounded and captured, writing later to his mother, praised his commander: 'Our Colonel was a wonder to see . . . he had no fear'. Private McElligot, Charrier's batman, who was also taken prisoner, pays perhaps the simplest and most eloquent tribute to Charrier: 'The Major died as he lived, a brave man.'[21]

After Charrier's death the heroic action of the Munsters, surrounded as they were by a ring of fire, was continued by old soldiers like Regimental Sergeant Major P. Cullinan, 'the third most senior warrant officer in the army', who fell wounded. After Captain C. R. Hall was wounded leading a bayonet charge, command of the battalion remnant fell to Lieutenant E. W. Gower who continued resistance from the orchard near the main road where a last stand was made with ammunition taken from the dead. By around 9.15pm he had to surrender with some 240 men, including many wounded and four unwounded officers; the Royal Field Artillery also lost heavily. After the battle it was discovered that Charrier's small force had been fighting nine German battalions for nearly twelve hours and by their resistance and sacrifice had been responsible for the safe withdrawal of Haig's I Corps. The Germans acknowledged this gallant resistance of so few against so many, albeit with annoyance when actual numbers became known: no less than 1,500 German wounded were assembled in Etreux the next day. Munster prisoners of war were allowed by the Germans to collect and bury their dead. Major Charrier was found 'lying as he had fallen, head towards the enemy'.

In reporting that Charrier was missing, the Kerry *Weekly Reporter* of 2 September 1914 reviewed his career as a professional soldier: 'He joined the 2nd Battalion Royal Munster Fusiliers in 1890, served in an Ashanti uprising of 1900, was wounded in action and mentioned in despatches. In South Africa 1902 he served with the Imperial Yeomanry, again mentioned in despatches (Queen's medal and two clasps), and from 1902–04 he was a Special Service officer in the operations against the Mullah of Somaliland (medal and clasp).' Charrier has been described as a 'hearty genial Kerryman', but he also, as Captain Jervis tells us, had French blood in his veins, with the suggestion that he was of Huguenot ancestry, equally at home in France and England, spoke fluent French and knew as much about the organization of the French Army as any British officer in France. Years later his grandson, Alexander McKee, said that in his family there were hints of a *Riddle of the Sands* type of adventure in which Charrier had been involved. He did not receive an award when, in 1920, the British Army recognized the bravery of the Munsters, officers, NCOs and men. Only the Victoria Cross can be awarded posthumously and at this time 'only when the act of gallantry was witnessed by a senior officer' as Charrier himself was.

Captain Jervis was among those brave men receiving awards. A career soldier in the Munsters, he was, in addition, a son of the regiment, his father having served with them. After his release from prisoner of war camp Jervis was promoted to Lieutenant Colonel and in June 1919 assumed command of the 2nd Battalion.[22] In November 1922 he published *The 2nd Munsters in France*.

Another intrepid Irish leader who lost his life in the retreat from Mons was Lieutenant Colonel the Honourable G. Morris of the 1st Irish Guards who were part of the rearguard of I Corps. On 1 September the pursuing Germans caught up with the battalion near Villers-Cottérêts, only some forty miles north-east of Paris. There, in the deep beech forests of that area, occurred the first major action of the war for the Irish Guards. They fell back into the forests on 'a rumour of advancing cavalry who turned out to be German infantry running through the fields of corn from stack to stack and filtering into the forest on their either flank'. Kipling, in his account, tells how the Germans were at first cautious because of the amazing fire-discipline of the Irish Guards which 'gave the impression that the forest was filled with machine guns, instead of mere trained men firing together sustainedly. . . . The action resolved itself into blind fighting in the gloom of the woods.'

When news first came that the Germans were approaching through the woods Private Stephen Shaughnessy from Tuam, Co. Galway, reported how his Colonel rode through the ranks shouting, 'Irish Guards, form up! Remember you are Irishmen !' Throughout the fight he continued to ride 'up and down smoking cigarette after cigarette in a long holder, chaffing and giving encouragement to his men until, as was inevitable, he was killed.' As Kipling wrote of Morris: 'He was an officer beloved and a man noticeably brave among brave men'. Lieutenant Colonel Morris's character, commented the *Galway Express* of 5 December when reporting his death, was 'marked by his Irish birth and Galway blood'. In his regiment Morris was 'a martinet with a strong Irish accent' whom his Guardsmen saw as 'a hard man, but a just one', someone who never failed 'to congratulate his men on their grit and vitality'.[23] In this so called 'skirmish' the Irish Guards lost nine officers, including their commander, his Second in Command, a company commander and one hundred and fifteen men. Morris left a month-old son, Michael, who would see service in the Second World War and later became Lord Killanin, president of the International Olympic Committee. Charrier and Morris were undoubtedly in the heroic tradition, although they would have said they were only doing their duty as professionals in the British Army.

Demonstrating anything but heroics on that retreat from Mons was Lieutenant Bernard Montgomery who would become Commander of the Eighth army in the Second World War, hero of the North African campaign, one of Churchill's famous Ulster generals and a future Field. Marshal. After Sandhurst Bernard, having failed to enter the Indian Army, was gazetted into the Royal Warwickshire Regiment and joined its 1st Battalion on the North West Frontier at Peshawar in 1908, too late for any action. On 26 August 1914 he was a young subaltern with his regiment somewhere between Cambrai and Le Cateau, near Haucourt, and what follows was his first action. When 12 Brigade abandoned a ridge, 'It was left to the Royal Warwickshires of 10 Brigade to retrieve the situation'. Colonel Elkington, their Commander, galloped forward immediately and sent two companies 'to attack and recapture the ridge.' No further orders were given, there was no reconnaissance, no plan, no covering fire. It was a suicidal charge into the fire of the enemy and no one had a clear idea how to attack. Montgomery dashed forward, leading his platoon in an action both comic and tragic: 'I tripped over my scabbard . . . and I fell flat on my face . . . By the time I had picked myself up and rushed after my men, I found that most of them had been killed.'

Montgomery redeemed himself later at Meteren on 13 October in the first Battle of Ypres. Again leading his platoon and again nearly losing his life, he avoided tripping over the scabbard and stormed a German trench to find a German soldier aiming his rifle up at him. Abandoning his sword, he flung himself through the air and 'kicked him as hard as I could. . . There is no doubt that the German was surprised and it must have seemed to him a new form of war; he fell to the ground in great pain, and I took my first prisoner.' Later that same day 'This wary tough little man with the cool darting brain', as he was later described, was shot by a sniper through the back when he 'stood up in the pouring rain to reorganize his men' and to see for himself, as he said, 'what the position looked like from the enemy point of view . . . I collapsed, bleeding profusely':

> A soldier from my platoon ran forward and plugged the wound with my field dressing . . . the sniper shot him . . . and he collapsed on top of me . . . . It was then 3p.m. and raining. I lay there all

the afternoon and I received one more bullet in the left knee. The
man lying on me took all the bullets and saved my life.

It was nightfall before anyone could get to him and fortunately he was
found alive. He survived, 'perhaps because he was Monty!' He was
promoted to captain in the field and later in hospital in England learned
he had won a DSO for turning the enemy out of the trenches with the
bayonet. Montgomery's fearlessness under fire became legendary in the
Warwickshires, but from February 1915 he would be a staff officer. It is
said that his experiences in the First World War would greatly influence
his policies in the Second; with great caution and calculation he always
made certain that sufficient forces were ready before mounting an attack,
and the care of his soldiers was for him of utmost importance.

Montgomery came from a prominent Donegal family who traced their
ancestry back to the Protestant Plantation from Scotland in the early
seventeenth century, a line of merchants, clergymen and administrators.
He was the first member of his family to join the British Army, which was
unusual among that elite group who reached high rank in the First and
Second World Wars. His decision surprised his parents as they expected
him to be a clergyman, following his father's example, the Reverend Henry
Montgomery, Anglican Vicar of St. Mark's, Kennington, in London
where Bernard was born. His mother's father was the Reverend Frederick
Farrar, later Dean of Canterbury and an eminent scholar. Close ties were
always maintained with Ireland where the family home of New Park,
Moville, Lough Foyle, in Co. Donegal, was the focal point for the large
Montgomery clan, and where Bernard spent many school holidays as well
as his army leave during 1914–18 and, later, whenever he could.[24]

Of that arduous retreat from Mons John Lucy of 2nd Irish Rifles wrote
that he and many of his fellows had fought three battles by the age of
twenty. On 6 September the British Army turned north and east in an
offensive against the Germans who were now the pursued. The Germans
rallied at the Aisne River and exhausted British troops dug in. For Lucy
the Battle of the Aisne was a holocaust, for in it he lost his young brother
Denis and poignantly records: 'Forward he went and out of my sight
forever.' The roll-call after the battle forcibly reminded him of Lady
Butler's sombre Crimean picture *The Roll-Call* (1874) where a sergeant
similarly records with his stubby pencil the names of casualties given by
the weary and wounded survivors.

The *Galway Express,* always ready to publish stories of the bravery of
the Connaught Rangers, reported on 26 September the deaths of two Irish
officers in the 2nd Battalion at the Aisne River, Lieutenant Robert de
Stacpoole and Major W. S. Sarsfield, Acting Commander of the battalion.

De Stacpoole, born at Mount Hazel, County Galway, was the fourth son of the Duke de Stacpoole and one of four serving brothers. He was well-known in the Galway Blazers (a fox-hunting club). Sarsfield, from a Cork family, is an important name in Irish history: his ancestor Patrick Sarsfield, Earl of Lucan, had fought for King James II in the seventeenth century in the Williamite War. Major Sarsfield's son, Lieutenant Patrick Sarsfield, also served in the Connaught Rangers. The year 1914 saw desperate fighting and the Rangers earned more battle honours than any other regiment.

Two Irish officers, in late October at Premesques, near Armentières, showed great initiative and daring in a most interesting escape after they were seriously wounded and captured. Both were from 'C' Company of the 2nd Leinsters. Captain G. de M. H. Orpen-Palmer lost an eye and was temporarily blinded in the other, while Captain F. E. Whitton was unable to walk:

> Too badly wounded to be sent to the rear when taken they were kept in a cottage during the fight and abandoned by the Saxons while the latter were streaming back in retreat. The two officers . . . stealing away in the misty dawn . . . eventually reached the new British line . . . having been without food or water or medical attention for over 24 hours.

This much of the story was told by Captain Whitton in his history of the Leinsters, for he later became the Regiment's historian. The full portent of their escape was revealed several years later by a sergeant in the Royal Irish Fusiliers to Captain F. C. Hitchcock MC, also of the 2nd Leinsters, who records in his *"Stand To" A Diary of The Trenches* how the Sergeant remembers seeing 'Leinster officers stumbling into their entrenchments; the blinded one . . . was being directed by the one he was carrying'.[25] Two Orpen-Palmer brothers served as captains in the Leinsters, known as OP1 and OP2, the sons of the Reverend Abraham Orpen-Palmer, a noted biblical scholar and Church of Ireland rector. Both would rise in rank to command battalions: G. Orpen-Palmer as Lieutenant Colonel of the Royal Irish Fusiliers, his brother R. A. H. Orpen-Palmer as Colonel of the 2nd Leinsters, who along the way was awarded the DSO.

Captain F. C. Hitchcock was a southern Irishman and also the son of a Church of Ireland rector, at Kinnitty, County Offaly (then Queen's County). As a Second Lieutenant he joined the 2nd Battalion in France in late May 1915. Hitchcock wrote his *Stand To* as a diary of the day-to-day events of his battalion 'at fire trench and parapet level', and in its quiet recital it takes its place among the more in-depth memoirs of the war. A noted horseman, he also wrote on equestrian affairs in his book *Saddle Up*. Amidst all the suffering of the war Hitchcock was one of those who survived unscathed, winning an MC while engaged in the Loos Section during the winter of 1916–1917. Sons of many Irish clergy would find careers in the British Army.

In recording what the 'Old Contemptibles' endured in the terrible slaughter of 1914 John Lucy's personal and heartrending account tells how he and his 2nd Irish Rifles in late November came out of the line in the First Battle of Ypres: 'Forty left out of 250 and only about three weeks ago there were only forty six out of an entire battalion. . . . I was too weary to appreciate my own good luck.' As they marched towards food and shelter, he wrote of being cheered by their field gunners, and the bare-armed workers of the guns, and feeling embarrassed by the tribute from fighting soldiers. The historian Tom Johnstone records that in 1914 no Irish regiment suffered heavier losses than the 2nd Royal Irish Rifles.

All Irish battalions had to be reinforced several times during the war. Irish Guards losses were such that by 8 November 'the remnant were made into two shrunken companies'. As Kipling wrote of the old regular army: 'In training, morale, endurance, courage and devotion, the earth did not hold its like, but it possessed neither the numbers, guns, nor equipment necessary for the type of war that overtook it.'[26]

That there were heroes in the old regular army of 1914 is clear, but also contributing to its professionalism were men like 'the redoubtable John Ring', the Irish Regimental Sergeant Major of the 2nd Battalion, Royal Munster Fusiliers. NCOs are the backbone of the army and there is no better example than John Ring, who survived the war. When the Munsters were heavily attacked on 12 November near Zillebeke and the senior NCO of the battalion, Quartermaster Sergeant Fitzmaurice, was killed, John Ring as Regimental Sergeant Major was left to hold this important position throughout the entire war 'with unexampled brilliance'. Famous in his Regiment, he was known throughout the army, 'all . . . recognized his sterling worth and splendid services'. He also volunteered to go into action and gained an MC, DCM and Bar. Born in Limerick, Ring enlisted at Tralee in 1897 and survived 'five consecutive years fighting, refusing promotion time after time rather than leave the battalion'.[27]

The well-known story of the Christmas truce of 1914 ends this period on a joyful note. M. J. Corbally, historian of the Royal Irish Rifles, records how on Christmas Eve Germans came out of their trenches and said they would not fire if the British did not. Some Riflemen spoke with German soldiers, many of whom spoke good English. The Commander of 8th Division, in which were the 1st Irish Rifles, had no objection to the truce itself, but gave orders that no Germans were allowed near British trenches.

On Christmas Day both sides were out in the open, but the Riflemen kept near their own parapet and warned off any Germans who approached. On Boxing Day one British field artillery battery received from German soldiers tobacco and cigars; the Dublin Fusiliers gave them a tin of jam. When the short-lived truce ended the killing began again. William Grattan of the Connaught Rangers relates a similar 'amicable enemies' incident in the Peninsular War. In the period before the Battle of Salamanca in July 1812 Picton's 3rd Division and the French 7th Division were encamped on either side of the Douro River:

> Each day the soldiers of both armies used to bathe together in the same stream and an exchange of rations . . . was by no means uncommon. . . . The French officers said to us on parting . . . As 'friends' we received each other warmly – as 'enemies' we shall do the same.

Ten days later the British 3rd destroyed the 7th French at the Battle of Salamanca.[28]

The Irish in Kitchener's New Armies

In those disastrous early months of the war Irish regular soldiers in the British Army fought and died in their historic Irish regiments that were nearly destroyed in Flanders. For John Lucy the arrival in France of reinforcements composed mainly of Reservists meant for him the end of the old army of 1914, the 'Old Contemptibles'. He writes of the remnants: 'We backed each other up . . . and by doing this we preserved and passed on the diluted *esprit de corps* of our regiment'. Kipling observed of the old Irish Guards that a leaven remained and worked on the rest.

Other Irishmen responded to Lord Kitchener's call to support the war and joined the New Army Divisions in the British Army. There were no *new* regiments for the Irish Divisions, instead the historic Irish regiments in the British Army were expanded to form service (S) battalions. How would the old army view the newcomers? When it was discovered that the New Army 'civilian warriors' could fight, John Lucy and his regulars forgot their prejudices.

Sinn Fein, the political wing of extreme Irish Nationalism, continued to oppose Irish recruitment and to brand any Irishman who enlisted in a Crown regiment as 'a traitor to his country'.[29] Despite this, Ireland as a whole identified with the British military campaign against the Central Powers. There was a flood of recruits spurred on by reports of the heroic stands of Irish soldiers and Irish regiments fighting in the retreat from

Mons, the Munsters at Etreux and the Irish Guards at Villers-Cottérêts. Old soldiers enlisted and even pre-war deserters were accepted and given a royal pardon, as Captain Jourdain found when recruiting his 5th (S) Battalion, Connaught Rangers.

At this time there was a growing consciousness of Irish identity and it was a matter of some pride that the 10th (Irish) Division was among the first to be authorized in Kitchener's 'first 100,000'. The term 'Irish' was initially merely a territorial designation, but the 10th soon became 'unique', the first definitely Irish Division in the British Army and one almost entirely composed of Irish battalions.[30] British Army officers and NCOs came out of retirement to train and lead these new divisions. General Sir Bryan Mahon, the Anglo-Irish hero who led a column to relieve Mafeking in the Anglo-Boer War, would command the 10th and the *Galway Express* of 29 August 1914 was pleased to report his appointment as 'A Galway man'. An active fifty-two-year-old, Mahon seems to have had a rapport with his men: 'Everything about him appealed to them, his great reputation, the horse he rode, his Irish name and his Irish nature.' Other officers appointed were either Irish or had experience with Irish troops. Brigadier General R. J. Cooper, CVO, leading 29 Brigade, came from a prominent Anglo-Irish family of County Sligo and had been the first Commanding Officer of the newly formed Irish Guards. Brigadier General L. L. Nicol, commanding 30 Brigade, was a Scot who had done the bulk of his service in the Rifle Brigade, but had learned his soldiering in the 94th Foot, later 2nd Battalion, Connaught Rangers. Brigadier F. F. Hill, CB, DSO, commanding 31 Brigade, had a long and distinguished career in Royal Irish Fusiliers.[31]

At battalion level was Lieutenant Colonel Lord Granard, KP, commanding 5th (S) Royal Irish Regiment. He was from a well-known seventeenth century Anglo-Irish military family in County Longford. At company level was Bryan Cooper, who had joined the 5th Battalion, Connaught Rangers, as a Captain, recommended by his uncle Brigadier R. J. Cooper. Bryan was one of the Markree Castle, County Sligo Coopers, a military and land-owning family that had been powerful in the county for some three hundred years. His mother, also of Anglo-Irish stock, was a soldier's daughter. He was a Woolwich-trained gunner largely influenced by his father, a gunner who had been stationed in India where Bryan was born. A Special Reserve officer in the Royal Artillery, Bryan had resigned in May 1914 partly because of the Curragh Incident, but also none too pleased with the life. Despite his family's military tradition, his interests had always been more literary and political; by temperament he was not a soldier, yet when training after he enlisted he threw himself into his new duties 'with passion and determination'. Later, in Gallipoli, he would be mentioned in despatches for his splendid handling of his company.[32] Cooper had great sympathy for the cause of the ex-soldier, particularly for any Connaught Ranger. His very valuable book *The Tenth (Irish) Division in Gallipoli* (1918) is one of the earliest accounts of the Gallipoli Campaign.

After the first rush enlistment slowed and recruits from England provoked criticism that the 10th (Irish) Division was Irish in name only, until it was discovered that these 'Englishmen' were Irish Roman Catholics rejoicing in such names as Dalton, Doyle and Kelly, the sons and grandsons of Irish who had settled in England, many working in industry or down the mines. Cooper makes the point that: 'there has never in past history been such a thing as a purely and exclusively Irish (or Scotch) battalion'. He concluded that the Englishmen who were drafted to the 10th Division became imbued with the utmost loyalty to their battalions and wore the shamrock on St Patrick's Day with much greater enthusiasm than the born Irishmen. He estimated that in the Division's Infantry ninety per cent of the officers and seventy per cent of the men were either Irish or of Irish extraction.[33]

An exception to the working-class background of most of the 10th Division's recruits was 'D' Company, 7th (S) Battalion, Royal Dublin Fusiliers. The Footballers, or Pals as they were soon known, came together through appeals to serve their country by F. H. Browning, President of the Irish Football Union, to the rugby football clubs in the Dublin district. The response inaugurated the Irish Football Union Volunteers and membership was soon extended to all other athletic clubs. Among young professional men of the middle and upper classes who answered the call were barristers, solicitors, businessmen, civil servants, many Trinity College Dublin graduates and men such as Ernest Julian, recently Reid Professor of Law at Trinity College, Stanley Cochrane of Woodbrook, son of His Majesty's Lord Lieutenant for County Wicklow, Poole H. Hickman, a barrister from County Clare educated at Trinity College, R. G. Douglas, well known in sporting circles, and Michael Fitzgibbon, a law student, son of the Nationalist MP for South Mayo. All trained vigorously, thanks to Browning, who, with General Sir Bryan Mahon, then urged these volunteers to join Kitchener's New Army. The way was made easy for them by Browning's old friend Lieutenant Colonel Geoffrey Downing, Commander of 7th (S) Battalion, Royal Dublin Fusiliers, well-known in football circles as Captain in 1883 of the first fifteen Monkstown Football Club. He agreed to keep open for them a special 'D' Company in his battalion. Drafted to the Curragh camp, the Footballers soon became identified with the traditions of the Royal Dublin Fusiliers, proud to be the 'Young Toffs' in the 'Old Toughs', the old regimental nickname of 2nd Battalion. Some, like Poole Hickman and Ernest Julian, received immediate commissions. Hickman by January 1915 was promoted Captain and then Commander of 'D' Company. Others were selected by their peers to be NCOs. Henry Hanna KC tells their story in his *The Pals at Suvla Bay*, a moving tribute to the citizen soldiers of 'D' Company who so willingly enlisted and who within a few months were almost annihilated in the disastrous Gallipoli campaign in 1915.[34]

The *Irish Times* of 1 May 1915 describes the tumultuous departure from Dublin for England and the war of the 7th (S) Battalion, Royal Dublin Fusiliers, who had the honour to represent the 10th Division. Crowds lined the Dublin streets to cheer them as they were led by their commanding officer, Lieutenant Colonel Downing, 'a man of unusual height and girth', who marched them right through the centre of Dublin with bands and pipes playing and both Union Jack and Irish flags carried. The newspaper particularly commented on the Pals and their famous 'D' Company, 'mainly composed of footballers':

> It is naturally regarded as being typical of the spirit that animates the country as a whole. Its composition is symbolic of the part that sport plays in war. Men . . . now have thrown aside their interest in sport and devoted themselves purely to the affairs of war in order that Ireland and other parts of the Empire may be kept free from the horrors of war.

With the 10th (Irish) Division was Francis Ledwidge, a young Irish poet and an outspoken Nationalist, who surprised everyone by enlisting and chose the 5th Royal Inniskilling Fusiliers. Before the war he was discovered and encouraged by Lord Dunsany, another Irish poet, and together they prepared Ledwidge's first book of poetry, *Songs of The Field,* which, to Ledwidge's great surprise and pleasure, was published in autumn 1915 while he was serving in Salonika. Later, writing of his origins, he claimed to have heard his mother say, 'I am of a family who were ever soldiers and poets'. Born in Slane, County Meath, he was the eighth child of an evicted tenant farmer whose early death meant that at age twelve Ledwidge had to work as a farm labourer and he early became involved in the rural labour movement. Ledwidge also joined and helped to organize those Irish Volunteers in Slane who were opposed to John Redmond and the Irish Parliamentary Party over the issue of enlistment, against which he frequently spoke and was even accused of being pro-German. Why then did he enlist ? The Irish writer Patrick McGill, from Donegal, who served in the London Irish Regiment, claims that 'few men could explain why they enlisted'. The articulate Ledwidge does so, echoing that thinking of many Irish Nationalists like Tom Kettle and Willie Redmond who became soldiers:

> I joined the British Army because she stood between Ireland and an enemy common to our civilization and I would not have her say that she defended us while we did nothing at home but pass resolutions.

Ledwidge became disillusioned with the Irish Volunteers who were increasingly dominated by Sinn Fein and who continued to proclaim against the war. But another and perhaps compelling reason for his enlistment was a disappointing love affair. He was jilted by a girl he had hoped to marry and the desire to get away from the wagging tongues of his small community was very strong. Rejection in love was not an uncommon reason for young men to enlist in the army. Ledwidge even writes of it in a poem:

> I'm wild for wandering to the far-off places
> Since one forsook me whom I held most dear.[35]

The army, as it turned out, suited Francis Ledwidge. He wrote to a friend in February 1915 that the army had shown him how to live and how to deserve all he loved.

By April 1914 the Ulster Volunteer Force (UVF) in Northern Ireland had been fully armed, thanks to a famous night gun-running episode that brought in guns from Europe to Larne on the east coast of Ulster. Then, in July of those anxious pre-war days, Erskine Childers, whom we met in the HAC in the Boer War and was now in sympathy with Home Rule aspirations of the Southern Irish Volunteers, was part of a group who decided that as a measure of self-protection more arms were needed to counterbalance the Ulster Volunteers. A skilled yachtsman, Childers, in a daring enterprise, brought in guns from Europe on his yacht, *Asgard*, to Howth Harbour at Dublin right under the nose of the British fleet. A clash leading to civil war in Ireland was very possible in that volatile situation, but the First World War intervened and temporarily settled the political problem. These Volunteers chiefly formed the other two divisions of citizen soldiers that Ireland sent to the war: 36th (Ulster) and 16th (Irish) Divisions, who became the 'standard bearers at the front of Unionism and Nationalism respectively'.[36]

When the two political leaders, Sir Edward Carson representing the Ulster Volunteers and John Redmond MP representing the Irish Volunteers, decided to support the war, both men hoped their Volunteers 'would earn the right to make political demands once the war was over'. Lord Kitchener was not at all sympathetic to any politicizing, but he was well aware of the formidable qualities of the UVF, seen as the best-prepared civilians in the British Isles, and so he sent his famous message to Carson: 'I want the Volunteers'. With the government's promise that the Home Rule Bill, although passed, would be held in abeyance until after the war, Carson could invite his Volunteers to sign up in the British Army for service abroad, but not until he had successfully campaigned to keep his Ulstermen together and, as he announced on 3 September, the word 'Ulster' would accompany the number 36 when a division was proposed to him. Most of the Ulster Volunteers who had signed the Ulster Covenant now enlisted in the 36th, however distrustful they were of the British government over Home Rule. Their division was 'to be an expression of Protestant Ulster power, pride, and independence . . . committed as much to the collective survival of Protestant Ulster as to the survival of the Britain they fought for and were part of'. Their 'special political oath' defining their separate status sanctioned by the War Office made 36th (Ulster) Division unique in the British Army.[37] Also unique was that its infantry was 'formed on perhaps the most strictly territorial basis of any Division in the New Armies'. From small communities, towns and countryside of Northern Ireland, 'a platoon would have five Armstrongs or Wilsons or Elliots, a company half a dozen Irvines or Johnstones, a battalion half a score of Morrows or Hannas'.[38] These Pals formations, like an enlarged family, brought a great moral force, but after the fatal Battle of the Somme entire Ulster communities were devastated.

Without James Craig MP, whom we remember as a Captain in the 13th (Irish) Battalion Imperial Yeomanry fighting in South Africa, it was said there would never have been an Ulster Division. It was due to his efforts in purchasing uniforms that the 36th was in khaki long before many of the new divisions. His prominent Unionist family had a strong sense of service to Ulster and James, together with Sir Edward Carson MP, had organized the first resistance to Home Rule, which became the UVF. He was one of five middle-aged brothers serving simultaneously in the British Army in the First World War, three of whom were in the Ulster Division. James, however, was unable to go to France with the 36th; having worked hard for the Division, his health was undermined.[39] Major-General C. H. Powell, a former Indian Army officer who was appointed Commander of the 36th, came from an army family who seemed not to have had any political leanings, which is probably why he was chosen.

Meanwhile John Redmond, Parliamentary leader of the Irish Nationalist Party, inspired by the news of the passing of the Home Rule Bill, even if for after the war, and by the forming of the 36th (Ulster)

Division, urged his Volunteers to enlist in the Imperial Army and to serve abroad. In September Redmond reminded the press that 'nothing less than an identifiable "Irish Brigade" would satisfy the ambitions of his countrymen who wanted to gain national credit for their deeds and . . . that she too has contributed an army bearing her name in this historic struggle'.[40] Redmond's symbolic title 'Irish Brigade' deliberately evoked romantic historical memories of other Irishmen, those Wild Geese who had fought as mercenaries in continental armies in the eighteenth century in *their* Irish Brigade. Indeed, Redmond believed that the Irish people were endowed with a genuine military spirit which produces born soldiers and commanders. In early October a brigade in the 16th Division, forming in the New Army under General Sir Lawrence Parsons, was kept for Redmond's Volunteers. Redmond wanted more. Emulating Carson, he continued to petition Kitchener that his Irish Volunteers should be kept together to form a distinctive separate Irish Division within the British Army. Kitchener was not sympathetic to Redmond's romantic notions nor to his Home Rule aspirations and, although he regarded the fighting qualities of Irish troops highly, he tended to see the Volunteers 'as rebels in sheep's clothing', harbouring the old suspicions of having armed Irish soldiers trained on Irish soil: rebellious Irishmen could be only too ready to use their guns against the British. But the War Office took the risk of training Irish soldiers in Ireland and, as *The Times* of 20 October 1914 reports, Redmond agreed to regard the 16th Division as the Irish Brigade. It was not, however, until nearly a year later that the 16th would be *officially* recognized as the 16th (Irish) Division, a tardiness that affected recruiting. Among Kitchener's reasons for granting concessions that would provide the Irish in the army with a sense of national identity was his admiration for Redmond's 'doggedness' and his own genuine concern that those brave Irishmen in the Dublin and Munster Fusiliers in Gallipoli in April had not been given sufficient recognition.[41]

That Anglo-Irish Protestant officers should lead Irish Catholic soldiers was not unusual in the British Army, but the Protestant Sir Lawrence Parsons' appointment as Commander of the largely Catholic 16th (Irish) Division was a very difficult one. General Parsons was proud to be called an Irishman, coming, he said, from an ancient family who had deep roots in King's County. He had been brought out of retirement, having seen distinguished service in the Sudan, India and South Africa where we met him as an Artillery Officer. He was a traditionalist of the old school of officers, adhering to regimental rather than divisional tradition. The political aspect of Redmond's Irish Brigade caused him great trouble. Serious differences surfaced between Parsons the soldier and Redmond the politician, particularly over the problem of commissions when lobbyists in the Irish Parliamentary Party besieged Parsons for commissions for friends and relatives. He was accused of snobbery, discrimination and even bigotry that he would not take Catholics as officers. On these grounds it was said Parsons refused Redmond's own son, William Archer Redmond, Nationalist MP for Tyrone and later Waterford, home of the Redmonds. Recent scholarship has exonerated Parsons on the Catholic question, pointing out that Catholic schools and universities did not have Officer Training Corps (OTC), and Parsons preferred officers with experience or some training (such as OTC) rather than someone with only a political background, even if they were professional men. To get around this problem Parsons instituted a specially formed Cadet Company for aspiring officers in 7th (S) Leinster Battalion where men first joined as privates. Young Redmond refused to accept this training like other candidates and demanded a commission, clearly a touchy situation because of his father's political position. He eventually obtained a commission, but with the Royal Dublin Fusiliers, transferring to the Irish Guards where he greatly distinguished himself and won a DSO, so there was 'good stuff' there after all. As for the cadet company in the Leinsters, it flourished: of the cadets passing through it who would become officers in the 16th Division most were Catholic and Nationalist.

Another knotty problem was the type of badges to be used. Redmond wanted a distinct badge for the 16th Division, whereas Parsons thought the traditional time-honoured insignia of the historic Irish regiments were sufficient to maintain loyalty and fighting spirit. Terence Denman, the Irish historian, claims that Parsons, in stressing the regimental traditions in the British Army, gave his Irish citizen soldiers something to adhere to when nationalist political ideals, as represented in the Division, faltered in the ensuing political upheavals in Ireland.[42]

Through Lady Parsons, who openly loved Ireland and had sympathy for John Redmond and his Volunteers, General Parsons found a greater (if uneasy) appreciation of his Nationalist citizen soldiers, although he himself did not approve of their political aspirations. Among them was a group prominent in Irish society, men unusually articulate and literate, MPs in the Irish Parliamentary Party such as Tom Kettle who had resigned his seat for East Tyrone in 1910 and was well known in pre-war Ireland as a National University professor in Economics, an orator and an essayist. Kettle was a complex, charming, brooding man, an Irish patriot and a strong advocate of both Home Rule and a united Ireland, but through parliamentary and constitutional means. Nevertheless, in the summer of 1914 he agreed to go to Europe to buy guns for the Irish Volunteers and was in Belgium when war broke out. Quickly the deal ended, but he remained as a war correspondent for *The Daily News*. His news reports overflowed with sympathy for the Belgians when he saw at first hand the desecration of the German advance and the consequent 'courage and anguish of this glorious little nation fighting now for its life'.

For Kettle Catholic Belgium, as an oppressed small nation, became analogous to Ireland. Belgium and the rights of small nations became the key to his support for the war and a cause also espoused by John Redmond and his IPP. Equally important for Kettle was that as a traveller in Europe he had become a lover of European civilization and was not interested in narrow nationalism. Now with Belgium/Europe threatened, and by inference Ireland, his duty was plain, to fight for liberty: 'I care for liberty more than I care for Ireland,' he confessed. In Europe he could have stayed on and become a leading war correspondent but chose to return to Ireland to volunteer for what he called the 'army of freedom'. He would, he said, 'rather see the war through as a sixth-rate soldier than as a first-rate man of letters'. Kettle was thirty-four years old when he enlisted and placed in Parsons' Cadet Company, but because of his age, his poor health and his undoubted oratory skill, he was used immediately on recruiting tours where his constant theme was 'Come and help Belgium, the latest and greatest of evicted tenants'.[43] Parsons befriended Kettle, concerned about his health and drinking, realizing that army life was not easy for him. He at first refused Kettle a commission, then relented and Kettle was commissioned in the 9th (S) Battalion, Royal Dublin Fusiliers.

Stephen Gwynn, another Nationalist MP, was devoted to his political chief John Redmond but also, as Nora Robertson, General Parsons' daughter writes, he 'became personally attracted and attached to my father'. Gwynn fully realized the opposing ideals of the politician and the soldier and has recorded the conflict most fairly in his book *The Last Years of John Redmond*. He and his fellow MPs, Kettle and Willie Redmond, John Redmond's brother, had been actively opposed to Irish soldiers' involvement in the Boer War. As late as 1906 Gwynn continued to chide his constituents in Galway, including soldiers of the Connaught Rangers at their depot, for having joined the British Army. Now in 1914 these quite remarkable Irish Nationalists supported the war, threw themselves behind John Redmond's recruiting campaign and enlisted in the British Army. Gwynn became a frequent companion of Tom Kettle on recruiting drives in 1914 and later wrote of Kettle that his was 'the most variously gifted intelligence I have ever known'.

Gwynn himself was a 'delightful litterateur . . . a man of European habits, and that rarity, a Protestant MP'. He grew up in Church of Ireland (Protestant) circles in which his father became Bishop of Raphoe and then Professor of Theology in their Divinity school in Dublin. Gwynn was a journalist, novelist, critic and poet, the worthy grandson of William Smith

O'Brien, founder of the famous United Irish League. After his enlistment Stephen went through the 16th's Cadet Company as a Private, receiving in April 1915 a lieutenancy, followed by a captaincy in the 6th (S) Battalion, Connaught Rangers. Serving on the Western Front, by May 1916 he had three dugouts blown in on him. Sent home because of ill health, he repeatedly petitioned to return to the trenches and finally did so in October of that year; he was now fifty-two years old. One of those civilian soldiers who found such appeal in his British Army regiment Gwynn would write: 'I was prouder of my company than of any earthly thing'.[44] Amazingly, he survived the war.

Willie Redmond was the most best-known of this group of prominent Irish Nationalist MPs, older men who supported the war and enlisted in the British Army. He had sat for the Borough of Wexford, his father's old seat, from 1883 and in the Commons he had frequently criticized the many campaigns of Empire that involved the British Army and Irish soldiers. Although he objected to the Boer War, in Parliament in February 1900 he applauded the bravery of Irish soldiers fighting in South Africa, 'as gallantly as Irishmen always have done'. He went on to speak in the House of Commons of the political loyalty of soldiers, mostly from southern Ireland, serving in the Irish regiments of the British Army; 'They are Catholics by religion, and in politics they are nationalists and Home Rulers like we are'. Because they are in the army does not mean that 'they are not in sympathy with us, because they are'.

In other words, like John Lucy, they were capable of holding a dual allegiance. In his excellent study of Major William Redmond, MP, Terence Denman explains how Willie's conflicting attitudes may be traced to his boyhood love of soldiering and to his Catholic gentry family's background of military service in the Austrian, French and British Armies. His mother, of Protestant stock, was the daughter of General Hoey of the Wicklow Rifles. A combination of influences therefore led him to join the City of Wexford militia battalion of the Royal Irish Regiment where he was commissioned in 1879 and thus was always able to temper his criticism of the British Army. After campaigning enthusiastically for John's Irish Volunteers and then the 'Irish Brigade', he announced at the end of 1914, 'I am going for the Irish Brigade. I can't stand asking fellows to go and not offer myself'. He enlisted in the British Army in February 1915, despite being fifty-four years old, and was gazetted as a temporary Captain in the 6th (S) Battalion, Royal Irish Regiment. His military training of many years earlier fulfilled General Parsons' prerequisite for military experience for his officers. Willie threw himself into soldiering with a kind of religious enthusiasm but did not immediately go to front-line service. He was sent to the divisional staff, not taking kindly to the suggestion that he remain in Ireland for recruiting purposes: 'I did not join the army to make recruiting speeches but to go to the front with my men'. Although there was a move to keep him from the front because of his age, by February 1916 he was writing home from France, appalled 'at the destruction, havoc and suffering I have encountered'. On leave in March 1916 he spoke in the House of Commons 'eulogizing the spirit of the men in France and deploring the failure to recognize specifically the services of the Irish troops'.[45]

Willie Redmond particularly enjoyed a warm friendship with Lady Parsons, corresponding with her frequently from the trenches. His death was a personal sorrow to her and the family. General Parsons had worried that Willie's 'unwarlike habit of mind' might cause casualties in France. However, Stephen Gwynn claims that Willie Redmond was instinctively a soldier and Nora Robertson writes that, 'he did extremely well in the . . . static trench warfare'.[46] Given their age and backgrounds, Redmond's, Kettle's and Gwynn's enthusiasm for the soldiers serving under them and for the life of camaraderie and discipline was unexpected. Their idealism was not an uncommon reason for enlisting among New Army Irish soldiers, whereas professionals in the British Army usually enlisted for a career. Willie Redmond truly believed that reconciliation between north and south Ireland after the war, between Protestants and Catholics, would be achieved through the shared experience of fighting in the trenches in a bond of common sacrifice. This was his constant theme. He was a devout Catholic and Nationalist and it is interesting that his hopeful view was shared by the Protestant Major Bryan Cooper, who wrote in his *Tenth (Irish) Division in Gallipoli* (p. 253):

> Catholic and Protestant, Unionist and Nationalist, lived, fought and died side by side like brothers. . . . It is only to be hoped that the willingness to forget old wrongs and injustices and to combine for a common purpose that existed in the 10th Division may be a good augury for the future.

Daniel Sheehan was another Irish Nationalist MP who vociferously denounced Britain for her past and oppressive treatment of Ireland, yet when war broke out in 1914 he too joined the British Army. He believed strongly in 'the justice and righteousness of the Allied cause' and at the same time he wanted 'to advance the cause for Irish freedom'. At the age of seven his family had been evicted from their farm and all his relatives were Fenian. Sheehan entered politics in 1901 to press Labour's claims in the House of Commons, but, not a believer in Home Rule, he was expelled from Redmond's Irish Parliamentary Party and then won his seat as an Independent Nationalist in the General Election of 1910. In the war crisis Sheehan threw himself enthusiastically into recruiting and claimed to have recruited nearly every soldier in the 9th (S) Battalion, Munster Fusiliers, under the slogan 'Fight for Right and Duty, Home and Motherland', conducting tours throughout the regimental district, which included Cork, his home and his constituency. Appointed a lieutenant in the 9th, he was later promoted to captain. Of his three sons who enlisted two were killed in action. After the war Sheehan wrote:

> I served and I suffered and I sacrificed, and if the results were not all that we intended . . . we enlisted for worthy and honourable motives and we sought . . . the ultimate good of Ireland in doing so.

For the first time in the long centuries of service to the British Army, many Irishmen in the First World War saw themselves as fighting for Ireland's cause. For Sheehan, 'Willie Redmond offered his life as surely for Ireland as any man who ever died for Irish liberty'.[47]

Neither General Parsons of the 16th (Irish) nor General Powell of the 36th (Ulster) took their divisions to France; both were considered too old. Powell was succeeded by Major General Sir O.S.W. Nugent, a career soldier and the son of a general. Commissioned into the King's Royal Rifle Corps, Nugent had been on the North-West Frontier and in South Africa, where he was severely wounded. He was brought from commanding a brigade in France and therefore he conformed with the War Office policy for active and experienced officers for the New Armies. From an Anglo-Irish Protestant family whose home was at Mount Nugent, County Cavan, Nugent, in 1914, had been involved with the County Cavan UVF, but increasingly he shared with many officers a contempt for all politicians. As for the Curragh Incident, he thought the 'arming' of Ulster had been 'a great mistake'.[48]

Major-General William Hickie, CB, a Catholic from an old Irish military family from County Tipperary, succeeded General Parsons. Hickie, a great talker, was a career soldier who, after graduating from Sandhurst in 1885, was commissioned into the Royal Fusiliers. He had had staff jobs in the South African War, but he always preferred 'regimental life with its opportunities for action and sport'. Promoted Brevet Lieutenant Colonel, he commanded a mobile column against the Boer commandos. As a Brigadier General he had had recent experience commanding a brigade on the Western Front (1914–15) where he was wounded. In commanding the 16th Hickie took political considerations into account, but his Division 'became no more Nationalist . . . than it was under Parsons'. He did emphasize the 16th Division's Irishness, giving out on parade parchment certificates sketched by his own hand with a shamrock and the words 'The Irish Brigade' in Celtic lettering. They were awarded, he told the troops, for 'meritorious deeds so that the heritage worth preserving might be passed on to future generations to the glory of the Irish Brigade'. He himself advocated Home Rule, disagreeing with Parsons, but as a professional soldier he respected what General Parsons had done for the 16th and he designed a monogram for the division, LP, as a tribute to him. If Parsons thought he was replaced to make way for a Catholic, Hickie's family believed that he had not been promoted above the rank of Major General because he *was* an Irish Catholic and referred to Field Marshal Sir Henry Wilson's view that he had gone far enough.[49]

Not all Irishmen who enlisted in the British Army as citizen soldiers had political affiliations; forty-eight thousand had no stated Volunteer connections. One such young man, George Lindsay, from County Derry, enlisted in a cyclist company in the 36th (Ulster) Division because he loved cycling.[50] Many Irishmen, not willing to wait for the Irish/Ulster Divisions to form while the politicians argued, went to England to enlist, which is clear from the lists of VCs won by Irishmen in English regiments. Many Ulstermen also joined Scottish regiments that early vigorously recruited in Ulster.

News of Irish heroes was essential at this time when the Irish divisions were forming and Irish identity was being sought. When Lance Corporal Michael O'Leary of the 1st Battalion, Irish Guards, won his VC at Cuinchy, France, on 1 February 1915, he was hailed as a hero in the British press and returned home 'the darling of all Ireland'. Feted as the first Irish VC in the war, which, while not true, was undoubtedly because of the great notoriety that attended his award, O'Leary was indeed the first VC for the Irish Guards. Born to humble parents in County Cork, his coolness and bravado became legendary in single-handedly killing five Germans who were holding the first barricade and then attacking a second barricade, killing three more and taking prisoners, thus practically capturing the enemy's position by himself. He and his parents participated in a private recruiting campaign never before seen in Ireland. An O'Leary Fund was set up to look after widows and orphans of Irish troops. Important for recruiting in Ireland was the appearance of his face on recruiting posters, which up to 1915 had no Irish content, appealing mainly to Empire loyalty. This was the first poster designed to counteract Sinn Fein anti-war propaganda and is 'an early reference to Ireland's fighting tradition with emphasis on valour'.[51] O'Leary, on his return to France, was given a commission in the 1st Connaught Rangers and finished the war as a Captain.

April 1915 – The Irish Regulars in Gallipoli

The Allied operation in the Gallipoli Peninsula in the spring of 1915 revealed the great bravery of Irish soldiers who fought in an impossible situation in a far-off land little known about since ancient times. This operation was intended to defeat the Turks who had entered the war on the side of the Central Powers and was largely the brainchild of Winston Churchill, First Lord of the Admiralty, who wanted to break through to Constantinople by forcing the Dardanelles Straits with the Allied Fleet. Kitchener's insistence that the British Army would not be involved soon changed.

In February and early March the fleet successfully bombarded the outer forts of the Dardanelles; marines were landed, but with casualties, and strong Turk resistance resulted in withdrawal and deadlock. An anxious Kitchener in London now realized that the Fleet would need an army to get the job done and appointed Boer War veteran General Sir Ian Hamilton as Commander-in-Chief of the Mediterranean Expeditionary Force, which utimately consisted of the British 29th Infantry Division, a Royal Naval Division, an ANZAC Corps (a term used from 1915 for Australians and New Zealanders) and an attached French Division. When Hamilton and his hastily assembled staff left England his vague orders were to engage in military operations only if the Fleet did not get through. A renewed attack on 18 March on the Turkish Narrows was ordered by the Allied Fleet Commander, Vice Admiral de Robeck. Batteries were silenced, but suddenly de Roebeck lost a third of his force from supposedly floating mines and broke off his naval action. In a conference that followed with General Hamilton, he decided he needed the co-operation of the army. Hamilton eagerly agreed and thus the decision for a combined naval-army operation was taken, not by the Cabinet or the War Council in London but by these two commanders on the spot. Before Hamilton's force could be ready for action in April the Turks, helped by the Germans, were well prepared. It was a campaign that started in confusion and ended in disaster.[52]

Regular Irish soldiers in the 1st Royal Munster, 1st Royal Dublin and 1st Royal Inniskilling Fusiliers were among the 75,000 troops who, on Sunday 25 April 1915, simultaneously assaulted a series of beaches designated S, V, W, X, Y on the Gallipoli shore. Munster and Dublin Fusiliers landed at the crescent-shaped V beach at Cape Helles, the southernmost tip of the peninsula, where on the right was an old castle (or fort) and the village of Sedd-el-Bahr, which was their objective, as was Hill 141 beyond. High cliffs rose on the left where Turks lay in wait hidden in trenches under the wire-protected crest, while heavy wire entanglements protected the beach itself. The suicidal attack occurred in daylight and Munsters and Dublins were slaughtered. The 1st Inniskilling Fusiliers landed successfully without casualties further north at X beach, but as they advanced inland from the beach their casualties were severe. The ANZAC Corps gained a precarious foothold at Anzac Cove, fourteen miles up the coast, while Royal Naval and French Divisions carried out diversionary tactics. The Turks, fighting bravely for their own land, remained firmly entrenched on the high ground overlooking the coast. Nowhere could the Allies get far inland.

No action in the Gallipoli campaign has gripped the imagination more than the landing at V beach, where four companies of Munsters, one of Dublins and two of 1st Hampshires (a regiment that had a close connection with the Irish) were packed into the holds of the *River Clyde*, an old collier transformed into a troop carrier and assault ship, and deliberately beached about three hundred yards from the shore. The analogy of the Trojan Horse was most apt. The *River Clyde*, and indeed V beach, will be for ever associated with the Irish. At 5.00 am a naval bombardment from two battleships pounded the Turkish defences around the village. The Turks remained silent until around 6.30 when the *River Clyde* was run gently aground near the shore by Captain Unwin; their murderous fire then opened on her and caught three companies of Dublin Fusiliers crammed into cutters towed by sailors, heading for shore on either side of the collier. They were perfect targets; the Turks could not miss and the sea was soon red with blood. Among the horrendous casualties the Dublins lost Colonel Rooth shot dead; Major Featherstonhaugh, second-in-command, was mortally wounded in his boat and Captain Anderson was shot dead on the beach. Many memoirs and letters were written home to families about this terrible experience. Sergeant J. Colgan of the 1st Dublin Fusiliers writes in a letter to his wife from the Royal Naval Hospital, Malta, where he had been sent after being wounded:

> I received 3 wounds, 2 only scratches. . . . nearly everyone you knew is killed, both sergeants and privates. All the 'Heals' were killed including Father Finn by 'Heals' he meant the Medics . . . there were 32 in my boat and 6 escaped alive. . . . Then came the job to swim with the pack, and one leg useless . . . bullets whipping around . . . [53]

The Father Finn Colgan refers to was the Catholic chaplain of 86th Brigade. Though urged to stay aboard the *River Clyde*, he insisted on going on shore with his soldiers: 'The priest's place is beside the dying soldier'.

He was killed as soon as he landed. A few brave Dublins reached the shore.

Meanwhile the Munsters on the *River Clyde* watched the slaughter of the Dublins and the difficulties of Captain Unwin's sailors who, amid Turkish fire, were trying to place barges into position for the troops to walk on to shore, some Munsters helping. When Captain Unwin informed Colonel Tizard of the Munsters that the gangways were ready, he ordered Captains Geddes and Henderson to advance and all poured out of sally ports cut into the collier's side and tried to dash for the shore under the tornado of fire. Gangways and barges were quickly choked with dead and wounded. A barge broke away and immediately Captain Geddes jumped into the water and swam the twenty yards to shore. His men followed and many drowned with the weight of their equipment. Such was the slaughter that Captain Geddes wrote later, 'Men who were at Mons and La Bassée say it was sheer child's play to what we've gone through here'. The very few who got ashore sheltered behind a bank about eight feet high ten yards from the water's edge, barbed wire on their front and the beach swept by cross-fire.[54] Geddes then tried to move his remaining men to protect the right flank under the base of the fort; two survived, he himself was shot in the shoulder. He was joined by Captain T. S. Tomlinson and Sergeant Ryan, with three men of 'Z' Company. Fourteen Dublins also joined them.

Young Lieutenant Henry Desmond O'Hara of the 1st Dublins was among those who safely landed from the *River Clyde* later at night in darkness. The Reverend O. Creighton, Anglican chaplain of 86 Brigade, met this quietly brave young Irishman and greatly admired him. In his book *With the 29th Division in Gallipoli* he writes that O'Hara was little more than a boy [aged about twenty-three] when he landed on 25 April. Major H. M. Farmer, DSO, Lancashire Fusiliers, later summed up O'Hara's achievements when he went to consolidate the position after the end of April and found only this one officer of the Dublins left: 'Lieutenant O'Hara who rose to every occasion with the greatest coolness and competence, from commanding a platoon at the terrible landing from the *River Clyde* to the command of a company the next day, and after 28 April to commanding the battalion'. O'Hara was awarded a well-deserved DSO, gazetted 3 June 1915. Creighton writes of O'Hara's acute sense of loneliness with all his brother officers dead. Of those terrible days of fighting in the Krithia area at the end of April and on 1 May, O'Hara wrote to his fiancé:

> This whole business is too horrible for words. I don't expect to come alive through it for an instant – it is a miracle for anyone who does. . . . the survivors of us were . . . bordering on lunacy.

His misgivings about his chances for survival were correct; he died on the hospital ship *Arcadia* on 29 August of wounds received on 12 August and was buried in the military cemetery at Gibraltar.[55]

Henry Desmond O'Hara was commissioned in the Royal Dublin Fusiliers in 1912. Born at Thomastown, County Kilkenny, into an Irish Protestant family of church and community commitments in both the north and south, his father, W. J. O'Hara, was the resident magistrate (RM) Ballincollig, County Cork, and his mother was the daughter of Peter Carnellon JP, of County Kilkenny. His paternal grandfather was the Reverend James Dunn O'Hara of Portstewart, and an uncle was the Bishop of Cashel. There were many young men in the First World War like O'Hara who had command thrust on them at an early age. Robert Graves of the Royal Welch Fusiliers would write that: 'No officer in [his] Company was more than twenty-two or twenty-three years old'.[56]

Lieutenant Robert Bernard was another brave young officer of the 1st Dublins. Very early on the day after the landing he was killed while leading his men in a bayonet charge in a ferocious fight which took the fort of Sedd-el-Bahr and the village, together with detachments of Hampshires, Munsters and Dublin Fusiliers, all under Lieutenant Colonel CHM Doughty-Wylie. Commissioned, like Desmond O'Hara, in 1912, Robert was a younger son of the Protestant Archbishop of Dublin.

Early that same afternoon Corporal William Cosgrove of the 1st Munster Fusiliers performed a remarkable feat that won him a VC. Men on the beach, now under Captain Stoney, of the King's Own Scottish Borderers, were still pinned down. He, seeing the attack being made on the right, led his men forward to support it, but they found their way barred by heavy wire entanglements that had resisted the naval bombardment and all attempts to cut it. Cosgrove, 'an Irish giant' over six feet tall and of exceptional strength, now volunteered and proceeded single-handedly and under heavy fire to pull down the posts of the enemy's high-wire entanglements, wrenching them out of the ground and clearing a way through. Cosgrove's feat was witnessed from the *River Clyde* by Surgeon P. Burrows Kelly, RN, DSO, who recorded his admiration in his diary: 'with his officers and brother Tommies dying and dead around him. . . . The manner in which the man worked out in the open will never be forgotten by those who were fortunate enough to witness it'. Cosgrove, after his Sergeant Major had been killed, led the Munstermen in the successful but fierce attack to take Hill 141. He was hit in the spine and was invalided home to Ireland to a hero's welcome. Cosgrove was the son of a small farmer in County Cork and as a young man in 1910 had enlisted in the 1st Munster Fusiliers with whom he had seen service in India. A modest man, when recuperating later at the family's farm and describing his action, he willingly gave credit to his fellow Munsters: 'The boys that were left with me were every bit as good as myself and I do wish that they all got some recognition'. He also had a good word to say about the Turks: 'We met a brave, honourable foe in the Turks'. Promoted to Sergeant, Cosgrove saw no further action because of his wound.[57]

These regular Irish soldiers continued to fight in isolated engagements throughout the spring and summer of 1915, and Captain 'Mickey' Gerald O'Sullivan, 1st Inniskilling Fusiliers, became a legend in the Gallipoli Peninsula. On 1 and 2 July he and Corporal (later Sergeant) James Somers of the same regiment, both 'wonderful bombers', won their VCs assisting Gurkhas whose trenches were penetrated by the Turks. O'Sullivan volunteered to lead a party of bomb-throwers to recapture it and:

> under a very heavy fire, and in order to throw his bombs with greater effect he got up on the parapet where he was completely exposed to the enemy. . . . He was finally wounded but not before his inspiring example . . . which resulted in the recapture of the trench.

Although the empty portion of the trench was subsequently reoccupied by the Turks, which happened frequently, Captain O'Sullivan's gallantry was recognized in his award. Born near Douglas, County Cork, he was the son of the late Lieutenant Colonel George L. O'Sullivan of the 91st Argyll and Sutherland Highlanders, an example of the many Irish in Scottish regiments. He spent much of his boyhood in Dublin, and from Sandhurst was gazetted to the Inniskillings in May 1909.

In his section Corporal Somers, of County Cavan, remained on the spot fighting with his rifle until a party brought up much-needed bombs. His citation states that he then climbed over into the Turkish trench and bombed the Turks with great effect. Some of his officers had said it was impossible to put the Turks out, but by his coolness and bravery he succeeded in doing so and was promoted Sergeant in the field. Somers was later gassed and invalided home to Tipperary where he died in May 1918.[58]

As in France, this kind of fighting degenerated into stalemate with the high ground still held by the Turks and the Allies chiefly settled on a narrow strip along the coast. In August General Sir Ian Hamilton made elaborate plans to break this stalemate with a fresh landing at Suvla Bay.

The 10th (Irish) Division in Gallipoli, August 1915

'When one thinks of Gallipoli one thinks first of graves.'

Major Bryan Cooper, *The Tenth (Irish) Division in Gallipoli*
London, 1918, p. 243

On 6 and 7 August Irish citizen soldiers in General Sir Bryan Mahon's 10th (Irish) Division were first thrown into battle. The 10th, a 'green division' in General Sir Frederick Stopford's IX Corps, was to effect a surprise landing at Suvla Bay, take the Kiretch Tepe Sirt Heights in the north of the Peninsula and then link up with the ANZACs precariously established on the coast, in order to break out east and inland to capture Sari Bair Ridge, considered the key. Anglo-Irishman General Sir Alexander Godley, GOC 1st Australian and New Zealand Division, commanded this attack under General Birdwood, GOC the ANZAC Corps. Godley, after the Anglo-Boer War, where we first encountered him in charge of Mounted Infantry and later at Mafeking, had been GOC the forces in New Zealand. Known as a determined officer, he was unpopular with his New Zealanders because of insensitivity.

Of Lieutenant General Sir F. Stopford, IX Corps, Bryan Cooper writes: 'We knew little of him, but we knew he was an Irishman and were prepared to take him on trust'. A professional soldier, Stopford had served as ADC in Egypt and the Sudan in the 1880s, and had been military secretary to General Buller in the early bleak months of the Anglo-Boer War. At sixty-one Stopford was not in good health and had been living in retirement since 1909. He seems to have been a man of considerable charm and a keen student of military history, but he had never commanded troops in battle and through no fault of his own his experience of actual fighting was minimal. He arrived in the peninsula only in July and was sent to Cape Helles to gain some battle experience.[59]

On 6 August Brigadier Cooper and his 29 Brigade were detached from General Mahon's 10th Division and sent to reinforce the ANZACs at Anzac Cove where, after landing, they met with further subdivision, going into action as isolated units. General Mahon would later write that his Irishmen had to fight 'under officers that did not know them', which was 'damaging to an Irish formation where officers and men traditionally struck up close ties of personal loyalty'. It was also a great disappointment that they were not to fight as a division, considering their high hopes and the hopes of those at home that these Irishmen were fighting for the honour of Ireland as the first Irish Division ever to do so. Historian Myles Dungan suggests that the 10th (Irish) Division 'suffered more than most

. . . never fighting as a single unit . . . at one point operating under three separate commands'.[60]

The 6th Leinsters were first attached to 1st Australian Division as a reserve in what is known as the Battle of Sari Bair from 7–10 August. The Australians appreciated the eagerness with which the Irish detachments carried out their duties, while the Irish admired the splendid physique of the Australians who, unlike the Irish, wore shorts and were deeply tanned by the Gallipoli sun. They appeared to be without nerves, very good men to fight alongside. On the 9th the Leinsters relieved the New Zealanders, who had been holding the rocky, steep Rhododendron Spur, an outcrop of the main Sari Bair ridge; there shrapnel killed several at the foot. At daybreak the next day the Turks launched a counter-attack, pouring over the crest of the Chunuk Bair and overwhelming the two British battalions on the Leinsters' right and left. Colonel Craske, DSO, leading his 6th Leinsters into action, drove the Turks back after a desperate struggle at close quarters. He and several officers were wounded, and three subalterns were killed. Captain J. C. Parke was hit in the arm, which was very tragic for him; before the war he was 'one of the greatest lawn tennis players in the British Isles and had represented the UK in the Davis Cup'. Helped by the guns of the Fleet and the artillery at Anzac Cove, the ridge remained in British hands, but the next morning, when the Turks could be seen massing for a determined final effort, the Leinsters launched their counter-charge: 'With a ringing yell, the line of bayonets surged forward . . . to prove again that to attack is not only the best defensive policy but is that best suited to the Irish temperament'. The Turks were driven back temporarily. The 6th Royal Irish Rifles were driven to ground in this their first action when two hundred yards short of their objective. They hung on all night in their precarious position, suffering agonies of thirst. The next day, in a fierce Turkish counter-attack, their line broke only when all the officers but three had become casualties, including Colonel Bradford. The entire 29 Brigade staff were casualties in these actions; Brigadier General R. J. Cooper fell severely wounded in the lungs. His life was saved when General Godley later found him on the beach, lying wounded on a stretcher, and had him carried immediately to a lighter.[61]

Meanwhile, early on the morning of 7 August the remaining battalions of the 10th Division were among some 20,000 troops landed at Suvla Bay, no small feat; it is little wonder there was confusion. For many Irish the wide semicircular bay and the beautiful coast looked very much like Dublin Bay, but the sunbaked land was strange and unfamiliar. Turkish resistance was at first slight; there were losses from snipers hidden in the scrub, but there seemed to have been no haste by commanders to get inland. Orders were given, then countermanded. The historian Robert

Rhodes James paints an extraordinary picture of infantry milling about or bathing in the sea, the bay crowded with warships and transports. His judgement was that 'A single act of resolute leadership would have secured the capture on very easy terms of the . . . Kiretch Tepe'. General Mahon's 10th was now further broken up; his 31 Brigade under Brigadier General F. F. Hill was diverted by the navy because of landing difficulties to land on the wrong side of Suvla Bay, *away* from Kiretch Tepe Sirt Ridge, the Division's objective. A confused Hill was taken to General Stopford's headquarters aboard his yacht *Jonquil* anchored in the bay. Stopford knew nothing of the situation on the shore and ordered Hill to assist General Hammersley and his New Army 11th Division. 'No one,' writes James, 'seems to have thought of consulting Mahon.'[62]

The Irish under General Hill were prominent in the capture of Chocolate and Green Hills, the first major success in the peninsula. In their advance inland through the noon of a tropical day burdened by rifles and ammunition all were exhausted and in need of water. Losses from land mines and shrapnel fire were unceasing. To reach the northern shore of the now dry Salt Lake and link up with 11th Division, the Irish troops had to pass over a narrow neck of land raked by enemy artillery. Leading the way was the towering figure of Colonel Geoffrey Downing of the 7th Dublins, who inspired all by his calm fearlessness: 'He stood in the centre of the bullet-swept zone quietly twirling his stick . . . As an old soldier he knew there were times when an officer must be prepared to run what would otherwise appear unnecessary risks.' Looming ahead was Chocolate Hill; only one hundred and sixty feet high, it was a strong defensive position, its sides seamed with trenches. For these 'freshies of the Irish brand', as an ANZAC captain called these New Army soldiers, it was a challenge.[63]

At dusk after a heavy naval bombardment the Irish attack on the hill began and the 6th Inniskillings and 6th Irish Fusiliers on the flanks pressed forward. In the centre was the wild boisterous charge of the 7th Dublins who raced in competition with each other towards the crest, Major R. S. M. Harrison, a Dublin Fusilier regular officer leading 'A' Company, and Captain Poole Hickman, the New Army Irishman, leading the Pals of 'D' Company. A former 'D' Company officer describes how: ' "D" Company came into our ditch with a dash for all the world like a wild forward rush at Lansdowne Road' [their Dublin sports ground]. Fatigue and thirst were forgotten as they gained the crest in an amazingly brave charge that would be enacted time and again by Irish troops in the peninsula. To honour the Dublin Fusiliers, Chocolate Hill would be known as 'Dublin Hill'. Casualties included an 'old soldier', Major Tippett of the 7th Dublins, who, along with several senior officers, died that day. Tippett had served for years in the old Dublin City Militia and had left the security of his comfortable position as a political agent in England to die in his old regiment. The death of Lieutenant Ernest Julian, one of the New Army 'Toffs' in 'D' Company, was a great loss for academic circles in Dublin. The 5th Royal Irish Fusiliers also suffered severely, taking the smaller Green Hill, losing their Major Garstin.[64]

On 7 August General Mahon, landing at a new beach, Suvla Point, had only four battalions under his command, one of them, the 5th Royal Irish Regiment, the Divisional Pioneers, being assigned to beach duty, so he was without support troops, divisional artillery and engineer field companies. Landing at Suvla late that morning, the 6th Munster Fusiliers encountered Turkish fire and a beach sown with mines that exploded on contact, injuring several; the 7th Munsters arrived a little later without casualties. Both battalions had orders to climb the Kiretch Tepe Sirt Ridge at its western end and push forward along the crest. Under a relentless sun the Munsters passed through a difficult terrain of gullies covered with dense oak and holly scrub and soon came upon fly-infested corpses, indications of a nasty fight waged by the 11th Manchesters whom they were to meet. The Manchesters had landed by 3.00 am despite prevailing confusions and now an exhausted remnant had established a position on the Ridge, their Colonel wounded. By nightfall the 6th Munsters had succeeded in advancing to within one hundred yards of the Turks on the crest, but darkness prevented them from going further and even this advance was costly. Their war diary is very brief and the last entry for 7 August states: '22:00. Retirement completed. Battalion entrenched S. slopes of Pt. 165. Casualties, Lt. J. B. Lee killed. Lt. G.W. Haynes wounded. (Other ranks killed, wounded, missing)'. Lieutenant Joseph Bagnall Lee was the first officer of the 6th Royal Munster Fusiliers killed in action; his younger brother, Alfred Tennyson Lee, was wounded the following day.

The Lee brothers were typical of the idealistic Irish middle class who enlisted like the Pals of the Dublin's 'D' Company. Joseph Lee, at twenty-seven years old, had been a successful Barrister at Law and had published two books on that subject. Both he and his brother Alfred had been eager to enlist and received their temporary commissions through Trinity College, Dublin, in September 1914. The diary of the 6th Munsters is in the Public Record Office in Kew, London, and Michael Lee, a grand-nephew and writer on military subjects, writes with some emotion how seventy-five years later he was the first of his family to see it. He also, in 1993, went to the Gallipoli Peninsula where:

> I found myself on West Beach, standing probably somewhere close to where my two granduncles stood, looking at the Kiretch

Tepe Sirt, my thoughts continually wandering back in time to that
fateful afternoon of August 7th, 1915, trying to imagine what it
was like for these two young men from Dublin, who like their
comrades had never seen war of any sort, let alone the hell they
were now experiencing.[65]

On 8 August the 6th and 7th Munsters dug in at Jephson's Post, a knoll
captured under the 6th's Major Jephson. In capturing half Kiretch Tepe
Sirt Ridge, the Munsters lost forty-eight all ranks killed and over one
hundred and fifty wounded. With the 5th Inniskillings, who had arrived
later in the day and relieved the 11th Manchesters, they held on for a week
on that bare Kiretch Tepe Sirt suffering from the heat and acute water
shortage; the stench of unburied bodies was everywhere.[66]

At the end of that gruelling time, on 15 August, a general advance along
the Kiretch Tepe Sirt Ridge was ordered. At least for this attack General
Hill's 31 Brigade was restored to Mahon's command, but by the time
Mahon attacked the Turks had brought up reinforcements. Canon
McLean, Protestant Chaplain for 30 Brigade, reported in his diary how
he watched the final 'brilliant charge of the 6th Dublins and 6th Munsters
going forward to secure the Kiretch Tepe Sirt. It was a wonderful sight to
see the men deployed in open order, their cheers, the charge'. Watchers
from the Gulf of Saros in the Salt Lake area heard the sound of the 'Irish
triumphal cry' and added their own excited shouts of victory. Amidst
heavy fire, Major Tynte of the 6th Munsters led the rush of these 'green'
Irish soldiers that brought them, with gleaming bayonets, to the Turkish
position and the whole of the northern slope of Kiretch Tepe Sirt as far as
and beyond the 'Pimple' was cleared. The Turks fled in the face of this
onslaught.[67]

For the Irish on the right, or southern, landward side of the Ridge it was
a different story. The 5th Inniskillings, supported by the 6th Inniskillings,
were now entrusted with taking Kidney Hill, a place of precipitous slopes
and thick scrub. Well-placed Turkish machine guns and artillery had
perfect observation of the open plain in front of the hill. The attack that
followed was the 5th Battalion's 'first bitter taste of war'. It was also a kind
of forlorn hope, as Bryan Cooper notes: 'For against modern weapons . .
. a frontal attack by daylight on an entrenched position a thousand yards
away is certain to fail', and fail it did. Kidney Hill was not taken nor was
the southern slope cleared and heavy casualties resulted: Commanding
Officer Lieutenant Colonel Vanrenen and five officers of the 5th
Inniskillings were killed, their total casualties, including missing, were
more than half the total strength they had had on landing at Suvla Bay.
The young Inniskillings held on and even though the battalion was

shattered they would not leave their positions. Lieutenant G. B. Lyndon of the 6th Inniskillings won the MC for courageously going out after sunset to bring in many of these little parties.[68]

The result of this failed attack was that the 7th Dublins and the 6th Royal Irish Fusiliers, both in reserve, and the 6th Munsters were hurried to the Ridge. Along the way Lieutenant Colonel Downing of the 7th Dublins was shot in the foot by a sniper and had to be relieved by Major Harrison. The Irish battalions were established in an uneven line just under the crest when late that night they were engaged in a sudden sharp bayonet and musketry fight, but managed to drive off the Turks. Before dawn, however, the invisible Turks began lobbing grenades over, a veritable rain of bombs from their side of the Ridge where they could skilfully hide behind large boulders. By early morning of 16 August the Irish were fed up with their helpless position: 'On every side men had fallen . . . the strain on the survivors was appalling' and they were without grenades with which to retaliate. A party of the Pals was only too eager to attempt a bayonet charge under Captain Poole Hickman when ordered to do so by Major Harrison. They dashed up the hill to meet a storm of fire and Captain Hickman was mortally wounded. Major Harrison took his place and was struck by a grenade. Only four men made their way back over the crest.

A few remaining officers of the 7th Dublins, bravely trying to encourage and calm their men, exposed themselves to snipers; lost in this way was Captain Richard Patrick Tobin, son of Lieutenant-Colonel R. F. Tobin, Royal Army Medical Corps. Here, too, fell Lieutenant Michael Fitzgibbon, the law student, and Lieutenant Edward Weatherill, descendant of one of King William's aides at the Boyne, a boy conspicuous for his courage. Brave Private Wilkin of the 7th Dublins threw Turkish bombs back at the enemy five times before they exploded, to be blown to pieces on the sixth. The 6th Irish Fusiliers, with the 5th sent to reinforce them, were both almost annihilated; nearly all the Irish Fusilier officers fell, including the 5th's Regimental Sergeant Major Mulligan, killed. Captains Panton and Kidd and 2nd Lieutenant Heuston earned the Military Cross, Heuston probably killed. For the Pals of 'D' Company, which had arrived at Suvla with 239 men, casualties during the night reduced it to 108. Only seventy-nine would leave the peninsula in September.[69]

These untried citizen soldiers had been in the peninsula only two weeks and were expected to fight like regulars. Immediately thrust into battle, they were not introduced gradually nor trained sufficiently, as were the New Army Division soldiers in the 36th and 16th Divisions in France. Despite the inadequacies and confusion in the Gallipoli command, Irish soldiers fought with great bravery and heroism in a lost cause. In

Bryan Cooper's list of awards for the 10th (Irish) Division there is no Victoria Cross.

One of the stretcher-bearers bringing in wounded was the young Irish poet Francis Ledwidge. An infantryman in the 5th Inniskillings, he had volunteered to help the Medical Corps, who could not cope with all the wounded. One soldier he brought in was his friend Robert Christie whose voice he recognized in the dark; they spoke only briefly, then Ledwidge was off to carry in more wounded. Ledwidge was appalled at the suffering of his fellow Fusiliers, yet amazed at their bravery as he wrote to his friend and mentor Lord Dunsany:

> It was Hell! Hell! No man thought he would ever return. Just fancy out of 'D' Company 250 strong, only seventy-six returned. By Heavens, you should know the bravery of these men. . . . It was a horrible and a great day. I would not have missed it for worlds.

Christie, after months in hospital, was discharged from the army and sent back to Belfast on crutches. The friendship of Christie, a Northern Ulsterman, and Ledwidge, a Southern Irishman, would have gladdened the heart of Bryan Cooper, who had hoped for reconciliation in Ireland between Unionist and Nationalist after the war. Ledwidge, writing to Christie after the Easter Rising in 1916, expressed their common love of Ireland:

> Yes poor Ireland is always in trouble. Tho' I am not a Sinn Feiner and you are a Carsonite do our sympathies not go to 'Cathleen ni Hoolihan'?[70]

Very brave were the two chaplains of 30 Brigade, Canon McLean, sometimes called the jewel of the Protestant chaplains, and Father Murphy, his courageous Roman Catholic counterpart. Canon McLean, called that dear old Irishman from Limerick, was sixty-one years old and had been rector of the Church of Ireland at Rathkeale, County Limerick. Father Murphy, twenty years younger than Canon McLean, described him as his 'splendid colleague', while McLean always paid great tribute to Father Murphy: '[I] cannot express the admiration and affection I have always felt for his sterling character, he was always looking after me'.

A Service was customary for any who could attend and on 15 August Canon McLean recorded in his diary that he had celebrated Holy Communion at Divisional HQ for Lord Granard's Pioneer Regiment (5th Royal Irish) and for the 6th and 7th Dublins in the trenches before the attack. Before an advance of his Irish regiments Canon McLean would always celebrate Holy Communion in the firing line, frequently placing himself in danger, sniped at several times. Father Murphy also celebrated mass for the 7th Dublins on 15 August; Lady Day was an important Church festival for all Roman Catholics. Indeed, both chaplains faithfully attended the wounded and the dying; no danger or hardship was too great. As one officer wrote of them and whose sentiments were repeated in the many soldiers' letters sent home: 'They put a great spirit in the men, who love them both . . . . Catholic and Protestant are hand in hand, all brought about by the gentleness and undaunted courage displayed by these two splendid soldiers of Christ'.[71]

Robert Graves, in his *Goodbye to All That*, was very hard on the Protestant clergy, maintaining that the soldiers had very little respect for the Anglican regimental chaplains who obeyed orders 'to avoid getting mixed up with the fighting and to stay behind with the transport'. Roman Catholic chaplains were 'not only permitted to visit posts of danger but definitely enjoyed to be wherever fighting was . . . to give extreme unction to the dying'. Canon McLean clearly exemplifies the number of Protestant chaplains who ignored the ban, as does the high number of casualties among them. The rule in fact was relaxed in 1916, which Graves seems not to have known about, 'but the troops continued to label Anglican Chaplains as cowards'.[72]

The great bravery and spirit of the Irish was never more in evidence than in the memorable charge of the 5th Connaught Rangers at the Kabak Kuyu Wells on 21 August. In a battle that in terms of numbers has been called the greatest battle fought in the Campaign, the Connaught Rangers were part of a coordinated attack by ANZAC forces and those of IX Corps to capture Hill 60 and the two important wells of Kabak Kuyu. The wells were the objective of the Rangers and their first main action. Like all battalions, the Rangers had already suffered casualties, whether on fatigue duty, carrying water, bringing in the wounded or burying the dead; no place was safe in the peninsula. Lieutenant Colonel H. F. N. Jourdain, who had raised the battalion in Ireland in August 1914 would lead them. Major General Alex Godley visited the Rangers waiting in their gully and told them what was expected of them: the 9th Worcesters had attempted to take the wells on 12 August and failed, and he now looked to the Rangers to carry the position 'by the cold steel . . . and an Irish yell'. His words, spoken in the spirit of General Picton to his 'Devil's Own' before the battle of Ciudad Rodrigo, were calculated to appeal even to modern-day Connaught Rangers. Dysentery and enteric fever were rampant among the troops, but no one reported sick that morning, not wanting to miss the fight.

At last the bombardment ceased at 3.40pm, the order came to advance and the rush was on to be first into the enemy's trenches; that honour fell to 2nd Lieutenant T. W. G. Johnson, a Platoon Commander in the 5th Connaughts, who had gained Amateur International Colours for Ireland at Association Football. He and the leading platoon dashed forward exuberantly and met heavy rifle fire which no one stopped to return. They ran across 400 yards of open country with bayonets levelled. Before Johnson's platoon caught up with him 'he had bayoneted six Turks and shot two more.'[73] For his part in this action and for other gallant deeds Johnson was awarded the Military Cross. Both the wells and the trenches guarding them were in the hands of the Rangers.

Seeing some New Zealanders in difficulties at the well-fortified Hill 60, Lieutenant Colonel Jourdain immediately sent the Rangers' 'A' Company to their assistance who were joined by eager men from all companies; 'their Irish blood was aflame', but, tragically, in the heavy Turkish fire, the Rangers storming Hill 60 fell and died. The Turks held on in Hill 60's top trenches. In the fierce fighting that continued during the night Sergeant Nealon, an old soldier from Ballina who had re-enlisted for the war, took over when Lieutenant Blake was killed. He led a group of Connaughts and New Zealanders to an abandoned trench and held it until relieved. His stout figure, writes Bryan Cooper, concealed the spirit of a hero.[74]

It was the action of the Connaught Rangers in capturing the Kabak Kuyu Wells that brought notoriety and recognition of their bravery. In November 1915 John Redmond, while 'showing a party of Australian convalescent soldiers over the House of Commons, asked them if they had seen anything of the 10th (Irish) Division. They had, and 'in their opinion the charge made by the Connaught Rangers at Kabak Kuyu Wells was the finest thing they had seen in the War'. This was no mean praise from Australians who were themselves known for bravery and dash. The capture of the wells was originally attributed to the Indian Brigade by General Hamilton in his official *Despatches* of December 1915, published in January 1916. On reading this, Lieutenant Colonel Jourdain complained at once in high dudgeon to General Godley, who assured Jourdain that Hamilton would be notified and the mistake rectified, and this was later confirmed by Godley. Two hundred and fifty Connaught Rangers, however, did receive recognition and praise from General Sir Ian Hamilton in his despatch for their spirited charge in an ANZAC final attack on Hill 60 a week later, which reads in part [they] 'excited the admiration of all beholders by the switfness and cohesion of their charge' but at midnight before fresh troops could arrive, he adds, 'the Irishmen had been out-bombed'.[75]

Meanwhile Irish regulars had again been in battle when the 29th Division, now known as the 'Incomparable' since the 25 April landings, was brought from Cape Helles to assault Scimitar Hill simultaneously with the ANZAC attack on Hill 60 on 22 August. With them were he 11th Division and the 2nd Dismounted Yeomanry Division. The 1st Inniskillings reached the crest, but were beaten back. Captain G. O'Sullivan died here before receiving his VC for his earlier actions at Helles. Once more he displayed great courage, appealing to his little remnant of Inniskillings to attack the crest again: 'One more charge, for the honour of the Old Regiment'. From a band of fifty, only one returned. 'The name of Captain O'Sullivan VC', writes Sir Frank Fox, the Inniskilling historian, 'will live as a type of the true soldier's spirit'.[76] Casualties in this terrible battle were particularly heavy in the 29th Division and the Yeomanry; among them was the brave Irish Brigadier General Lord Longford KP. The failure of the attacks on Scimitar Hill and Hill 60 signalled the end of the Allies' Gallipoli offensive.

The day of crisis in this ill-fated campaign had been 15 August at Suvla. General Liman von Sanders, the German commander of the Turkish Fifth Army, saw it as such, writing later in his memoir: 'If, on August 15 and 16, the British had taken the Kiretch Tepe they would have outflanked the entire Fifth Army and final success might have fallen to them'.[77] That is, had General Mahon's 10th (Irish) Division remained together at Suvla on the 7th, this might have happened. Moreover, General Hamilton chose 15 August to change his senior command, a sorry tale that concerns Mahon. Hamilton relieved General Stopford of IX Corps, along with General Hammersley of 11th Division and Brigadier General W. H. Sitwell, and sent them home. Major General H. de Lisle, GOC 29th Division, was temporarily appointed in Stopford's place. General Mahon was then asked to waive his seniority and serve under de Lisle who was junior to him in rank. He refused, resigned and was sent to Lemnos to think things over, accused of putting his own dignity above his duty to his fighting soldiers. Robert Rhodes James writes: 'Mahon, seething with rage and suffering from the strain of a terrible week on the Kiretch Tepe Sirt, left Suvla while his brave Irishmen were locked in their desperate battle on the craggy and exposed ridge. Mahon hated de Lisle and made it clear that he would have willingly served under anyone else; after a few days' reflection, he cooled off and returned to command his severely mauled division'.[78] Lord Granard, commander of the 10th's 5th Royal Irish Regiment, told a different story. He claimed that Mahon was also sacked at the same time as Stopford and that, for political reasons, Kitchener intervened to restore Mahon to his command; Mahon, not wishing to serve under de Lisle, *then* resigned, but changed his mind. Mahon undoubtedly retained his command because his dismissal would have caused adverse reaction in Ireland, connected as he was with this very first Irish Division and a popular figure there. Many in the 10th thought that Mahon had been unfairly treated and Lord Granard himself considered resigning in his support.[79]

Personal jealousies were no new thing in the British Army and Tom Johnstone suggests, in a most interesting conjecture, that in this case they went back to the Boer War where Mahon had been a hero in the relief of Mafeking, while Hamilton had been highly criticized by Kitchener for a failure at Oliphant's Nek and was only 'saved' by General Roberts. Mahon was consequently not welcome in Gallipoli by Hamilton. Johnstone further suggests that this may have been why the 10th had been so broken up and its battalions fighting piecemeal. Even the mild Bryan Cooper of the 5th Connaught Rangers, who wished to avoid any controversies in writing his *The Tenth (Irish) Division in Gallipoli* could not refrain from commenting on Mahon's 'extraordinary position'. He was a Lieutenant General of three years' standing, had commanded a division for more than six years, now he was 'entering into action with only four battalions the . . . rest of his Command having been diverted elsewhere'.[80]

For a division that was formed without political overtones, what happened to the 10th in Gallipoli certainly brought political repercussions and a drop in recruitment in Ireland. Little recognition by the military authorities of the 10th's bravery and sacrifice was evident. As an example, for the regular Irish soldiers at Cape Helles in April there did seem to be a scarcity of awards, considering their suffering in that slaughter.

A final trial for these Irish soldiers was the tremendous Great Flood and Blizzard, an ice-storm that swept over the Gallipoli Peninsula at the end of November 1915 in a succession of gales, dropping temperatures and floods, where men drowned in trenches that suddenly became raging torrents. Suffering greatly were those regulars in the 29th Division, 1st Munsters, 1st Dublins and 1st Inniskillings; the 10th (Irish) Division had left for Salonika in September. The storm inflicted 5,000 casualties in the Suvla area alone, and among the more than 1,000 evacuated with frost-bite and ailments connected with extreme cold was Lieutenant J. C. R. Delmage of the 1st Munsters, son of a Huguenot family from County Limerick. Major Guy Geddes DSO, in the 1st Munsters, who had come ashore from the *River Clyde* in April, records in his diary how 'men lay dead from exposure including Private Bulger DCM, a veteran of the South Africa War . . . a magnificent shot'. Geddes had to be forcibly evacuated under General de Lisle's instructions and sent to Mudros with the first batch of invalids from Suvla.[81]

Even before this disaster occurred Kitchener arrived in the peninsula to assess the Gallipoli situation for himself and, appalled at the conditions, gave assent for the army to evacuate. With amazing secrecy, by 20 December troops had left Suvla and Anzac on barges and small boats, and the evacuation of Cape Helles could proceed, which was carried out over 7/8 January 1916. The survivors who had landed at V Beach finally leaving the peninsula saw the *River Clyde* still anchored offshore; unlike their arrival, there was only sporadic firing by the Turks that soon tapered off.

As for the young New Army Irish soldiers in the Gallipoli Peninsula, whatever their limitations 'without knowledge or experience of war' and fighting in a lost cause, Bryan Cooper would write of them:

> Officers and men did all that was required of them. They died. There was no fear or faltering, there was no retirement without orders. They make no claim to exclusive glory, to have done more than it was their duty to do . . . they have no cause to be ashamed.[82]

CHAPTER TEN

The Irish in the Great War
1916 – 1918

It is too late now to retrieve
A fallen dream, too late to grieve
A name unmade, but not too late
To thank the gods for what is great;
A keen-edged sword, a soldier's heart,
Is greater than a poet's art.
And greater than a poet's fame
A little grave that has no name,
Whence honour turns away in shame.

From *Soliloquy*, Francis Ledwidge
5th Royal Inniskilling Fusiliers

The Irish in the British Army in the Easter Rebellion – 1916

While Irish soldiers serving in France were preparing for the great Somme offensive of 1916, back home in Ireland, mostly in Dublin, a minority of Irish Volunteers in a bid for independence on 24 April suddenly broke out into what is known as the Easter Rebellion or Rising. While the 16th (Irish) Division, John Redmond's beloved 'Irish Brigade', suffered greatly in gas attacks at Hulluch on 27 and 29 April Irish soldiers in Ireland were dying while fighting rebellious fellow Irishmen. No wonder that the troops, quickly brought in when the fighting began in the streets of Dublin, were 'as bewildered as were the civilian crowds'.[1]

About noon on that Easter Monday a mixed group of Irish Citizen Army and Volunteers marched to the General Post Office on O'Connell Street, Dublin, and occupied it as the headquarters of the insurrection. The insurgents, numbering fewer than 1,000 and joined by some 800 a day later, 'showed from the start they were prepared to go to extremes: policemen were shot in St. Stephen's Green, the Castle and elsewhere within minutes of the outbreak of the revolt . . . the insurrection took the government and the military authorities by surprise'.[2] In all parts of Dublin sympathy was initially not on the side of the rebels; there were far too many Dubliners fighting with Irish regiments in France and elsewhere for the population to feel that this was the right moment to embarrass England.[3] Captain Stephen Gwynn in the 6th Connaught Rangers and now attached to the 10th (S) Royal Dublin Fusiliers in Dublin, asked the Fusiliers how their scouting worked during the conflict. Their answer was: 'We needed no scouts, the old women told us everything.'[4] Many Irish soldiers had Irish Volunteer connections, but, encouraged by John Redmond, had enlisted to support the war. Gwynn writes: 'The first volley that a company of this battalion [10th Dublins] encountered killed an officer who was strongly Nationalist in his sympathies . . . others had been active leaders in the Howth gun-running episode under Erskine Childers and here they were in the British Army'. Again the ambiguities of Irish soldiers fighting for the Crown are apparent.

Some 2500 British Army troops were available for action in Dublin against the rebels. All infantry were Irish and many were recruits still undergoing training in reserve battalions stationed throughout the city: 3rd (Special Reserve) Royal Irish Regiment and 3rd Royal Irish Rifles, a strong Ulster militia battalion. A detachment of the 18th Irish Rifles, a reserve battalion from 36th (Ulster) Division under their Colonel R. G. Sharman Crawford, took part in the capture of 'Liberty Hall' in Dublin. A section of the 'inlying piquet' of the 10th Dublin Fusiliers under Lieutenant D. O'M. Leahy suffered loss when it came under heavy fire from across the River Liffey and had to retire. The 4th Battalion sent a detachment to defend Dublin Castle; the 5th Battalion sent another from the Curragh camp to occupy the Guinness buildings. The Dublin Fusiliers suffered eleven killed and thirty-five wounded. It was to the Dublin Fusiliers that Captain Sean Heuston of the rebel Volunteers surrendered. Captain Henry de Courcy-Wheeler of the Dublins, an Irishman from County Kildare, took the surrender of rebels in the Royal College of Surgeons, Dublin, where the famous Countess Constance Markievicz, clad in the dark green uniform of the Irish Volunteers, was second-in-command. 'So small was the Ascendancy world that he was connected to Constance through marriage.'[5]

A detachment of the 5th Leinsters came under fire around Dublin Castle and, in operations that continued over the next few days, Private C. Moore was killed and buried in the Provost's Garden, Trinity College. Many subaltern officers of the 3rd Leinsters were with the Young Officers Corps at Fermoy and on the outbreak of the rebellion they were sent to guard the munitions factory at Wexford. Later the Corps was divided into flying columns and engaged in rounding up suspects, all of which gained practical experience for active service to come.[6] Irish newspapers praised the actions of these British Army troops in the Rising, at the same time lauding the bravery and suffering of Irish troops fighting in France.

The Anglo-Irish Captain John Bowen-Colthurst, however, earned a reputation as a monster. During Easter week in Dublin he ordered the execution of Francis Sheehy-Skeffington, an Ulster Protestant and Tom Kettle's gentle, pacifist and extreme Nationalist brother-in-law. While engaged in his 'self-appointed non-combatant role of trying to prevent looting in the streets' Sheehy-Skeffington was apprehended and taken to Portobello Barracks where Bowen-Colthurst was in charge. On the following day Bowen-Colthurst, 'on hearing Sheehy-Skeffington's political convictions, saw him as a dangerous rebel and had him summarily shot'. Sheehy-Skeffington had strenuously objected to Kettle's enlistment; he sympathized with the rebels and his pacifism had earlier led to imprisonment. Bowen-Colthurst should never have been placed in charge; posted to Dublin to recover from shell-shock, the events of the rebellion had proved too much for his disordered mind. He himself shot a man and two boys in the streets. In between his rampagings, he suffered remorse and said, 'It's a terrible thing to shoot one's own countrymen, isn't it?' Eventually sent to Broadmoor prison in England because of his wild activities during Easter week, Bowen-Colthurst afterwards emigrated to Canada. In the guerrilla war that developed in Ireland from 1919 between the Irish Republican Army (IRA) and the British military, his home in County Cork, where his mother and sister lived, was one of the first houses to be burnt.[7]

The battles of Easter week were a military failure for the rebels says the Irish historian Hayes-McCoy, but after a week of severe fighting and the executions of rebel leaders, which created martyrs for the rebels' cause, Irish public opinion 'soon saw that the Rising was something to be proud of'.[8] This small but significant event was a violent step on Ireland's road to independence and crucial in Irish history. Most Irish soldiers serving at the front, when they heard of the Rebellion 'felt a greater sense of betrayal than patriotism . . . especially when many found their leave postponed as a result of the troubles'. Regulars in the 2nd Irish Guards, although supporters of Home Rule, were not sympathetic towards the rebels; they themselves were 'risking their lives for a greater cause'.[9] John Lucy, home on sick leave at this time, expressed this prevalent opinion: 'My fellow soldiers had no great sympathy for the rebels, but with ambivalent feelings they got fed up when they heard of the executions of the leaders'.

Tom Kettle, in Dublin that Easter with his family, was astounded to hear the news that the rebels had risen in arms. His enlistment, spurred on by ideals, had not been easy as he had criticized Britain's ambiguous stance towards Home Rule and continued to have many misgivings about wearing the uniform of the British Army. He was outraged at Britain's handling of the rebels. Many leaders were his friends and their execution and that of Francis Sheehy-Skeffington prompted his famous bitter remark: 'These men will go down in history as heroes and martyrs and I will go down – if I go down at all – as a bloody British Officer'. Nevertheless, frustrated by his inactivity at home, in July 1916 he left for France to join his unit, the 9th Royal Dublin Fusiliers.

Francis Ledwidge, the Irish poet in the 5th Inniskilling Fusiliers, heard about the Rebellion while he was recuperating in a Manchester Hospital, sent there from Salonika suffering from inflammation of the gall bladder. The news both shocked him and sorely tried his patriotic spirit, as many of the leaders had been heroes to him, especially Thomas MacDonagh who was also a good friend. Back in County Derry for the summer, war to him became increasingly futile, but when an Inniskilling comrade offered to help him to desert to the Irish Volunteers he refused: 'it was against his principles'.

Recruitment after the Rising again took a decided drop. There was also frequent open hostility in Ireland towards British Army soldiers after 1916: 'In Dublin no local girl dared walk the streets with a man in uniform,' observed a Dublin Fusilier. 'But,' writes Peter Verney of the Irish Guards, 'it is an incredible fact that the allegiance and loyalty of the many Irishmen fighting in the British services were not more affected by the strife which was taking place in their beloved country and by the political issues involved.'[10]

The Irish in The Battle of The Somme – 1916

> War seen at the front is hell . . .
> but it is a hell inhabited not by devils but by heroes . . .
>
> George A. Birmingham, *A Padre in France*
> London, n.d., p. 17

The 36th (Ulster) Division, 1 July 1916

Frank McGuinness, the modern Irish playwright, had been raised to believe strongly in the Easter Rising of 1916 as 'the foundation of my country . . . a triumphalist event and the triumphalism was so strongly Catholic'. A Catholic from Donegal, his anger was very great when, in his twenties in Dublin, he discovered the number of [Protestant] Ulster lives lost at the Battle of the Somme, 1 July 1916. He realized that that battle and the 'psychic blow it delivered to a part of the population of this island . . . has as effectively shaped our destinies as anything that happened on Easter Sunday [Monday]'. His reaction was to write his poignant play *Observe the Sons of Ulster Marching Towards the Somme* that opened in Dublin in February 1985.[11] In it eight young Protestant soldiers from 36th (Ulster) Division set off for war, return on leave and then set off again towards the Somme and annihilation. Before they leave they explore their relationships with each other and try to understand their love for the country for which they were fighting and for which all but one will die.

The response to this play was emotional and varied and one critic even asked why 1 July should be seen as so important – 'more people died in the flu epidemic after the war'! For Ulster Protestants, however, 1 July 1916, when the 36th (Ulster) Division went 'over the top', is observed as 'one of their holy days'; it happens to coincide with the anniversary of the Battle of the Boyne, that defining event in the seventeenth century when the Protestant William III of Orange, King of England, defeated the Catholic King James II, 'a victory seen as the cornerstone of the Protestant heritage in Ireland'.[12] The New Army Ulster soldiers understood this and, as Rifleman Edward Taylor of the 9th Royal Irish Rifles recalls, on that Saturday morning they followed their Company Commander, Captain George Gaffikin, who took out an orange handkerchief and, waving it around his head, shouted, 'Come on boys, this is the first of July'. 'No surrender!' roared the men, the same answer given to King James and the besieging Jacobites by the gallant defenders of the city of Derry. Some Ulstermen, it is said, acquired for their tunics 'orange lilies, the symbolic flowers of the Battle of the Boyne', and orange sashes, stowed away by a few, were now placed 'around their shoulders', consoling symbols of their 'corporate identity'.[13] In their attack astride the River Ancre and along the lower slope of Thiepval Ridge Ulstermen faced a defensive German network of strong points, particularly the notorious Schwaben Redoubt, a formidable system of trenches fortified by the machine guns of Thiepval that could swing around on the attacking Ulstermen. 'The slopes of Thiepval run red with the blood of Ulstermen,' writes young Sergeant Jim Maultsaid of the 14th Royal Irish Rifles. American-born of Irish parents and raised in Donegal, his words are more sombre than the light-hearted and lively sketches he made of his fellow Ulstermen, sketches used effectively by Philip Orr in his *The Road to The Somme*. Maultsaid had become an 'unofficial war artist' and when hit in the arm on that day he worried about his ability to sketch again. He was saved, however, by two unknown infantrymen.[14]

The painting celebrated in Northern Ireland, *The Charge of the Ulster Division, July 1, 1916* by James Prinsep Beadle, is a well-known 'over the top' theme that has come to typify World War I on the Western Front. Lieutenant Francis Thornley, the young officer in the centre of the painting, beckons on the Ulstermen of the 11th Royal Irish Rifles in the midst of black smoke and falling shells; soldiers already hit are lying in the trench.[15] Many years later Gardiner S. Mitchell, as a small boy sitting in Sunday School in Victoria Hall, Londonderry, would gaze in fascination at a print of this painting, realizing that the charge of the Ulster Division on 1 July 1916 was 'a very special event – away back in history'. Equally fascinating to him were the reminiscences of his Great Uncle Jim Donaghy from Londonderry and Leslie Bell of Moneymore, two of the few survivors of that fierce battle. Their memories were 'incredibly accurate', even after seventy-five years, and form the basis of Gardiner's book *Three Cheers for The Derrys!*, his tribute to the bravery of that band of young men of the 10th Battalion, Royal Inniskilling Fusiliers who were known as the Derrys. It is their story that follows – only one of the many of that fatal day.

Jim Donaghy and Leslie Bell were two very ordinary young Ulster infantrymen typical of their comrades, underage and often undersize, who had 'never travelled outside Ulster before'. Going to France would be a great adventure. From tightly knit communities, before the war they went to the same schools, played on the same streets and knew each other's families. Jim Donaghy knew his commanding officer, Lieutenant Colonel Ross Acheson Smyth, JP, having worked as an assistant gardener at Smyth's home near Londonderry. Smyth was a typical regular officer in the First World War; commissioned in the Royal Irish Regiment in 1885, he had served in India and in the Anglo-Boer War with the mounted infantry where he was mentioned in despatches, received the Queen's medal with five bars and awarded a brevet majority. In Ulster Smyth had been involved in the formation of the UVF in the Londonderry area and came out of retirement at age fifty-four to command the Derrys. He never got into the fight that morning, for while crossing the River Ancre on a pontoon bridge an explosion startled his horse and he fell off, damaging his leg; his active war was ended.

Leslie Bell also had a short war. As a bomber in 'D' Company his job was to carry bombs in a canvas bucket and pass them to his fellow bomber Duncan Jordan. When his time came to go 'over the top' he vividly remembered:

> My Platoon got thirty yards when a big shell exploded above us wiping out the whole lot. I was badly hit in the legs. . . . Captain

Robertson was running up with his Platoon and as he ran past, gave me a kick to see if I was still alive.

Bell lay there all afternoon and 'watched the battle with men constantly falling as they were hit by the hail of machine-gun bullets or tossed into the air by exploding shells'. He was finished as an infantryman and never fully recovered, ending his war as a driver for the Army Service Corps.

After seven days of British artillery bombardment Jim Donaghy's 'B' Company on 1 July was in position from 1.00am, their lines constantly shelled. He remembers that at 7.00am Stokes (Trench) Mortars started a terrific hurricane bombardment on the German front line [for wire-cutting prior to zero hour]:

> The Germans now opened up . . . in retaliation . . . the noise was unbelievable. . . . Men had their wee bibles out and were reading them. . . . Just before the first units went into no-man's- land . . . we all said the Lord's prayer. . . . We sang hymns even though we could hardly hear our own voices.

In the first wave, he records how 'A' and 'B' Companies went out into no-man's-land at 7.15am, *before* zero hour of 7.30 where, as the German trenches were being heavily bombed, no one shot at them. There they awaited the whistle to advance, a successful plan of the 36th's Commander, General Nugent.

The Derrys' next obstacle was the notorious heavily fortified Schwaben Redoubt where, taking many casualties, they advanced behind the artillery barrage. About 9.00am the Derrys took 'C' or third line, their objective the German north-east corner of the Redoubt which they stormed with a wild Irish yell. The Derry's should have halted at the third line, but they joined the 14th Irish Rifles, who were ordered to continue on. Jim Donaghy and a very small band of exhausted men now composed of a mixed group of different battalions of 109 Brigade, reached and fought at the German 5th line trenches. 'We were consolidating ourselves running from dugout to dugout. We had no officers.' Then suddenly Jim and his group were caught in the open by a heavy barrage of 5.9" shells, possibly their own: 'I was hit twice and lost so much blood I looked like a red tunicked soldier.' His wounds were not life-threatening and when a brave runner brought a message to retire, Jim and the battered remnants limped back towards their own line helping each other, the air still filled with shrapnel. Along the way Jim rescued a badly wounded sergeant, dragging him in on a groundsheet. The Derrys 'had been to Hell – and back' writes Mitchell: Only 10 of the 22 officers and 336 of the 742 other ranks who went into action on 1 July returned to roll call at Martinsart the next day.[16]

Lieutenant-Colonels H. C. Bernard, Commander of the 10th Royal Irish Rifles, and Percy Crozier of 9th Royal Irish Rifles ignored a divisional order that senior officers should not accompany their men in the assault.[17] Bernard was killed leading his men on their path through Thiepval Wood which bombardments had denuded of foliage. Casualties were severe; they had come under machine-gun fire from front and rear at the same time before even arriving at their jump-off positions. Other battalions suffered less, writes Cyril Falls, being further from the Thiepval guns and screened by foliage. Crozier's batman, Corporal David Starret, an Ulsterman from Belfast, reports how Crozier frantically rallied the remainder of Colonel Bernard's men and some who were retreating and, inflamed by the sight of battalions wiped out he, shouting and dashing forward, led them on:

> He walked into bursts, he fell into holes, his clothing was torn by bullets . . . he again and again rallied his men.[18]

Percy Crozier was undoubtedly a brave man; he was also controversial and one of the colourful figures of World War I who was not without his critics. From an Anglo-Irish military family who also had members in the church, he was not tall enough to join the army until the South African War gave him the opportunity to enlist abroad. In the West African Frontier Force fighting in Nigeria he developed a problem with alcohol. After treatment he went to Canada, 'helped raise a squadron of Saskatchewan Light Horse . . . and finally became a teetotaller' to be subsequently aggressive against offenders. He returned to Britain in 1912 and joined the UVF, raising a Special Service section of the West Belfast Volunteers. He gained a 'healthy respect for his raw and fearsome Shankill recruits' and when they became the 9th Royal Irish Rifles he was appointed Major and Second in Command.[19] Crozier led an adventurous life and in the First World War rose to Brigadier General, CB, CMG, DSO. He also gained a reputation as callous and overbearing. His *Brass Hat in No-Man's-Land*, one of many memoirs of this war that appeared in the 1930s, was well received, but his second book *The Men I Killed* was considered to be in very poor taste.

Colonel Bernard was a regular career officer, the son of the late Robert Bernard MD, Royal Navy, Deputy Inspector General of Hospitals and Fleets and Honourary Surgeon to the Queen, a family with service to the church and the military; a cousin was the Anglican Archbishop of Dublin. After passing through Sandhurst as Queen's Cadet he was commissioned in the 67th Hampshire Regiment in 1884. A year later he joined the Indian Army, serving in Burma until 1905 when he joined the 45th Sikhs, commanding the regiment from 1909–14. When war broke out he was given command of the 10th Royal Irish Rifles. Bernard, like a good regular soldier, 'hated politics' and in conversation with Crozier the evening before the 1 July attack said he 'knew nothing about them' but he expressed the hope that:

> this war will settle the Irish question. The Ulster and the Irish Divisions, shoulder to shoulder in France should consolidate the home front afterwards, despite the Rebellion.

Unlike Willie Redmond, who espoused similar views, Bernard rather cynically saw the Irish Question as 'an unreal politically inspired game of bluff and office-seeking expediency'.[20]

Four of the nine VCs awarded for that 1 July, the blackest day in the history of the British Army, were won by the 36th (Ulster) Division. The first was awarded to twenty-one-year-old Billy McFadzean of the 14th Royal Irish Rifles, who enacted his brave deed of self-sacrifice in the last moments before zero hour in a tragic accident. The Rifles' trench was filled with men making their final preparations as bombardiers and, while handing out bombs, a box of grenades slipped and two safety pins fell out. Billy, understanding the danger and without a moment's hesitation, heroically threw himself on top of the bombs, giving his life for his comrades. Billy McFadzean's story of bravery is often told and was an inspiration in his battalion and in the army. Billy was a young Ulsterman from Cregagh where his father was a JP. An indifferent student at school but a keen rugby player, he was also an enthusiastic member of the Young Citizen Volunteers in the Ulster Volunteer Force.[21]

Two VCs were awarded for bringing in wounded under fire, to Rifleman Robert Quigg of the 12th Royal Irish Rifles and Lieutenant Geoffrey St George Shillington Cather of the 9th Royal Irish Fusiliers. Quigg had advanced to the assault with his platoon three times. The next morning Quigg, on hearing a rumour that his platoon officer, the twenty-year-old 2nd Lieutenant Sir Harry Macnaghten, 6th Baronet, reported missing on 1 July, was lying out wounded, went seven times to look for him under heavy shell and machine-gun fire, each time bringing back a wounded man, the last man found only a few yards from the enemy's wire. Exhausted after several hours engaged in this gallant work he finally had to give up the search. Sir Harry, seconded to the 12th Irish Rifles from the Black Watch, had twice re-formed what was left of his company in no-man's-land and led it through gaps in the German wire to be killed on the second occasion.[22] Before the war Quigg was a worker on the Macnaghten estate in County Antrim at Bushmills, famous for its whisky and very near the Giant's Causeway where Quigg was born, another example of the close community connections in the 36th (Ulster) Division. Many men from the little town of Bushmills enlisted in the 12th Royal Irish Rifles and on 1 July twenty-three of them died, of whom only six have known graves. 'The other decorations won by Bushmills men by 1918 would number two Military Crosses, seven Military Medals, two Distinguished Conduct Medals and one Croix de Guerre.'[23] Rifleman Quigg was not only renowned for his devotion to his officer, he had the distinction of being the sole survivor of the 36th's Victoria Cross winners of 1 July.

Lieutenant Cather's VC was awarded for his actions near Hamel. He searched no-man's-land for several hours and brought in four wounded men under direct machine-gun fire; finally he was killed bringing water to another man. Born in London, he had family connections in Portadown, Northern Ireland, and in the Irish Methodist Church. He obtained his commission in May 1915 and joined an uncle and cousin from Portadown, also serving in the 9th Royal Irish Fusiliers. At twenty-five Cather was the adjutant of his battalion, which was said to be one of the best in the division.

Captain Eric N. F. Bell of the 9th Royal Inniskilling Fusiliers won his Victoria Cross for a truly heroic performance outside the scope of his duties as commander of a trench mortar battery. He advanced with the infantry into the Schwaben Redoubt and as his citation reads:

> On no less than three occasions . . . he went forward alone and threw trench mortar bombs among the enemy. When he had no more bombs . . . he stood on the parapet under intense fire and used a rifle with great coolness. . . . Finally he was killed rallying and reorganizing infantry parties which had lost their officers.

Not yet twenty-one years old, Eric Bell was another of those youthful and brave officers of World War I. Born in Enniskillen into a military family, he was one of three brothers serving in the Ulster Division, sons of Captain E. H. Bell formerly of the Inniskillings who was then serving in Egypt in a garrison battalion of the Royal Irish Regiment.[24]

1 July 1916 was both victory and failure for the Ulstermen; elements of the 36th broke through the German lines and advanced farther than any other major unit of this size, undoubtedly because they ran, not walked, and 'without forming up in waves adopted by other divisions, they rushed the German front line' to capture it through a combination, Middlebrook claims, of 'sensible tactics and Irish dash'. Theirs was a remarkable feat, he adds, when it is considered that 'the Ulster Division had no Regular battalions attached to it as "stiffeners" as had some of the New Army divisions'.[25] Their gains could not be exploited, as their outstanding

success, in which they had overrun the most formidable and reputedly impregnable positions on the Western Front, had created a deep, narrow salient that left them in an isolated position and the Ulstermen had to retire. On this costliest day the Ulster Division lost more than half the men who attacked. When it was taken out of the line two days later, it lost its distinctively Ulster Protestant nature by the necessary addition of drafts of English, Welsh and Scottish recruits that even included Irish Catholics. After the war, when the Free State of Ireland was formed, it was said that because of the sacrifice of the Ulster Division 'most of Ulster was not forced into the unwanted union with the Catholic South'.[26]

Among Ulstermen serving on 1 July in other divisions was Major Alan Brooke. His artillery plan ensured that his 18th Division was the most successful of any of the attacking divisions that day. He 'adapted a French idea, the creeping bombardment, which was designed to keep pace with the advancing infantry and give them support', a tactic of General Buller's that Colonel Lawrence Parsons had employed in the Anglo-Boer War. Brooke also 'decided to use trench mortars instead of shrapnel to cut the barbed wire in no-man's-land; this technique proved extremely effective' and he was awarded a DSO for his contribution to the Somme fighting. This talented artilleryman would be the future Field-Marshal Viscount Alanbrooke, Chief of the Imperial General Staff in World War II and one of Churchill's valued generals. Brooke came from an Ulster Protestant land-owning family of Colebrooke, County Fermanagh, a most prominent military family; twenty-six Brookes served in the First World War and twenty-seven in the Second.[27]

The Tyneside Irish 1 July 1916

The story of the Irish in the British Army in the Battle of the Somme must also include that of the Tyneside Irish Brigade who showed all the courage and tenacity of the Irish in an attack that John Keegan called 'a bizarre and pointless massacre'. General Parsons had not wanted these Irish recruits from Britain's industrial centres, some of whom he referred to as 'slum birds'. The Tyneside Irish, with War Office approval, formed a brigade of their own (103) as part of the 34th Division; it was too late for 16th (Irish) Division to recruit on Tyneside. Staunchly Irish and Catholic, these Tynesiders were the descendants of Irishmen who in the nineteenth century had fled the famine in Ireland to find work in the industrial north of England. They had sympathies for John Redmond's Nationalist political struggles for Home Rule for Ireland and when war came they pressed for a strictly Irish Tyneside force like Redmond's 'Irish Brigade', wanting, with similar romantic sentiments, 'Ireland to have the credit of the powerful assistance she is giving in this War'.[28] Many of the Tyneside Irish officers had been born in Ireland and many had seen service with Irish regiments. Indeed, Denman records that when the 16th (Irish) Division was forming it was found that 'in junior officers [it] is already over establishment' and it was suggested that 'nationalist officer candidates might like to join the Tyneside Irish'. From early 1915 many did.[29]

In an unusual decision Lieutenant General I. Williams, CB, the 34th's Divisional Commander, 'decided to move all twelve of his battalions simultaneously towards the German front', leaving none in reserve. 101 and 102 Brigades left from their front trench, but when 103, with its four Tyneside Irish battalions, left the support line, the Tara-Usna line, to cross the Avoca Valley (names poignantly associated with Ireland), it had 'a mile of open ground to cover before it reached its own front line'. It was here that the Tynesiders were cut down. The German guns of La Boiselle had not been destroyed by the bombardment and Sergeant J. Galloway, 3rd Tyneside Irish, recalled:

> I could see away to my left and right long lines of men. Then I heard the 'patter, patter' of machine-guns in the distance. By the time I'd gone another ten yards there seemed to be only a few men left around me; by the time I had gone twenty yards I seemed to be on my own. Then I was hit myself.

Very few in the 2nd and 3rd Tyneside Irish battalions reached the British front line. The 1st and 4th pushed on, losing men all the way. A few brave Tynesiders not only reached their own front line but, ever mindful of orders to follow the leading brigades, crossed no-man's-land and managed to reach the German front line. Instead of sheltering there with troops who were holding out, they set off yet again 'to fight their way into the German rear completely on their own'. Well into German lines, 'Incredibly the C.O. of the 4th Tyneside Irish was still with them, but he was now recalled . . . needed at brigade HQ.' This was Lieutenant Colonel G. R. V. Steward, DSO, a career soldier who had served in the Royal Inniskilling Fusiliers in both the Anglo-Boer War and in Europe 1914–15. A small remnant reached Contalmaison, their original objective; the order to retire had not reached them. Luck, which had surely been with them to get this far, ran out. Thirty or so men 'could not tackle a German village fortress completely on their own . . . and survive.' Those few who survived the brief fight tried to return, but it was too late. They had advanced farther than any other unit that day and 'died 2,000 yards inside the German lines'. Most of the Tynesiders, however, lay in the British zone, dead 'before the battle had begun'.[30]

The 16th (Irish) Division on the Somme, 2–10 September 1916

Ulstermen remember 1 July 1916 as the day so many in their 36th Division lost their lives in the Somme Battle of Thiepval; the time of remembrance for many southern Irish is Easter Monday 1916, the Irish Rising in Dublin. Only a few months later, in September, Irish soldiers in the 16th (Irish) Division fought and died in two major Somme battles, Guillemont and Ginchy, that became the graveyards of the Irish Brigade. Few remember them, Terence Denman sadly notes.[31]

Guillemont was a triumph for the troops of Southern Ireland: 'The men of Munster, Leinster and Connaught broke through the intricate defences of the enemy as a torrent sweeps down rubble,' the author John Buchan wrote. He might have added 'men of Ulster'. One of two Victoria Cross winners in the 16th (Irish) Division, Private Thomas Hughes of the 6th Connaught Rangers, was an Ulsterman from County Monaghan, then one of the historic nine counties of Ulster. All battalions of the Division's 47 Brigade received Ulster Nationalists, the 6th Connaughts and 7th Leinsters in particular relied heavily on them,[32] and these two battalions would bear the brunt of the brigade's attack to capture the ruined village of Guillemont on 3 September. Taken from the 16th at the last moment and attached to the weakened 20th Division, 47 Brigade was part of a large assault force, but it is not too much to say that 'Guillemont was devastated by an avalanche of Irish troops. . . . We swept through the Germans like the Dublin Mail going through Westport,' a Connaught Ranger said.[33] When the Germans fell back, however, the message the wounded brought, 'The English are in Guillemont', would have greatly annoyed the Irish/Ulstermen in 47 Brigade had they heard it.[34]

At Guillemont companies of the 7th Leinsters, the Fighting Seventh, 'went over in perfect lines through enemy shelling. . . . The Germans were taken completely by surprise and before they could leave their dugouts or get their machine guns into position, the Leinsters were on top of them'. It was here that the daring Lieutenant John Vincent Holland, the battalion bombing officer, won the Victoria Cross: 'Not content with bombing hostile dugouts . . . Holland fearlessly led his bombers through our own barrage and cleared a great part of the village in front. He started out with twenty-six bombers and finished with only five after capturing some fifty prisoners . . . . He was far from well at the time and later had to go to hospital.' Captain Hitchcock of the 2nd Leinsters wrote to Lieutenant Holland to express the Leinsters' pride that this was the Regiment's first Victoria Cross in the war, and this remarkable twenty-seven-year-old Irish lieutenant was not a professional soldier. From Athy, County Kildare, his father was a past President of the Royal College of Veterinary Surgeons of Ireland and he himself was a pre-war veterinary student. His nickname was 'Tin-Belly' because he had served as a trooper in the Life Guards before receiving his commission in the 3rd Leinsters where Hitchcock met him. An adventurous young Irishman, he had been employed by the Central Argentine Railway and at the outbreak of war he enthusiastically hurried home to Ireland to enlist. A story about him tells of his lively spirit: 'The night before the engagement [of Guillemont] he made a bet of five pounds with a brother officer that he would be the first over the parapet . . . He won the bet, the Victoria Cross, and in addition was made a Chevalier of the Legion of Honour and of St. George of Russia.' The bravery of the other bombers was also recognized; the Leinster historian lists the names of two DCMs, six MMs, as well as naming those killed and wounded. Private John Ford was recommended for a battlefield commission. A happy event occurred in early 1917 when Holland was married at the 3rd Leinsters' Base at Queenstown (present day Cork). He also survived the war.[35]

The 6th Connaught Rangers also went over the top with 'flair and dash' before zero hour and surprised the Germans. But 200 of them were casualties before they left their trench, their own projectiles having fallen short. They reached their third objective, North Street, and in this mêlèe Private Thomas Hughes of the 6th Connaughts won the Division's second VC. Though wounded in the attack, he returned at once to the firing line after having his wounds dressed. Later, seeing a hostile machine gun, he dashed out in front of his company, shot the gunner and, single-handed, captured the gun. Again wounded, he brought back three or four prisoners. A man of small stature, before the war Hughes had been a jockey attached to Ireland's Curragh racing stable. He returned to the front as a corporal and survived the war.

A great loss both to the army and the 6th Connaught Rangers was their popular commander, Lieutenant Colonel J. S. M. Lenox-Conyngham, who was killed at Guillemont. At the moment of the charge he sprang forward to lead and, in the spirit of Wellington at Waterloo, who directed his hidden Foot Guards towards the oncoming French with the memorable words: 'Up guards! Make ready – Fire!', Lenox-Conyngham pointed to the German lines with his cane, turned, and said, 'That, Connaught Rangers, is what you have to take'. The next moment he was shot dead. His men, ignoring machine-gun fire, were off to the attack and the rest we know. Lenox-Conyngham, a career soldier from an Ulster Protestant military family, was the son of Colonel Sir William Lenox-Conyngham of Spring Hill, County Derry. Three brothers also served in the army as colonels. Like many regulars, Lenox-Conyngham came out of retirement from the army reserve of officers and, after thirty years service with the Rangers, was appointed to command the 6th (S) Battalion when it was formed in October 1914 and had the honour of leading it into action. He was known for his concern for his men and Captain Stephen Gwynn, a Nationalist in the 6th Connaughts, generously paid tribute to him: 'No commanding officer was more beloved by those he commanded . . . I have known no better Irishman than this son of an Ulster house whose kindred were deep in the Ulster covenant.' Lenox-Conyngham was buried in a little churchyard behind the lines. Later a memorial to him was erected by his wife in the Royal Irish Fusiliers Memorial Chapel of St Patrick's Anglican Cathedral, Armagh, together with the wooden Celtic cross from his grave at Guillemont.[36]

On 5 September General Hickie took over command of the front before Ginchy, another German stronghold about a mile from Guillemont and the fortified Quadrilateral to the south. When it came time to plan the Ginchy attack Hickie found that his battalions were scattered, taken from him after Guillemont and fed piecemeal to British divisions. Like General Mahon with his 10th (Irish) Division in Gallipoli, it could only have infuriated General Hickie to see his battalions used like this. In the fighting around Leuze Wood during the week of 4 September when the 7th and 8th Royal Irish Fusiliers were attached to 5th Division, casualties were so high that one officer of the 8th wrote: 'The remnant of the battalion came out of the battle on a lorry'. At Leuze Wood Lieutenant Colonel H. N. Young of the 7th Inniskillings was seriously wounded, as was Major A. R. Reid, the new Commanding Officer, and four others of the HQ staff. Galling for the Irish, the credit for taking Leuze Wood was given to the Devonshires.[37] One may ask again if it mattered in which division the Irish soldiers fought. From the time the Irish divisions were formed it was important to them that they should be given credit for their deeds as Irish soldiers fighting in the British Army and, as we have seen, recognition of their contribution to the war was especially important for the Irish at home.

General Hickie finally managed to get his depleted and tired brigades together to fight as a division on 9 September. Hickie assigned 48 Brigade to the capture of Ginchy while 47 Brigade, in consideration of its rôle and losses at Guillemont, would assault the Quadrilateral, mistakenly thought to be the weaker position. A German trench opposite, reported unoccupied, worried Lieutenant Colonel R. C. Feilding, who assumed command of the 6th Connaught Rangers on the death of Lenox-Conyngham. An Englishman and special reserve officer of the Coldstream Guards, Feilding was from an old Catholic family and seems to have won immediately the trust of his Catholic Irish soldiers who called him

'Snowball' because of his white hair. In turn he developed a great sympathy and respect for his Rangers. Another of those Englishmen who became completely devoted to their Irish soldiers was Lieutenant Guy Nightingale. He had served with the 1st Battalion, Royal Munster Fusiliers, since before the war and wrote to his family his now oft-quoted comment:

> I would sooner be in an Irish regiment with Irish soldiers behind me in a scrap than any English or Scotch unit they would like to produce.[38]

John Lucy in fact 'preferred Irish officers, who were more friendly than the English – more democratic or at any rate less feudal in outlook'. Yet his Captain, an Englishman called Thom, was 'greatly respected by the troops. . . . in all matters he was extremely strict and very just'.

To return to the Battle of Ginchy, plans were changed at the last-minute and the Irish brigades were ordered to wait for an extra two minutes after zero hour of 4.45pm so that a final longer bombardment of the German trenches might take place. 47 Brigade duly waited in their trenches which meant the Germans were now well prepared when the barrage lifted and in the attacking waves Colonel Curzon of the 6th Royal Irish was killed, and, with the 8th Munsters, both battalions were swept back by a torrent of machine-gun fire from the supposedly derelict trench. The 6th Connaught Rangers and 7th Leinsters, coming on behind, were also massacred in this hurricane of steel and lead and, as the Leinster historian writes,

> The only thing to do was drop into the [crowded] trench and get any cover possible. In a very short time all the company officers with the exception of Lieutenant V. J. Farrell and Lieutenant Keating had been killed.

Farrell earned an MC when, later that evening, seeing the useless slaughter of his men, he withdrew the remainder of the battalion to the Guillemont-Bapaume road. For the 7th Leinsters 9 September was their most 'disastrous day'.[39]

48 Brigade either did not get or ignored the order to wait and went ahead swiftly to find the Germans still under cover, but they suffered greatly from enfilade fire and from 'unders' (their own shells falling short). Old regulars in the 1st Munsters, however, only recently transferred from the 'incomparable' 29th Division to 48 Brigade, showed their battle experience. Second Lieutenant D. J. Bailey, when all the company officers

were either killed or wounded within the first fifty yards of the trenches, took command of 'X' Company, pushed forward, but, finding the right flank exposed, he wheeled to the right and dug in; only twenty-eight men were left to him. Company Sergeant Major Harris, of Munster's 'Z' Company, also demonstrated great leadership. In the advance, when his commander was wounded he took over, wheeled the left of his company and charged, driving the enemy out of their trench. On continuing the advance he found the enemy again strongly entrenched so dug in opposite them and, 'with the assistance of one machine gun, held his position until relieved', thus preventing Germans cutting through on the right. New Army Irish soldiers in the 7th Royal Irish Rifles supported by the 7th Royal Irish Fusiliers also fought with great spirit and successfully reached the German line in the western part of Ginchy. Together with the other Irish troops, they 'drove the Germans out of Ginchy with such gusto that it was difficult to find enough Irishmen to begin the necessary work of consolidating the line around the ruined village'.[40]

Lieutenant Tom Kettle was killed in this same attack, leading his Company of the 9th Royal Dublin Fusiliers, by a rifle bullet in the upper chest 'above a protective steel waistcoat'. His friend and fellow officer eighteen-year-old Lieutenant Emmet Dalton, following behind, 'was horrified to see him fall. . . . Dalton paused to press a crucifix into his hand . . . Kettle was obviously dying'. Young Emmet, the 'boy hero of Ginchy', then took command of two companies without officers and led them to their final objective . . . After dark . . . with only one sergeant escorting' he captured an officer and twenty men, winning the Military Cross for his bravery and leadership. Tom Kettle, in France only since mid-July, had very little battle experience though he had, as his biographer writes, 'taken many risks' in the battle around Guillemont where 'he came through unscathed as if he had a charmed life'. He ought not to have been in the battle at all because of his poor health, aggravated by conditions in the trenches. He had turned down a staff appointment, insisting on staying with his Dublin Fusiliers whose 'radiant valour' he constantly praised when writing home. His men loved him, as Father Felix Burke, Roman Catholic chaplain with the Dublin Fusiliers wrote, 'We all looked up to him as a towering genius and a storehouse of information'. It was said that this most talented and complicated Irishman 'hardly cared what happened to him, welcoming in France the blood sacrifice Pearse, leader in the 1916 Irish Rebellion, sought in Dublin'. His biographer thinks otherwise and quotes Kettle's letter to his brother: 'I am calm and happy . . . but desperately anxious to live' and Kettle, Lyons also tells us, was planning a book on the war and the 16th (Irish) Division, and to work for 'perpetual peace' after hostilities. The writer Tim Cross claims that Kettle's vision was of

an Ireland 'at parity with Britain as a free European nation' and he quotes
Kettle: ' My only counsel to Ireland is that in order to become deeply Irish,
she must become European '.[41] 9 September was a day of loss for literary
Ireland.

Sir Philip Gibbs wrote 'that the capture of Ginchy by the Irish Brigade
deserved to be recorded not in a journalist's prose but in heroic verse'.[42]
It was 'no wonder', wrote Father William Doyle SJ, chaplain, that 'an
angry German officer called the 16th (Irish) Division 'a pack of devils'.
Born in Dublin, Father Doyle became one of the well-known and loved
First World War chaplains receiving, on 15 November 1915, his appointment from the War Office to the 16th. A gentle young man of indifferent
health, he was always to be found as close to the front line as possible,
saying Mass, tending the wounded and the dying and, consequently, he
had many narrow escapes. Doyle's letters to his father in Ireland reveal his
experiences of the horrors of the First World War. Neverthless for him:

> War may be horrible but it certainly brings out the best side of a
> man's character; over and over again I have seen men risking their
> lives to help or save a comrade and these brave fellows knew the
> risk they were taking.

Through all the suffering and ghastliness he encountered shines his great
love and admiration for 'my brave Irish boys' who had 'all the dash and
go of the hot-blooded Celtic race, the courage of lions, and a strong deep
faith'. His is a very human picture of his Irish Catholic soldiers:

> They curse like troopers all the day, they give the Germans hell,
> purgatory and heaven all combined at night, and next morning
> come kneeling in the mud for Mass and Holy Communion.[43]

For the Somme battles Father Doyle was awarded the MC for his bravery.
Apart from two VCs, there were some three hundred decorations awarded
in the 16th. This was at heavy cost: 'Over 1,000 men of the 16th Division
had been killed on the Somme. The majority of the casualties had been in
the Irish infantry battalions'.[44]

In the action of 15 September by the Guards Division, which renewed
the offensive capturing Ginchy Telegraph and the Quadrilateral, was the
Ulsterman Captain the Hon Harold Alexander of the 2nd Battalion, Irish
Guards. A fearless soldier, he had been in command of 1st Company, 2nd
Battalion at the Battle of Loos in September 1915 where he won an MC,
after which he was temporarily in command of the 1st Battalion. Now at
Ginchy, again in command of his old 1st Company, 2nd Battalion, he led

forward '120 men of all units of the Brigade and about five other officers'. For a gain of eight hundred yards casualties were severe: Alexander and one other were the only officers to escape unhurt. For his leadership he was awarded an immediate DSO, his citation reading: 'He was the life and soul of the attack'.

'Alexander,' wrote Valentine Williams, a junior officer in his battalion, 'was the only man I knew who appeared to enjoy the battle of the Somme.' In fact, he enjoyed the First World War and was not ashamed to admit it. His courage became a byword in the Irish Guards and a fellow Guardsman has paid tribute to him:

> He was entirely free from fear, superior airs or snobbery. . . . He was fitter than anyone else in the Regiment. He was the most perfect man morally, physically, mentally that I have ever met. These things enabled him to be superb in the face of danger. . . .

He was in fact aware of fear, but he overcame it with a strong sense of duty and honour.

Harold Alexander was 'a perfect Anglo-Irish gentleman of a type that had officered the British Army for centuries'. From the time he was a very young man he knew what he wanted to do. His biographer Nigel Nicolson tells us that his aristocratic Anglo-Irish family of Protestant Ulster stock can be traced back to the Plantation in Ireland during the reign of James I, a cadet branch of the Earls of Stirling. The first Earl of Caledon (1730–1802), who made his fortune in the East India Company serving under Clive in Bengal and Warren Hastings, built Caledon Castle, the great family estate in County Tyrone, Northern Ireland, where Alexander grew up. His father, the fourth Earl of Caledon, who died when Harold was only six had joined the Life Guards and later became a major in the Royal Inniskilling Fusiliers. He also took part in the Egyptian Campaign of 1882. After Harrow and Sandhurst, Alexander had no hesitation in choosing to join the 1st Battalion, Irish Guards, and from then on he was committed to service in the British Army, finding time for his considerable talent as a painter. There was a political and military tradition in the family, the latter not particularly distinguished until Harold's illustrious career; his brothers Herbrand in the Royal Irish Lancers and William in the Irish Guards both won DSOs in the First World War.[45] In the Second World War Alexander would be prominent as one of Churchill's Field Marshals.

The Irish in The Battle of Messines – 1917

> O let the Orange lily be
> Your badge, my patriot brother.
> The everlasting green for me,
> And we for one another.
>
> John Lucy, *There's a Devil in the Drum*,
> p. 358 quoting an old Colour Sergeant from Limerick
> to Orange chums on 12 July.

A day of significance for Ireland was 7 June 1917 when, at the Battle of Messines, Irishmen and Ulstermen fought side by side in the 16th (Irish) and 36th (Ulster) Divisions. This coming together of soldiers from both North and South was viewed by many as symbolic of future reconciliation in that land. This was 'an Irish day'. The capture of Messines Ridge was a battle, Cyril Falls writes, that was 'the first completely successful single operation on the British front. . . . the most elaborately and carefully "mounted" action ever fought by British Arms'. There were five days of intensive bombardment; concealment of the attack was not a question as the Messines Ridge was already under constant enemy observation. However, the detonation of nineteen mines in the very early morning of 7 June was a surprise to the Germans. In Father Doyle's words, 'There was a deep muffled roar, the ground in front of where I stood rose up, as if some giant had wakened from his sleep . . . and then I saw seventeen huge columns of smoke and flames shoot about a hundred feet into the air . . . I never before realized what an earthquake was like for not only did the ground quiver and shake, but actually rocked backwards and forwards.' About the same time 'with one monstrous roar, every British gun upon ten miles of front opened fire . . . General Nugent, returning to his command post on Kemmel [Hill] from the observation post a hundred yards away, declared the sight he had seen was "a vision of hell" '.[46]

Enthusiasm to be first over the top was marked by everyone and the death that day of the irrepressible Captain H. Gallaugher was deeply regretted in the 11th Inniskillings. He 'had hardly left the trench leading his men when a shell shattered his right arm. He refused to go back . . . dropped the rifle which he could no longer carry and, with revolver in his left hand, went forward. Only when the task of the day was done would he go back to the dressing station . . . and as he went back he was killed by another shell.' The Inniskillings' Commanding Officer, Lieutenant Colonel A. C. Pratt, writing to Gallaugher's father, voiced the esteem the battalion felt for Gallaugher: 'He was a true soldier and a great leader and organizer'. Henry Gallaugher, from Manorcunningham, County Donegal, had been a Company Commander in the local branch of the Ulster Volunteer Force and on the outbreak of war enlisted in the 11th Inniskillings, later to become Battalion Transport Officer. Wanting more action, he volunteered to go 'over the top' in the Somme battle, 1 July 1916. All that day he had fought gallantly 'at one time he met single-handed and killed six Germans'. Two nights later Lieutenant Gallaugher, Captain W. Moore and twenty men from the ranks 'volunteered to go out into the storm of shells on rescue work and brought in twenty-eight wounded men'. For these actions Gallaugher was awarded the DSO.[47]

Major Willie Redmond's death at Messines was also greatly mourned in the 16th (Irish) Division, in his regiment and throughout Ireland where even by his 'political enemies' his Parliamentary career as a Nationalist MP was respected. Willie Redmond, like his friend and fellow Nationalist Tom Kettle, should not have been in a front-line trench at all; at fifty-six he was too old and he was not physically fit. Like several of the older Irish soldiers he wanted to get into action and he had been 'deeply hurt by letters from Ireland accusing him of cowardice'. General Hickie finally gave him permission to go into the attack with the 6th Royal Irish Regiment, on the condition that he return when the first objective was achieved. He was wounded in the leg and wrist shortly after leaving the trench, not life-threatening wounds, but he died shortly after at the aid post. That it was stretcher bearers from the 36th (Ulster) Division who brought him to the aid station would have pleased him greatly, as he would have seen this as representing his constant theme for reconciliation between north and south Ireland, between Unionists and Nationalists, Protestants and Catholics. A recently discovered diary of a Rev Redmond (no relation), who was a Protestant Church of Ireland clergyman, reveals that he was the last chaplain to talk to the wounded Redmond and this would have been seen as another symbolic happening. His burial in the garden of the convent at Locre was attended by chaplains of both the 16th (Irish) and 36th (Ulster) Divisions. Willie Redmond, reports Terence Denman, expected his death in battle: 'He could not expect to do anything more for poor old Ireland, unless to die for her'.[48]

The Irish in the Third Battle of Ypres –1917

After Messines a big British offensive was planned for the summer of 1917 and on 31 July began the Third Battle of Ypres, a series of battles that lasted until 20 November in a slaughter collectively known as Passchendaele, the most ghastly in the whole campaign and indeed in the annals of the British Army to that time. Two Irishmen who were killed were Lieutenant Colonel Eric Greer, MC, 2nd Battalion, Irish Guards, only twenty-five years old, and Corporal Francis Ledwidge, the promising Irish poet now in the 1st Inniskilling Fusiliers. On 31 July Greer was killed instantly by shrapnel while standing outside his advanced battalion head-quarters' dugout in the first objective line. The Greer family home was in County Tyrone near Caledon, the home of his boyhood friend Harold Alexander, who succeeded him as another 'boy-colonel'. Here Eric grew up, the son of Captain (afterwards Sir) Harry Greer of the National Stud and later a Free State Senator in Ireland, a man who lost two sons in the war. Eric and Harold had trained together as athletes and in 1911 on the same day had joined the 1st Battalion, Irish Guards. At the end of their preparatory training 'they had come to be regarded . . . as the most promising young officers of the regiment'. Kipling would write of Eric Greer:

> Men and officers together adored him for his justice, which was exemplary and swift; for the human natural fun of the man; for his knowledge of war . . . and for his gift of making hard life a thing delightful.[49]

On that same day Francis Ledwidge's death was another loss for literary Ireland. After recuperating in Ireland from his illness he, along with other drafts from Derry, was posted to France to 'B' Company, 1st Inniskilling Fusiliers, to fill their depleted ranks. At the beginning of July 1917 the Inniskillings were ordered to the Ypres Salient and on the 31st found that Pilckem Ridge was their objective. Ledwidge was in reserve when his battalion went forward, engaged with a work party in road- building where the Germans continued to hurl shells. One exploded beside Ledwidge, killing him instantly, 'blown to bits' as Father Devas wrote in his diary, along with seven others killed and twelve wounded. Father Charles Devas SJ was also a poet and he and Ledwidge had been friends since they first met at Suvla Bay where the chaplain had won the DSO. They often read their poems to each other and right up to his death Ledwidge was writing his poems at any free moment he could find. In the spring of 1917 he had received an enquiry from an American admirer, Professor Lewis N. Chase of the University of Wisconsin, requesting biographical information and poems to use in a series of lectures he was giving on contemporary poets. Ledwidge's reply to Professor Chase was written, as he said, in moments snatched 'between watches for I am in the firing line'. In it he expresses his hope, very reminiscent of Irish Nationalists like Tom Kettle and Willie Redmond, that, after the Rising 'a new Ireland will arise from her ashes in the ruins of Dublin, like the Phoenix'. He goes on to voice the ambiguity that he and some Irish felt as serving soldiers in the British Army: 'I tell you this in order that you may know what it is to me to be called a British soldier while my own country has no place amongst the nations but the place of Cinderella'.

Ledwidge's moving poem, written on the execution of his Nationalist friend Thomas McDonagh after the Irish Rebellion, was his own fitting epitaph and is on the plaque to his memory in his birthplace at Slane:

> He shall not hear the bittern cry
> In the wild sky, where he is lain,
> Nor voices of the sweeter birds
> Above the wailing of the rain.[50]

The Irish in the 36th (Ulster) and 16th (Irish) Divisions now in Gough's Fifth Army were again fighting together in the Third Ypres Salient. On 31 July the opening phase began. The rains started and the wettest August in years followed, turning the battlefield into a sea of mud where the ground's natural drainage had been destroyed by prolonged bombardment to produce swamp-like conditions as had been predicted. It is said that General Kiggell, an Irishman from Limerick and Haig's Chief of Staff, 'wept when he eventually reached the mere edge of the battlefield and exclaimed, "Did we really send men to fight in this ?" '[51] After the first failed offensive of 31 July the attack was postponed for two weeks, but troops in the 16th and 36th Divisions stayed in the line in the unrelenting rain and mud because of Fifth Army's policy that troops were not relieved before an attack. Subjected to continual bombardment, diseases like trench foot and trench fever, and fatigue duties, the soldiers were exhausted before the attack resumed. Each division lost a third of their attacking troops before the Battle of Langemarck began on 16 August.

At this time the troops also had to contend with a new German method of defence in depth, strong concrete pill-boxes mounted with machine guns, first encountered on the Messines Ridge. Captain Frank Hitchcock of the 2nd Leinsters explains: 'The waterlogged soil in the Ypres sector made defence of deep trenches impossible, so the problem of holding their ground was solved by [Germans] erecting the pill-boxes.' He likened one he found to 'a miniature Martello Tower, (so very common on the southern coasts of England and Ireland) it stood only some six feet off the ground on deep foundations, . . . walls of about three feet in thickness were built on a steel framework . . . impregnable to the ordinary barrage of field artillery . . . room inside for a garrison of about fifteen men'. To put a pillbox out of action by 'posting' a bomb through the firing slit, the Inniskillings found courage was needed to crawl through the deadly mud while machine gunners with perfect observation sprayed bullets.[52]

On 16 August at Langemarck the 16th (Irish) and 36th (Ulster) divisions led the assault. The exhausted Irish went forward over a quagmire of craters and churned-up ground; small parties gained a footing on the objectives, 'but were then too weak to resist the German counterattacks.' Already attacking under strength, casualties in the 7th and 8th Inniskillings were so severe that they had to be amalgamated into one battalion, the 7/8th. As Sir Philip Gibbs writes: 'The two Irish Divisions were broken to bits and their brigadiers called it murder. They were violent in their denunciation of Fifth Army'. Several senior officers in Irish battalions were casualties: Lieutenant Colonel Pratt of the 11th Inniskillings was killed as the battalion was moving off. Lieutenant Colonel R. P. Maxwell, leading his 13th Royal Irish Rifles, was severely wounded and Lieutenant-Colonel S. J. Somerville, commanding officer of the 9th Royal Irish Fusiliers, was mortally wounded when his battalion was trying to dig in on Hill 35. Cyril Falls laments, 'The 36th Division . . . failed once only in attack, in the Battle of Langemarck', and Terence Denman reports, 'The 16th Division was forced back to its starting line.'[53]

General Sir Hubert Gough has been held responsible for the disastrous Langemarck battle which, it is said, he should have halted. He had been given command of Fifth Army in Flanders by Sir Douglas Haig, the Commander in Chief of the British Army, seemingly a good choice: Gough, with a reputation for boldness, was, at 47, the youngest army commander. One of many criticisms against Gough was that he did not 'grasp the strategic fundamental of the Ypres battle'. He pursued it relentlessly and arrogantly disregarded warnings from his own commanders of adverse conditions. Hickie, for example, warned him the men were not fit. Gough even sent dissidents home. It was claimed that his main fault was permitting or not noticing poor staff work, so that 'battalion officers and divisional staffs raged against the whole of the Fifth Army organization'. When, at the end of 1917, Haig finally informed Gough of the reputation of his Fifth Army throughout the BEF and that there were divisions that did not wish to serve under him, he was very surprised. He was always courteous and seen as a 'shrewd general, personally popular, who cared for his troops and, unlike some, lived a spartan existence'.

Gough continued to 'make further and usually ill-prepared attempts' to win ground. General Plumer's biographer, Geoffrey Powell, however, claims that Gough was acting against his better judgement. When he 'protested to Haig that success was impossible in such foul conditions, the latter insisted that operations must continue . . . [for] strategic imperatives', that is, to attack while the Germans held so much of Belgium. Gough would later admit that Plumer, with his long experience on the

Ypres front, was the right man for the job and that Haig had been mistaken in not initially choosing him. By September Haig did pass the command of the main battle back to General Plumer and Second Army.[54]

Father William Doyle SJ, the much-loved Irish chaplain, was among the dead, losing his life, it is thought on 17 August on Frezenberg Ridge. Amidst the confusion and carnage of that day authentic information was difficult to obtain. Father Doyle had gone out to minister to wounded lying in an exposed position, although he had been ordered to stay behind the lines. When the bombardment increased in violence he began to retire with some officers and all were killed by a shell. Corporal Raitt confirmed that Private McInespie, Father Doyle's runner, came staggering into the Regimental Aid Post (RAP) and, when able to speak, said, 'Father Doyle has been killed'. Father Doyle's biographer writes of a rumour that his body was buried by some retiring Dublins, but the grave has not been found. He had become known for the constant risks he took to bring spiritual help to 'his boys' in the front line, as he himself wrote, 'We with the Irish regiments live in the thick of it'. Newspapers in Ireland and England carried tributes to Father Doyle and a generous appreciation by a Belfast Orangeman appeared in the Glasgow *Weekly News* of 1 September 1917: 'We couldn't possibly agree with his religious opinions but we simply worshipped him for other things. He didn't know what bigotry was. He was as ready to risk his life to take a drop of water to a wounded Ulsterman as to assist men of his own faith and regiment . . . none were readier to show their marks of respect to the dead hero priest than were our Ulster Presbyterians.' Although recommended for the VC, Father Doyle instead received the MC.

A month earlier Father Doyle had preached his last sermon in St. Omer Cathedral where 2,500 soldiers of the 16th (Irish) Division were present, Dublin Fusiliers filling the nave. In his sermon:

> He spoke wonderfully of the coming of the old Irish Brigade in their wanderings over the Low Countries. It was here that he touched daringly, but ever so cleverly, on Ireland's part in the war. Fighting for Ireland and not fighting for Ireland, or rather fighting for Ireland through another.

Father Doyle's historical references to the Irish Brigade that had fought against England were tactful and diplomatic and greatly appreciated by General Hickie and his staff, including Protestants, 'the men particularly, *they* were delighted.'[55]

In that autumn at Passchendaele occurred the death of Lieutenant Colonel Alfred Durham Murphy, DSO, MC, of the 2nd Leinsters. The son of Lieutenant Colonel E. W. Murphy and Mary Ellen Murphy of Ballinamona, Cashel, County Tipperary, his valour and leadership have caught the attention of military historians. In a daring action in June Lieutenant Colonel Murphy, as Brigade Commander, and his Brigade Major had captured a German officer and his orderly. However, 6 November was the saddest day for the Leinsters. Murphy was with the Medical Officer and other battalion staff attending to the wounded in a building that served as headquarters mess when a shell exploded among them. Murphy, the Medical Officer and six men were killed. The sole survivor, a Captain Warner, was wounded. Only twenty-seven years old, Murphy was about to be promoted to Brigadier General. The Leinster historian devotes unusual words of praise to this highly esteemed young officer:

> Thus perished . . . the most remarkable officer who served in the Battalion in the Great War. . . . Absolutely fearless, modest but firm. . . . a born leader of men. . . . a just commander . . . an upright man, the memory of Alfred Murphy will remain.

And so it did. Captain Frank Hitchcock, who served under Murphy, notes that a year later 6 November was remembered as 'the anniversary of Colonel Murphy's death; the men had not forgotten him'.[56]

On 10 November the 1st Canadian Division took the village of Passchendaele on top of the ridge. This Pyrrhic victory and the foul weather influenced Haig to close the battle down.

Severe losses in the 1917 Third Ypres battles pointed up the problems of manpower and recruitment that had been present for the Irish from the Gallipoli campaign in 1915, the Easter Rising and the Somme battles of 1916. The sensitive political situation in Ireland had always ruled out conscription, although some Irish commanders, like General Nugent of the 36th (Ulster) Division, recommended it. Drafts of non-Irish troops to Irish formations had been an option, but by late 1916 Irish MPs were not alone in making demands that 'the national character' of units be maintained: 'the Welsh and Scottish MPs and the Territorial associations were others lobbying for special treatment within the army'. Already the British Army in 1916 had permitted the transfer of thousands of Irishmen from non-Irish to Irish units. Also there was the transfer of regular Irish battalions to the New Army Irish divisions, beginning in 1916 when the 1st Royal Munster Fusiliers went to the 16th (Irish) Division and fought in the Somme Battle of Ginchy in September. Later in that same year the 2nd Royal Irish and 2nd Royal Dublin Fusiliers were transferred to the 16th. Similarly, in 1917 the 2nd Royal Irish Rifles and 1st Royal Irish

Fusiliers were transferred to the 36th (Ulster) Division, replacing two service battalions.[57] With these regulars and English reinforcements the 36th (Ulster) Division, as happened in 1916, could no longer be seen as the Protestant fulfillment of the Ulster Volunteer Force, nor could the 16th (Irish) Division,which in general expressed the ethos of the National Volunteers, be seen as Redmond's Irish Brigade.

Initially there was some objection by regular Irish soldiers to leaving their existing formations, but particularly they resented being sent to divisions considered to have 'political' associations. On learning that they were being transferred to the 36th (Ulster) John Lucy of the 2nd Irish Rifles wrote that many southern officers considered the Division 'poisonously loyal'. Consequently, when Lucy went home to Ireland on leave he was requested to bring back Irish flags with harps only inscribed on them. Lucy was commissioned in June 1917 and when his regiment was host to a great dinner before the Battle of Cambrai in November and 'invited a good many officers of the Ulster Division to join us . . . they affected no surprise at our very Irish table decorated with green flags and other national emblems and we had a very merry evening'.

Amalgamation of Irish battalions was another way to keep them alive without non-Irish reinforcements. When a regular Irish battalion like the 2nd Leinster Regiment with the 24th Division absorbed their 7th Service Battalion, the nationality and regimental *esprit de corps* were preserved and an Irish connection was further reinforced by orders in January 1918 to join the 16th (Irish) in the Somme country.[58]

The political situation in Ireland again affected Irish soldiers in 1917. Home on leave, they not only met continued hostility by Irish Nationalists, but from January 1918 they could no longer bring their rifles. Some reserve battalions reported the loss of arms and ammunition, which led to Irish units being transferred out of Ireland. Despite this home situation, the fighting spirit of Irish soldiers in the British Army did not seem to be seriously affected, though many were undoubtedly confused and loyalties were often strained.[59]

10th (Irish) Division in Palestine – 1917

While Irish soldiers were dying in the devastating battles of Third Ypres, Irish soldiers in the 10th (Irish) Division sent from Salonika were about to help in defeating the Turks in Palestine and in capturing Jerusalem as a 'Christmas present' for the British people, as suggested by Prime Minister Lloyd George. General Sir Edmund Allenby, Commander of the Egyptian Expeditionary Force in the Palestine Campaign, was a cavalry-man known as 'the Bull'; not an Irishman, he had been commissioned in the 6th Inniskilling Dragoons and had commanded the Royal Irish Lancers. In his force were Irishmen like Major General John Longley, commander of the 10th from December 1915. He was the son of an Indian Civil Service official and his wife was from County Clare. Commissioned in the East Surrey Regiment, he had been a Brigade Commander in the 27th (Regular) Division. The Anglo-Irishman Brigadier General R. S. Vandeleur, who commanded 29 Brigade, had been with the 10th since Gallipoli. Known as 'Vandy', he was a strict disciplinarian as to the appearance of his soldiers and their equipment, carrying out 'a multitude of inspections' that were anything but mild, in contrast to Allenby who wasted little time on inspections. General Sir Edward Bulfin, Commander of XXI Corps, was from Rathfarnham, County Dublin, educated at Stonyhurst and Trinity College Dublin; the Irish Major General John Shea, Commander of 60th Division, had first been commissioned in the Royal Irish Regiment.[60]

In the opening Third Battle of Gaza Beersheba fell to the Allies on 31 October. The 10th (Irish) Division was in reserve in these actions, but a most vital if inglorious role of supplying water to men and horses of XX Corps had been allotted to the 1st and 6th Leinsters under Colonel Craske. The Irishmen, working day and night, had to fill with water some 34,000 *fanatis* (containers), chlorinate them and load them on camels. When Beersheba was captured the wells became available and the Leinsters watered thousands of horses mad with thirst. On 6 November they were relieved and joined their 10th Division.

On that day Irishmen came into action when the 5th/6th and 2nd Irish Fusiliers, supported by the 5th and 6th Inniskillings, led a dashing attack on the left of John Shea's 60th Division, driving the Turks out of their trenches with the bayonet and across the Wadi Sheria. The Turks fled to their last stronghold on the Gaza-Beersheba Road, the Hureira Redoubt. The next day 10th Division was ordered to capture this important high ground and the honour of the assault was assigned to the 2nd Royal Irish Fusiliers, plus two companies of their 5th/6th, with the 6th Inniskillings in a subsidiary role. Lieutenant Colonel G. de M. H. Orpen-Palmer, whom we have already met, commanded the Faughs when they headed for the redoubt early in the morning. Suffering machine-gun fire, they pressed on until halted near the redoubt. A company of Faughs and Inniskillings moved round the flanks and most of the Turks fled. As soon as the fire slackened the Faughs 'rushed the hill taking, 28 prisoners and 4 large mortars'. The fight lasted three hours and caused total Faugh losses of 166 killed and wounded in all ranks. Casualties could have been reduced if time had been allowed for an artillery bombardment.[61] After Gaza (city) fell to General Bulfin's XXI Corps and Jaffa was entered on

16 November, Turk forces were able to retreat into the shelter of the Judean Hills that run like a spine up the middle of Palestine.

By 8 December Allenby halted his advancing divisions south of Jerusalem, both British and Turkish commanders ensuring that there would be no fighting around the ancient Holy City of Jerusalem. During the night the Turks in Jerusalem evacuated the city, streaming north and east towards Nablus and Jericho, and next morning the city surrendered to the British. A comic touch was when the mayor had difficulty in finding someone to whom to hand over the keys of the city. Major General John Shea finally accepted them. Allenby formally entered Jerusalem on 11 December, walking, like a pilgrim of old, solemnly through the historic Jaffa Gate. London Irish troops lined part of his way up the Jaffa Road and outside the Gate on either side was an honour guard of English, Scottish, Irish, Welsh and ANZAC troops, inside French and Italian. Henry Harris writes that the occupation of the Holy City made a 'deep impression' on the troops.[62] Their 'Christmas present' was greatly praised in newspapers in England.

Fighting continued against the Turks and in late December in a double advance the 10th (Irish) Division formed the centre and left attack, its objective the Kereina Ridge, north-west of Jerusalem. All Irish regiments in the 10th endured severe fighting in the rugged Judean Hills, and Henry Lamb's famous painting *Irish Troops in the Judean Hills Surprised by a Turkish Bombardment* (Imperial War Museum, London), in bright Mediterranean colours, portrays the grim aftermath of a Turkish attack on this rock-terraced terrain. Lamb, already an artist and now a Medical Officer with the 5th Inniskilling Fusiliers, was among the first to see the devastation in his battalion's encampment in which four of his comrades were killed and eight wounded. The Inniskilling historian Sir Frank Fox describes this kind of fighting as reminiscent of Gallipoli: 'Companies and platoons . . . struggled down slopes which were swept by machine-gun and rifle fire, and along the bottom of wadis raked by enfilade fire, and then faced ascents precipitously steep . . . finally to expel the enemy from the summits in hand to hand fighting'.[63] The 6th Inniskillings, at the end of December, captured Kereina Peak and during the fight Fusilier James Duffy, a stretcher-bearer from County Donegal, was awarded the VC for bringing in seriously wounded men with an utter disregard to danger under heavy fire. Then, on 2 January 1918, Brigadier General Vandeleur visited the 5th Connaught Rangers and awarded the Military Medal to Private P. Madigan for 'conspicuous bravery in the field', when he carried messages for two hours under heavy machine-gun and rifle fire.[64]

The Palestine Campaign was the last time the 10th, formed as the first Irish Division in the British Army, fought as an Irish formation. After the disastrous German offensive of 21 March 1918 reinforcements for the Western Front were badly needed and in the early summer of that year Irish infantry battalions in the 10th were sent to France. Only three battalions of Irish Infantry remained, one in each of the division's brigades, and in what was called the 'Indianization' of Allenby's divisions Indian Army Infantry replaced the departing battalions. Irishmen in the reorganized 10th Division, in the 1st Royal Irish Regiment, 1st Leinsters, 2nd Royal Irish Fusiliers and the 1st/2nd Connaught Rangers (who had arrived with the Indian Division) continued fighting and losing their lives in Palestine until the armistice with Turkey on 31 October 1918.

The Irish in The Great Retreat of 1918

The German offensive that began 21 March 1918, *Die Kaiserschlact*, the Kaiser's Battle, as the German commander General Ludendorff called it, was an onslaught of overwhelming violence, the name indicative of its importance to the Germans. Criticism has been levelled against General Gough's Fifth Army, particularly his Irish soldiers, that they did not put up a 'reasonable resistance' to the German attack, but as Martin Middlebrook writes: 'No army of the British Expeditionary Force ever had to face an assault on the scale or with the ferocity of that sustained by Fifth Army on this day'. At the end of it, says Middlebrook, 'it had not acquitted itself badly'.[65]

Gough's Fifth Army was considered the weakest in the British Army. Historians agree that his prepared defences were far from adequate due to labour shortages and lack of time for construction, and his sector, taken over from the French, had the longest front – forty-two miles – to be covered by twelve infantry and three cavalry divisions, in effect a long line too thinly held. Gough would later claim that shortage of manpower was the chief cause of the resulting retreat. When, almost on the eve of the German attack, he requested permission to move divisions forward GHQ refused him; such moves were premature. Moreover, battalions and divisions had been reduced in numbers in a reorganization put in place from January 1918 by which a division would now have nine rather than twelve battalions, in three rather than four brigades, thereby limiting the number of actual fighting men that commanders had at their disposal. Soldiers had to spend a longer time in the front line and, when relieved, were further exhausted by manual labour in building defences. Battalions such as the 2nd Dublins and 1st Munsters had been in the line for over a month. Colonel Feilding of the 6th Connaught Rangers was one of several commanders who saw that the tired men in 16th Division 'sorely needed a rest and above all training'. The training he refers to was a new system

of 'defence in depth', recently initiated in the British Army: a lightly held
Front or Forward Zone with a series of strongpoints rather than a trench
line, a Battle Zone for the main defence (some three thousand yards
behind) to which troops would retire after dispersing enemy attacks and,
finally, some miles behind that a Reserve or Rear Zone. Many brigade or
battalion commanders, and indeed ordinary soldiers, did not understand
the new system in which counter-attacks were not expected to recover the
Forward Zone. Commanders were not fully briefed on the idea of 'elastic
yielding' that 'in certain circumstances there might be an ordered
retreat'.[66]

There had been much speculation as to the exact time and place of the
German attack. 'The 16th (Irish) Division's staff never became convinced
that the Germans were planning an offensive'.[67] There was enough
evidence building up, however, through intelligence reports, prisoners
taken and his own observations, that General Gough eventually realized
when the blow would fall on his Fifth Army sector. On 19 March he wrote
to his wife, 'I expect a bombardment will begin tomorrow night, last six
to eight hours, and then will come the German infantry . . . on March
21st'. He was right.[68] On that morning at 4.30am a terrible German
bombardment erupted over the British Army positions and fell not only
on the Forward but on the Battle Zone, aimed not so much at destruction
as dislocation, which happened. Communications were soon cut and units
became isolated; the soldiers' sense of isolation was increased as they
struggled behind their gas masks or staggered sick and blinded towards
aid posts. Shortly after 9.30, out of the enveloping fog that hid them and
magnified the terrifying sounds of battle, came the German 'storm troops',
swarming, confident, fresh. The British Army was up against a new kind
of war that virtually saw the end of trench warfare: the Germans simply
swept by prepared positions and carried on to leave 'mopping-up' for
other fresh troops. This, along with the use of gas, meant that in a matter
of hours 'The Fifth Army lost the bulk of its fighting power in its swamped
Forward Zone and part of the Third Army gave way as well'. 'Most were
prisoners or were tied down in the positions that still held out but all were
as good as completely lost to . . . commanders'.[69]

That some divisions lost their entire Battle Zone during the first day of
the virulent German attack is known. Haig's often-quoted criticism of the
16th (Irish) Division in his 22 March war diary calls attention to the Irish:
'Our 16th (Irish) Division which . . . lost Ronssoy village is said not to be
so full of fight as the others . . . and gave way immediately the enemy
showed'. But Martin Middlebrook includes the 36th (Ulster) and 51st
(Highland) Divisions, who also early lost their Battle Zones and elicited
his comment that possibly these 'Celtic' divisions [whose] 'troops . . . all

had such fine reputations in offensive operations did not have the temperament for defence'. Terence Denman objects to this, calling it a 'lame
conclusion', and Middlebrook himself adds that Haig's judgement on the
16th Division was only partly justified. Some Irish battalions did break,
but only 'after suffering numbers of men killed exceeded by only three
other divisions during the day'. At Ronssoy practically all the officers of
the 7/8th Inniskillings, including their commanding officer, Lieutenant
Colonel Walkley, were wounded, killed or captured, and hundreds of
Fusiliers were casualties or missing. Important also was that the 16th's
front line was so heavily manned. This was because Gough's VII Corps
Commander, Lieutenant General Sir W. N. Congreve, insisted that five
battalions should be in the Front or Forward Zone when two or three
would have been enough and only one in the Battle Zone, and Gough
backed him up. When objected to by the 16th's new commander Major
General Hull, a competent Englishman, Gough's famous reply was: 'The
Germans are not going to break my line'. Henry Harris suggests a reason
for Gough's blunt statement: 'This strong manning of the Forward Zone
had been judged necessary because the Division's front was somewhat of
a salient and therefore difficult to defend'. Nine German divisions, with
another three in support, were against the tired 16th Division;[70] no wonder
the Irish positions were quickly overrun.

Haig's criticism was undoubtedly influenced by prevalent attitudes
towards Irish soldiers in the British Army and the growing suspicions of
their loyalty, due to the political situation in Ireland where there was talk
by John Redmond, already losing authority, of a limited Home Rule for
Ireland, and where Sinn Feiners were winning by-elections. Irish soldiers
were easy targets for criticism. Ever since the Easter rebellion in 1916 they
had been taunted by the Germans and as recently as February 1918 the
2nd Leinsters had received an aerial dart urging Irishmen to desert. Their
response had been 'a hurricane of rifle grenades and small-arm ammunition directed at the German line'. There were also examples of fellow
British troops shouting taunts, 'There go the Sinn Feiners', against the 1st
Munsters, as Captain Guy Nightingale reported. This occurred in spite of
the 'military authorities threatening court martial for anyone spreading
slander against Irish troops'.[71]

In the midst of battle chaos and despite war weariness many Irish
performed brave deeds. In the 16th's sector Private R. Barry of the 7th
Royal Irish singlehandedly captured a German machine gun, and Sergeant
Rudge and Private Brown silenced a machine gun with grenades. All three
won the Military Medal. Brave stands, if in vain, also took place. When
the Germans broke through at Ronssoy one example is that of Major F.
Coll commander of the 7th Royal Irish, who, with his small remnant and

joined by one platoon of the 2nd Royal Irish, held a desperate position from 1.00 to 4.00 p.m.. Their grenades finished, machine-gunned from both flanks, they were captured when rushed by the Germans.[72]

The brave action of the counter-attack near St Emilie of the 6th Connaught Rangers can only be called a 'forlorn hope' and possibly was the only one carried out on 21 March. In the mid-afternoon the 6th Connaughts, along with the 1st Munster Fusiliers, were ordered to retake Ronssoy. A new order from the 16th's headquarters cancelling the attack reached the Munsters but not the Connaught Rangers. The heroism of their singlehanded action was costly: only a remnant of some thirty stragglers joined their 47th Brigade Headquarters. Among many killed was Captain Tommy Crofton, leading 'A' Company, heir to one of the oldest baronetcys in Connaught. The next day Lieutenant Ulic Moore was killed after surviving a wound with the 6th Connaughts at Guillemont. From an ancient family in Ireland, he was the son of Colonel Sir Maurice Moore, who had had a distinguished career in the Connaught Rangers, retiring in 1906 to become known in Nationalist circles as the military commander of the Redmondite Volunteers.[73]

In the 36th (Ulster) Division's sector by noon on 21 March the redoubts in their Forward Zone had been cut off or had fallen; the men were taken in the rear without warning by Germans who outnumbered them three to four times. It was believed at the time that all these troops had been quickly overwhelmed, but from the evidence of returned prisoners it appears there was 'at least one magnificent defence . . . though then unknown'. Captain L. J. Johnston and 'C' Company his counter-attack Company of the 12th Royal Irish Rifles, had fought gallantly all morning at Foucard trench, even taking prisoners, and had held on for four hours, repulsing Germans after savage hand-to-hand fighting. When the fog suddenly lifted Germans could be seen thronging about Jeanne D'Arc Redoubt a mile to the rear that held the battalion headquarters and 'B' Company. The unnerving sight of a long column of German transport advancing some four hundred yards to their right propelled 'C' Company into further action and their Lewis-gun fire quickly brought total confusion to the column. Attacked on both flanks Johnston withdrew his company to Le Jeune Trench five hundred yards to the rear where he was reinforced by heaquarters men from Le Ponchu Quarry; his little force now numbered about one hundred and twenty. A magnificent stand was made here. A German Company, evidently believing the trench was lightly held, was soon seen advancing from the rear. In tried and true British Army style Johnston had his men hold their fire until the Germans reached point-blank range and then gave them such a volley that 'Captain Johnston believes that not a man escaped. The position, however, was now hopeless.' The Germans sent in a tank firing into Johnston's trench in enfilade and simultaneously a whole battalion advanced from the front. They were surrounded. Johnston, with only about a hundred men alive, many of them wounded, had no choice but to surrender. Their indomitable courage was recognized and after the war Johnston was awarded the Military Cross; in all there were two Distinguished Conduct Medals and four Military Medals awarded to the survivors of the Company.[74]

That there were also 'premature surrenders' or 'negotiated surrenders' is certain. One such was that of Lieutenant Colonel Lord Farnham from County Cavan, Commander of the 2nd Inniskilling Fusiliers at the Boadicea Redoubt near St Quentin in the 36th Ulster's Forward Zone. Boadicea Redoubt, which held the Inniskillings' headquarters and at least one company, seemed to have missed the heavy German bombardment and the story of its fall, discovered by Martin Middlebrook in the history of the 463rd German Regiment, is most unusual. Their second battalion invested the redoubt, guns were brought up and the redoubt was surrounded. A deputation of men who spoke English approached under a white flag and Lord Farnham was told that, unless he and his defenders surrendered, heavy artillery would bombard them. The Germans seemed reluctant to embark on such a slaughter, which may explain what followed. Farnham knew he could not expect help from his division's Battle Zone where the Germans had broken through. Middlebrook asks: 'What choice did Lieutenant-Colonel Lord Farnham have? Fight on? . . . Surrender, and save much life but risk shame? . . . The officers who surrendered while still unwounded risked court-martial, and all had to face courts of enquiry on their return to England after the war'. So Lord Farnham negotiated his surrender: he asked for and was given a document stating that he had put up a good fight before surrendering. Carrier pigeons brought both this message and news of the fall of the Boadicea Redoubt to 36th Division's headquarters. The Inniskillings' historian Sir Frank Fox, in reporting this action, comments how 'The German officer who took over paid high compliments to Lt.-Col. Farnham and his men on their gallant resistance', and added, 'There were very few of the defenders left alive and unwounded'. Clearly Fox did not know the full story at the time he wrote his history, but admits that he was somewhat mystified as to why messenger pigeons were sent, for they homed on 36th Division's headquarters: 'Whether this was due to a mistake by the Germans or to an intention on their part to let the British Army know the fate of our garrison cannot be determined'. Of officers who surrendered like Lord Farnham, Middlebrook asks were they not the more 'civilized, realistic and humane in the circumstances'? Perhaps Lord Farnham was not, to use that phrase of Cyril Falls, a man 'of triple brass', as some writers saw soldiers, but a man 'of less durable material'. His very human influences were that 'he was possibly wounded in this action. Earlier in the war, he had suffered a personal tragedy when two of his young sons died at the same time through a sudden illness at home.' Middlebrook writes, 'It was a tired war-weary army'. 'There were cases of weakness in the days that followed among the troops of the 36th Division, as among other troops.' But, as Falls goes on, 'Their achievements must be measured by the standard of their cruel and heartbreaking task'.[75]

On that same afternoon Second Lieutenant Edmund De Wind from Comber, County Down, Commander of the smaller Race Course Redoubt near Grugiés, demonstrated that he *was* a man 'of triple brass'. Twice wounded, he and his 15th Royal Irish Rifles held out for nearly seven hours. They did not surrender until after his death. For his consummate leadership and valour he was awarded a posthumous Victoria Cross, his citation recording:

> On two occasions with two noncommissioned officers only, he got out on top under heavy machine gun and rifle fire and cleared the enemy out of the trench, killing many. He continued to repel attack after attack until he was mortally wounded and collapsed.

At thirty-five De Wind was old to be a second lieutenant, but he had joined the Canadian Army as a private at the outbreak of the war and had not been commissioned until 1917 when, as a native of County Down, he joined his native Ulstermen.[76]

A full account of the chaos on that first day can never be known. Gough worried about the course of the battle and, learning from air reconnaissance that masses of German troops were still heading towards his front, set out by car to visit his corps commanders to learn for himself what was happening. So disheartened by lost ground and without significant reserves or hope of reinforcements, or French help, on returning to his headquarters he decided that 'it was more important to keep together what was left of his battered divisions in the south than to hold ground'. His early decision to pull back more than three divisions over the Crozat Canal was a bold move that saved lives. Haig agreed with this principle of withdrawal before the battle, although it was much earlier than expected. Gough's decision would affect his career.[77] When he spoke to GHQ by telephone that night no one seemed to understand that Fifth Army's danger would only worsen without reinforcements.

Gough was then forced to pull his entire Fifth Army back behind the Somme, as Haig discovered when he visited him on 23 March at his headquarters at Villers-Brettoneux. Haig later recorded in his diary his surprise that Gough's troops 'are *now behind* the Somme. . . . I cannot make out why the Fifth Army has gone so far back without making some kind of stand'. The possibility for a fighting withdrawal of Gough's Fifth Army to the Somme had been considered in early February and a memorandum to Gough from GHQ stated: 'Your policy should be to secure and protect at all costs the important centre of Péronne and the River Somme to the south of that place'. Moreover, Gough was to construct a defensive system there and along the Somme, projects that proved to be impossible with his inadequate forces. That they were expected of Gough was another mis-understanding and confusion in communications between GHQ and Gough's Fifth Army.[78] Gough also had difficulties with the French, whose forces, promised to support him, were tardy in getting into action; Marshal Pétain had other priorities, despite his offer of help. By 24 March the Germans 'had advanced fourteen miles in four days, the greatest gain in territory since 1914'. Very soon in London rumours were flying about before any facts were known that 'the greater part of the Fifth Army had run away'.[79] From 23 March, pursued by the Germans on the line of the Somme, battalions became isolated in the great retreat and fought on bravely until their ammunition gave out and they were forced back. On 24 March came a magnificent stand by the 2nd Royal Irish Rifles of the 36th (Ulster) Division, west of the town of Cugny. Runners sent by Lieutenant Colonel McCarthy-O'Leary of the 1st Irish Rifles to Captain J. C. Byans to withdraw never arrived and the 2nd Rifles, after being attacked all morning and early afternoon, succumbed only after the final attack and an heroic hand-to-hand struggle. There were only three survivors.[80]

Another of the many stories on that retreat is that of a gallant band from the 16th (Irish) Division of reduced battalions of Munster and Dublin Fusiliers and Royal Irish Regiment, who, by 27 March, had fallen back to the east of Mericourt and, after repeated attacks when the Germans were successful in occupying a gap, organized a counter-attack. It was led successfully by Munstermen Second Lieutenant C. E. A. O'Callaghan, Corporal Gallagher and Private Douglas, with Regimental Sergeant Major John Ring volunteering to join them. By evening the Irishmen were surrounded and the three commanding officers decided to withdraw in a hazardous night march and fight a way through. At about 8.00pm, in dark-ness, the four-hundred-strong column, led by the Dublins, headed for the north bank of the Somme, erroneously presuming to cross it to safety. To cover the withdrawal Corporal Padfield of the Munsters was left alone in the trenches with a Lewis gun with orders to fire occasionally until 10.00pm and then to withdraw. His feat was recognized with the award of the Military Medal in January 1920. After unsuccessful attempts to find a bridge, the march continued, passing through Morcourt, which was in flames, and headed to the bridge at Cérisy, found to be held by the Germans. There Captain Stitt of the Dublins, who spoke German, learned the countersign and a bold move occurred. Major Wheeler of the Dublins records how he ordered up his batman, Fusilier Byrne, a heavyweight boxer, and placed him in the leading section of fours, 'curiously' without his rifle. Fusilier Byrne knew what to do. 'We moved off,' writes Wheeler, 'Captain Stitt and I leading. We were within some 15 yards of the Germans when they challenged. We rushed forward, Fusilier Byrne knocking out two with a right and left. A couple of revolver shots accounted for two more and so completely surprised was this piquet that they retired.' The column marched on and a sharp fight occurred at Sailly-Lorette. Captain Jervis of the Munsters writes: 'The whole country seemed to be swarming with the enemy . . . so it was finally decided to leave the river and work westwards . . . steering by the stars. At any moment the German front line might be met', therefore it was with great relief when, about 3.30am near Bois de Hamel, the sentry the exhausted column finally stumbled upon was English. After marching twelve miles through enemy territory the remnant of about two hundred had reached the British line and at Hamel fell into welcome billets. Among their losses was the brave Second Lieutenant O'Callaghan, taken prisoner after his party lost touch with the main body.[81]

During this time, in a reorganization with the French, GHQ informed Gough that he would take orders directly from French General Fayolle and Fifth Army would be in Fayolle's group of armies. Gough could cheerily write, 'Placing the Fifth Army under Fayolle's group of armies made no material difference. He issued no orders to me and I only saw him once for a few minutes'. General Butler's III Corps would be under French General Pellé and General Congreve's battered VII Corps north of the Somme came under the command of General Byng's Third Army. The writer William Moore has seen in these changes the beginning of the end for Gough: 'It was almost as though GHQ had decided to disown Gough and his men'.[82]

The Somme line gone, Haig, aware that the battle was going against him and realizing that the French Commander-in-Chief Marshal Pétain', priorities were to protect Paris, saw that a strong unified command was imperative. He wired London to have Sir Henry Wilson, Chief of the Imperial General Staff, come at once to France and the important conference at the little town of Doullens on 26 March was the result. Attended by the French High Command and President Poincaré, Haig suggested that French General Foch be chosen as the Supreme Commander of the Allied Armies on the Western Front, something

Wilson had long worked for, as his diary suggests. When Fifth Army was mentioned, it is reported that Pétain, Commander in Chief of the French, blurted out: 'Alas it no longer really exists. It is broken . . . from the first they have refused to engage the enemy . . . they have run like the Italians at Caporetto'. Haig let the remark pass, but it brought a sharp retort from the Francophile Henry Wilson. Pétain's were unfortunate words because a report was already in Haig's hands that General Maxse's XVIII Corps and General Watts's XIX Corps, remaining under Gough, were still in the line and everywhere fighting advancing Germans. Gough, unaware of Foch's appointment until Foch arrived at his headquarters that same day, was immediately attacked 'in a most regrettable interview', all the more unforgivable in that Foch's brusque words seemed to question Gough's personal courage. Foch hurled questions at Gough in French without waiting for answers: 'Why I was at my Headquarters and not with my troops in the fighting line ?' and 'Why did the army retire ?' To the question 'What were my orders to the Army?' Gough attempted to reply, 'To fight a rearguard action and thus gain time for the Allies to send up their reserves'. Not inquiring into Fifth Army's strength or condition, Foch only said in a loud and excited manner, 'There must be no more retreat . . . and then walked out of the room'. Even allowing for Gough's perhaps biased account, written in retrospect some years later, it is not difficult to agree with Haig that 'Foch had spoken most impertinently'.[83] Foch's appointment, however, was generally well received.

Events were piling up against Gough. Sir Henry Wilson and Lord Milner (Secretary of State for War), who had Prime Minister Lloyd George's ear, also now censored Gough. On 28 March Haig's Military Secretary, General Ruggles-Brise, arrived at Gough's headquarters and gave him the 'painful' news that he would be replaced by General Rawlinson who took over as Commander of Fourth Army. This change of number from Fifth to Fourth was interpreted to mean that Fifth Army had been destroyed. Although shrunk to a single corps, Gough's Fifth Army was in fact 'bent but not broken' and, with few reinforcements, had 'fought a fine German Army of sixty-four divisions to a standstill', undoubtedly helped by the fact that the German Somme drive was running out of steam, thanks in part to hungry Germans discovering British liquor and supplies. After a marked defeat on 5 April Ludendorff reluctantly broke off the attack on Amiens, persuaded that 'the enemy's resistance was beyond our powers'. Before the tide was turned Gough had been sacked, sent home on half-pay: 'A hard fate after conducting a skilful week-long fighting retreat on a scale without precedent in the history of the British Army'. Criticism had centred on him for sanctioning a retreat early in the battle; as Middlebrook wrote of Gough's decision to withdraw, in the 'more than three years' tradition and philosophy of the Western Front . . . British generals simply did not give up ground'.[84]

Political expediency, as well as internal criticism, seems to have dictated what happened to Gough. As Haig records in his diary, Lloyd George told him he 'is looking out for a scapegoat for the retreat of Fifth Army'. Haig concluded that Lloyd George expected to be attacked in the Commons for the manpower problem. Answering Lloyd George's intense criticism of Gough, Haig, on 3 April, reminded the Prime Minister that Gough 'had very few reserves, a very big front entirely without defensive works recently taken over from the French, and the weight of the enemy's attack fell on him . . . In spite of a most difficult situation, he had never really lost his head'. This was a fair appraisal, but with Haig's own position under threat 'he did not go to great lengths to defend Gough'[85] ,who would later regret that there was not an inquiry, as was suggested, as he could not then defend the honour and bravery of his courageous soldiers. After the war these veterans proudly formed a Fifth Army Association. They were in sympathy with Gough and resented the denigration of their fighting abilities.

So ended the British Army career of this controversial Anglo-Irish soldier. Looking back, it is possible to see what had contributed to his sacking. The Asquith government had never forgiven Gough for his part in the Curragh Mutiny in 1914, nor for the 'damage' it had done to civil-military relations. Gough also undoubtedly inherited a legacy of his handling of the disastrous Third Ypres battles of 1917, for which many believed him responsible. Since May 1916 Gough had been the youngest commander in the British Army, but in 1918 this did not help his cause with Sir Henry Wilson, CIGS, who thought that he himself should have commanded Fifth Army. In 1918 Gough was considered the unluckiest commander in either the British or French forces.

An exoneration of Gough appeared in the British *Official History* (1918 – Vol. 2, p. 458), but it was not until the 1930s that Gough's name was publicly cleared of blame for the retreat of Fifth Army in March 1918. In 1930 Lord Birkenhead published a vindication of Gough in his book *Critical Points in History*, a minor sensation, which received attention in the *Evening News* of 17 October. In 1936 Lloyd George, on the publication of his *Memoirs*, wrote to Gough:

> facts which have come to my knowledge since the War have completely changed my mind as to the responsibility for that defeat. You were completely let down and no general could have won that battle under the conditions in which you were placed.[86]

Hubert Gough died in 1963 at the age of ninety-two, having outlasted them all.

In Gough's Fifth Army the 16th (Irish) and 36th (Ulster) Divisions had suffered grievously in the Great German March offensive. An exhausted remnant was all that was left of the 36th when, on 30 March, it was moved north to the area of Gamaches on the Normandy Coast for reorganization. With English reinforcements, even if mostly conscript boys, the division entered the line in July, once again a fighting force. The 16th (Irish), after the final unsuccessful advance by the Germans on Amiens, was moved to England in June and was finished as 'a separate and Irish fighting unit'. There were 'sad amalgamations and disbandments'; Irish battalions were dispersed to other divisions and soldiers from one regiment were absorbed by another. 'Most officers and men accepted this change philosophically, but some Connaught Rangers were upset. When shoulder titles were exchanged for those of the Leinsters, one Connaught Ranger was heard to say, 'I've been a Ranger for eighteen years and my father was a Ranger before me – I shall always be one.'[87]

By July 1918, when the 16th Division was reconstituted and returned to France, the 5th Royal Irish Fusiliers was its only Irish battalion. Why? As Stephen Gwynn pointed out, by the summer of 1918 'sufficient Irish units serving on the western front' could have been transferred to the 16th. In addition, those New Army Irish battalions in the 10th (Irish) Division returned from Palestine could have been added to make the 16th an Irish Division again, and similarly added to the 36th (Ulster) Division. Policy considerations in the army and the political situation in Ireland were certainly factors. The outcry in southern Ireland against a conscription bill in April 1918 and the consequent 'growing Nationalist sentiments towards Sinn Fein' were all reasons that made 'appeasing Nationalist opinion' in Ireland unnecessary for the War Office to maintain an 'unsustainable' Irish identity for 16th Division. Tom Johnstone goes further and points to General Sir Henry Wilson, who was staunchly Protestant and Unionist, anti-Catholic and anti-Irish Nationalist, and who, as Chief of the Imperial General Staff, would have been responsible for such decisions at GHQ involving battalions and divisions.[88]

In a final effort to encourage Irish voluntary recruitment, a new Irish Recruiting Council was set up in Ireland and to assist it Nationalist MPs serving in the British Army, such as Stephen Gwynn and Arthur Lynch, appeared on recruiting platforms, but audiences were hostile. From the beginning of June to mid-October 1918 approximately 10,000 Irishmen enlisted, but less than half went into the army.[89]

The Irish were well represented in the British Army of Occupation, which, after the Armistice on 11 November 1918, began its march into

Germany, composed of the Guards Division, the 'incomparable' 29th (Regular), 15th Scottish (New Army), and 1st and 2nd Canadian Divisions. On 13 December three Divisions triumphantly crossed the Rhine simultaneously at different bridges, the place of honour going to the Regulars. At Cologne, in the 29th, were the 2nd Leinsters wearing their saffron kilts and the 1st Dublin Fusiliers, the famous 'Blue Caps'. 'The enemy press,' writes Captain Frank Hitchcock of the 2nd Leinsters:

> alone testified to our splendid appearance, remarking on the physique and turn out of the 'khaki-clad 29th Division'. They refused to believe it was composed of troops who had been engaged in the recent fight and said it had been obviously raised and formed recently in England for this event! They also remarked that the British battalions crossed over to well-known English marching airs . . . all played 'The British Grenadiers', but they omitted to mention that the 2nd Leinster Regiment were played over to 'Paddy McGinty's Goat!'

When the Guards Division arrived in late December, the drums of the Irish Guards played "Brian Boru" as they entered the Hohenzollern Ring. Irish identity in Irish regiments seems to have continued to be important for the Irish soldier. Hitchcock writes on 21 December with some pride that the 2nd Leinsters was still 'overwhelmingly Irish . . . I record this as I have heard it stated that at the end of the war the Irish Regiments were Irish only in name'.[90]

The First World War saw the end of the British Army in Ireland. As Henry Harris observes: 'The red coat disappeared from the scene of Ireland never to be seen again, except in the north'.[91]

EPILOGUE

The First World War was not the end of that great service that Irish soldiers have given to the British Army. It was truly a phenomenon that in the Second World War the officially neutral Republic of Ireland provided over 43,000 recruits of whom 32,778 were in the army at the end of 1944 and who joined the 38,000 Ulstermen fighting for the crown.[1] Moreover, there were six Irish Field Marshals: Sir John Dill, Lord Gort, Sir Alan Brooke, Sir Harold Alexander, Sir Bernard Montgomery and Sir Claude Auchinleck, all career soldiers, veterans of the First World War now in senior positions in the Second. There were also six Irish Regiments in the British Army fighting in all theatres. One of the most significant formations in the Second World War was the Irish Brigade, made up of Irish line regiments. Its first Commander was the distinguished Royal Irish Fusilier from West Cork, the Anglo-Irishman Brigadier the O'Donovan. He immediately recognized the historical significance of the term the 'Irish Brigade' and on his appointment told a friend that [he] 'felt the mantle of Sarsfield had fallen on his shoulders'.[2] The Irish Brigade under Brigadiers Nelson Russell and Pat Scott, both, like O'Donovan, 'Faughs', became a byword for excellence in the war, but that is another story.

After the First World War in the turmoil of the emerging state of Ireland Field Marshal Sir John French was the Lord Lieutenant, appointed May 1918. His aim was to get rid of Sinn Fein so that Home Rule could safely be granted. Recognizing the complexities of this, he believed that necessary social and economic reforms in Irish society must include a military offensive 'against the "physical force" elements of Sinn Fein'. French had no real understanding of the present situation in Ireland and consistently underestimated the strength of Sinn Fein in the country. A little over six months after his arrival Sinn Fein won a landslide victory in the general election in December 1918, followed, in January 1919, by a Parliament, Dáil Éireann, set up in Dublin, that demanded sovereign independence for Ireland. The existing Irish Volunteers became 'the standing army of the republic' or 'Irish Republican Army' (IRA).[3] A guerrilla war soon broke out between British forces and the IRA and French became a target, as his death would advertize their cause. In December 1919 Sir John narrowly escaped being killed by the IRA when, in a convoy of cars returning to the Viceregal Lodge, the wrong car was shot up. French certainly was 'brave as a lion', as Sir Henry Wilson admitted. He loved Ireland and intended to live in the country after independence. But as French continued to demand military rather than political policies against Sinn Fein, he was asked to relinquish his post in April 1921, praised at the same time by Prime Minister Lloyd George for his bravery. 'It is perhaps surprising,' his biographer writes, 'that French had survived at Viceregal Lodge for as long as he had.'[4]

Rejection of Irish soldiers serving in the British Army by extreme Irish Nationalists was long-standing. After the First World War soldiers returning to Ireland for demobilization found their heroic contribution to the British Army and their sacrifice in the trenches savagely condemned by unforgiving Nationalist hatred. Intimidation began in the spring of 1919 and during the War of Independence (1919–21) Irish ex-servicemen were major civilian targets for IRA assassins; houses were burned and almost one-third of the civilians killed in the first months of 1921 alone were former British Army soldiers. One such was Lieutenant Colonel J. Peacocke DSO of the 9th Royal Inniskilling Fusiliers in 36th (Ulster) Division who was murdered in his home near Cork on 1 June 1921.[5]

Uncounted Irish veterans changed their allegiance and joined revolutionary forces in the cause of Irish independence, finding opportunity to express their martial spirit in paramilitary organizations. Unemployment after the First World War was undoubtedly a factor, but there was also a nostalgia for the fellowship of the trenches and for military life; the flag they fought under was not important. One interesting example was that of the very brave Company Sergeant Major Martin Doyle born in New Ross, County Wexford, who was awarded the Victoria Cross while serving in France with 1st Battalion, Munster Fusiliers. On 2 September 1918 command of the Company devolved on him due to officer casualties and his citation includes several brave actions, among them how he single-handedly saved a tank crew, silenced a machine gun firing on it, capturing it with three prisoners, and then carried a wounded man to safety. Within a year after his service in France he was 'providing the [Irish] Volunteers with "information" while working in the Ennis military barracks'.[6] Tom Barry, often referred to by historians, was an ex-British Army soldier who joined the Irish Volunteers and gained a fearful reputation as a guerrilla fighter commanding a West Cork flying column.

Lieutenant Emmet Dalton, MC, formerly in Royal Dublin Fusiliers, was also in sympathy with the Irish revolutionary movement and reached high rank when he helped his friend Michael Collins to organize the Irish National Army authorized by the Irish Free State that came into being in January 1922. The new Irish Army greatly benefited from the professionalism of these ex-British Army officers who joined it.[7] They were again particular targets in the civil war that erupted in June 1922 between Republican forces and the Free State Army. Field Marshal Sir Henry Wilson's startling assassination at his home in London in June of that year was another violent result of these troubled times. After forty years of soldiering in the British Army, becoming MP for North Down as well as military advisor to the Ulster Executive, Wilson was shot by two Irishmen, former British Army soldiers identified by Robert Kee as Reginald Dunne and Joseph O'Sullivan. Both were connected to the London Brigade of the IRA.[8] In historian Peter Karsten's opinion, 'On balance Irish veterans of World War I tended to be less sympathetic to Sinn Fein and the IRA than were others in the southern Irish population'. During these revolutionary years virtually all the Irish regiments in the British Army remained quiet and loyal and over 20,000 Irishmen continued to enlist in the British Army. Anti-British sentiment, as usual, did not affect the behaviour of Irish soldiers.[9]

With partition established in Ireland from 1922 and drastic cuts already put in place in the British Army, in June the five historic Irish Regiments territorially associated with southern Ireland were disbanded: Connaught Rangers, Royal Irish Regiment, Royal Dublin and Royal Munster Fusiliers and the Leinster Regiment. Thanks to earlier efforts of Sir Henry Wilson three Ulster Regiments were 'saved': Royal Ulster Rifles, Royal Inniskilling Fusiliers and Royal Irish Fusiliers. The Irish Guards also remained in the army. Cavalry regiments were reduced (not disbanded) and several were amalgamated. In December the British Army left Ireland (apart from troops remaining in the 'Treaty Ports') handing over barracks, military establishments and equipment to the new National Irish Army.

Some former senior Irish officers of the British Army accepted the new Irish Free State, contributing to its political life. General Sir William Hickie, General Sir Bryan Mahon and Colonel the Earl of Granard became senators in the first Irish Parliament (the Dáil). But, as Mark Bence-Jones points out, it took some courage to join the Senate. In the civil/guerrilla war of 1922–23 Liam Lynch, Chief of Staff of the Republican forces, ordered, on 30 November 1922, 'that the houses of all Senators should be burnt'. Mullaboden, Mahon's country house in County Kildare, was burnt and Lord Granard's family home, Castle Forbes in County Longford, was extensively damaged by a land-mine. Also Major Bryan Cooper's home Markree, in County Sligo, was damaged. As one of many ex-Unionists to accept the new order, Cooper represented his old constituency of South County Dublin in the Dáil from 1923 and 'enjoyed the political life of the new Ireland', serving as an Independent. He brought to the Irish Parliament 'his passionate desire that Ireland should forget old quarrels and look to the future rather than the past'. Appropriately, at his funeral his 'coffin was draped with both the Irish Tricolour and the Union Jack . . . and all commands were in Irish'.[10]

General Hickie worked for the welfare and support of Irish veterans and was active in organizing an Irish Battlefield Memorial Committee in Dublin to erect three Celtic crosses at significant sites for the 16th (Irish) Division, his design based on the original wooden cross at Ginchy. On 22 August 1926 the first cross, at Wytschaete, was unveiled by Sir Bryan Mahon and the next day Marshal Foch of France unveiled a similar cross at Guillemont; a wreath was also laid at the 36th (Ulster) Division's memorial at Thiepval.[11] A third cross was later erected at Salonika to honour the fallen of the 10th (Irish) Division. In Paris, in November 1928, Foch delivered a glowing tribute to those Irish soldiers who had served under him in the First World War: 'The soldiers of Ireland fought with the rare courage and determination that had always characterized the race on the battlefield. . . . We [in France] shall try to ensure that generations that come after shall never forget the heroic dead of Ireland'.[12]

In the new Republic of Ireland attitudes towards the Irish in the British Army were slowly changing. During the inter-war years annual Armistice Day celebrations by the British Legion (in which Irish veterans were affiliated) took place in Southern Ireland, but were met by strong opposition from Republicans who engaged in rowdy activities and sent letters to Irish newspapers continuing to voice bitter criticism of the November ceremonies they saw as confirming British Imperialist values. In these years an Irish government representative attended some of the annual Armistice day celebrations demonstrating a certain reluctance in Ireland to commemorate the war. For many still only the Easter Rising of 1916 was worthy of commemoration. In Northern Ireland, however, official Armistice Day ceremonies were annually celebrated, but in a chiefly Protestant setting that tended not to include the common sacrifices of both Catholics and Protestants in the war.[13]

As late as 1960 a memorial bust of Tom Kettle, who had served in the Dublin Fusiliers and died in action 1916, was removed at night from its pedestal in Dublin's St. Stephen's Green and dumped into a pond. On the fiftieth anniversary of the Easter Rising in 1966 Sean Lemass, the Irish Prime Minister, who himself had fought in the Rising, in a speech he gave in Dublin in the presence of President de Valera, the British Ambassador and the U.S. Ambassador (whose grandfather had been the Lord

Lieutenant in 1916) reminded his audience of 'generous young Irishmen who [like Tom Kettle] . . . had volunteered enthusiastically to fight as they believed for the liberty of Belgium'. Lemass added:

> In later years it was common – and I also was guilty in this respect – to question the motives of those men who joined the new British armies formed at the outbreak of the war, but it must, in their honour, and in fairness to their memories, be said that they were motivated by the highest purpose, and died in their tens of thousands in Flanders and Gallipoli, believing they were giving their lives in the cause of human liberty everywhere, not excluding Ireland.[14]

On 11 November 1998 at Messines in Belgium an unprecedented event occurred when the heads of state, Britain's Queen Elizabeth and the Irish President Mary McAleese, together with Belgium's King Albert, took part in the first joint memorial service to the First World War dead of Ireland, North and South. All three laid wreaths at a Peace Tower constructed in a newly laid-out Peace Park dedicated to the memory of all Irish soldiers who suffered and died. Now past wrongs were being put right and the 'collective amnesia', as Colonel Jimmy Hughes of the British Legion called it, that forbade remembering the valour of Irish soldiers who died serving in the British Army, was hoped to be a thing of the past. The theme of reconciliation was at the heart of the project and the ceremony was organized by two Irishmen, Glenn Barr of the Reconciliation Trust and Paddy Harte, MP for Donegal in the Irish Government. The site was chosen because, in the Battle of Messines Ridge of 7 June 1917, Irishmen in the 16th (Irish) and Ulstermen in the 36th (Ulster) Divisions attacked side by side, which became a symbolic message that Irishmen from both north and south *could* join in a common cause after the war. The tower itself is a very ancient Irish image; tall and straight round towers were first built in Ireland in the tenth century as belfries and places of refuge. The stone was brought from Mullingar, Ireland, and was a joint building project for students from both north and south. Irish clergy from all denominations participated in the ceremonies and music was provided by military bands from the Irish Army and the present Royal Irish Regiment in the British Army. Also not forgotten was the Irish National Memorial at Islandbridge, Dublin. Billy Irvine of the Somme Association, when interviewed in the Belfast studio in conjunction with the day's ceremonies, expressed the hope that it would be visited again.[15] And so with reference to that important memorial, we have come full circle in this study of the Irish in the British Army.

Notes

Preface (pp xi – xvii)

1. Foster, R. F., *Modern Ireland, 1600–1972,* London, 1988, p. 472
2. *Irish Times,* 24 February, 1988
3. Leonard, Jane, 'Lest we Forget: Irish War Memorials' in *Ireland and the First World War,* Trinity History Workshop, Dublin, 1986, pp. 60, 65, 66, 67
4. Knowles, David, *Historian and Character,* Cambridge, 1954, p. 3
5. Murtagh, Harman, 'Irish Soldiers Abroad – 1600–1800', p. 313 in *A Military History of Ireland* Eds. Bartlett, Thomas and Jeffery, Keith, Cambridge, 1966; see Farwell, Byron, *Mr. Kipling's Army,* New York, 1981; De Watteville, Colonel H., *The British Soldier,* London, 1954
6. Karsten, Peter, 'Irish Soldiers in the British Army, 1792–1922: Suborned or Subordinate?' in *Journal of Social History,* 1983, XVII, p. 36
7. Harries-Jenkins, Gwyn, *The Army in Victorian Society,* London, 1977, pp. 41–43; Bartlett, Thomas; Jeffrey, Keith; 'An Irish military tradition ?' pp. 6, 7, and Spiers, E.M., 'Army organization and society in the nineteenth century'; pp. 341, 342 both in *A Military History of Ireland,* Cambridge, 1996
8. O'Malley, Ernie, *Army Without Banners,* London, 1967, p. 21; Asherwood, Paul and Spencer-Smith, Jenny, *Lady Butler – Battle Artist 1846–1933,* Exhibition Catalogue, National Army Museum, 1987, pp. 74–76, 156
9. Harris, Henry, *Irish Regiments in the First World War,* Cork, 1968, p. 5
10. Denman, Terence, 'The Catholic Irish Soldier in the First World War: the Social Environment' in *Irish Historical Studies,* Vol. XXVII, No. 108, November 1991, p. 352
11. Harris, Henry, *The Royal Irish Fusiliers,* London, 1972, p. 9
12. Harris, *Ibid.,* p. 1

Chapter 1 (pp 1 – 12)

1. Hughes, Kathleen, *Church in Early Irish Society,* London, 1966, p. 8
2. Newark, Tim, *Celtic Warriors,* London, 1988, pp. 116–117; Heath, Ian &

Sque, David, *The Irish Wars 1485–1603,* London, 1993, pp. 8, 9. Spelling also galoglas, gallowglass

3. White, D.G., 'Henry VIII's Irish Kern in France and Scotland, 1544–1545,' *Irish Sword,* 1957–1958, III, p. 223; cf. Ferguson, K., 'Development of a Standing Army in Ireland', *Irish Sword,* 1982, XV, pp. 153–58

4. Newark, *Celtic Warriors,* p. 123; Hayes-McCoy, G.A., *Irish Battles,* London, 1969, p. 117

5. Malcolm, J.L., 'All the King's Men: The Impact of the Crown's Irish Soldiers on the English Civil War', *Irish Historical Studies (IHS),* 1979, XXI, p. 263; Irwin, Margaret, *The Stranger Prince,* London, 1937, p. 320; and her *The Proud Servant, The Story of Montrose,* London, 1934, 315–321, Most of the Macdonalds had been driven out of Scotland by the Campbells, their hereditary foes.

6. Lindley, K.J., 'Impact of the 1641 rebellion upon England and Wales, 1641–1645' *I.H.S.,* 1972, XVIII, p.153, cf. Fitzpatrick, Brendan, '*Seventeenth Century Ireland: the War of Religions',* Dublin, 1988, p. 215

7. Ascoli, David, *A Companion to the British Army 1660–1983,* London, 1983, pp. 14, 15

8. Guy, Alan, J., 'The Irish Military Establishment,1660–1776' in *A Military History of Ireland,* p. 212.; Ascoli, David, *Companion,* p. 20

9. Gretton, Lieutenant-Colonel G. Le M., *The Campaigns and History of the Royal Irish Regiment.,* London, 1911, Appendix 9, and pp. 423–24.

10. McGuire, James, 'James II and Ireland 1685–90' in *Kings in Conflict,* Ed. W. A. Maguire, Belfast, 1990, p. 46

11. Gretton, *Royal Irish Regiment,* pp. 2, 3

12. Garland, J. L., 'Regiment of MacElligot, 1688–1699,' *Irish Sword,* 1949–1950, I, pp. 121–25; Miller, John, 'The Glorious Revolution' in *Kings,* p. 35

13. Simms, J.G., *The Siege of Derry,* Dublin, 1966, p. 4

14. Miller, 'The Glorious Revolution', p. 43; Murtagh, H., 'The War in Ireland'; p. 61 both in *Kings.*

15. Gretton, *Royal Irish Regiment,* p. 6

16. Murtagh, 'War In Ireland' in *Kings,* p. 62, 64; Hayes-McCoy, *Irish Battles.,* pp. 240–242

17. Evans, Roger, *The 5th Inniskilling Dragoon Guards,* Aldershot, 1951, pp. 9,13, 14,15. Dr. Leslie, after commanding at the Boyne, had religious scruples about fighting and relinquished his command to his son who was killed at Aughrim in 1691.

18. Murtagh, 'War in Ireland' in *Kings,* p. 83

19. *Ibid.,* p. 85; *Inniskilling Fusiliers.,* pp. 23, 24; The name Inniskillen is derived from the ancient name of the parish of Enniskillen and in 1741 was officially adopted as the title of the Enniskillen regiments. Following the example of the regiment's history we will use the title Inniskilling from the outset.

20. Evans, *5th Inniskilling Dragoon Guards,* p. 16

21. Murtagh, *op. cit.*, pp. 90, 91; O'Callaghan, J.C., *History of the Irish Brigade in the Service of France,* Glasgow, 1886, pp. 62–64

22. Gretton, *Royal Irish Regiment,* pp. viii, 22, 21,54. In 1832 the Royal Irish finally received official permission to emblazon their motto on their Colours.

23. Hayton, D.W., 'Anglo-Irish Attitudes: changing perceptions of national identity among the Protestant ascendancy in Ireland. c. 1690–1750,' in *Studies in Eighteenth Century Culture,* London, 1987, XVII, pp. 146–50; and his 'The Propaganda War' in *King's,* pp. 120–121

24. Connolly, S.J., 'The Penal Laws' in *Kings,* p. 166

Chapter Two (pp 13 – 38)

1. cf Brereton, J.M., *History of the Royal 4th/7th Dragoon Guards,* Catterick, 1982, p. 85; Johnston, Major S. H. F., 'The Irish Establishment' in *Irish Sword,* Vol. I, No. 1, 1949–50, pp. 33–36; Bartlett, Thomas, 'Army and Society in Eighteenth Century Ireland', p. 173 ff.

2. Brereton, *The British Soldier,* London, 1986, pp. 26; Hastings, Max, Ed, *The Oxford Book of Military Anecdotes*; Oxford, 1985, pp.141–143, quoting Dictionary of National Biography (authorship attributed to Daniel Defoe), and pp. 146, 147, James Settle

3. Brereton, *4th/7th Dragoon Guards,* p. 86

4. Wall, Maureen, 'Catholic Loyalty to King and Pope', *Catholic Ireland in the Eighteenth Century: Collected Essays of Maureen Wall,* Dublin, 1989, pp. 107, 109

5. Bartlett, T., 'Arms and Society', *Kings in Conflict,* p. 180; Catholic officers could not be commissioned until 1793 and then only in Irish regiments

6. *Royal Inniskilling Fusiliers History from December 1688 to July 1914,* London, 1934, pp. 86, 123

7. Brereton, *4th/7th Dragoon Guards,* pp. 86, 94, Ligonier was another French Huguenot who gave such service to the British Army that he rose to be commander in chief and field marshal; Neuburg, Victor, *Gone for a Soldier,* London, 1989, p. 155

8. Brereton, *4th/7th DragoonGuards,* p. 141

9. Lynn, F. J., 'Ireland, the Jacobite Rising of 1745,' *Irish Sword,* 1979, 13, pp. 339–52; Wood, Stephen, *The Auld Alliance,* Scotland and France, the Military Connection, Edinburgh, 1989, p. 86

10. Sheppard, E. W., *Coote Bahadur, Life of Lieutenant-General Sir Eyre Coote;* London, 1956, p. 28. It was General Hawley with no confidence in his men and they in him who led the dispirited 27th to Edinburgh; *Inniskilling Fusiliers,* p. 78

11. Reid, Stuart, *Wolfe, The Career of General Wolfe from Culloden to Quebec,* Staplehurst, 2000, pp. 19, 39, 40

12. Stacey, C. P., *Quebec, The Siege and the Battle 1759,* London, 1957, pp. 125–132. Reid,*Wolfe,* p. 188, 195, 197; Knox, Captain John, *An*

Historical Journal of the Campaigns in North America, 3 vols., first published 1769, Ed. Doughty, A G, Champlain Society 1914–16, Vol. 2, p. 101

13. Lecky, W. E. H., *History of Ireland in the Eighteenth Century,* II, London, 1881, pp. 188–89; Guy, Alan J., 'The Irish Military Establishment', in *A Military History of Ireland,* p. 229

14. Laurie, George Brenton, *History of the Royal Irish Rifles,* London, 1914, pp. 79, 80, 83; Anonymous; 'Sir Henry Keating, KCB', in *Journal of the Society for Army Historical Research,* Vol. 20, 1941; Hayes-McCoy, *Irish Battles,* pp. 214, 215

15. Leyburn, J. G., *Scotch-Irish,* Chapel Hill, 1962, p. 192

16. Caton, Alan, 'The Causes of the Conflict – A British Historian's View' in *The American War of Independence 1775–1783,* 20th Anniversary Booklet, Eds. John Williams, Alan Caton, London, 1974, p. 8

17. Ketchum, R. M., *Winter Soldiers,* N.Y., 1973, p. 341; Doyle, D.N., *Ireland, Irishmen and Revolutionary America,* Cork, 1981, pp. 73, *passim.*

18. Graves, Robert, Ed. *Proceed Sergeant Lamb,* London, 1941, pp. 47–49, and passim.

19. Bartlett, Thomas, 'Defence, Counter-insurgency and Rebellion: Ireland 1793–1803 in *Military History of Ireland,* pp. 247–254

20. McAnally, Sir Henry, *Irish Militia 1793–1816,* London, 1949, p. 40 quoting Major Ross Lewin, *With the Thirty-Second,* ed. Professor Wardell,1904, p. 2

21. Chart, D. A., 'The Irish Levies during the Great French War', *English Historical Review,* Vol. 32, 1917, pp. 497–516; Oman, C., *Wellington's Army, 1809–1814,* London, 1912, p. 209; McAnally, *Irish Militia,* pp.152, 182

22. Spiers, E. M., 'Army Organization and Society in the Nineteenth Century' in *A Military History of Ireland,* pp. 335, 336

23. McAnally, *Irish Militia,* p. 102,136

24. Grove-White, James, *Account of the Yeomanry of Ireland,* Cork, 1893, pp. 6–8 re Ballinamuck; Hayes-McCoy, *Irish Battles,* pp. 314, 277; Bartlett, Thomas, 'Defence, Counter-insurgency and Rebellion' in *Military History of Ireland,* pp. 286

25. Bence-Jones, Mark, *Clive of India.,* London, 1974, pp. 176,166; Sheppard,*Coote Bahadur;* p. 63, On leaving the 39th Foot Forde asked for £5000 from the Company in compensation for losing his commission. The Company paid only half, Clive paid the rest.

26. Sheppard,*Coote,* pp. 48–51

27. Bence-Jones,*Clive.,* p. 194; Sheppard, *Coote,* p. 61

28. Sheppard,*Coote,* p. 64, 65; Bence-Jones, *Clive* pp. 168, 180–182

29. McCance, Captain S, *History of the Royal Munster Fusiliers,* I, Aldershot, 1927, pp. 23, 24, 26, 66

30. Sheppard, *Coote,* p. 93; Mason, Philip, *A Matter of Honour,* London, 1974, p. 152

31. Sheppard, *Coote,* pp. 138, 141,164

32. Sheppard, *Ibid.,* pp.192 (quoting Sir John Fortescue, *History of the British Army,* III),193,194

33. McCance, *Munster Fusiliers*, I, pp. 46–48
34. Bidwell, Shelford, *Swords For Hire, European Mercenaries in Eighteenth Century India,* London, 1971, pp. 85–87, 208, 209, 211
35. Longford, Elizabeth, *Years of the Sword,* London, 1969, p. 45, 61, 65; Wilson, Joan, *Wellington's Marriage,* London, 1987, pp. 10–15
36. Hibbert, Christopher, *Wellington, a Personal History,* London, 1998, p. 14
37. Hibbert, *Ibid.* p. 23
38. Hibbert, *Ibid.* pp. 28 – 31. Some historians claim that Generals Baird and Harris were credited with defeating Tippu and that Wellesley's importance in taking Seringapatam has been exaggerated. See Dalrymple, William, *White Mughals,* London, 2002, footnote p. 193
39. Longford, *Wellington – Sword.*, p. 282
40. Bartlett, 'Defence, Counter-insurgency and Rebellion' in *A Military History of Ireland,* p. 257

Chapter Three (pp 39 – 72)

1. Longford, *Wellington, Sword*, p. 161; Hibbert, *Wellington,* p. 53
2. Wilson, *Wellington's Marriage,* London, 1987, pp. 13, 27, 30, 31
3. Guedalla, Philip, *The Duke,* London, 1931, p. vii
4. Hibbert, *Wellington,* pp. 68, 69
5. Longford, *Wellington, Sword*, pp. 201; Hibbert, *Wellington,* p. 78
6. Parkinson, Roger, *Moore of Corunna,* London, 1976, pp. 201, 212, 233, 234
7. Hibbert, Christopher, *Corunna,* London, 1972, pp. 189,190
8. Hibbert, *Wellington*, p. 94, ft. note; Pack-Beresford, D. T., *Memoir of Major General Sir Denis Pack,* Dublin, 1908, p. 2 ff: Law, H. W., *Book of the Beresford-Hopes,* London, 1925, p. 27
9. Bryant, A., *Jackets of Green,* London, 1972, pp. 22, 23, 31; Parkinson, *Moore,* pp. 125–27
10. Hibbert, *Wellington,* p.82; Bryant, *Jackets of Green,* pp. 30 footnote
11. Longford, *Wellington, Sword,* p. 247, 249; Wilson, *Wellington's Marriage,* p. 124. Wellington was the name of a village in Somerset (England) from where the family were said to originate, chosen by his brother William.
12. Grattan, William, *Adventures with the Connaught Rangers 1809–1814,* London, this edition 1989, pp. 17–20; Myatt, Frederick, *Peninsular General,* p. 78; Hibbert, *Wellington,* p. 170; Laurie, *Royal Irish Rifles,* pp. 138, 139
13. Gates, David, *The Spanish Ulcer, A History of the Peninsula War,* London, 1986, pp. 33–35
14. Parkinson, *The Peninsular War,* London, 1973, p. 109
15. Parkinson, *ibid,* p. 115
16. Longford, *Wellington, Sword,* p. 395
17. Harris, Rifleman, *Recollections of Rifleman Harris,* Ed. Curling, H., London, 1929, pp. 8–11,166–67
18. Hibbert, *Wellington,* p. 95,96
19. Longford, *Wellington, Sword,* pp. 319, 320; Gates, *Spanish Ulcer,* p. 272

20. Cunliffe, Marcus, *The Royal Irish Fusiliers, 1793–1950*,Oxford, 1952, pp. 95, 96,101, 107, 108

21. Grattan, *Connaught Rangers*, p. 67,69; Longford, *Wellington, Sword*, p. 318

22. Grattan, *Connaught Rangers*, pp. 147,149, 152–154; Myatt, Frederick, *British Sieges of the Peninsular War*, Tunbridge Wells, 1987, pp. 69, 71; Gates, *Spanish Ulcer*, p. 330

23. Grattan, *Connaught Rangers*, pp. 194, 196,197

24. Grattan, *Connaught Rangers*, p. 201; Fletcher, Ian, *In Hell Before Daylight*, Tunbridge Wells, 1984, pp. 64, 92, 93 *quoting Edward Costello's Adventures of a Soldier, 1841*

25. Fletcher, *In Hell*. p. 73 quoting Joseph Donaldson, *Recollections of the Eventful Life of a Soldier (1856);* 74, 79; Grattan, *Connaught Rangers*, p. 200

26. Grattan, *Connaught Rangers,* p. 205

27. Blakeney, Robert, *A Boy in the Peninsular War*, Ed. Julian Sturgis, London, this edition1989, pp. 273, 274, Intro. IX

28. Grattan,*Connaught Rangers*, pp. 242–50; Anglesey, Marquess of, *A History of the British Cavalry*, Vol. 1, London, 1973, pp. 54–55.

29. Gates, *Spanish Ulcer*, p. 358

30. Grattan,*Connaught Rangers*, p. 293, 311

31. Cunliffe, *Royal Irish Fusiliers*, pp.116,117, 118

32. Myatt, *Picton*, pp.168–69, Wellington later estimated that about a million pounds went into the pockets of the soldiers.

33. Longford,*Wellington, Sword*, p. 402–404; Hibbert, *Wellington*, p. 138

34. Myatt, *Picton*, p. 194, 195; Grattan, *Connaught Rangers*, pp. 334,338

35. Morton, Desmond, *A Military History of Canada*, Edmonton, 1985, p. 53, 55

36. Fitz Gibbon, Mary, A., *Veteran of 1812: the Life of James FitzGibbon*, Toronto, 1894, pp. 81–94, 139, 151, 163, 268; Morton, *Military History of Canada*, p. 61, 74

37. Phillips, R. B., *Patterns of Power: The Jasper Grant Collection and Great Lakes Indian Art of the Early Nineteenth Century*, Kleinburg, 1985, p. 22

38. *Royal Inniskilling Fusiliers*, pp. 243–248, Hitsman, J. M., *The Incredible War of 1812*, University of Toronto Press, 1965, p. 24; Morton, *Military History of Canada*, p. 68

39. Hitsman, *Incredible War*, p. 231

40. Whitton, F. E., *History of the Prince of Wales Leinster Regiment*, Aldershot, 1924, I, p. 28, 29, 32, 33; accounts vary, says Whitton.

41. Whitton, *Leinster Regiment*, p. 39; Hitsman, *Incredible War*, p. 172, 195, 196

42. Cunliffe, *Royal Irish Fusiliers*, pp. 148–152; Graves, Donald, E., ed., *Fighting for Canada*, Toronto, 2000, p. 133; Greenhous, Brereton, 'Militia Roots 1627–1867', in *We Stand on Guard*, An Illustrated History of the Canadian Army, ed. Marteinson, John, 1992, p. 13; 'Regulars' included Canadians whom Greenhous identifies as fencible regiments who were subject to harsh British discipline except they were not required to serve outside their own colony or province.

43. Maguire, W. A., 'Major General Ross and the Burning of Washington' in *Irish Sword*, vol. XIV, Winter 1980, no. 55, pp. 117–28; Hitsman, *Incredible War*, pp. 208–212 notes that the President's residence in Washington was rebuilt subsequently and received the name 'White House' since the walls were white-washed to hide the marks of the fire.

44. Spiers, Edward M., *Radical General, Sir George De Lacy Evans,* Manchester, pp. 4–13; Longford, *Wellington, Sword,* p. 465, footnote

45. Myatt, *Picton,* p. 204; Holmes, Richard, *Redcoat,* London, 2001, p. 344 claims Picton begged Wellington not to take him . . . his nerves were shattered.

46. Myatt, *Picton,* p. 214; Roberts, Andrew, *Napoleon & Wellington,* London, 2001, pp. 155,158, 169

47. *Irish Times,* 9 January, 1929. Graham's son served in the 89th Foot; Pericoli, Ugo, Glover Michael, *1815 – The Armies at Waterloo,* 1973, p. 44

48. Longford, *Wellington, Sword,* pp. 556 – 557 Myatt, *Picton,* p. 222; Anglesey, *British Cavalry,* 1, pp. 58, 59. The figure of an Inniskilling Dragoon is part of the magnificent Wellington memorial, Hyde Park Corner, London.

49. Anglesey, *British Cavalry,* 1, p. 60; Howarth, David, *Waterloo: Day of Battle,* New York, 1968, pp.205, 206

50. Howarth, *Waterloo,* pp. 178, 181,182; Roberts, *Napoleon & Wellington,* p. 183; Longford, *Wellington, Sword,* pp. 574–577

51. Kincaid, J., *Adventures in the Rifle Brigade,* London, 1830, pp. 341–52; *Royal Inniskilling Fusiliers,* pp. 267, 268, 271; The 27th wore a replica of the castle at Enniskillen on their shako badges.; Longford, *Wellington, Sword.,* p. 579, 590; Keegan, John, *The Face of Battle,* Penguin, 1976, 128, 129

52. Verner, Ruth, *Reminiscences of William Verner (1782–1871),* London, 1965, pp. 57–8; cf. Richardson, E. M., *Long Forgotten Days,* London, 1928, p. 384

53. Longford, Elizabeth, *Wellington: Pillar of State,* London, 1972, p. 5: de Lancey, *A Week at Waterloo in 1815,* Ed. Major B. R. Ward, London, 1906, p. 14

54. Hibbert, *Wellington,* pp. 185; Butler, Elizabeth, *An Autobiography,* London, 1922, p.36

55. Brett-James, Antony, 'Wellington's Army' in *The History of the British Army,* Eds., Young, Peter, & Lawford, J.P., London, 1970, p. 127

56. O'Callaghan, J. C., *History of the Irish Brigades,* London, 1886, pp. 615–616, footnote

57. Longford, *Wellington, Pillar,* p. 114

Chapter 4 (pp 73 – 90)

1. *Royal Inniskilling Fusiliers,* p. 272; Costello, Edward, *Adventures of a Soldier,* London, 1852, pp. 207–13

2. *Royal Inniskilling Fusiliers,* p. 278; Myatt, Frederick, *The British Infantry 1660–1945.,* Poole, 1983, pp. 104, 107

3. Spiers, E. M., 'Army Organization and Society' in Bartlett and Jeffery *A Military History of Ireland,* pp. 336, 339; Cunliffe, *Royal Irish Fusiliers,* p. 231;

Cockerill, H. W., *Sons of the Brave, the Story of Boy Soldiers*, London, 1984, p. 95

4. Ascoli,*Companion to the British Army*, Preface p. 9
5. Dinwiddy, J. R., 'Early Nineteenth Century Campaign against Flogging in the Army', *E H R* 1982, XCVII, pp. 308–31; Bonham-Carter, V., *Soldier True*, London, 1963, p. 7; MacMullen, J. M., *Camp and Barrack Room*, London, 1846, p. 142–144; Anglesey, *British Cavalry*, 1, p. 141, quoting the Duke of Wellington in 1829
6. O'Malley, James, *Life of James O'Malley*, Montreal, 1893, p. 16–37
7. Faughnan, Thomas, *Stirring Incidents in the Life of a British Soldier*, Toronto, 1882, p. 99
8. Brewer, J. D., *Royal Irish Constabulary*, Belfast, 1990, p. 3; Broeker, *Rural Disorder and Police Reform in Ireland 1812–1836*, London, 1970, pp. 33, 86, 239; Barrington, Sir Jonah, *Personal Sketches of His Own Times*, London, 1869, II, pp. 327–328, 344; O'Connell, P., *Irish Faction Fighters of the Nineteenth Century*, Dublin, 1966, p. 113; James N. Healy, *Percy French and his Songs*, Dublin, 1966, p. 132 Cornelius, however, had other ideas . . . .
9. Bardon, Johnathan, *History of Ulster*, Belfast, 1992, p. 247.
10. Harris, *Royal Irish Fusiliers*, p. 59; Cunliffe, *Royal Irish Fusiliers*, p. 194
11. Kipling, Rudyard, *The Complete Barrack Room Ballads*, ed.by Charles Carrington, London, 1974, p. 36
12. Cadell, Patrick, 'Irish Soldiers in India' *Irish Sword* 1950–51, I No. 2, pp. 75–80; Spiers, E. M., 'Army Organization of Society in the Nineteenth Century' in *A Military History of Ireland*, p. 336
13. Murray, R. H., *History of the VIII King's Royal Irish Hussars, 1693–1928*, I, 1928, p. 363; Anglesey, *British Cavalry*,1, pp. 68, 69 192; Newbolt, Henry, *Poems Old and New*, London, 1917, p. 57; Farwell, Byron, *The Gurkhas*, London, 1985, p. 29
14. Shipp, John, *The Path of Glory: Being the Memoirs of the Extraordinary Military Career of John Shipp*, Ed. Stranks, C.J., London, 1969, pp. 101, 106, 115, 116; Judy Flanagan's name for the 87th 'the Fogs', came from the 2nd 87th 'The Faughs', which in turn came from their battle cry at Barossa 'Faugh a Ballagh' (clear the way).
15. Hervey, Albert, *Soldier of the Company: Life of an Indian Ensign, 1833–1843*, first published 1853, ed. Allen, Charles, London, 1988, pp.179–184; Brereton, *The British Soldier*, pp. 83–88; Moriarty, Maurice 'an Irish NCO in India 1845–48' in Notes – *Irish Sword*, Vol. II, #9, 1956
16. Farwell, Byron, *QueenVictoria's Little Wars*, London, 1972, pp. 6–9
17. Farwell, Byron, *Mr. Kipling's Army*, London, 1981, p. 80; MacMullen, *Camp and Barrack Room*, pp. 134–136, 163–169, 207, Father Mathew was the renowned Irish temperance preacher
18. Morris, James, *Heaven's Command*, Penguin Books, 1973, pp. 177
19. Featherstone, *India*, pp. 16, 20, 22; Morris, *Heaven's Command*. p. 180
20. Featherstone, *India*, pp. 51–52; McCance, Royal Munster Fusiliers, I, pp. 118, 119; Harries-Jenkins, *The Army in Victorian Society*, p. 15

21. Mason, *A Matter of Honour*, p. 231; Featherstone, Donald, *All For a Shilling a Day*, London, 1966, p.106 and his *India*, p. 86

22. Farwell, *Eminent Victorian Soldiers*, p. 59; cf. Crawford, E. R., 'The Sikh Wars, 1845–1849' in *Victorian Military Campaigns*, ed. Brian Bond, N.Y. 1967; Featherstone, *India*, p. 96 quoting *Punch*.

23. Mason; *Matter of Honour*, p. 529

24. Gretton, *Royal Irish Regiment*, pp. 155, 156

25. Longford,*Wellington, Pillar*, pp. 372–374.

Chapter 5 (pp 91 – 101)

1.   MacDonagh, Oliver, 'Irish Emigration to the United States of America and the British Colonies During the Famine', in *Great Famine*, eds. Edwards, R. D. and Williams, T. D., Dublin, 1962, p. 328

2.   Harries-Jenkins, G., *Army in Victorian Society*, p. 204 – 205; Prebble, John, *Highland Clearances*, London, 1963, pp. 180–185, 295–302. Only three Highland regiments went to the Crimea, 42nd, 79th and 93rd.

3.   Judd, Denis, *The Crimean War*, London, 1975, p. 28

4.   Griffin, Brian; 'Ireland and the Crimean War' in *The Irish Sword*, Vol. XXII, #89, 2001, pp. 281–312

5.   Gretton, *Royal Irish Regiment*, p. 164

6.   Murray, R. H.,*VIIIth Royal Irish Hussars*, II, p. 407; Tisdall, E. E. P., *Mrs. Duberly's Campaigns*, London, 1964, p. 26

7.   Evans, R., *5th Royal Inniskilling Dragoon Guards*, pp. 68, 69

8.   Judd,*Crimean War*, pp. 38–40,120; Russell, W. H., *Despatches From the Crimea*, Ed. Nicolas Bentley, London, Panther Edition, 1970, pp. 12–14

9.   Lehmann, Joseph, *The Model Major-General*, Boston, 1964, p. 25

10. Holmes, *Redcoat*, pp. 62–63

11. Brereton, *4th/7th Royal Dragoon Guards*, p. 221

12. Russell, *Despatches*, p. 122; Anglesey, *British Cavalry*, 2, pp. 74, 75

13. Moyse-Bartlett, H., *Louis Edward Nolan*, London, 1971, for early life; Anglesey, *British Cavalry*, 2, pp. 83, 84, 94, 96,108; Pemberton, W. B., *Battles of the Crimean War*, London, 1968, p. 120; Woodham-Smith, C., *The Reason Why*, London, 1958, pp. 241–251

14. Calthorpe, S. J. G., *Cadogan's Crimea*, N.Y., 1980, p. 100; Pemberton, *Battles of the Crimean War*, p. 173

15. Cunliffe, *Royal Irish Fusiliers* pp. 210; Pemberton, *Battles of the CrimeanWar*, pp. 185

16. Gretton, *Royal Irish Regiment*, pp. 177, 178; Pemberton, *Battles of the Crimean War*, pp. 213, 214

17. Faughnan, Thomas, *Stirring Incidents in the Life of a British Soldier*, Toronto, 1882, p. 216 – 218

18. Steevens, Lt. Col. N., *The Crimean Campaign with the Connaught Rangers*, London, 1878, pp. 4, 23, 227, for the 'exuberance' of even the Connaught Rangers' women who stopped Turks running from Cossacks at Balaclava;

Jourdain, H.F.N. and Fraser, Edward, *Connaught Rangers,* III, London, 1928, pp.179 – 181; Griffin, Brian; 'Ireland in the Crimean War' p. 294 quoting Cork Examiner, *Irish Sword,* 389

19. Holmes, *Redcoat,* p. 249; Russell's Despatches, p.153
20. *Belfast Telegraph* 4 November 1985 and 14 April 1988 remembered VC exploits and notes. John Byrne was often in the cells when not at war.

Chapter Six (pp 102 – 121)

1. Montgomery, Brian, *Monty's Grandfather,* Poole, 1984, pp. 30, 31, 41, 44, and, *A Field-Marshal in the Family,* New York, 1974, p. 38; Hibbert, Christopher, *The Great Mutiny,* Penguin Books, 1978, pp. 217, 218; Morris, James, *Heaven's Command,* pp. 182, 183 re George Lawrence.
2. Pearson, Hesketh, *The Hero of Delhi, The Life of John Nicholson,* Penguin Books, New York, pp.153–156, 148
3. Moorhouse, Geoffrey, *India Britannica,* London, 1984, pp. 85, 86; refers to *From Sepoy to Subedar,* the memoirs of Sita Ram Pande, ed. James Lunt, London, 1970
4. Anglesey, *British Cavalry,* 2, 1851–1871, p. 150
5. Hibbert, *The Great Mutiny,* pp. 130, 131
6. Anglesey, *British Cavalry,* 2, pp. 150–154, 157. Guides are said to be the first soldiers to wear khaki.
7. Featherstone, Donald, *Colonial Victorian Warfare – India,* London, 1993, pp. 123–125; Hibbert, *Great Mutiny,* pp. 175, 177, 189, 191–196
8. Pearson, *Hero of Delhi,* p. 235; Lehmann, *Model Major-General,* p. 51
9. Pearson, *Hero of Delhi,* pp. 67, 76, 94, 95, 177; Allen, Charles, *Soldier Sahibs,* New York, 2001, p. 218
10. Harris, John, *The Indian Mutiny.,* London, 1973, pp. 134–36; Pearson, *Hero of Delhi,* pp. 234–237, accounts vary; McCance, *Munster Fusiliers,* 1, pp. 153–154
11. Hibbert, *Great Mutiny,* p. 424, quoting from Roberts, *Forty-one Years in India,* London, 1897, p. 130 and from Wilberforce, R.G., *An unrecorded Chapter of the Indian Mutiny,* London, 1894, p. 201; Callwell, Major-Gen. Sir C. E., *Field Marshal Sir Henry Wilson, His Life and Diaries,* London, 1927, I, p. 53 and II, p. 321
12. MacCauley, J. A., 'The Dublin Fusiliers' in *Irish Sword,* no. 25, Vol. VI, 1964, p. 265
13. Hibbert, *Great Mutiny,* p. 200
14. Annand, M. K., 'Lucknow Kavanagh and the 1st European Bengal Fusiliers, 1858' in *Journal for Army Historical Research,* 1966, XVIV, No. 179, pp. 178–82
15. Lehmann, *Model Major-General,* pp. 64, 65, 67
16. Harris, *Indian Mutiny,* pp. 191,198 quoting from Russell's *My Indian Mutiny Diary,* London, 1951
17. *The Victoria Crosses and George Crosses of the Honourable East India Company*

and Indian Army 1856–1945 – a National Army Museum Publication, May 1, 1962, pp. 13, 15

18. Anglesey, *British Cavalry*, 2, p. 235
19. Dooley, Thomas P., *Irishmen or English Soldiers?*, Liverpool, University Press, 1995, p. 43
20. Swinson, Arthur, *North-West Frontier*, London, 1969, pp. 222–224; Anglsey, *British Cavalry*, 3, pp. 266–267
21. Kipling, *Barrack Room Ballads*, p. 92
22. Mason, Philip, A *Matter of Honour*, London, 1974, pp. 347 (quoting Roberts, *Forty-one Years)*, 348
23. Dooley, *Irishmen or English Soldiers ?*, p. 43
24. Caball, John, *Rose of Tralee*, Tralee, 1864, pp. 24, 25; a verse not always included in anthologies of Irish verse.
25. General Sir O'Moore Creagh, *Autobiography*, London, 1925, pp. 147–150,`162, 183
26. Brereton, *4th/7th Dragoon Guards*, pp. 268–69, cf, Younghusband, George, *Soldiers Memories in Peace and War*, London, 1917, pp. 294–95
27. Kipling, *Barrack Room Ballads*, Carrington, Charles, Intro. p. 12
28. Kipling, Rudyard, 'With the Main Guard' in *Soldiers Three*, Frome, this edition 1986, pp. 50–64
29. McCourt, Frank, *Angela's Ashes*, N.Y., 1996, p. 120.

Chapter Seven (pp 122 – 158)

1. Reid, Brian, 'The Battle of Ridgeway, June 2, 1866' in *Fighting for Canada, Seven Battles 1758–1945*, Graves, Donald E., Ed., Toronto, 2000, pp. 137–181
2. Lehmann, *Model Major-General*, pp. 132–33
3. McCourt, *Remember Butler*, Toronto, 1967, pp. 40–42
4. Butler, Sir William; *Autobiography*, London, 1913, p. 113
5. McCourt, *Remember Butler*, pp. 43, 44
6. McCalmont, Sir Hugh, KCB, CVO, *Memoirs*, Ed. by Major-General Sir Charles Calliwell, KCB London, 1924, p. 47.
7. McCourt, *Remember Butler*, pp. 50–54
8. Lehmann, *Model Major-General*, p. 158
9. McCourt, *Remember Butler*, pp. 59, 80
10. *Ibid.*, p. 94; Featherstone, *Africa*, p. 28
11. *Inniskilling Fusiliers*, pp. 290, 292–300
12. *Ibid.*, p. 302, and footnote quoting MacLean anecdote from *Sprig of Shillelagh*, August 1, 1893; pp. 303, 304, 312
13. Lehmann, *Model Major-General*, pp. 159–162; Abolition of Puchase Bill was passed in House of Commons in the summer of 1871.
14. McCourt, *Remember Butler* p. 91
15. Featherstone, *Africa*, p. 30
16. Lehmann, *Model Major-General*, p. 177

17. McCourt, *Remember Butler*, p. 108
18. Lehmann, *Model Major-General*, p. 187. Regulars sent: one battalion each of the Black Watch (42nd Highlanders), Rifle Brigade, Royal Welch Fusiliers, and units of Royal Artillery and Royal Engineers.
19. Featherstone, *Africa*, p. 34; Lehman, *Model Major-General*, pp. 192, 197, 207
20. McCourt, *Remember Butler*, pp. 110, 111
21. *Ibid.*, p. 114; Lehmann, *Model Major-General*, p. 210
22. Lehmann, *Model Major-General*, p. 217 quoting Sir John Robinson, *A Lifetime in South Africa*, London, 1900, p. 39
23. McCourt, *Remember Butler*, p. 118
24. Morris, Donald R., *Washing Of the Spears*, London, this edition 1968, pp. 168–69
25. Farwell, Byron, *The Great Anglo-Boer War*, N.Y., 1976, pp. 121–22
26. Morris, *Washing of the Spears*, pp. 216–217, 227
27. Barthorp, Michael, *The Zulu War, A Pictorial History*, London, 1988, pp. 40, 45; Morris, *Washing of the Spears*, pp. 309, 331
28. Featherstone, *Africa*, p. 119
29. Morris, *Washing of the Spears*, pp. 360, 362, 364; Knight, Ian, *Brave Men's Blood, The Epic of the Zulu War, 1879*, London, 1990, pp. 58, 60
30. Morris, *Washing of the Spears*, pp. 371, 375, 378; Knight, *Brave Men's Blood*, p. 66; Featherstone, *Africa*, p. 129
31. Morris, *Washing of the Spears*, p. 385
32. *Ibid.*, p. 619; Barthorp, *Zulu War*, p. 67
33. Barthorp, *Zulu War*, pp. 66, 67; Morris, *Washing of the Spears,* pp. 387, 388, 589. Lt. Higginson reported their brave feat making possible their VC (posthumously).
34. Barthorp, *Zulu War*, p. 87
35. Yorke, Edmund, *Rorke's Drift,* Gloucestershire, 2001, pp. 39, 149
36. Barthorp, *Zulu War*, p. 77; Whitton Col. F.E., *Rorkes Drift, The Zulu War of 1879,* reprinted from Blackwood's magazine January 1879
37. Lehman, *Model Major-General,* pp. 245, 246, Admiral Nelson was the Hero of the Battle of Trafalgar in 1805.
38. *Ibid.*, pp. 253, 254; Chelmsford later claimed he thought Cetshwayo would have surrendered, as did Wolseley who in his correspondence referred to Chelmsford's stupidity in not pursuing Cetshwayo.
39. Morris, *Washing of the Spears*, pp. 563, 572
40. McCourt, *Remember Butler*, p. 139
41. Maurice, Major General Sir F., *Life of Wolseley,* London, 1924, pp. 120, 123
42. Lehmann, *Model Major-General*, pp. 272, 277
43. Farwell, *Eminent Victorian Soldiers*, p. 222; Lehmann, *Model Major-General*, p. 288
44. Harries-Jenkins, Gwyn, *The Army in Victorian Society*, Great Britain, 1977, pp. 82,192
45. Farwell, *Anglo-Boer War*, pp. 17–19; Barthorp, Michael, *The Anglo-Boer Wars*, Poole, 1987, pp. 35, 36, 39, 42

46. Morris, James, *Heaven's Command.*, p. 443; McCourt, *Remember Butler*, p. 141

47. McCourt, *Remember Butler*, p. 150; Butler, *Autobiography*, p. 219

48. McCourt, *op. cit.*, p. 151

49. Gretton, *Royal Irish Regiment*, p. 247; Cunliffe, *Royal Irish Fusiliers*, p. 237

50. *Lady Butler, Battle Artist 1846–1933*, Exhibition Catalogue, National Army Museum, London, 1987, p. 88

51. McCourt, *Remember Butler*, p. 159; Strachey, Lytton, 'The End of General Gordon' in *Eminent Victorians*, Penguin Books, 1948, pp. 264, 265; MacGregor-Hastie, Roy; *Never to be Taken Alive*, London, 1985, p. 160

52. McCourt, *Remember Butler*, p. 168; Butler, Sir William, *Charles George Gordon*, London, 1889, p. 252; Morris, James, *Heaven's Command*, p. 497

53. McCourt, *Remember Butler*, pp. 167–168

54. Preston, A., *In Relief of Gordon, Lord Wolseley's Campaign Journal of the Khartoum Relief Expedition 1884–1885*, London, 1967, p. 171; McCourt, *Remember Butler*, p. 173

55. Gretton, *Royal Irish Regiment*, pp. 263, 264, 270

56. Anglesey, *British Cavalry*, 3, p.332; Barthorp, Michael, *War on the Nile*, London, 1984, p. 103. Except the Hussars, all were on camels, Guards, infantry of the 1st Royal Sussex, 2nd Essex, sailors and gunners. and Beresford was on a white pony.

57. Kipling, *Barrack Room Ballads*, p. 56

58. Barthorp, *War on the Nile*, p. 107

59. MacGregor-Hastie, *Never to be Taken Alive*, p. 175.; Barthorp, *War on the Nile*, pp. 109,112; McCourt, *Remember Butler*, p. 177

60. McCourt, *Remember Butler*, pp. 182–84, 186

Chapter Eight (pp 159 – 195)

1. *Royal Inniskilling Fusiliers*, p. 382; O'Brien, Joseph V., *Dear Dirty Dublin, a City in Distress 1899–1916*, London, 1982, p. 243; Fitzpatrick, 'Militarism in Ireland 1900–1922' in *A Military History of Ireland*, p. 380

2. McCourt, *Remember Butler*, p. 220

3. *Ibid.*, pp. 225, 229, 242

4. Lehmann, *Model Major-General*, p. 386

5. Cunliffe, *Royal Irish Fusiliers*, pp. 249–251; Farwell, Byron, *Anglo-Boer War*, pp. 63, 64, 67

6. Holmes, Richard, *The Little Field Marshal, Sir John French*, London, 1981, pp. 15–20, 64, 66

7. Anglesey, *British Cavalry*, 4, pp. 52–57; Farwell, *Anglo-Boer War*, p. 73

8. Holmes, *Little Field Marshal*, p. 68

9. Cunliffe, *Royal Irish Fusiliers*, pp. 253–55; Kruger, *Dolly Gray*, pp. 91–95

10. Kee, Robert, *The Green Flag*, London, 1972, pp. 443, 444, 575; Fitzpatrick, 'Militarism in Ireland 1900–1922' in *Military History of Ireland*, p. 380

11. Godley, Sir Alexander, *Life of An Irish Soldier*, London, 1939, pp. 66, 87

12. Judd, Dennis, *The Boer War*, London, 1977 p. 108; Pakenham, Thomas, *Boer War,* London, 1982, p. 397

13. Grinnell-Milne, Duncan, *Mafeking*, London, 1957, p. 72; Neilly, J. E., *Besieged with B-P*, London, 1900, p. 91

14. Grinnell-Milne, *Mafeking*, pp. 108–111; Pakenham, *Boer War*, p. 405

15. O'Meara, Lt/Col W. A., CMG, *Kekewich in Kimberley*, London, 1926, p. 120

16. Laurie, *Royal Irish Rifles*, pp. 371 – 375

17. Harries-Jenkins, *Army and Victorian Society*, pp. 54–55

18. Kruger, *Dolly Gray,* p. 140; MacCauley, James, A., 'The Dublin Fusiliers' in *Irish Sword*, VI, pp. 267–269

19. Todd, Pamela, Fordham, David, Eds., *Private Tucker's Boer War Diary*, London, 1988, p. 33

20. Pakenham, *Boer War*, pp. 214, 235

21. Pakenham, *Boer War,* pp. 229, 361; Robertson, Nora, *Crowned Harp,* Dublin, 1960, pp. 21–30

22. Callwell, Maj/Gen. Sir C. E., KCB, *Field-Marshal Sir Henry Wilson, Bart., GCB., DSO, His Life And Diaries*, Vol. I, London, 1972, I, pp. 29, 33; Ash, Bernard, *The Last Dictator, Field Marshal Sir Henry Wilson*, London, 1968, p. 33; Head, Lt/Col. C. O., DSO, *The Art of Generalship*, Aldershot, n.d., p. 137

23. Lehmann, *Model Major-General*, p. 387

24. Kipling, *Barrack Room Ballads*, pp. 92–94 'an'arder' means 'and a half', Bahadur – (Indian), refers to bold knight or hero, courageous; Farwell, *Anglo-Boer War*, p. 153

25. Lehmann, *Model Major General*, p. 387, 388; James, David, *Lord Roberts*, London, 1954, p. 232; McCourt, *Remember Butler.*, p. 257

26. Barnett, Correlli, *Britain and Her Army 1509–1970*, Penguin Books, 1970, pp. 314–15; Royle, Trevor, *The Kitchener Enigma*, London, 1985, pp. 10, 41, 153

27. Holmes, *Little Field-Marshal*, p. 84

28. Pakenham, *Boer War*, p. 333

29. Gretton, *Royal Irish Regiment*, p. 365; Corbally, Lt/Col. M. J. P. M., *The Royal Ulster Rifles, 1739–1960*, Belfast, 1960, p. 88

30. Maxse, Colonel F. I., CB, DSO, *Seymour Vandeleur The Story of a British Officer*, London, 1905, pp. 263, 249

31. Holmes, *Little Field Marshal*, pp. 85, 92

32. Anglesey, *British Cavalry*, 4, p.136; Pakenham, *Boer War*, p. 327; Holmes, *Little Field-Marshal*, pp. 92, 93

33. *Royal Inniskilling Fusiliers*, pp. 419–422, 441; Barthorp, *Anglo-Boer Wars*, pp. 114, 115

34. *Royal Inniskilling Fusiliers*, p. 443, 444, 445; Pakenham, *Boer War*, p. 358

35. Cunliffe, *Royal Irish Fusiliers*, p. 259; Barthorp, *Anglo-Boer Wars*, p. 116, A combined account of these actions. Caton-Woodville's painting 'My Brave Irish' depicts this last charge.

36. Farrar-Hockley, *Goughie,* London, 1975, p. 52; Farwell, *Anglo-Boer War,* p. 233
37. Beckett, Ian W., *Johnnie Gough, VC,* London, 1989, pp. 51, 66
38. Cunliffe, *Royal Irish Fusiliers,* p. 260
39. Barthorp, *Anglo-Boer Wars,* p. 108; Royle, *Kitchener* pp.169–171; Farwell, *Anglo-Boer War,* p. 216, wonders if Kitchener's more aggressive tactics might has saved lives despite high casualties.
40. Pakenham, *Boer War,* pp. 341, 342, information from Kelly-Kenny's diary which Pakenham says had not been revealed before.
41. Kruger, *Dolly Gray,* p. 247
42. Verney, Peter, *The Micks – The Story of the Irish Guards,* London, 1970, pp. 1–3, 7
43. Powell, Geoffrey, *Plumer, The Soldier's General,* London, 1990, p. 69; Kruger, *Dolly Gray,* p. 297
44. Pakenham, *Boer War* p. 415; Grinnell-Milne, *Mafeking,* pp. 176,179; Farwell, *Anglo-Boer War,* p. 271
45. Anglesey, *British Cavalry,* 4, pp. 176, 177; Ervine, St. John, *Craigavon – Ulsterman,* London, 1949, pp. 55,58,61; Pakenham, *Boer War,* p. 436
46. Anglesey, *British Cavalry,* 4, pp. 177–182
47. Ervine,*Craigavon,* pp. 63, 64
48. Wilkinson, Burke, *The Zeal of the Convert – The Life of Erskine Childers,* Sag Harbour, N.Y., 1976, pp.1–16, 43, 48–51
49. Pakenham, *Boer War,* pp. 433–434, 441–444, 451; Barthorp, *Anglo-Boer Wars.,* pp. 128–129
50 Pakenham, *Boer War,* p. 455; *Royal Inniskilling Fusiliers,* pp. 465, 469, 470
51. James, *Roberts,* pp. 358,59
52. Pakenham, *Boer War,* p. 448; Roberts's ADC, Lord Kerry, admitted that Roberts's hard line was probably due to Lady Roberts who was hostile to Boer women and children.
53. Gretton, *Royal Irish Regiment,* p. 351
54. Maxse, *Seymour Vandeleur,* pp. 281–287
55. Farrar-Hockley, *Goughie,* pp. 66,68; Anglesey, *British Cavalry,* 4, pp. 264, 265
56. Holmes, *Little Field Marshal,* p. 112
57. Robertson,*Crowned Harp,* pp. 55,56

Chapter Nine (pp 196 – 241)

1. Jourdain, Lt-Col. H. F. N., *Ranging Memories,* Oxford, 1934, pp.15, 16, 148; Denman Terence,*Ireland's Unknown Soldiers,* Blackrock, 1992, p. 117 refers to Jourdain's Anglo-Irish Protestant stock.
2. Lucy, John, *There's a Devil In The Drum,* Dallington, this edition1992, pp. 15, 37, 68, 69. Quotes from John Lucy will be from this work unless otherwise stated.
3. Kee, *The Green Flag,* pp. 486, 488

4. Beckett, *Johnnie Gough, V.C.*, pp. 153, 167
5. Foster, R. F., *Modern Ireland 1600–1922*, London, 1988, p. 469
6. Beckett, *Johnnie Gough,V.C.*, p. 151
7. Gough, Sir Hubert, *Soldiering On*, London, 1954, p. 100
8. Holmes, *Little Field Marshal*, pp. 193–94
9. Ash, *Last Dictator*, p. 108; Beckett, *Johnnie Gough, V.C.*, p. 173
10. Holmes, *Little Field Marshal*, pp. 203, 209
11. Meehan's War Service Record, *Charrier File 6307/86/1105* I.W.M. read by author at National War Museum; Fitzpatrick, 'Militarism in Ireland 1900–1922', *A Military History of Ireland*, p. 388
12. Whitton, *Leinster Regiment*, II, p. 12
13. Harris, *Irish Regiments in The First World War*, p. 12
14. Verney, Peter, *The Micks, The Story of the Irish Guards*, London, 1970, pp. 15–17; p. 36 re RIC; Grayson, T.H.H., *A Short History of the Irish Guards 1900–1927*, Colchester, 1931, p. 50; Bence-Jones, M., *Twilight of the Ascendancy*, London, 1987, p. 57 for Morris family.
15. Barthorp, Michael, *The Old Contemptibles*, London, 1989, p. 3
16. Coombs, Rose, MBE, *Before Endeavours Fade,* 'Guide to the Battlefields of The First World War', London, first published 1976, p. 108; Brereton,*4th/7th Royal Dragoon Guards*, pp. 310–311
17. Ascoli, David, *The Mons Star, British Expeditionary Force 1914*, London, 1981, p. 65; Bence-Jones, *Twilight of The Ascendancy*, p. 51; Lavery, Felix, compiler in 'Irish Heroes of the War' military section, London, 1917, pp. 262, 263
18. Ascoli, *Mons Star*, p. 4
19. Johnstone, Tom, *Orange, Green & Khaki, The Story of the Irish Regiments in the Great War 1914–18*, Dublin, 1992, pp. 18, 71
20. Holmes, *Little Field Marshal*, p. 217
21. *Charrier File #6307/86/1105*, IWM (Imperial War Museum)
22. McCance, *Royal Munster Fusiliers*, II, pp. 114–19; Johnstone, *Orange Green and Khaki*, pp. 33–34; Staunton, Martin, *The Royal Munster Fusiliers in the Great War 1914–19*, unpublished thesis for MA National University of Ireland, University College, Dublin, 1986, p. 121; *Charrier File*, McKee Correspondence; Jervis, H. S., *The 2nd Munsters in France*, Aldershot, 1922, p.2
23. Kipling, Rudyard, *The Irish Guards in the Great War*, I, Toronto, 1923, pp. 10–12; MacDonagh, Michael, *The Irish at The Front*, London, 1916, p. 26; Verney, *The Micks*, p. 25
24. Hamilton, Nigel, *Monty, The Making of a General 1887–1942*, London, 1981, pp. 78–79, 87–89; Montgomery, Brian, *A Field Marshal in the Family*, New York, 1974, p. 159; Carver, Michael, 'Field Marshal Viscount Montgomery' in *Churchill's Generals*, Ed. John Keegan, London, this edtion1995, pp. 150, 151
25. Hitchcock, Captain F. C., MC, *"Stand To" A Diary of the Trenches*, London, 1937, pp. 12, 261; Whitton, *Leinster Regiment*, II, pp. 67, 68

26. Kipling, *Irish Guards, I*, p. 42, p. X
27. McCance, *Royal Munster Fusiliers*, II, pp. 122, 123
28. Corbally, M. J., *The Royal Ulster Rifles*, Glasgow, 1960, p. 104; Macdonald, Lyn, *1914 –1918 Voices and Images of the Great War*, Penguin Books,1991, pp. 47, 48; Grattan, *Connaught Rangers*, pp. 230, 231
29. Denman, *Ireland's Unknown Soldiers*, p. 31
30. Cooper, Major Bryan, *The Tenth (Irish) Division in Gallipoli*, London, 1918, Foreword by John Redmond pp. VIII, XII
31. Cooper, *10th (Irish)*, pp. 4–6
32. Robinson, Lennox, *Bryan Cooper*, London, 1931, pp. 27, 28, 91, 98
33. Cooper, *10th (Irish)*; pp. 13–15
34. Hanna, Henry (KC), *The Pals at Suvla Bay*, The Record of 'D' Company of the 7th Royal Dublin Fusiliers, Dublin, 1916, pp. 14–23, 58
35. Curtayne, Alice, *Francis Ledwidge: A Life of the Poet 1887–1917*, London, 1972, pp. 15, 84; Cross, Tim, *The Lost Voices of World War I*, London, 1988, p. 37
36. Perry, Nicholas, 'Nationality in the Irish Infantry Regiments in the First World War' in *War and Society*, Vol. 2, Number 1, May 1994, p. 77
37. Orr, Philip, *The Road to the Somme*, Belfast, 1987, pp. 41, 45
38. Falls, Cyril, *The History of the 36th Ulster Division*, London, pp. 12,13
39. Ervine, St John, *Craigavon, Ulsterman*, p. 298, 310
40. Royle, Trevor, *The Kitchener Enigma*, pp. 271, 272; A group of Irish Volunteers disagreeing with Redmond's support of the war broke away while the Redmondite rump became the Irish National Volunteers.
41. Denman, *Ireland's Unknown Soldiers*, p. 40; Royle, *Kitchener*, p. 274
42. Denman, *Ireland's Unknown Soldiers*, p. 179; Dooley, Thomas P., *Irishmen or English Soldiers?*, Liverpool, 1995, p. 196. Some writers thought that the New Army soldiers' loyalty to the regiment was transferred to the division by 1915.
43. Lyons, J. B., *The Enigma of Tom Kettle*, Dublin, 1983, pp. 252, 267, 278
44. Gwynn, Stephen, *Experiences of a Literary Man*, London, 1926, pp. 241, 302
45. Denman, Terence, 'A voice from the lonely grave': the death in action of Major William Redmond, MP, 7 June 1917', in *Irish Sword*, Vol. XVIII, No. 73,1992, pp. 286, 288, 291, 292
46. Gwynn, Stephen, *The Last Years of John Redmond*, p. 183; Robertson, Nora, *Crowned Harp*, Dublin, 1960, pp. 126, 127,133
47. Dooley, *Irishmen or English Soldiers?*, pp. 198, 199; Sheehan, Daniel, *Ireland Since Parnell*, London, 1921, pp. 287–288; Gwynn, Stephen and Kettle, T. M., *Battle Songs for the Irish Brigade*, Dublin, 1915, Preface p. V
48. Johnstone,*Orange Green & Khaki*, p. 221; Perry, Nick, 'Politics and Command: General Nugent, the Ulster Division and Relations with Ulster Unionism 1915–17' in *'Look to Your Front'*, Brian Bond et al, Staplehurst, 1999, pp. 105–107
49. Johnstone, *Orange Green & Khaki*, p. 203; Dooley, *Irishmen or English Soldiers?*, pp. 194, 195

50. Denman, *Ireland's Unknown Soldiers*, p. 36; Orr, *Road to the Somme*, p. 73
51. Verney, *The Micks*, p. 35; O'Leary was also called Canada's first VC of the War. He went on the Reserve and, emigrating to Canada, joined the North-West Mounted Police. On the outbreak of the war O'Leary was recalled to the Colours to the 1st Battalion Irish Guards in France.; *See* Lavery, Felix, *Irish Heroes in the War*, p. 256; Tierney, Mark; Bowen, Paul; Fitzpatrick, David, 'Recruiting Posters' in *Ireland and The First World War*, Trinity History Workshop, Dublin, 1990, pp. 57ff.
52. James, Robert Rhodes; *Gallipoli*, London, 1984, This edition 1984, pp. 58, 65, 68; Johnstone, Tom, *Orange, Green & Khaki*, p. 100
53. 'The Dublins in the Dardanelles' in *Royal Munster Fusilier Association Journal*, No. 6,1995, p. 23
54. Dungan, *Irish Voices*, p. 41; McCance, *Munster Fusiliers*, II, p. 49; Johnstone, *Orange Green & Khaki*, pp. 103,104
55. Clark, Brian, 'Lieutenant Henry Desmond O'Hara, D SO, The Royal Dublin Fusiliers', in *Irish Sword*, Vol. XVIII, #73, 1992, pp. 305, 306; Creighton, Rev. O., *With the 29th Division in Gallipoli.*, London, 1916, p. 74
56. Graves, Robert, *Goodbye to All That*, Penguin Books, 1957, p. 146
57. McCance, *Munster Fusiliers*, II, p. 50 and appendices p. 212; Lavery, *Irish Heroes*, pp. 260, 261
58. Johnstone, *Orange Green & Khaki*, p. 112; Lavery, *Irish Heroes*, pp. 278, 280
59. Cooper, *10th (Irish)*, p. 53; James, *Gallipoli*, pp. 240–41
60. Denman, Terence, 'The 10th (Irish) Division 1914–15', *Irish Sword*, Vol. XVII, #66, 1987, p. 22; Dungan, *Irish Voices*, p. 53
61. Whitton, *Leinster Regiment*, II, pp. 191–193; Corbally, *Royal Ulster Rifles*, pp. 108, 111; Godley, General Sir Alexander, *The Life of an Irish Soldier*, p. 188
62. James, *Gallipoli*, pp. 281, 280; Dungan, *Irish Voices*, p. 58 claims Mahon knew Hill was to support Hammersley but was unable to get a message to Hill.
63. Cooper,*10th Irish*, pp. 128, 129; MacDonagh, *Irish at the Front*, p. 9
64. Cooper, *10th (Irish)*, pp. 135, 139; Hanna, *Pals*, p. 76
65. Lee, Michael, 'Lieutenants Joseph Bagnall Lee and Alfred Tennyson Lee and the 6th Battalion Royal Munster Fusiliers at Suvla Bay, Gallipoli, August 1915' in *Royal Munster Fusiliers Association Journal*, #7,1995, pp. 17–20. All Information on Lee brothers from this work.
66. Cooper, *10th (Irish)*, pp. 144–145; Johnstone, *Orange, Green & Khaki*, p.130
67. Hanna, *Pals*, p. 136; Cooper, *10th (Irish)*, p.165
68. Cooper, *10th (Irish)*, pp. 166–168; Fox, *Royal Inniskilling Fusiliers*, pp. 193, 194
69. Cooper,*10th (Irish)*, pp. 170–177; Cunliffe, *Royal Irish Fusiliers*, p. 297; Hanna, *Pals*, pp. 106, 113
70. Curtayne, *Ledwidge*, pp. 126, 127, 151; Cathleen ni Houlihan is a symbolic figure of Ireland; Dungan, *Irish Voices*, p. 73
71. Hanna, *Pals*, pp. 132, 136
72. Graves, *Goodbye To All That*, p. 158; Leonard, Jane, 'The Catholic Chaplaincy' in *Ireland and The First World War*, Dublin, Trinity History

Workshop, 1986, p.10, numbers of casualties among Anglican Chaplains (88) and Roman Catholics (30).

73. Cooper, *10th (Irish)*, pp. 189, 191
74. *Ibid.*, pp. 192, 195
75. *Ibid*, pp.197, 205; Jourdain, Fraser; *Connaught Rangers*, III, pp. 46–51, 71; Johnstone, *Orange, Green & Khaki*, p. 147
76. Fox, *Inniskilling Fusiliers*, pp. 196,197; James, *Gallipoli*, p. 309; the term 'incomparable' for 29th Division was used by General Hamilton in his Force Order of 29 June 1915.
77. Moorehead, Alan, *Gallipoli*, London, 1963, p. 273
78. James,*Gallipoli*, pp. 306, 307; Moorehead, *Gallipoli*, p. 274
79. Johnstone, *Orange Green & Khaki*, p. 152; Denman, 'The 10th (Irish) Division', *Irish Sword*, no. 66, p. 22; James, *Gallipoli*, p. 307
80. Johnstone, *Orange Green & Khaki*, p. 151; Cooper, *10th (Irish)*, p. 140
81. McCance, *Munster Fusiliers*, II, p. 60
82. Cooper,*10th (Irish)*, p. 254

Chapter Ten (pp 242 – 282)

1. Ryan, A. P., 'The Easter Rising 1916' in *History Today*, XVI, #4, April 1966, pp. 234–42
2. Hayes-McCoy, G.A., 'A Military History of the 1916 Rising' in *The Making of 1916, Studies in the History of the Rising*, Ed. Kevin B. Nowlan, Dublin, 1969, pp. 266–67
3. Ryan, Desmond, *The Rising*, Dublin, 1949, p. 3
4. Gwynn, Stephen, *The Last Years of John Redmond*, London, 1919, p. 227
5. Hayes-McCoy, 'A Military History of the 1916 Rising', p. 267; MacCauley, James, A., 'The Dublin Fusiliers', Part II, in *Irish Sword*, Vol. X, No. 38, 1971, pp. 62–63; Bence-Jones, *Twilight of The Ascendancy*, p. 177; Falls, *36th (Ulster) Division*, p. 11
6. Whitton, *Leinster Regiment*, II, p. 263, 264, 272
7. Bence-Jones, *Twilight of the Ascendancy*, pp. 176,196–197
8. Hayes-McCoy, *Military History of the 1916 Rising*, pp. 303, 304; Casualties among troops and police were 132 killed and 397 wounded, for the rebels 60 killed (not counting executions) and more than 120 wounded; for civilians 300 killed and as many as 2,000 wounded, among them H. F. Browning, President of Irish Football Union who was associated with the 'Footballers', 'D' Company 7th Dublins.
9. Verney, *The Micks*, pp. 45–46
10. Denman, *Ireland's Unknown Soldiers*, p. 148; Verney, *The Micks*, p. 73

11. Frank McGuinness interview with Charles Hunter, *Irish Times*, 15 February 1985

12. Keegan, John, *Face of Battle*, Penguin Books, 1976, p. 259; Orr, *Road to The Somme*, p. 161

13. MacDonagh, Michael, *The Irish on The Somme*, London, 1917, pp. 36–37; Orr, *Road to the Somme*, pp. 164,165

14. Dungan, *Irish Voices*, pp. 120, 121

15. Colonel Ian Gailey, Chairman of the Royal Ulster Rifles Association, paper about J. P. Beadle's painting 'The Battle of The Somme', a copy of which was sent to the authors in January 1985 by Lieutenant-Colonel W. R. H. Charley, JP, Regimental Association Secretary, Regimental Headquarters (Belfast), The Royal Irish Rangers, Waring Street, Belfast. The painting hangs in Belfast City Hall.

16. Mitchell,Gardiner, S. *Three Cheers For The Derrys!*, A History of the 10th Royal Inniskilling Fusiliers in the 1914–18, Derry, 1991, pp. 1, 2, 16, 90–107; Hall, Michael, *Sacrifice on the Somme*, Newtownabbey (N.I.), 1993, pp. 10–12

17. Dungan, *Irish Voices*, p. 105; see Middlebrook, Martin, *First Day on the Somme*, New York, 1972, appendix 3 for list of senior officer casualties on 1 July.

18. Dungan, *Irish Voices*, p. 118 re Starret memoir discovered by him in the Imperial War Museum; Falls, *36th (Ulster) Division*, p. 55

19. Orr, *Road to the Somme*, pp. 19, 47, Shankill Road in Belfast, a Protestant area.

20. Crozier, F. Percy, *A Brass Hat in No-Man's-Land*, London, 1930, p. 101

21. Orr, *Road to the Somme*, p. 49

22. Falls, Captain Cyril, 'An Historical Note', p. 10 in Booklet; *Commemoration of the 50th Anniversary of the Battle of the Somme, Government of Northern Ireland Review and Drumhead Service, Balmoral, July 4, 1966*

23. Evans, Martin M., *The Battles of The Somme*, Toronto, 1996, pp. 29–30

24. MacDonagh, *The Irish on the Somme*, pp. 49, 50

25. Middlebrook, *First Day*, pp. 155,160, only elements of Tyneside Irish and Royal Scots near Contalmaison went as far as the Ulstermen.

26. Middlebrook, *First Day*, p. 291

27. Fraser, David, 'Alanbrooke, Field-Marshal Viscount Alanbrooke' in *Churchill's Generals*, ed. by John Keegan, London, 1992, pp. 89 ff; Doherty, Richard, *Irish Generals*, Belfast, 1993, pp. 179,181

28. Johnstone, *Orange Green & Khaki*, p. 196; Keating, Joseph, 'Tyneside Irish Brigade History of its Origin and Development' in Lavery, Felix, compiler, *Irish Heroes in the War*, p. 89

29. Denman, *Ireland's Unknown Soldiers*, pp. 44, 45

30. Middlebrook, *First Day*, pp. 122, 123, 148, 149; Keegan, *Face of Battle.*, p. 249

31. Denman, *Ireland's Unknown Soldiers*, p. 102

32. Johnstone, *Orange Green & Khaki*, p. 254, quoting Buchan in Nelson's

History of the Great War; Denman, Terence 'An Irish Battalion at War: From the Letters of Captain J. H. M. Staniforth, 7th Leinsters, 1914–18' in *Irish Sword*, Vol. XVII, no. 68, 1989, p. 165

33. Lyons, J. B., *The Enigma of Tom Kettle*, Dublin, 1983, p. 300;Westport, a town in the west of Ireland.

34. Harris, *Irish Regiments,* p. 95

35. Whitton, *Leinster Regiment*, II, pp. 309, 320, 376; Hitchcock, *"Stand To"*, pp. 129; MacDonagh, *Irish on The Somme*, pp. 156–57

36. Jourdain and Fraser, *Connaught Rangers*, III, pp. 221, 222; Johnstone, *Orange Green & Khaki*, pp. 241–244; Denman, *Ireland's Unknown Soldiers*, p. 82

37. Cunliffe, *Royal Irish Fusiliers*, p.312; Fox, *Royal Inniskilling Fusiliers*, p. 75; Johnstone, *Orange Green & Khaki*, p. 247

38. Perry, *Nationality in Irish Infantry Regiments*, p. 88

39. Whitton, *Leinster Regiment*, II, pp. 315–316; Johnstone,*Orange Green & Khaki*, p. 251

40. McCance, *Munster Fusiliers*, II, pp. 65–66; Cunliffe, *Irish Fusiliers*, pp. 311, 312

41. Lyons, *Tom Kettle*, pp. 298, 301; McDonagh, *Irish on the Somme*, pp. 155–156; Cross, *Lost Voices*, p. 43

42. Lyons, *Tom Kettle.*, p. 301, quoting Gibbs, P., *The Germans on the Somme*, London, 1917

43. O'Rahilly, Professor Alfred, *Father William Doyle, SJ*, London, 1930, p. 440; General Picton's term for the Connaught Rangers was 'the Devil's Own'; see too pp. 443, 439, 412

44. Denman, *Ireland's Unknown Soldiers*, p. 101

45. Nicolson, Nigel, *Alex The Life of Field Marshal Earl Alexander of Tunis*, London, 1973, pp. 5–11, 40, 41, 42

46. O'Rahilly, *Father William Doyle, SJ*, p. 511–12; Falls, *36th Ulster Division*, pp. 82, 92

47. Fox, *Inniskillings*, pp. 97, 69, 70; Dungan, *Irish Voices*, pp. 116, 161

48. Denman, Terence, 'A voice from the lonely grave': in *Irish Sword*, No. 73, pp. 294–296

49 Bence-Jones, *Twilight of the Ascendancy*, p. 184; Nicolson, *Alex*, p. 28; Kipling, *Irish Guards* II, pp. 146–47

50. Curtayne, *Francis Ledwidge*, pp. 188, 180, 128

51. Warner, Philip, *Passchendaele, The Story Behind the Tragic Victory of 1917*, London, 1987, p. 2; Terraine, John, *Douglas Haig*, London, 1990, p. 387

52. Hitchcock, *"Stand To"*, p. 290; Fox, *Inniskilling Fusiliers*, p. 100

53. Johnstone,*Orange Green & Khaki*, p. 296 quoting Sir Philip Gibbs, *Realities of War*; Cunliffe, *Royal Irish Fusiliers*, p. 326; Falls, *36th (Ulster) Division*, p. 299; Denman, *Ireland's Unknown Soldiers*, p. 123

54. Terraine, *Haig*, pp. 337, 387; Powell, Geoffrey, *Plumer*, London, 1990, pp. 203, 209, 210

55. O'Rahilly, *Father William Doyle SJ*, pp. 552, 556–57, 522

56. Whitton, *Leinster Regiment*, II, pp. 365, 373–74; Hitchcock, *"Stand To"*, p. 306
57. Perry, 'Nationality in the Irish Infantry Regiments', pp. 81, 84
58. Whitton, *Leinster Regiment*, II, p.442
59. *Ibid.*, pp. 377, 378; Denman, *Ireland's Unknown Soldiers*, pp. 150, 152
60. Johnstone, *Orange Green & Khaki*, pp. 186, 318, 321; Whitton, *Leinster Regiment*, II, p. 323
61. Cunliffe, *Royal Irish Fusiliers*, pp. 335–336
62. Johnstone, *Orange Green & Khaki*, p. 328; Harris, *Irish Regiments*, p. 140, says Brigadier General C. F. Watson commanding 180th Infantry Brigade 'rode up and accepted the surrender'.
63. Fox, *Royal Inniskillings*, p. 216
64. Jourdain and Fraser, *Connaught Rangers*, III, p. 179
65. Middlebrook, Martin, *The Kaiser's Battle*, Penguin Books, 1983, pp. 274, 332
66. Harris, *Irish Regiments*, p. 164; Middlebrook, *Kaiser's Battle*, p. 81
67. Denman, Terence, 'The 16th Irish Division on 21 March 1918: Fight or Flight' in *Irish Sword*, vol. XVII, no. 69, 1990, p. 275
68. Gough, Sir Hubert, *The March Retreat*, London, 1934, p. 57. He had learned that the 18th Army of the successful German General Von Hutier was building up opposite him.
69. Barnett, *Britain and Her Army*, p. 406; Middlebrook, *Kaiser's Battle*, p. 204
70. Middlebrook, *Kaiser's Battle*, pp. 324, 326; Harris, *Irish Regiments*, p. 157; Denman, 'Fight or Flight', *Irish Sword*, #69, p. 283; Fox, *Inniskilling Fusiliers*, p. 40
71. Whitton, *Leinster Regiment*, II; p. 443; Denman, 'Fight or Flight?', *Irish Sword*, #69, p. 285
72. Johnstone,*Orange Green & Khaki*, pp. 357–358
73. Dungan, *Irish Voices*, p. 187; Jourdain and Fraser, *Connaught Rangers*, III, pp. 267, 418, 498; Denman, *Ireland's Unknown Soldiers*, p. 82
74. Falls, *36th (Ulster) Division*, pp. 195–197
75. Middlebrook, *Kaiser's Battle*, pp. 267, 268, 337, 338; Fox, *Inniskilling Fusiliers*, pp. 137, 138; Falls, *36th (Ulster) Division*, p. 209
76. Moore, William, *See How They Ran*, London, 1970, p. 60
77. Middlebrook, *Kaiser's Battle*, p. 277 – 278
78. Terraine, *Haig*, pp. 409, 417; Farrar-Hockley, A.; *Goughie*, London, 1975, p. 292
79. Everett, Suzanne, *World War I, An Illustrated History*, Greenwich, USA., 1980, p. 202; Farrar-Hockley, *Goughie*, p. 291
80. Dungan, *Irish Voices*, p. 189; Corbally, *Royal Ulster Rifles*, p. 126
81. McCance, *Munster Fusiliers*, II, pp. 153–155 quoting Colonel H. S. Jervis's '2nd Munsters in France'; MacCauley, 'The Dublin Fusiliers', Part II, *Irish Sword*, #38, p.166. Accounts vary.
82. Gough, *March Retreat*, p. 128; Moore, *See How They Ran*, p. 122
83. Farrar-Hockley,*Goughie*, p. 302; Gough, *March Retreat*, pp. 152–154; Terraine, *Haig*, p. 427

84. Harris, *Irish Regiments*, p. 185; Terraine, *Haig*, p. 417; Gray, Randal, *Kaiserschlacht 1918*, London, 1991, p. 68; Middlebrook, *Kaiser's Battle*, p.279

85. De Groot, Gerard J., *Douglas Haig 1861–1928*, London, 1988, p. 376

86. Farrar-Hockley,*Goughie*, p. 359, Gough's own books, *Fifth Army and The March Retreat* were published in the early 1930s.

87. Harris, *Irish Regiments in the First World War*, p. 186, 187; Denman, *Ireland's Unknown Soldiers*, p. 172; Jourdain and Fraser, *Connaught Rangers*, III, pp. 274, 275

88. Johnstone, *Orange Green & Khaki*, p. 395; Perry, *Nationality in the Irish Infantry Regiments*, p. 89

89. Denman,*Ireland's Unknown Soldiers*, p. 174

90. Hitchcock, *"Stand To"*, pp. 315, 327, 331; Kipling, *Irish Guards, I*, p 331

91. Harris, *Irish Regiments*, p. 11

Epilogue (pp 283 – 287)

1. Jeffery, Keith, 'The British Army and Ireland Since 1922' in *A Military History of Ireland*, p. 438

2. Doherty, Richard, *Clear the Way! A History of the 38th (Irish) Brigade, 1941–47*, Dublin, 1993, pp. 7, 8. The regiments were 1st Royal Irish Fusiliers, 6th Royal Inniskilling Fusiliers, 2nd London Irish Rifles.

3. Holmes,*The Little Field-Marshal*, p. 347; Fitzpatrick, David, 'Militarism in Ireland 1900–1922' in *A Military History of Ireland*, p. 401

4. Holmes,*The Little Field-Marshal*, p. 358; Kee, *The Green Flag*, p. 626

5. Leonard, Jane, 'Getting Them At Last, The I.R.A. and Ex-servicemen', in *Revolution? Ireland 1917–1923*, Trinity History Workshop, Dublin, 1990, pp. 118–129; Falls, *36th (Ulster) Division*, London,1922, p. 38.

6. Fitzpatrick, 'Militarism in Ireland 1900–1922' in *A Military History of Ireland*, p. 401; McCance, *Munster Fusiliers*, II, p. 213.

7. 'The Irish Volunteers of 1913 are frequently described as the forerunners of the national army' but behind them was a long Irish military tradition. See O'Halpin, Eunan, 'The army in independent Ireland' in *Military History of Ireland*, p. 407

8. O'Brien, Conor Cruise & Maire, *A Concise History of Ireland*, London, 1972, p. 151. names them as John O'Brien and James Connolly; Kee, *The Green Flag*, p. 739

9. Karsten, Peter; 'Irish Soldiers in the British Army 1792–1922: Suborned or Subordinate?' in *Journal of Social History*, #17,1983, p 54; Fitzpatrick, 'Militarism in Ireland 1900–1922' in *Military History of Ireland*, p. 399

10. Bence-Jones,*Twilight of the Ascendancy*, pp. 232, 251; Robinson, *Bryan Cooper*, p. 153; Harris, *Irish Regiments*, p. 208

11. Denman, *Ireland's Unknown Soldiers*, p. 175

12. Clarke, Brian, Royal British Legion, Ireland, letter to *Irish Times,* November

5, 1983 quoting Marshal Foch in a special number of The British Legion Annual of 1941.

13. Jeffery, Keith, *The Great War in Modern Irish Memory*, Eds. Jeffery, Keith, Fraser, T. G., *Historical Studies*, XVIII,1991 p.153;

14. Harris, Henry, *Irish Regiments*, pp. 211–212, *Irish Times*, April,1966

15. RTE programme of the filming of 11 November 1998 memorial ceremonies in Messines, Belgium.

BIBLIOGRAPHY BOOKS

Allen, Charles, *Soldier Sahibs,* New York, 2001

Anglesey, Marquess of, *A History of The British Cavalry,* 8 Vols., London, 1973 –1986

Ascoli, David, *A Companion to the British Army 1660–1983,* London, 1983

——, *The Mons Star,* London, 1984

Ash, Bernard, *The Last Dictator, Field-Marshal Sir Henry Wilson,* London, 1968

Asherwood, Paul, Spencer-Smith, Jenny, *Lady Butler – Battle Artist 1846–1933,* Exhibition Catalogue, National Army Museum, 1987

Bardon, Jonathan, *History of Ulster,* Belfast, 1992

Barnett, Correlli, *Britain and Her Army 1509–1970,* Penguin, 1970

Barrington, Sir Jonah, *Personal Sketches of His Own Times,* London, 1869

Barthorp, Michael, *The Zulu War, A Pictorial History,* London, 1988

——, *War On The Nile,* London, 1984

——, *Anglo Boer Wars,* Poole, 1987

Bartlett, Thomas and Jeffery, Keith, Eds., *A Military History of Ireland,* Cambridge, 1966

Beckett, Ian W., Johnnie Gough VC, London, 1989

Bence-Jones, Mark, *Clive of India,* London, 1974

——, *Twilight of The Ascendancy,* London, 1987

Bidwell, Shelford, *Swords for Hire – European Mercenaries in Eighteenth Century India,* London, 1971

Blakeney, R., *A Boy in the Peninsular War,* Ed. Julian Sturges, London, this edition 1989

Bond, Brian, et al, *'Look To Your Front',* Staplehurst, 1999

Bonham-Carter, V., *Soldier True,* London, 1963

Brereton, J. M., *History of the 4/7th Dragoon Guards,* Catterick, 1982

——, *The British Soldier,* London, 1986

Brewer, J. D., *Royal Irish Constabulary,* Belfast, 1990

Broeker, *Rural Disorder and Police Reform in Ireland 1812–1836,* London, 1970

Bryant, Arthur, *Jackets of Green,* London, 1972

Butler, Lieut. General The Rt. Hon. Sir W. F., CGB, *An Autobiography,* London, 1913

Callwell, Major-General Sir C. E., KCB, *Field Marshal Sir Henry Wilson, His Life and Diaries,* 2 volumes, London, 1927

Calthorpe, S. J. G., *Cadogan's Crimea,* Illustrated by General the Hon. Sir George Cadogan, New York, 1980

Cockerill, H. W., *Sons of the Brave, The Story of Boy Soldiers,* London, 1984

Coombs, Rose, MBE, *Before Endeavours Fade,* London, 1983

Cooper, Bryan, *The 10th (Irish) Division In Gallipoli,* London, 1918

Corbally, Lt. Col. M. J. P. M., *The Royal Ulster Rifles 1793–1960,* Belfast, 1960

Costello, Edward, *Adventures of a Soldier,* London, 1852

Creagh, General Sir O'Moore, *Autobiography,* London, 1925

Cross, Tim, *The Lost Voices Of World War I,* London, 1988

Crozier, F. Percy, *A Brass Hat In No Man's Land,* London, 1930

Cunliffe, Marcus, *The Royal Irish Fusiliers 1793–1950,* London, 1952

Curtayne, Alice, *Francis Ledwidge: A Life Of The Poet 1887–1917,* London, 1972

Denman, Terence, *Ireland's Unknown Soldiers,* Dublin, 1992

Dooley, Thomas, P., *Irishmen or English Soldiers?,* Liverpool, 1995

Doyle, N. B., *Ireland and Irishmen and Revolutionary America,* Cork, 1981

Dungan, Myles, *Irish Voices From The Great War,* Dublin, 1995

Edwards, R. D., Williams, T. D., Eds., *Great Famine,* Dublin, 1962

Ervine, St John, *Craigavon – Ulsterman,* London, 1949

Evans, Roger, *The 5th Inniskilling Dragoon Guards,* Aldershot, 1951

Everett, Suzanne, *World War I, An Illustrated History,* Greenwich, USA, 1980

Falls, Cyril, *The History of the 36th (Ulster) Division,* London, this edition 1996

Farrar-Hockley, General Sir Anthony, *Goughie,* London, 1975

Farwell Byron, *Eminent Victorian Soldiers,* London 1985

——, *The Armies of The Raj,* London, 1989

——, *The Gurkhas,* London, 1985

——, *The Great Anglo-Boer War,* London, 1976

——, *Queen Victoria's Little Wars,* London, 1972

Faughnan, Thomas, *Stirring Incidents in the Life of a British Soldier,* Toronto, 1882

Featherstone, Donald, *All For a Shilling a Day,* London, 1966

——, *Victorian Colonial Warfare Africa,* London, 1993

——, *Victorian Colonial Warfare India,* London, 1993

Fitzgibbon, M. A., *Veteran of 1812: The Life of James Fitzgibbon,* Toronto, 1984

Fitzpatrick David, Ed., *Ireland and The First World War,* Trinity History Workshop, Dublin, 1986

——, *Revolution? Ireland 1917–1923,* Trinity History Workshop, Dublin, 1990

Fletcher, Ian, *In Hell Before Daylight,* Tunbridge Wells, 1984

Foster, R. F., *Modern Ireland 1600–1972,* London, 1988

Fox, Sir Frank, OBE, *The Royal Inniskilling Fusiliers in the World War,* London, n.d.

Gates, David, *The Spanish Ulcer, A History of the Peninsular War,* London, 1986

Godley, Sir Alex, *Life of An Irish Soldier,* London, 1939

Gough, Sir Hubert, *Soldiering On,* London, 1954

——, *The March Retreat,* London, 1934

Gratton, William, *Adventures With the Connaught Rangers 1809–1814,* London, this edition 1989

Graves, Donald E., Ed., *Fighting for Canada,* Toronto, 2000

Graves, Robert, *Goodbye To All That,* Penguin, 1960

——, *Proceed Sergeant Lamb,* London, 1985

Gretton, Lt. Col. G. Le M., *The Campaigns and History of the Royal Irish Regiment,* London, 1911

Grinnell-Milne, Duncan, *Mafeking,* London, 1957

Grove-White, James, *Account of the Yeomanry of Ireland,* Cork, 1893

Guedalla, Philip, *The Duke,* London, 1931

Gwynn, Stephen, *Experiences Of A Literary Man,* London, 1926

——, *The Last Years of John Redmond,* London, 1919

Hall, Michael, *Sacrifice On The Somme,* Newtownabbey, 1993

Hanna, Henry (KC), *The Pals At Suvla Bay,* The Record of 'D' Company of the 7th Royal Dublin Fusiliers, Dublin, 1916

Harries-Jenkins, Gwyn, *The Army in Victorian Society,* London, 1977

Harris, John, *The Indian Mutiny,* London, 1973

Harris, Henry, *Irish Regiments in the First World War,* Cork, 1968

——, *The Royal Irish Fusiliers,* London, 1972

Harris, *Recollections of Rifleman Harris,* Ed. Curling, Henry, London, 1929

Hastings, Max, Ed., *The Oxford Book of Military Anecdotes,* Oxford, 1985

Hayes-McCoy, G. A., *Irish Battles,* London, 1969

——, 'The Making Of 1916', *Studies In The History Of The Rising,* Ed. Nowlan, Kevin. B., Dublin, 1969

Healy, James N., *Percy French and His Songs,* Dublin, 1966

Heath, Ian, Sque, David, *The Irish Wars 1485–1603,* London, 1993

Hervey, Albert, *Soldier of the Company: Life of an Indian Ensign 1833–1843,* Ed. Allen, Charles, this edition London, 1988

Hibbert, Christopher, *Wellington, a Personal History,* London, 1998

——, *The Great Mutiny India 1857,* Penguin, 1978

Hitchcock, Captain F C, *"Stand To" A Diary Of The Trenches 1915–1918,* Norwich, This Edition 1988

Hitsman, J. M., *The Incredible War of 1812,* Toronto, 1965

Holmes, Richard, *The Little Field-Marshal, Sir John French,* London, 1981

——, *Redcoat,* London, 2001

Howarth, David, *Waterloo, Day of Battle,* New York, 1968

Hughes, Kathleen, *Church in Early Irish Society,* London, 1966

Irwin, Margaret, *The Stranger Prince,* London, 1937

——, *The Proud Servant, The Story of Montrose,* London, 1934

James, Robert Rhodes, *Gallipoli,* London, this Edition 1984

Johnstone, Tom, *Orange Green And Khaki,* Dublin, 1992

Jourdain, H. F. N., Fraser, Edward, *History of the Connaught Rangers, 3Vols,* London, 1928

——, *Ranging Memories,* Oxford, 1934

Judd, Denis, *The Crimean War,* London, 1975

Kee, Robert, *The Green Flag,* London, 1972

Keegan, John, *The Face of Battle,* Penguin, 1976

Ketchum, R. M., *Winter Soldiers,* New York, 1973

Kincaid, J., *Adventures in the Rifle Brigade,* London, 1830,

Kipling, Rudyard, *Complete Barrack Room Ballads,* Ed. and Introduction, Carrington, Charles, London, 1974

——, *Soldiers Three,* Frome, this edition 1986

——, *The Irish Guards In The Great War,* Toronto, 1923

Knowles, David, *Historian and Character,* Cambridge, 1954

Kruger, Rayne, *Goodbye Dolly Gray,* London, 1983

Laurie, Lt. Col. George Brenton, *History of the Royal Irish Rifles,* London, 1914

Lavery, Felix, Compiler, *Irish Heroes In The War,* London, 1917

Law, H. W., *Book of the Beresford-Hopes,* London, 1925

Lecky, L. E. H., *History of Ireland in the Eighteenth Century,* Vol. II, London, 1881

Lehmann, Joseph, *The Modern Major-General,Biography of Field-Marshal Lord Wolseley,* Boston, 1964

Leyburn, J. G., *Scotch-Irish,* Chapel Hill, 1962

Longford, Elizabeth, *Wellington, Years of the Sword,* London, 1971

——, *Wellington, Pillar of State,* London, 1972

Lucy, John, *There's a Devil In The Drum,* Dallington, this Edition 1992

Lyons, J. B., *The Enigma Of Tom Kettle,* Dublin, 1983

MacDonagh, Michael, *The Irish At The Front,* London, 1916

——, *The Irish On The Somme,* London, 1917

MacDonald, Lyn, *1914–1918 Voices And Images Of The Great War,* Penguin, 1991

MacMullen, J. M., *Camp and Barrack Room or the British Army as it is,* London, 1846

Maguire, W. A., Ed., *Kings in Conflict,* Belfast, 1990

Marteinson, John, Ed., *We Stand on Guard, An Illustrated History of the Canadian Army,* Montreal, 1992

Mason, Philip, *A Matter of Honour,* London, This Edition 1974

Maurice, Maj Gen. Sir F., *Life of Wolseley,* London, 1924

Maxse, F. I., CB, DSO, *Seymour Vandeleur, Brevet Lieutenant-Colonel, DSO,* London, 1905

McAnally, Sir Henry, *The Irish Militia 1793–1816,* London, 1949

McCalmont, Sir Hugh, Major-General, KCB, CVO, *Memoirs,* Ed. Sir C. E. Callwell, KCB, London, 1924

McCance, Captain S., *History of Royal Munster Fusiliers*, 2 volumes, Aldershot, 1927

McCourt, Frank, *Angela's Ashes*, New York, 1996

McCourt, Edward, *Remember Butler*, Toronto, 1967

McGregor-Hastie, Roy, *Never To Be Taken Alive, A Biography of General Gordon*, London, 1985

Middlebrook, Martin, *First Day On The Somme*, New York, 1972

———, *The Kaiser's Battle*, Penguin, 1983

Mitchell, Gardiner S., *"Three Cheers For The Derrys!"*, Derry, 1991

Montgomery, Brian, *Monty's Grandfather*, Poole, 1984

———, *A Field-Marshal in the Family*, New York, 1974

Moore, William, *See How They Ran*, London, 1970

Moorhead, Alan, *Gallipoli*, London, 1963

Moorhouse, Geoffrey, *India Britannica*, London, 1984

Morris, James, *Heaven's Command*, Penguin, 1979

Morris, Donald, *Washing of The Spears*, London, this Edition 1968

Morton, Desmond, *A Military History of Canada*, Edmonton, 1985

Moyse-Bartlett, H, *Louis Edward Nolan*, London, 1971

Murray, R H, *History of the VIII King's Royal Irish Hussars 1693–1927*, 2 volumes, 1928

Myatt, Frederick, *Peninsular General, Sir Thomas Picton 1758–1815*, London, 1980

———, *The British Infantry 1660–1945*, Poole, 1983

———, *British Sieges of the Peninsular War*, Tunbridge-Wells, 1987

Neuburg, Victor, *Gone For a Soldier*, London, 1989

Newark, Tim, *Celtic Warriors*, London, 1988

Nicolson, Nigel, *Alex, The Life of Field-Marshal Earl Alexander of Tunis*, London, 1973

Orr, Philip, *The Road To The Somme*, Belfast, 1987

O'Brien, Joseph V., *Dear Dirty Dublin, A City in Distress 1899–1916*, London, 1982

O'Brien, Conor Cruise and Maire, *A Concise History of Ireland*, London, 1972

O'Callaghan, J. C., *History of the Irish Brigades*, Glasgow, 1886

O'Connell, P., *Irish Faction Fighters of the Nineteenth Century*, Dublin, 1966

O'Malley, James, *Life of James O'Malley*, Montreal, 1893

O'Malley, Ernie, *Army Without Banners*, London, 1967

O'Meara, Lt. Col. W. A., CMG, *Kekewich in Kimberly*, London, 1926

O'Rahilly, Professor Alfred, *Father William Doyle SJ*, London, 1930

Pack-Beresford, D. T., *Memoir of Major-General Sir Denis Pack*, Dublin, 1908

Pakenham, Thomas, *The Boer War*, London, 1982

Parkinson, Roger, *Moore of Corunna*, London, 1976

Pearson, Hesketh, *The Hero of Delhi, The Life of John Nicholson*, New York, 1939

Pemberton, W. B., *Battles of The Crimean War*, London, 1968

Pericoli, U., and Glover, M., *The Armies at Waterloo*, New York, 1973

Phillips, R. B., *Patterns of Power: The Jasper Grant Collection and Great Lakes Indian Art of the Nineteenth Century,* Kleinburg, 1985
Powell, Geoffrey, *Plumer, The Soldier's General,* London, 1990
Prebble, John, *Highland Clearances,* London, 1963

Reid, Stuart, *Wolfe,* Staplehurst, 2000
Roberts, Andrew, *Napoleon and Wellington,* London, 2001
Robertson, Nora, *Crowned Harp,* Dublin, 1960
Robinson, Lennox, *Bryan Cooper,* London, 1931
Royal Inniskilling Fusiliers History from December 1688 – July 1914, London, 1934
Royle, Trevor, *The Kitchener Enigma,* London, 1985
Russell, W. H., *Russell's Despatches From the Crimea,* Ed. Bentley, Nicholas, London, 1970

Sheppard, E. W., *Coote Bahadur,* London, 1956
Shipp, John, *Path of Glory, Being the Memoirs of the Extraordinary Career of John Shipp,* Ed. Stranks, C. J., Ed., London, 1969
Simms, J G, *The Seige of Derry,* Dublin, 1966
Skelley, Alan Ramsay, *The Victorian Army at Home,* London, 1977
Spiers, Edward, *Radical General, Sir George De Lacy Evans,* Manchester, 1983
Stacey, C. P., *Quebec 1759,* London, 1957
Swinson, Arthur, *North-West Frontier,* London, 1969

Terraine, John, *Douglas Haig The Educated Soldier,* London, this edition 1990
Todd, Pamela, Fordham, David, Eds., *Private Tucker's Boer War Diary,* London, 1988

Verner, Ruth, *Reminiscences of William Verner (1782–1871),* London, 1965
Verney, Peter, *The Micks, The Story of the Irish Guards,* London, 1970

Warner, Philip, *Passchendaele, The Story Behind The Tragic Victory Of 1917,* London, 1987
Whitton, Lt Col., *The History of the Prince of Wales's Leinster Regiment,* 2 volumes, Aldershot, 1924–1926
Wilkinson, Burke, *The Zeal of The Convert, The Life of Erskine Childers,* New York, 1976
Wilson, Joan, *Wellington's Marriage,* London, 1987
Woodham-Smith, C, *The Reason Why,* London, 1958
Woods, Stephen, *The Auld Alliance,* Edinburgh, 1989

Yorke, Edmund, *Rorke's Drift 1879,* Stroud, 2001

ARTICLES

Annand, M. K., 'Lucknow Kavanagh and the 1st European Bengal Fusiliers', *Journal of the Society for Army Historical Research,* XVIV, #179, 1966

Anonymous, 'Sir Henry Keating, KCB', *Journal of the Society for Army Historical Research,* #20,1941

Cadell, Patrick, 'Irish Soldiers in India', *Irish Sword,* I, #2, 1950–51

Chart, D. A., 'The Irish Levies During The Great French War', *English Historical Review,* #32, 1917

Clark, Brian, 'Lieutenant Henry Desmond O'Hara, DSO, The Royal Dublin Fusiliers', *Irish Sword, XVIII, #73, 1992*

Denman, Terence, 'The Catholic Irish Soldier in the First World War: The Social Environment', *Irish Historical Studies,* XXVII #108, 1991

——, 'A Voice From The Lonely Grave: The Death in Action of Major William Redmond, MP, 7 June, 1917', *Irish Sword,* XVIII, #73, 1992

——, 'The 10th (Irish) Division 1914–15', *Irish Sword,* XVII, #66, 1987

——, 'An Irish Battalion at War: From the Letters of Captain J H M Staniforth, The Leinsters 1914–18', *Irish Sword,* XVII, #68, 1989

Dinwiddy, J. R., 'Early Nineteenth Century Campaigns Against Flogging in the Army', *English Historical Review,* XCVII, 1982

Griffin, Brian, 'Ireland and the Crimean War', *Irish Sword,* XXII, #89, 2001

Karsten, Peter, 'Irish Soldiers in the British Army 1792–1922 Suborned or Subordinate ?', *Journal of Social History,* XVII, 1983

Lee, Michael, 'Lieutenant Joseph Bagnall Lee and Alfred Tennyson Lee and the 6th Battalion

Royal Munster Fusiliers at Suvla Bay, Gallipoli, August 1915, *Royal Munster Fusilier Journal,* #7, 1995

Maguire, W. A., 'Major-General Ross and The Burning of Washington', *Irish Sword,* XIV, #55, 1980

Malcom, J. L., 'All the King's Men: The Impact of the Crown's Irish Soldiers on the English Civil War', *Irish Historical Studies,* XXI, 1979

Perry, Nicholas, 'Nationality in the Irish Infantry Regiments in the First World War', *War and Society,* Vol. 12, #1, 1994

Ryan, A. P., 'The Easter Rising 1916', *History To-day,* XVI, #4, 1966

MANUSCRIPT SOURCES

Charrier File 6307/86/1105, Imperial War Museum

Staunton, Martin, *The Royal Munster Fusiliers In The Great War 1914–19,* unpublished thesis for University College Dublin, 1986

Index

Alexander, Capt. the Hon. Harold MC, DSO, 2nd Bn. Irish Guards, at Ginchy 15 Sep 1916, 259, character & family background, 260

Allenby, Gen. Sir Edmund, Cmdr. Egyptian Expeditionary Force, in Palestine, 270

Anderson, Col. Paul (later Lt. Gen.) at Corunna, 41

Arabi, Col. Ahmed, Egyptian Army, defeat at Tel el Kebir, 152

Baden-Powell, Col. Robert, 5th Dragoon Guards, 272, Mafeking, 273–275

Barré, Maj. Isaac, 32nd Foot, at Quebec, 18

Barry, Pte. John, VC, 1st Royal Irish Regiment, death at Monument Hill, 192

Barry, Pte. R., MM, Royal Irish Regiment, March 1918 German offensive, 273

Bell, Capt. Eric N. F., VC, 9th Royal Inniskilling Fusiliers, killed on Somme 1 July 1916, 251

Bell, Pte. Leslie, 1st Royal Inniskilling Fusiliers, Somme Battle 1 July 1916, 247, 248

Beresford, Capt. Lord Charles, RN, Gordon Expedition, 154, at Abu Klea, 156, rescues Wilson, 157

Beresford, Capt. Lord William de la Poer, VC, 9th Lancers, Zulu War, 145, 146

Beresford, Maj Gen. William Carr, Marshal of Portuguese Forces, Peninsular War, 42, 48, 57

Bernard, Lt Col. H. C., 10th Royal Irish Rifles, killed on Somme 1 July 1916, 249, 250

Bernard, Lt. Robert, 1st Royal Dublin Fusiliers, killed Gallipoli, 228

Bowen-Colthurst, Capt. John, Easter Rising, Dublin 1916, 244

Blakeney, Ensign Robert, 28th Foot, at Badajoz, 53, 54